VITALLY USELESS INFORMATION

An Incredible Collection of Irrelevance

WEST SIDE PUBLISHING

Contributing Writers: Jeff Bahr, Diane Lanzillotta Bobis, Tim Frystak, Tom Harris, Noah Liberman, Matt Modica, David Morrow, Dan Rafter, Terri Schlichenmeyer, Pat Sherman, Donald Vaughan, Vivian Wagner, Jodi Webb

Cover Illustrator: Adrian Chesterman

Fact Checkers: Marci McGrath and Chris Smith

Louis Weber, CEO
Publications International, Ltd.
7373 North Cicero Avenue
Lincolnwood, Illinois 60712

Permission is never granted for commercial purposes.

ISBN-13: 978-1-60553-916-4
ISBN-10: 1-60553-916-3

Manufactured in USA.

8 7 6 5 4 3 2 1

Contents

❖ ❖ ❖

❖ ❖ ❖

❖ ❖ ❖

Drum Roll, Please

It is with great pleasure that we introduce to you the newest member of the Armchair Reader™ family—*Vitally Useless Information.* This legendary book is the culmination of hundreds of hours of work on the part of our fabulous team of editors, writers, researchers, and artists. We've truly outdone ourselves this time.

So, what is vitally useless information? Perhaps the better question is: What *isn't* vitally useless information? About one thing, you can be certain: The articles, statistics, facts, and lists we've compiled for this book are not ordinary or expected or commonplace or mundane. You'll find it impossible to refrain from saying "Hey, did you know...?" to anyone within hearing distance. Trust us on this one—we've sent countless e-mails to spouses, friends, coworkers, and Facebook acquaintances heralding the nuggets of wonder we've discovered while compiling *Vitally Useless Information.* Our postal carriers and garbage collectors may never be the same.

Vital isn't a word we take lightly. It is indeed very important, fundamental, imperative, essential, critical, and of the essence that you read this book. After all, you wouldn't want to miss such riches as:

- Things you don't know (and didn't need to know) about *The Simpsons* (Can you guess what "Bart" is an anagram for?)

- Real names you probably wouldn't want to have (thank your parents for steering clear of Talula Does the Hula from Hawaii)

- How the birds and bees *really* do it

- Most dangerous toys (because it's only fun and games until someone loses an eye)

Can you survive without *Armchair Reader™: Vitally Useless Information?* In all honesty, we wouldn't recommend it.

Yours until next time,

Allen Orso

Allen Orso

All Dolled Up

Mattel Toys introduced the very first Barbie doll at the New York Toy Fair in 1959. Back then, Barbie was a simple, three-dimensional teenage fashion model based on the concept of paper dolls; her fabulous fashions sold separately for $1 to $5 each. As Barbie creator Ruth Handler wrote in her autobiography, "Barbie always represented the fact that a woman has choices." And as the popularity of Barbie grew, so did her closet, career options, and family tree.

Pals

Many have wondered: If Barbie is so popular, why do you have to *buy* her friends? Turns out a doll's entourage can be her most popular accessory. Barbie's inner circle includes more than 8 relatives and 32 close companions.

A few of her most notable peeps (in order of introduction):

1961: Ken, on-again, off-again boyfriend

1963: Midge, Barbie's BFF (best friend forever)

1964: Skipper, beloved younger sister

1967: Francie, first African American gal pal

Pets

Over the years, Barbie has taken care of 50 different pets, including Ginger Giraffe, Zizi Zebra, and enough horses for her own horse farm. No wonder she became a veterinarian in 1985, a zoologist in 2006, and a SeaWorld trainer in 2009.

Her most precious:

1971: Dancer, her first pet horse

1985: Prince, a French poodle with beret

1988: Tahiti, the tropical bird

1994: High Stepper Horse (it really walked...with the help of batteries)

Places

When Barbie's not busy being an astronaut, a rock star, or a presidential candidate, it seems she just wants to kick back with friends and be a regular girl. You can find her at the beach, the pool, the skating rink, the mall, or even mailing letters at the Barbie So Much to Do! Post Office.

The Doll's Dossier

- Barbie's real name is Barbie Millicent Roberts.
- Barbie hails from Willows, Wisconsin. She attended Willows High School.
- Barbie has represented 50 nationalities and more than 108 careers.
- Barbie's relationship status is single. She and Ken broke up on Valentine's Day 2004.

Fashionable Facts

- The very first Barbie wore a black-and-white striped swimsuit, gold hoop earrings, and a signature ponytail.
- Barbie has been outfitted by 70 famous designers, including Calvin Klein, Cartier, Gucci, Versace, and Vera Wang.
- It takes 100 people (designers, seamstresses, pattern makers, and stylists) to create a single Barbie outfit and look.
- Barbie has had one billion pairs of shoes over the years.

A Controversial Figure

- Barbie is 11½ inches tall, with measurements of 5 inches (bust), 3¼ inches (waist), and 5³⁄₁₆ inches (hips). She weighs 7¼ ounces.
- If the original Barbie were a "real" woman, at 5'6", her measurements would be 39–21–33.
- A real woman's chances of having Barbie's figure: less than 1 in 100,000.

Her favorite play scenes to be seen:

1976: *The Barbie Fashion Plaza*

1982: *Barbie Loves McDonald's*

1986: *The Great Shape Barbie Workout Center*

1995: *The Pretty Pet Parlor*

Properties

Barbie has owned more than 20 homes in various architectural designs and price ranges. Her first piece of real estate, the 1962 Dream House, was constructed entirely of paperboard. In 2008, Barbie moved into a fully furnished, three-foot tall, three-story Dream House complete with winding staircase, gourmet kitchen, and flushing toilet.

Her other not-so-humble abodes:

1974: *The Barbie Townhouse*

1983: *The Barbie Dream Cottage*

1985: *The Barbie Glamour Home*

1990: *The Barbie Magical Mansion*

Planes, Trains, and Automobiles

Barbie has been all over the world—and she certainly has the means. Her garage is filled with everything from Ten Speeder bikes and Around Town Scooters to Country Campers and too many Corvettes to count.

Barbie's passport to traveling in style:

1962: *An Austin Healy sports car with personalized license plate*

1972: *A United Airlines Barbie Friend Ship plane*

1994: *A Jaguar XJS convertible in dazzling pink*

2008: *A Barbie Party Cruise ship with water slide and "poolcuzzi"*

Ten Heaviest States

Why are some states heavier than others? Some speculate that there is a correlation between poverty level and obesity. That's because high-calorie, less healthful foods are usually cheaper. As you can see below, eight of the ten states with the greatest percentage of obese and overweight adults are in poor states in the South.

State	Percentage of Overweight/ Obese Adults	Poverty Rank
1. Mississippi	65.9	1
2. Alabama	64.1	7
3. Kentucky	63.8	8
4. West Virginia	63.7	4
5. North Dakota	63.3	33
6. Arkansas	63.1	6
7. Texas	62.9	5
8. Alaska (tied)	62.7	33
9. Louisiana (tied)	62.7	2
10. Tennessee	62.3	11

The following list examines the ten slimmest states, based on the percentage of obese and overweight adults and poverty rank.

State	Percentage of Overweight/ Obese Adults	Poverty Rank
1. Hawaii	51.6	44
2. Colorado	53.0	35
3. Massachusetts	54.5	40
4. Vermont	55.2	32
5. Utah	55.8	41
6. Arizona (tied)	56.4	15
Connecticut (tied)	56.4	48
8. Montana	57.1	13
9. Rhode Island	57.4	26
10. New York	57.9	18

Great Achievements in Medical Fraud

Have you fallen for pills, ointments, and gadgets that swear to make you thinner or more muscular, with thicker hair and rock-hard abs? Well, you're not alone. Read on for a look at some of history's most notorious medical shams and charlatans.

To the Rescue

If you were diagnosed at the turn of the century with lumbago, puking fever, black vomit, consumption, decrepitude, falling sickness, milk leg, ship fever, softening of the brain, St. Vitus's dance, trench mouth, dropsy, or—heaven forbid—dyscrasia, then chances are you were in big trouble. Not only did the "modern" medical community misunderstand most of these diseases, but it was also clueless as to how to treat them.

Facing a life of interminable pain and suffering, many sufferers of these diseases resorted to hundreds of unfounded medical treatments, which sometimes worked and sometimes didn't. Here's a brief list of some of the more popular medical treatments and the claims made by their originators:

- **The Battle Creek Vibratory Chair** Many people who enjoy a bowl of Corn Flakes in the morning are familiar with their inventor, Dr. John Harvey Kellogg of Battle Creek, Michigan. Dr. Kellogg also designed a number of therapeutic devices, including the Battle Creek Vibratory Chair. The patient was strapped in, then the chair would shake violently to "stimulate intestinal peristalsis" that was beneficial to digestive disorders. Prolonged treatments were also used to cure a variety of maladies from headaches to back pain.

- **The Toftness Radiation Detector** If the Toftness Radiation Detector looks suspiciously like the PVC piping and couplings found at a hardware store, that's because it is. By passing PVC tubing outfitted with inexpensive lenses over the patient's back, chiropractors listened for a high-pitched "squeak" that meant the device had detected areas of neurological stress, characterized by high levels of radiation. The device was widely used until 1984 when it was deemed worthless by the Food and Drug Administration (FDA).

- **The Foot Operated Breast Enlarger Pump** In the mid-1970s, silicone breast implant technology was still in its infancy. Instead, many women pining for larger breasts spent $9.95 for a foot-operated vacuum pump and a series of cups that promised "larger, firmer and more shapely breasts in only 8 weeks." As it turned out, more than four million women were duped into buying a device that produced nothing more than bruising.

- **The Crystaldyne Pain Reliever** In 1996, one of the most popular pain relievers on the market was nothing more than a gas grill igniter. When the sufferer pushed on the plunger, the device sent a short burst of sparks and electrical shocks through the skin to cure headaches, stress, arthritis, menstrual cramps, earaches, flu, and nosebleeds. After being subjected to FDA regulations, however, the company disappeared with thousands of dollars, falsely telling their consumers that "their devices were in the mail."

- **The Prostate Gland Warmer and The Recto Rotor** Even someone without the slightest bit of imagination would cringe at the idea of inserting a 4½-inch probe connected to a nine-foot electrical cord into their rectum. However, for thousands of adventurous consumers in the 1910s, the Prostate Gland Warmer (featuring a blue lightbulb that would light up when plugged in) and the Recto Rotor promised the latest in quick relief from prostate problems, constipation, and piles.

- **The Radium Ore Revigator** In 1925, thousands of unknowing consumers plunked down their hard-earned cash for a clay jar with walls that were impregnated with low-grade radioactive ore. The radioactive material was nothing more than that found in the dial of an inexpensive wristwatch, but the Revigator still promised to invigorate "tired" or "wilted" water that was put into it—"the cause of illness in one hundred and nine million out of the hundred and ten million people of the United States."

- **Hall's Hair Renewer** For as long as there's been hair loss, there have been hair-loss cures. One of the better-known snake oils in the 19th century was Hall's Vegetable Sicilian Hair Renewer, which Reuben P. Hall began selling in 1894. According to the inventor, an Italian sailor passed the recipe onto him; the results promised hair growth and decreased grayness. The first version was composed of water, glycerine, lead sugar, and traces of sulfur, sage, raspberry leaves, tea, and oil of citronella. Eventually, the formula was adjusted to include two kinds of rum and trace amounts of lead and salt. Of course, lead is poisonous, and the ingredients had to be changed once again. Still, the product sold into the 1930s. Perhaps it was its promise that "As a dressing it keeps the hair lustrous, soft and silken, and easy to arrange. Merit wins."

- **The Relaxacisor** For anyone who hated to exercise but still wanted a lithe, athletic body, the Relaxacisor was the answer. Produced in the early 1970s, the Relaxacisor came with four adhesive pads that were applied to the skin and connected by electrodes to a control panel. The device would deliver a series of electrical jolts to the body, "taking the place of regular exercise" while the user reclined on a sofa. All 400,000 devices were recalled for putting consumers at risk for miscarriages, hernias, ulcers, varicose veins, epilepsy, and exacerbating preexisting medical conditions.

- **The Timely Warning** In 1888, one of the most embarrassing and debilitating experiences a man could endure was an "amorous dream" or "night emission." Fortunately, Dr. E. B. Foote came up with the "Timely Warning," a circular, aluminum ring that was worn to prevent "the loss of the most vital fluids of the system— those secreted by the testicular glands." For better or for worse, no diagrams have been found to illustrate exactly *how* the device was worn.

Cash Curiosities

Beyond the standard money lore—that it's the root of all evil, makes the world go round, and (sadly) never grows on trees—there's a wealth of monetary trivia.

- Beginning around 9000 B.C., cattle were used as a form of money. The animals had consistent value, so it was simple to "spend" them.
- The original currency was the cowrie shell, first used in China around 1200 B.C.
- Before the American Civil War, banks—not the government—printed their own paper currency.
- The Treasury Department issued the first $1 bill in 1862. It featured a portrait of Treasury Secretary Salmon P. Chase. George Washington took his place in 1869.
- In 1934 and 1935, the United States printed $100,000 notes, the largest bill to date. They featured a portrait of Woodrow Wilson and were only used in transactions between Federal Reserve banks.
- In a typical year, 95 percent of new notes are printed to replace worn-out money.
- The average life expectancy of a $1 bill is 21 months, while $100 bills typically last 89 months.
- In the 2008 fiscal year, the U.S. Mint produced more than 10 billion coins, half of which were pennies.
- In 2008, it cost 1.67 cents to make one penny. Taxpayers spent more than $130 million making pennies that were worth $80 million.
- The $ sign likely originated on old pesos, which included a *P* and an *S* that eventually merged and evolved into the $ sign.

McDonald's Food Items that Didn't Make the Cut

If you remember "Two all-beef patties, special sauce, lettuce, cheese, pickles, onions on a sesame seed bun," you're familiar with McDonald's Big Mac—by far the chain's biggest hit. But standing in stark contrast to this celebrated sandwich are some wacky McDonald's offerings that even Ronald McDonald couldn't save.

Hulaburger Although veggie burgers and other meat replacements have gained ground over the years, people still prefer beef patties. Perhaps this explains why the Hulaburger dropped the hoop. In a move that's best described as fast-food folly, McDonald's targeted Catholic consumers (who couldn't eat meat on Fridays during Lent) with a sandwich featuring a sliver of *pineapple* instead of a meat patty. Rather than "hang loose" with this bizarre Hulaburger, consumers turned up their noses and hula-danced away.

McDLT Okay, you *think* you know where this is headed, but do you really? Yes, the McDLT featured lettuce and tomato, just like its BLT namesake, but that's where the resemblance ended. In McDonald's wacky version, the hot and cold portions were completely separated in a rather unwieldy box. Hungry consumers were then expected to combine the two before mastication commenced. The public balked, the McDLT walked, and the rest is history.

McPizza In a world that already featured Pizza Hut, Domino's, and a gazillion other local pizzerias, did McDonald's really believe it could sell pizza and prosper? You bet your pepperoni! But in the end, this McDonald's experiment failed for two key reasons: People preferred to dine at actual pizza parlors, and they craved the higher quality that such outlets promised. *Ciao*, McPizza.

McLean Deluxe First rule of contemporary food marketing: A healthful product should also taste good. This burger, which reduced fat by combining water with *seaweed* of all distasteful things, tasted awful. A savvy public allowed it to "sink."

McPasta Try though they did, McDonald's simply could not find an audience for its pasta-based menu. Even with popular dishes like lasagna, spaghetti, and Fettuccini Alfredo fronting for the red, white, and green, the fare never caught on. *Molto triste*.

McAfrika Well known for an enduring famine, the continent of Africa once found its name prominently featured in a McDonald's product. Traded as a "Limited Edition Olympic Games Burger," the McAfrika appeared insensitive to more than a few. When McDonald's realized its ghastly error, it installed famine relief donation boxes in outlets where the McAfrika was sold.

McHotdog Wieners being hawked at a burger joint? Isn't this akin to sacrilege? Available at select outlets throughout the world, the venerable hot dog never found an audience under Ray Kroc's golden arches. Perhaps potential customers were too busy wolfing them down at ballparks?

McLobster Most can see why this one failed, but if you haven't a clue, try this on for size: Lobster is generally found at more expensive dining establishments. Translation: People with a shellfish craving would likely *never* visit McDonald's. Toss in a relatively steep price, and the McLobster's fate was sealed. Even so, the sandwich maintains a claw-hold in Maine and in certain parts of Canada.

McGratin Croquette This Japanese-market sandwich featured fried macaroni, shrimp, and mashed potatoes. Sound pretty awful? Many diners agreed. This effectively doomed the sandwich to bit-player status. It remains a seasonal offering.

Arch Deluxe Billed as a sophisticated burger, the Arch Deluxe (featuring Spanish onions and a fancy bun) was aimed squarely at discriminating adults. But discrimination can cut two ways, as McDonald's soon found out. Despite a $100 million ad campaign, the burger for grown-ups flamed out. Many McHeads rolled after the giant misstep.

Ten Surefire Signs You're Living in a Dictatorship

1. Your president's face is staring back at you all the time.

Is your president's face on a banner in the town square? In framed photos in the dining room? How about on your currency? Yep, it's a dictatorship.

2. Your nation's leader sports interesting facial hair.

Stalin, Hitler, Hussein, Pinochet, Castro, Trujillo—all had trademark facial hair. The lesson? Vote for the clean-shaven candidate.

3. Your nation's artists and writers are in prison.

One of the first things to go under a dictatorship is freedom of speech. Have more poets in prison than in literary journals? You're probably living under a dictator.

4. Your nation's leader is getting progressively stranger.

Idi Amin declared himself "Conqueror of the British Empire" for no apparent reason and was rumored to have dined on his enemies. Kim Jong-Il wears oversize sunglasses and eats live lobsters with silver chopsticks. Hitler was a hypochondriac who hated moonlight and whistling. There's something about being a dictator that brings out the eccentricities in people.

5. Your president wears his army uniform in public.

Nothing says "dictator" like army uniforms weighed down by several dozen medallions and ribbons. See: Idi Amin, Manuel Noriega, Rafael Trujillo, Benito Mussolini, and Saddam Hussein.

6. The ruling party won "reelection" by an enormous margin.

By their very nature, political elections are hotly contested—unless you're a dictator rigging the polls. Never was this more obvious than in 2002, when 100 percent of nearly 12 million eligible Iraqi voters "voted" Saddam Hussein in for another seven-year term.

7. You catch your neighbor peeping through your curtains.

Oppressive regimes depend on their citizenry to help police the state. In Maoist China's "Cultural Revolution," for example, people who turned in their neighbors for uttering disparaging words about the government were hailed as patriots.

8. Your government talks about "Plans" and trumpets its successes.

Plans, usually of the five-year variety, have been a hallmark of dictatorships dating back to Josef Stalin. Another hallmark is trumpeting the successes of those plans—almost always fabricated—through government-run media outlets.

9. The president is the richest man in the country.

We all know that even in free countries, politics is dominated by the wealthy, but when your leader is using the nation's coffers as his personal bank account, you've got problems. Perhaps nowhere was this more blatant than in Nigeria, where from 1993 to 1998 dictator Sani Abacha reputedly pilfered billions from the national government.

10. Your leader was put in charge by a relative.

In democracies, rulers are voted in. In dictatorships, dictators hand the reins over to relatives, most often their children. See: Papa Doc and Baby Doc Duvalier.

Air Force One

According to the official White House Web page for Air Force One, Franklin Roosevelt was the first U.S. president to travel extensively by air. His trips to the Yalta Conference and other destinations in Europe were an essential part of the World War II effort, but left his staff scrambling to find ways to ensure his safety and security as well as to keep the nation running while he was abroad. His successor, Harry Truman, also flew frequently, but it wasn't until the final years of Truman's administration that the name "Air Force One" came into use. The term is actually a call sign rather than the name of a specific aircraft and is only used to identify the aircraft when the president is on board. Each president since Roosevelt has had a dedicated airplane at his disposal, but any Air Force jet that has a sitting president as a passenger uses the call sign Air Force One.

Specifications of Current Air Force One Aircraft

Model: Boeing 747–200B

Engine thrust rating: 56,700 pounds

Fuel capacity: 53,611 gallons

Range: 7,800 miles

Wing span: 195 feet, 8 inches

Length: 231 feet, 10 inches

Height: 63 feet, 5 inches

Maximum altitude: 45,100 feet

Interior floor space: 4,000 square feet

Special Amenities of Current Air Force One Aircraft

- Exercise room
- Full medical facility
- Retractable stairways
- Two galleys with capacity to prepare 100 meals in one sitting
- Shielded wiring to protect from electromagnetic pulses
- Classified defensive countermeasures technology
- In-flight refueling capability
- Safe for storing nuclear launch codes
- Two private bathrooms with showers
- Number of telephones: 85
- Number of televisions: 19

Famous Air Force One Moments

- **November 22, 1963:** Lyndon B. Johnson is sworn in as president on board Air Force One (the plane is on the ground at the time) after the assassination of John F. Kennedy.

- **August 9, 1974:** On the day of Richard Nixon's resignation, Gerald Ford is sworn in as president while Nixon is aboard Air Force One, making this the only time the plane changed its call sign in midflight.

- **September 11, 2001:** President George W. Bush uses Air Force One as a military command center following the 9/11 attacks.

- **April 27, 2009:** Without President Barack Obama's knowledge, his backup plane is flown at a low altitude around Manhattan for publicity photos, causing panic among unknowing New Yorkers who feared it was another 9/11–type attack.

The Truth About Mighty Mouse

Which Mighty Mouse is your favorite? Do you like the classic opera-singing Mighty Mouse and his famous call "Here I come to save the day!" Or do you prefer the more modern Mighty Mouse who came with his own sidekick, Scrappy Mouse? Whichever mouse you like most, you're sure to be surprised by some of these forgotten facts regarding everyone's favorite flying mouse.

1. Mighty Mouse was almost a housefly. When Terrytoons studio writer Izzy Klein first came up with the idea of a tiny superpowered creature, he designed a character called Superfly. Thankfully, cooler heads prevailed: Studio head Paul Terry changed our hero into a mouse. Good thing, too; no one likes flies. (As opposed to mice. We all love having a mouse for a houseguest, don't we?)

2. Even after he became a mouse, our hero still wasn't "Mighty." In his first two cartoon appearances, the flying mouse went by the name Super Mouse. Terrytoons changed the name to Mighty Mouse only after learning that a new comic book, *Coo Coo Comics*, had introduced its own Super Mouse character in 1943. Terrytoons renamed their mouse "Mighty Mouse" to avoid competition. The studio later altered Mighty Mouse's first two adventures upon re-release to reflect the change.

3. The first Mighty Mouse cartoon debuted in 1942. It was titled "The Mouse of Tomorrow."

4. Mighty Mouse's most famous villain is Oil Can Harry, a nasty cat. Oil Can, though, made his debut long before the flying mouse, starring in Terrytoons' 1933 cartoon "The Banker's Daughter." In that cartoon, he was a villainous human out to steal the virtuous Fanny Zilch from her stalwart lover, J. Leffingwell Strongheart.

5. During his early adventures, Mighty Mouse's girlfriend was the sweet Pearl Pureheart. Pearl usually managed to get captured by Oil Can Harry. The first Mighty Mouse cartoons were actually parodies of the silent-film serials that often featured heroines in

peril with the requisite strong-chinned heroes rushing to their rescue. Many Mighty Mouse cartoons started with the mouse and Pearl already in some trap devised by the nefarious Oil Can—say, tied to railroad tracks as a locomotive steamed toward them.

6. Mighty Mouse is known for his operatic cartoons, in which characters sing their lines. The first operatic Mighty Mouse episode titled "Mighty Mouse and the Pirates" aired in January 1945.

7. For the most part, Mighty Mouse has been slighted by the Academy. Only one of his cartoons, "Gypsy Life" (1945), was nominated for an Oscar. It didn't win.

8. Some of the original Mighty Mouse cartoons, especially the operatic cartoons, were rather violent for kiddie fare. Mighty Mouse would often pummel his enemies, mostly cats of some sort, until they fled the scene.

9. In some cartoons, Mighty Mouse boasts telekinetic powers, making objects fly through the air. In one adventure, he even managed to turn back time.

10. Mighty Mouse cartoons first aired as animated shorts that ran before feature films in movie theaters. In 1955, CBS brought the character and his old adventures to television screens. The network then replayed the old shorts for 12 years on the "Mighty Mouse Playhouse."

11. Famed animator Ralph Bakshi—who created the adult "Fritz the Cat"—created his own version of Mighty Mouse in the 1980s. Called "Mighty Mouse: The New Adventures," the cartoon shared elements of the flying mouse's backstory with viewers. For instance, when he wasn't fighting crime, Mighty Mouse posed as an ordinary mouse named Mike Mouse. He also gained a sidekick in this version, Scrappy Mouse.

12. The Bakshi version of the cartoon lasted only two seasons, but that was long enough for it to generate controversy. In one cartoon, Mighty Mouse sniffs a white powder. The Reverend Donald Wildmon, founder of the American Family Association, claimed the mouse was snorting cocaine. Bakshi denied this, saying the mouse was actually sniffing his lucky cheese. Later, Bakshi said Mighty Mouse was sniffing crushed flowers.

Surviving Life Behind Bars, Part 1

The trial is over, you've been sentenced to a term in prison, and even though you're feeling tough, you're scared to death. Here's what to do to survive and stay out of trouble.

- Do expect taunting, especially if you're young and innocent-looking. Pay attention, but remember that it's a way for the rest of the prison population to see what you're made of.

- Do keep your mouth shut. Watch and listen until you get a feel for the place. Don't try too hard to make friends. Allegiances will come naturally. Absorb jailhouse "law"—both inmate and official—before touching anything.

- Walk and talk with extreme respect. The words "excuse me" and "sorry" should be ready on your lips at all times.

- Although prison rape happens, understand that consensual sex is more common, particularly in male populations. Women should be aware that sexual favors from guards aren't worth the hassle in the end. If you're asked for sex and aren't interested, calmly say "no" and walk away. Be willing to fight, if necessary.

- Be discreet. Keep your eyes and ears open. Never forget that you're in jail with people who've done crimes like yours or worse.

- Always protect yourself. Be aware of prison weapons and projectiles, including feces and flammables. Remember that your personal safety is not the first thing on a guard's mind when something happens.

- Be willing to get a job. Prison employment gets you out of your cell, and it looks great on your record. Bonus: You get a little cash for the few things you need and can buy there.

- Do spend your time constructively. Take advantage of any schooling offered. Read everything you can, not just law books.

- Do remember that even though you're in jail, you still have some constitutional rights. Know what they are.

Bragging Rights

Nature's Nerds:
The World's Brainiest Animals

It's notoriously difficult to gauge intelligence, both in humans and animals. Comparing animal IQs is especially tricky, since different species may be wired in completely different ways. But when you look broadly at problem-solving and learning ability, several animal brainiacs do stand out from the crowd.

Great Apes Scientists generally agree that after humans, the smartest animals are our closest relatives: chimpanzees, gorillas, orangutans, and bonobos (close cousins to the common chimpanzee). All of the great apes can solve puzzles, communicate using sign language and keyboards, and use tools. Chimpanzees even make their own sharpened spears for hunting bush babies, and orangutans can craft hats and roofs out of leaves. One bonobo named Kanzi has developed the language skills of a three-year-old child—and with very little training. Using a computer system, Kanzi can "speak" around 250 words and can understand 3,000 more.

Dolphins and Whales
Dolphins are right up there with apes on the intelligence scale. They come up with clever solu-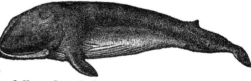tions to complex problems, follow detailed instructions, and learn new information quickly—even by watching television. They also seem to talk to each other, though we don't understand their language. Scientists believe some species use individual "names"—a unique whistle to represent an individual—and that they even refer to other dolphins in "conversation" with each other. Researchers have also observed dolphins using tools. Bottlenose dolphins off the coast of Australia will slip their snouts into sponges to protect themselves from stinging animals and abrasion while foraging for food on the ocean floor. Marine biologists believe whales exhibit similar intelligence levels as well as rich emotional lives.

Elephants In addition to their famous long memories, elephants appear to establish deep relationships, form detailed mental maps of where their herd members are, and communicate extensively over long distances through low-frequency noises. They also make simple tools, fashioning fans from branches to shoo away flies. Researchers have observed that elephants in a Kenyan national park can even distinguish between local tribes based on smell and clothing. The elephants are fine with one tribe but wary of the other, and for good reason: That tribe sometimes spears elephants.

Parrots People see intelligence in parrots more readily than in other smart animals because they have the ability to speak human words. But in addition to their famed verbal abilities, the birds really do seem to have significant brain power. The most famous brainy bird, an African gray parrot named Alex, who died in 2007, exhibited many of the intellectual capabilities of a five-year-old. He had only a 150-word vocabulary, but he knew basic addition, subtraction, spelling, and colors, and had mastered such concepts as "same," "different," and "none."

Monkeys They're not as smart as apes, but monkeys are no intellectual slouches. For example, macaque monkeys can understand basic math and will come up with specific cooing noises to refer to individual objects. Scientists have also trained them to learn new skills by imitating human actions, including using tools to accomplish specific tasks. They have a knack for politics, too, expertly establishing and navigating complex monkey societies.

Dogs If you're looking for animal brilliance, you might find it right next to you on the couch. Dogs are good at learning tricks, and they also demonstrate incredible problem-solving abilities, an understanding of basic arithmetic, and mastery of navigating complex social relationships. A 2009 study found that the average dog can learn 165 words, which is on par with a two-year-old child. And dogs in the top 20 percent of intelligence can learn 250 words. Border collies are generally considered the smartest breed, followed by poodles and German shepherds. One border collie, named Rico, actually knows the names of 200 different toys and objects. When his owners ask for a toy by name, he'll go to the next room and retrieve it for them.

What to Do When Your Single-Engine Plane Conks Out

1. Locate the nearest landing area. This can be anything from an airport to a cleared field or a parking lot. Roads and highways are also possibilities. Remember, the average single-engine plane flown at optimum glide speed will travel approximately 7,000 feet forward for every 1,000 feet it loses in altitude. Never give up!

2. Maintain level flight until airspeed is reduced to optimum glide speed (the speed at which the airplane can glide the farthest). Then, begin descent.

3. Continually adjust trim for best glide speed.

4. Check to see if the propeller is still spinning. This indicates that the engine has not seized, and a restart may be possible.

5. Perform flow pattern check and adjustment (right to left) of engine controls and instruments in an attempt to restart the engine. Necessary alterations such as enriching carburetor air-fuel mixture, engaging carburetor heat, changing throttle position, switching on backup electric fuel pump, switching magneto ignition systems, and switching fuel tanks should be performed as deemed necessary.

6. Set discrete transponder code (aka squawk code) to 7700. This shows up as an aircraft in distress on air traffic control radar.

7. Set communications radio to 121.50 MHz and verbally broadcast "MAYDAY." The closest air traffic controller should respond.

8. Adjust flight path as necessary. Example: Perform S-turns or circles to reduce altitude, lower flaps as required, and so forth.

9. On short final approach, shut down fuel and electrics. This lessens the chance of fire upon touchdown.

10. Finally, the best priority sequence during an engine failure or other in-flight emergency is aviate/navigate/communicate in that precise order.

Presidentially Speaking

With their riotous quips, intentional or otherwise, our chief executives have given comics a run for their money. This collection proves far and away that Washington's "top bananas" play "second banana" to no one.

"I have often wanted to drown my troubles, but I can't get my wife to go swimming."
—Jimmy Carter

"I never drink coffee at lunch. I find it keeps me awake for the afternoon."
—Ronald Reagan

"Our enemies are innovative and resourceful, and so are we. They never stop thinking about new ways to harm our country and our people, and neither do we."
—George W. Bush

"Solutions are not the answer."
—Richard Nixon

"Did you ever think that making a speech on economics is a lot like pissing down your leg? It seems hot to you, but it never does to anyone else."
—Lyndon B. Johnson

"Look, when I was a kid, I inhaled frequently. That was the point."
—Barack Obama

"Too many OB-GYNs aren't able to practice their love with women all across this country."
—George W. Bush

"Contrary to the rumors you have heard, I was not born in a manger. I was actually born on Krypton and sent here by my father Jor-El to save the Planet Earth."
—Barack Obama

"For seven and a half years I've worked alongside President Reagan. We've had triumphs. Made some mistakes. We've had some sex . . . uh . . . setbacks."
—George H. W. Bush

"Things are more like they are now than they ever were before."
—Dwight D. Eisenhower

"As yesterday's positive report card shows, childrens do learn when standards are high and results are measured."
—George W. Bush

"A conservative is a man who just sits and thinks; mostly sits."
—Woodrow Wilson

Feeling Stressed?

- Almost nine out of ten adults have suffered from severe stress. As many as four out of ten adults are so stressed out that it affects their health. It is reported that 75 to 90 percent of all visits to the doctor are for symptoms caused by stress.

- In the United States, tranquilizers, antidepressants, and medications for anxiety account for 25 percent of all prescriptions written.

- Studies show that 60 percent of all employee absences are due to stress. The number of employees who report that they are "highly stressed" is greater now than at any time in history. Stress strong enough to cause disability has doubled over the past decade.

- Job stress is estimated to cost U.S. industry $300 billion annually, as assessed by absenteeism, diminished productivity, employee turnover, and direct medical, legal, and insurance fees.

- In a 14-year study of stress among 12,500 Swedes, those who had little control over their work were twice as likely to develop heart disease. Those with little support at work were nearly three times as likely to develop heart disease.

- In the United States, about a million people each day are absent from work due to stress-related disorders.

- When you're under pressure and feeling tense or angry, stress hormones such as adrenaline and cortisol pour into your system. They make your blood pressure and heart rate rise. Your muscles tense, and your blood sugar increases. These physical changes affect you for hours after the stress has passed and can lead to poor health.

- Post-traumatic stress disorder (PTSD) is delayed stress that can occur when people are exposed to a disturbing or frightening experience. Any extremely stressful situation can result in PTSD, whether someone is directly involved or just an observer.

- PTSD is commonly experienced by people who are exposed to physical or emotional violence; a car or airplane crash; a hurricane, fire, or war; or any other imminent threat of death.

It Happened in ... January

- On New Year's Day 1907, President Theodore Roosevelt shook almost 9,000 hands—a record for the time.

- Is your calendar half empty or half full? January 1, 1950, was the official halfway point of the 20th century.

- Gesundheit: In January 1981, young Donna Griffiths of Pershore, England, began sneezing about every 30 seconds. She didn't stop until nearly three years later, kachooing an estimated one million times.

- Police arrested Karen Jane McNeil in January 2001 after she was discovered stalking singer Axl Rose. McNeil believed that Rose was communicating with her via telepathy. It was her second arrest for this offense.

- Remember the song "What Do I Get" by The Buzzcocks? Probably not, because in 1978, workers at the band's record-pressing plant refused to make the discs. It seems that the B-side's title contained a word that rhymes with "fit," and they didn't like it.

- Speaking of obscenities, Fleer, the makers of Orioles second-baseman Billy Ripken's 1989 baseball card were forced to recall thousands of packages of cards when the company discovered a four-letter word was clearly printed on the end of the bat in the photo. Annnnnnd... they're out.

- From the "We've Ignored It Ever Since Department": The first television broadcast of any session of Congress—in this case, the opening session—was shown on January 3, 1947.

- It might be cold outside, but we want you warm: January is Bath Safety Month, National Soup Month, and Oatmeal Month.

Smoke 'Em If You Got 'Em

Back in the days when smoking was fashionable, these now-defunct cigarette brands could light up a room. Today, most of these tobacco manufacturers are remembered through their highly collectible premium inserts, including pin-back buttons and cards featuring baseball players. Here are a few worth revisiting.

Chesterfield Cigarettes

A mainstay of the 1950s scene, the company featured advertisements by such luminaries as Lucille Ball, Dean Martin and Jerry Lewis, Ronald Reagan, and Rod Serling, and was once a sponsor of the police drama *Dragnet.* The brand is still manufactured but hasn't been advertised in the United States for several years. Dogged by declining sales, the product may soon join the ranks of the forever forgotten.

Duke Cigarettes

Extra Credit! The company was owned by industrialist James Buchanan Duke, whose establishment of The Duke Endowment encouraged a Durham, North Carolina, college to change its name to Duke University in honor of Duke's deceased father.

Fatima Cigarettes

This brand was a staple advertiser of 1940s radio programs, including *Dragnet*, with star Jack Webb appearing in several print and radio ads for the company. It was also purported to be the favorite of actress Jean Harlow.

Old Judge Cigarettes

Old Judge is best known by collectors for introducing the first major set of baseball cards in the late 1880s.

Other brands of days past include:

- Admiral Cigarettes
- American Beauty Cigarettes
- Broadleaf Cigarettes
- Champ's Cigarettes
- Clix Cigarettes
- Contentnea Cigarettes
- Cycle Cigarettes
- Emblem Cigarettes
- Gypsy Queen Cigarettes
- Hassan Cigarettes
- Hindu Cigarettes
- Kotton Cigarettes
- Lenox Mouthpiece Cigarettes
- Lloyd's Cigarettes
- Lord Salisbury Cigarettes
- Marvels Cigarettes
- Mino Cigarettes
- Mogul Cigarettes
- Mono Cigarettes
- Murad Cigarettes
- Obak Cigarettes
- Ogden's Cigarettes
- Old Mill Cigarettes
- Paul Jones Cigarettes
- Pet Cigarettes
- Picayune Cigarettes
- Pirate Cigarettes
- Player's Cigarettes
- Polar Tobacco
- Red Sun Cigarettes
- Turf Cigarettes
- Turkey Red Cigarettes
- Twenty Grand Cigarettes
- Wings Cigarettes
- Zira Cigarettes

20 Bizarre Causes of Death on *CSI*

If you've ever watched CBS's CSI: Crime Scene Investigation *series, you know that death isn't always a straightforward affair. Here are some of the more bizarre murders that have taken place on the show.*

Stiletto A visitor to a "special" nightclub is punctured in the neck with a spiked heel in "Lady Heather's Box."

Wooden Stake It worked on Dracula, though this one penetrated a non-vampire skull in "Lucky Strike."

Body Dysmorphic Disorder Excessive Botox, self-inflicted facial wounds, and a poor self-image do not mix in "The Hunger Artist."

Ricin Post-9/11 America saw new fears (and new prime-time story lines) including death by the toxin ricin in "Caged."

Lobster Bisque Delicious on a cold winter night but potentially deadly if you have an allergy to shellfish, as one character learned in "Alter Boys."

Organ Harvest She tried to blame it on a hungry dog in "Justice Is Served" but really it was a demented doctor who harvested human organs to use in yummy protein shakes.

Rabies Bat rabies, to be precise, used in a tattoo parlor, as shown in "The Gone Dead Train."

Toothpaste Brushing your teeth is good. Ingesting two tubes of toothpaste is bad. Lesson learned via "Deep Fried and Minty Fresh."

Tire Those 18-wheelers can be dangerous, especially when a tire explodes in the middle of a go-cart race and beheads a young driver in the aptly named "A La Cart."

Dandruff Shampoo Dry, itchy scalp? Watch out for your dandruff shampoo, an ingredient of which was the weapon of choice in the episode "Organ Grinder."

Meat Bullet Beef. It's what's for *murder*! In "Burden of Proof," Gil Grissom and company investigate the murder of a man shot with a frozen slug of meat.

Death by Gnawing Same-sex intrigue in "Jackpot"—and a guy who buried another guy in the desert, cut his cheek, and let the wild beasties of the Nevada wilderness have their way. One of them gnawed off his head.

Game Tiles Learning can be fun . . . and deadly . . . in "Bad Words" when a man is suffocated by six tiles, similar to those used in the board game SCRABBLE.

Blood Thinners The seedy side of sitcoms is revealed in "Two and a Half Deaths" as a comedy series costar slowly poisons the crabby star's mouthwash (where, naturally, she hid her booze). The star falls down, bangs her head, and bleeds to death.

Killer Mold It's not quite a 1950s B-movie thriller . . . a fitness trainer oozes black pus while undergoing an autopsy in "4 × 40." Creatures from another world? Nope. It was flesh stuck on a bullet lodged in a wall, upon which mold grew, releasing spores, killing the trainer who had a weakened immune system from steroid use.

Dry Ice A jealous ex-girlfriend kills the big man on campus and his girlfriend with fumes from dry ice. A toilet also explodes in "Iced."

Flesh-Eating Bacteria One expects a lot from an episode entitled "Pirates of the Third Reich." A girl is found dead in the desert, having starved to death after being injected with a flesh-eating bacteria. She also chewed off her hand. Oh, and one of the eyes loosely fitted in her socket belongs to someone else!

Embalming Fluid Just say no to drugs! Especially joints that are dipped in embalming fluid. They may not kill you, but the toxins and the pot may make you kill a guy (as evidenced in "Toe Tags").

Chain Saw Bonus! "Toe Tags" actually had two bizarre deaths. This one involved a chain saw! Though not the stuff of horror movies, the premise involved a man accidentally chopping off his friend's arm, then having the saw kick back into the first guy's chest. A two-fer!

All This and Cereal Too?

It's rare to find toys in cereal boxes today, but there was a time when no self-respecting kid would buy a breakfast cereal that didn't boast its own rubber spider or Fred Flintstone magnet hiding beneath all those corn flakes and marshmallow hearts.

Cardboard Records The cardboard record may be one of the most unusual cereal box toys of them all. You had to cut the record from the back of your favorite cereal box, which meant that you'd have to wait until you finished the cereal inside—if you were patient enough. You could then play these records on a real record player!

In 1954, General Mills offered some of the earliest cardboard records when the company released a series of 78-rpm children's songs that kids had to cut from the backs of Wheaties boxes. Some of the songs included in the series were "Take Me Out to the Ball Game" and "On Top of Old Smokey."

Other favorites include a cardboard record packaged on Alpha Bits with several songs from the Jackson 5, including "I'll Be There" and "Never Can Say Goodbye," and a Monkees record on Honeycomb cereal that included the songs "Pleasant Valley Sunday" and "I'm a Believer."

Vintage Space Adventure In the 1940s, Cheerios offered kids the chance to send away for a Moon Rocket Kit. They only had to mail in a Cheerios box top and a label from a can of V8 vegetable juice. That's right: They wanted kids to drink tomato juice.

The Moon Kit itself came with plastic astronauts, a rocket, and a poster of the moon that boasted different targets. Kids were supposed to shoot the astronauts at the highest-scoring targets.

A More Modern Take Kids eating Froot Loops, Apple Jacks, Frosted Flakes, or Cocoa Krispies in 2006 had the chance to win a real Ford Fusion, presumably for their moms and dads. That's because Ford Motor Company inserted 600,000 toy Fusion cars in select Kellogg's cereal boxes sold at Target department stores. Kids who found red toy cars with the Target logo won a real Ford Fusion.

Infamous Zoo Escapes

On Monday, November 9, 1874, New Yorkers awoke to shocking news. According to the New York Herald, *enraged animals had broken out of the Central Park Zoo the preceding Sunday. At that very moment, a leopard, cheetah, panther, and other beasts of prey roamed the park in search of hapless victims. Women and children huddled indoors. Men rushed out with rifles, prepared to defend their families. But it was all for naught—the whole story was a hoax perpetuated by a reporter irate at what he thought were lax security measures at the zoo. As it turns out, though, that reporter may have been on to something.*

Fast-forward to Sunday, July 5, 2009. More than 5,000 visitors were evacuated from Great Britain's Chester Zoo in the city of Liverpool. "Chimps Gone Wild!" the headlines screamed the next morning. Apparently, 30 chimpanzees had escaped from their island enclosure. This great breakout was certainly no hoax, but neither was it cause for alarm. The chimps got no further than the area where their food was kept. They gorged themselves until they had to lie down and rub their aching bellies. A little later, zoo wardens rounded them up, and the escapees returned to their island peacefully.

When it comes to zoo escapes, primates are often among the prime offenders. One of the greatest of all nonhuman escape artists was the legendary Fu Manchu of Omaha's Henry Doorly Zoo. Back in 1968, this orangutan confounded his keepers by repeatedly escaping from his cage no matter how well it was secured. Only when a worker noticed Fu slipping a shiny wire from his mouth did the hairy Houdini's secret come out. The orangutan had fashioned a "key" from this wire and was using it to pick the lock. What's even more impressive is that he had the sense to hide it between his teeth and jaw—a place no one was likely to look. Once officials realized what the cagey animal had been up to, they stripped his cage of wires. Though Fu Manchu never escaped again, he was rewarded for his efforts with an honorary membership in the American Locksmiths Association.

Oliver, a capuchin monkey in Mississippi's Tupelo Buffalo Park and Zoo, went Fu Manchu one better. In 2007, he escaped from his cage twice in three weeks. Both times he traveled several miles before being apprehended. Zookeepers suspected him of picking the lock, but they never figured out how he did it. Their solution was to secure his cage with three locks, a triple threat that has so far kept him inside. Word of Oliver's escapades drew so many visitors to the zoo that officials decided to capitalize on the capuchin culprit. A best-selling item at the zoo's gift shop is a T-shirt emblazoned with "Oliver's Great Escape" along with a map of his routes.

Evelyn, a gorilla at the Los Angeles Zoo, didn't need to pick a lock. She escaped on October 11, 2000, via climbing vines, à la Tarzan. After clambering over the wall of her enclosure, she strolled around the zoo for about an hour. Patrons were cleared from the area, and Evelyn's brief attempt to experience the zoo from a visitor's point of view ended when she was tranquilized and returned to her enclosure without further incident.

Juan, a 294-pound Andean spectacled bear at Germany's Berlin Zoo, had a much more amazing adventure on August 30, 2004. It started when he paddled a log across the moat that surrounded his habitat. He then scaled the wall and wandered off to the zoo playground. There, he acted just like a kid, taking a spin on the merry-go-round and trying out the slide. When he left in search of further amusement, clever animal handlers decided to distract him with a bicycle. Sure enough, Juan stopped to examine the two-wheeler as if he were contemplating a ride. Before he could mount it, however, an officer shot him with a tranquilizer dart, thus ending Juan's excellent adventure.

Struck by Lightning

There are about 25 million lightning strikes per year in the United States, and for every 83,000 flashes, there's one injury. For every 345,000 zaps, there's one death. Here are the states with the most lightning fatalities (since 1959).

Florida: 440

Texas: 200

North Carolina: 186

Ohio: 140

Tennessee: 139

Louisiana: 136

New York: 136

Colorado: 132

Maryland: 123

Pennsylvania: 126

- In any year in the United States, the odds of being struck by lightning are 1 in 700,000. The odds of being struck in your lifetime are 1 in 3,000.

- Ice in a cloud can contribute to the development of lightning. As ice particles swirl around, they collide and cause separation of electrical charges. Positively charged ice crystals rise to the top of the storm cloud, and negatively charged particles drop to the lower parts of the storm cloud. These enormous charge differences can cause lightning.

- If your hair happens to stand on end during a storm, it could indicate that positive charges are rising through you toward the negatively charged part of the storm. If this ever occurs, get indoors immediately.

- Every year, lightning-detection systems in the United States monitor some 25 million strikes of lightning from clouds to ground during approximately 100,000 thunderstorms. It is estimated that Earth is struck by an average of more than 100 lightning bolts every second.

15 People Who Somehow Got Their 15 Minutes of Fame

From Linda Tripp to John Wayne Bobbitt, this group proves that Andy Warhol was right on the money when he predicted that everybody would be famous for 15 minutes.

William Hung When is bad singing good? When the performance is entertainingly awful. In this regard, one-time *American Idol* hopeful William Hung has few peers. Hung never came close to winning the big prize, but it hardly mattered. A horrendous rendition of Ricky Martin's "She Bangs" won him a huge following that exists to this day. Sometimes wrong *can* be right.

Brian "Kato" Kaelin As O. J. Simpson's unofficial houseboy, Kaelin knew well the dealings of the gridiron star. After Simpson's arrest for the double murder of Nicole Brown Simpson and Ronald Goldman, Kaelin testified as a witness in Simpson's trial. Afterward, Kaelin became a Hollywood fixture, parlaying his notoriety into paying gigs as a radio personality, actor, and host of the TV series *Eye for an Eye*.

Paris Hilton The Hilton Hotel heiress has tasted many more than 15 minutes of fame. However, she makes this list because, like many *fifteeners*, she's famous for being famous. If mugging for cameras is an art form, Hilton ranks up there with Picasso.

Jessica Hahn When sexy church secretary Hahn accused televangelist Jim Bakker of rape, Bakker's world came crashing down. The scandal would lead to Bakker's imprisonment and the beginning of Hahn's 15 minutes. When the opportunity for celebrity arose, Hahn answered with a *Playboy* spread. She also accepted small roles in movies and on television. Regular appearances on *The Howard Stern Show* keep her name in the public sphere.

Donna Rice On the prophetically named yacht *Monkey Business*, married senator and presidential hopeful Gary Hart engaged in, well, monkey business. Unfortunately for Hart, his trysts with sexy model

Rice were discovered by a probing press—a situation that forced him to drop out of the race. In a supremely ironic turn of events, Rice went on to become the communications director and vice president of *Enough Is Enough*, an anti-pornography organization.

Ashley Dupre When New York Governor Eliot Spitzer was caught canoodling with a call girl, some found it hard to believe. After all, hadn't this former attorney general been a crusader *against* prostitution? Dupre became the bad girl of the moment. Attempting to capitalize on her sudden celebrity, Dupre, a former singer, went searching for record deals. Nothing as yet, but time will tell.

Jennifer Wilbanks A real-life runaway bride, Wilbanks went missing just before her planned nuptials. When her absence sparked a nationwide search, Wilbanks called her fiancé, claiming that she had been kidnapped. She would eventually admit that her story was a lie. Wilbanks received two years probation and 120 hours of community service for her deception. To date, she remains single.

Chesley B. Sullenberger III Many receive their 15 minutes for less-than-admirable reasons. Not so for airline captain Sullenberger. On January 15, 2009, the quick-thinking aviator ditched his stone-dead Airbus A320 in New York's Hudson River. Due to his cool head and uncommon skill, all passengers were able to walk away unscathed. Sullenberger's celebrity may fade with time, but his heroic status will not.

John Wayne Bobbitt Bobbitt gained fame when angry wife Lorena severed his penis. He promptly had the appendage reattached. After divorcing, Bobbitt embarked on a career as a porn star but found his equipment lacking. Enhancement surgery brought big results, but success still eluded him. Since then, Bobbitt has had numerous scrapes with the law, mostly for domestic battery.

Jayson Blair Blair hoodwinked *The New York Times* into believing he was a solid journalist. In reality, he could barely write and often plagiarized the work of others. When his dirty secret came out, the well-respected newspaper took a heavy hit. After resigning, Blair returned to college. He currently works as a life coach.

Evan Marriott Evan who? You wouldn't have asked this in 2003 when Marriott posed as a rich bachelor on the reality show *Joe*

Millionaire. Post-series, the strapping Marriott returned to his former job as a construction worker. He currently owns his own firm and maintains a low profile. "I'm just burnt from the whole thing," says Marriott about his moment in the sun. "I'm done with it."

Linda Tripp When Tripp brought the clandestine relationship of President Bill Clinton and Monica Lewinsky to the fore, she became at once admired and despised. After the incident, she had extensive plastic surgery and changed her address. Today, Tripp owns and operates a boutique in Middleburg, Virginia.

Chris Crocker In 2007, when everything in singer Britney Spears world was falling down, one chivalrous defender came to her rescue. A crying Crocker gained overnight fame on YouTube when he screamed: "Leave Britney alone!" Since then, the openly gay Crocker has released several more videos on YouTube. Some are funny, some tackle gay and social issues, but to date none have approached the popularity of his Spears rant.

Ken Jennings Are you smarter than Ken Jennings? Don't bet on it. During an unprecedented win streak of 74 games in 2004, Jennings earned more than $2 million on TV's *Jeopardy!* He currently produces trivia books and hopes to one day become an insignificant footnote to history.

Steve Bartman When this life-long Chicago Cubs fan reached for a foul ball during game six of the 2003 National League Championship series, he inadvertently denied Cubs right-fielder Moises Alou the chance to catch it. Although the Cubs were just a few outs away from a World Series berth, the Florida Marlins rallied to win the game and the series victory. Describing himself as "heartbroken" and "truly sorry," Bartman leads an intentionally private life. But Aisle 4, Row 8, Seat 113 of Wrigley Field still looms large in his mind. Perhaps it always will.

❖ ❖ ❖

"Wal-mart . . . do they like make walls there?"
—Paris Hilton

What's Up, Doc?

We may not like going to the doctor, but we love our TV docs. They consistently rank as most watched. So how closely were you paying attention? How well do you know your favorite TV doctor?

1. Bernie Kopell was simply known as "Doc" during his nine years on *The Love Boat*. But what was his character's real name?

   A. Burl Evans   C. Bob Crawford

   B. Adam Bricker   D. Tom McMann

   Answer: B.

2. What TV doctor starred in two different series—in the first he was a skirt-chasing young doctor, and in the second, he had aged 30 years and was a divorced chief of surgery.

   A. Ben Casey   C. John McIntyre

   B. B. J. Hunnicutt   D. R. Quincy

   Answer: C. From 1972 to 1975, Wayne Rogers played Trapper John McIntyre in M*A*S*H (set between 1950 and 1953) while Pernell Roberts played him in *Trapper John, M.D.* (set in the late '70s and early '80s) from 1979 to 1986. Ironically, Rogers refused the starring role in *Trapper John, M.D.* to play Dr. Charley Michaels in the sitcom *House Calls.*

3. Before George Clooney broke hearts and fixed bodies as Dr. Doug Ross on *ER* he played a doctor on which show?

   A. *St. Elsewhere*   C. *E/R*

   B. *Northern Exposure*   D. *House Calls*

   Answer: C. Clooney was Mark "Ace" Kolmar for the sitcom *E/R* from 1984 to 1985. He wasn't the only *E/R* veteran to show up on *ER*. Mary McDonnell, who starred in *E/R* as Dr. Eve Sheridan played Dr. John Carter's mother on *ER*.

4. St. Elsewhere was the nickname for an old, decrepit Boston hospital. What was its real name?

 A. St. Eligius   C. St. Ellison

 B. St. Edmund   D. St. Efrem

Answer: A.

5. What show focused on the lives of medical personnel in the Vietnam War?

 A. *Tour of Duty*   C. *M*A*S*H*

 B. *China Beach*   D. *Saved*

Answer: B. Tour of Duty also took place during Vietnam but was about combat soldiers.

6. Who played the teenage genius doctor Douglas "Doogie" Howser?

 A. Neil Patrick Harris   C. Kirk Cameron

 B. Jon Cryer   D. Brian Bonsall

Answer: A. Harris now plays Barney Stinson on the sitcom *How I Met Your Mother.*

7. Why does Dr. Joel Fleischman move from NYC to Cicely, Alaska?

 A. To "temporarily" help out a school friend.

 B. As a condition of his medical school scholarship.

 C. He's offered a generous salary by an eccentric Alaskan.

 D. A two-week adventure-vacation morphs into a job.

Answer: B. Turns out Dr. Joel never read the fine print in his scholarship.

8. What TV doctor was protested by gay activists after an episode about a teenage boy raped by his male teacher?

   A. Dr. Kildare

   B. Marcus Welby, M.D.

   C. Dr. Wayne Fiscus

   D. Dr. John Carter

Answer: B. Who knew sweet Dr. Welby was so shocking? These protests against equating homosexuality with sexual violence led to the creation of a media watchdog group: the Gay and Lesbian Alliance Against Defamation (GLAAD).

9. What do the following doctors have in common: Ben Turner, Doogie Howser, Addison Montgomery, and Sean McNamara?

   A. The characters were married to doctors or nurses.

   B. The characters practiced medicine in California.

   C. The characters were "fired" during the series.

   D. The actors who played them left their show before the last season.

Answer: B. Although Dr. Sean McNamara's *Nip-Tuck* was originally set in Miami, the show relocated to Los Angeles for the fifth and sixth seasons.

10. TV docs call some weird places home. Which of the docs below lived in an actual apartment?

   A. George Alonzo "Gonzo" Gates

   B. John "J. D." Dorian

   C. R. Quincy

   D. Derek Shepherd

Answer: B. Despite being a bit wacky, "J. D." of *Scrubs* actually lived in an apartment. Gonzo of *Trapper John, M.D.* and Dr. "McDreamy" Shepherd of *Grey's Anatomy* both lived in campers—Gonzo's was right in the hospital parking lot—while Quincy lived on a houseboat.

Curious Classifieds

Fur coats made for ladies from their own skin.

Sheer stockings. Designed for fancy dress, but so serviceable that lots of women wear nothing else.

And now, the Superstore—unequaled in size, unmatched in variety, un-rivaled inconvenience.

We will oil your sewing machine and adjust tension in your home for $1.00.

Don't stand there and be hungry … come in and get fed up.

Open house—Body Shapers Toning Salon—free coffee & donuts.

Rabbit fur coat, size medium, $45. Small hutch, $55.

Golden, ripe, boneless bananas, 39 cents a pound.

Get rid of aunts: Zap does the job in 24 hours.

Semi-Annual after-Christmas Sale.

Mother's helper—peasant working conditions.

Saturday Morning 10:30 A.M. Easter Matinee. Every child laying an egg in the doorman's hand will be admitted free.

Found: dirty white dog … looks like a rat … been out awhile … Better be a reward.

Registered Miniature American Eskimos, females—$150, male— $125. Ready to go.

Will trade fire, life, automobile insurance for anything can use. Want lady with automobile.

Wanted: A boy who can take care of horses who can speak German.

Dinner Special—Turkey $2.35; Chicken or Beef $2.25; Children $2.00.

For sale: a quilted high chair that can be made into a table, pottie chair, rocking horse, refrigerator, spring coat, size 8 and fur collar.

No matter what your topcoat is made of, this miracle spray will make it really repellent.

Marathons: By the Numbers

- The first Olympic Marathon took place in 1896 and was 40,000 meters (24.85 miles) in length. Greek postal worker Spiridon Louis completed the course in 2 hours, 58 minutes, 50 seconds. His average pace was 7.11 minutes per mile.

- The Olympic Marathon length was changed to 26 miles, 385 yards at the 1908 Olympic Games in London. The length encompassed the distance between Windsor Castle and White City Stadium (26 miles). The 385 additional yards were added to this number to facilitate a finish point in front of King Edward VII's royal box.

- The distance of 26.2 miles was officially established at the 1924 Olympics in Paris. It remains the standard to this day.

- The first New York City Marathon was held in 1970. It featured only 127 competitors. In 2007, 38,557 runners completed the NYC Marathon.

- The first Boston Marathon was held on April 19, 1897. The race's length of 24.5 miles (a distance linking Metcalf's Mill in Ashland to the Irvington Oval in Boston) would be lengthened to 26.2 miles in 1927 to conform to Olympic standards.

- Marathon deaths are rare. A 1996 study performed by the USA Track and Field Road Running Information Center estimates roughly 1 death for every 50,000 runners.

- Statistics for the annual NYC Marathon are staggering. At the starting line, volunteers will dispense more than 90,000 bottles of water, 40,000 cups of coffee, and more than 30,000 PowerBars. Some 2,500 members of the media are present, including photographers who snap 450,000 photos of the racers. As the race progresses, 62,370 gallons of water and 32,000 gallons of Gatorade will be consumed. Approximately 2.2 million paper cups will deliver these vital liquids to thirsty marathoners, and 41 medical aid stations outfitted with 13,000 adhesive bandages, 5 tons of ice, and 390 tubs of Vaseline will be at the standby—just in case.

Nine Facts About Scientology

1. "I'd like to start a religion. That's where the money is." So offered founder L. Ron Hubbard to fellow science-fiction writer Lloyd Eshbach in 1949. Despite the questionable quip, Scientology has enticed thousands into its fold.

2. New members must sign a legal waiver before the Church of Scientology admits them.

3. Scientologists believe that people are immortal spiritual beings who've lost track of their original purpose.

4. Scientologists tell of an alien warlord named Xenu who visited Earth 75 million years ago. The extraterrestrial deposited a rogue's gallery of misfits on Earth and set off volcanic eruptions that continue to poison the minds and bodies of humans.

5. Scientologists shun conventional medical treatments and believe that most—if not all—health problems are psycho-somatic, stemming from a person's "reactive mind."

6. To gain enlightenment, Scientologists use a form of spiritual counseling called *auditing.* The practice features "processes"— a series of questions supplied by an auditor. When a process yields a specific objective, it's ended and another is begun. Scientologists believe auditing frees them from barriers that obstruct their natural abilities.

7. To reach Scientology's top level of awareness, the faithful pay dearly with earthly funds. Actor and famed Scientologist Tom Cruise reportedly spent hundreds of thousands of dollars to reach level OT VII (the highest is OT VIII).

8. "Theta" refers to the Scientologist's spiritual and thought pro-cesses. Such energy is viewed as separate and distinct from the physical universe of matter, energy, space, and time.

9. "Squirreling," or the act of using Scientology's techniques in a form other than that originally outlined by L. Ron Hubbard, is considered a high crime within the religion.

Who Knew?

Too Much Web Surfing

Studies suggest that Internet addiction is becoming a growing concern in the United States. One report found that one out of every eight people is "addicted" to being online. Addiction, in this case, is defined as a behavior-altering, habit-forming, compulsive, physiological need to use the Internet.

Not So Mobile

The world's largest functioning mobile phone is the Maxi Handy, which measures 6.72 feet tall by 2.72 feet wide by 1.47 feet deep. This phone was installed at the Rotmain Centre in Bayreuth, Germany, on June 7, 2004, as part of the "Einfach Mobil" informational tour. Constructed of wood, polyester, and metal, the fully functional phone features a color screen and can send and receive text and multimedia messages. Just don't expect to slip it into your pocket.

Mining for Diamonds

It's finders keepers at the Crater of Diamonds State Park in Murfreesboro, Arkansas. This is the world's only diamond-producing site that's open to the public. Not only that, but visitors can keep any stones they dig up! The visitor center features exhibits and an audio/visual program that explains the area's geology. The center even offers tips on recognizing diamonds in the rough.

Made of Stone

The Washington Monument is the world's tallest freestanding stone structure not created from a single block of stone. The monument is composed of more than 36,000 separate blocks. It stands a whopping 555 feet tall and weighs approximately 90,854 tons! The outside is composed almost entirely of white marble, while the inside is granite.

Only on eBay...

It should probably come as no surprise that a company whose first sale was a broken laser pointer has become a marketplace for all manner of things ranging from gross, weird, and just plain useless. The broken laser pointer—sold for $14.83 to a person who collected broken laser pointers—proves that the company's slogan is true: Whatever it is, you can find it on eBay.

Remote Control Fart Machine #2 When you're talking fart machines, the #2 designation comes with the territory. This "new and improved" battery-operated gadget gives the buyer "15 fart sounds" and promises to be a real toot at parties, school, or the office. Apparently, it can also induce death—a solemn fact evidenced by its "You might die laughing!" warning. For the low $7.99 buy-it-now price, you, too, can become the vilest human being at a gathering. Progress!

Genuine Fart Exploding on the eBay scene, this listing brings new meaning to the term "full of hot air." As an extra treat for one's proboscis, the seller guarantees that his product is the smelliest ever experienced. For some reason, he stops just short of revealing its human creator, though we do have our theories. The scent bouquet comes trapped in a sealed jar creatively labeled "Fart-in-a-Jar." It's just the thing to place on one's coffee table when the boss drops in for a visit or the in-laws overstay their welcome.

Human for Rent An enterprising gentleman from Dinant, Belgium, offers up his bald pate as a sort of fleshy billboard. With a starting bid of $14,999, no one has yet taken him up on his offer. Too bad. It seems the fellow travels extensively and believes that his adorned noggin (Your Message Here!) is the future of advertising. "Don't hesitate," he cautions. "We can realise great things together." Uh-huh.

I Am Selling Myself Since eBay doesn't permit prostitution, we must accept this woman's word that she's "not selling sex"—even if she *is* pictured in a provocative minidress. For $15,000—a measly dollar more than the Human for Rent—the lady's offer appears to be the better deal. Billing herself as a "human pet," the heavily tattooed woman promises to do your shopping, errands, answer your phone, and hang out with you. However, the deal becomes null and void the very instant that you mistreat her. If such were to happen, we wonder whether she'd call the police or alert the ASPCA?

Picture of "Hedgie" the Hedgehog For a measly $0.15, crafty buyers not only snag a photo of this spiky little fellow taking nourishment, they also gain "positive feedback" (a much sought-after commodity in the eBay world) to boot. Talk about a square deal!

Jay Leno Peanut What can you buy for a Jay Leno fan who already has posters, autographs, and photos of the funnyman? The Jay Leno Peanut, of course. For a starting bid of $1.00, a fan might win this genuine peanut with a right-angle bend in it—a condition that mimics the comic's jutting chin profile. Of course, if someone gets a hankering for peanuts, Jay could instantly vanish. That's show biz.

New Male Stainless Metal Chastity Locking Cage Device Why should women be the only ones to have chastity forced upon them? This male "Penistentiary" is crafted of quality stainless steel and resembles, well, a penistentiary. The four-inch, tube-shaped cage (described as a "sexual Alcatraz") attaches to a steel ring. With a buy-it-now price of £30, the cage serves as a stylish deterrent for would-be Lotharios. It's an idea whose time has clearly come.

eBay by the Numbers

90 million: the number of active users eBay currently boasts

$60 billion: the total worth of goods sold on eBay in 2009 (that's $2,000 every second!)

$28,000: the sum paid for a partially eaten grilled cheese sandwich said to bear the image of the Virgin Mary

12 "Teaser" Quotes from *CSI: Miami*

Anyone who has watched CSI: Miami *is familiar with the trademark "teaser" lines that lead into the opening credits. Go ahead: Don your dark glasses and insert your own dramatic pauses . . . YEAHHHHH!!!*

Tripp: *"It looks like a mob hit, Horatio."*

Caine: *"Yes. And it's time—to hit back."*

Coast Guard official: *"It's been ten years since a Florida ship got pirated."*

Caine: *" 'til now."*

Dr. Alexx Woods: *"You don't fall three stories, get up, and run away."*

Caine: *"You do—if you've got something to hide."*

Tripp: *"She was famous for being famous. All eyes trained on her every move."*

Caine: *"All except—her last one."*

Woods: *"He died hours before this accident ever happened."*

Caine: *"So our accident—is not an accident at all."*

Tripp: "He's got quite a little business on his hands."

Caine: "He also has Murder One."

Caine: "Where is Patrick now?"

Sgt. Frank Tripp: "I don't know. He's missing from the scene. Maybe he took off."

Caine: "Or maybe—he got taken for a ride."

Eric Delko: "Do you think he's trying to get our attention?"

Caine: "I don't know. But he just got mine."

Tripp: "He was hauling ass."

Caine: "Yes, Frank. A dead body can have that effect on you."

Tripp: "The verdict's already in."

Caine: "The verdict is in, Frank, but the jury is out."

Gun-toting bad guy: "You're already dead, brother."

Caine (shooting and killing the suspect): "Join the club."

"So we have a victim that started the weekend Big Man on Campus and ended it Dead on Arrival."

Time Spent Wasting Time

You'd be amazed how much time you waste doing stuff!

Breathing Not exactly "wasted" time, considering the alternative. Numerically speaking, if you live to be 75 (and assuming that you expire at the same exact time you were born, mind you) that equates to 900 months or 3,900 weeks or 27,300 days or 655,200 hours or 39,312,000 minutes or 2,358,720,000 seconds. Who says you don't have time to take out the trash?

Eating Mmmmm ... food. Americans sure do love to eat! We stuff our faces an average of 67 minutes per day. Doing some quick math, that comes out to roughly 24,455 minutes—about 407 hours—per year.

Housework Ask the U.S. Department of Labor's Bureau of Labor Statistics and they'll tell you that married moms spend about two hours per day on activities such as housework, preparing dinner, and gardening. That's 36,500 hours, assuming a 50-year marriage. To the surprise of no wife anywhere in the United States, married men reported doing about half this amount of work.

Internet Thanks for finding time to read this book! No small task, since Americans spend about 10½ hours per month, or 126 hours per year, browsing Web sites while at home.

Sleeping By age 75, most people who sleep an average of 7 hours per night will have snoozed away 22 years of their lifetime—about a third of their existence. Incidentally, a 1900 news article put that total at 23 years and 4 months. Hopefully, you did something worthwhile with the time you've since accrued.

Stuck in Traffic You might want to bring along a good book (like this one!) the next time you head out on the open road. The Texas Transportation Institute conducted a study of 439 urban areas across the United States and found that all Americans spent a grand total of nearly 4.2 billion hours stuck in gridlock in 2007. Residents in larger urban areas with populations of more than one million people average 46 hours per year in traffic. The delay was worst in the Los Angeles area, where people spend about 70 hours per year staring at the brake lights in front of them. Take heart, Wichita, Kansas, residents…you spend a mere six hours per year cursing your fellow motorists.

Texting Thanks a lot, technology, for giving us something new to obsess over. According to research conducted by the Nielsen Company, U.S. teens sent or received an average of 2,272 text messages per month in 2008. That's about 80 texts per day. One girl in California girl reportedly sent or received 14,528 texts in a single month.

Watching Television The boob tube eats up 9 years of your life by the time you reach 65, given an average of 4 hours of viewing each day (so says A.C. Nielsen Research). Research has also shown that the TV is on nearly 7 hours each day in the average household. Not only that, but the average American now spends 35 percent more time watching TV *while* using the Internet (way to multitask, America!) than they did a year ago. Of course, since you're reading this book, these statistics probably don't apply to you!

Working How does 89,784 hours sound? That's given an average 8-hour workday at a career that spans 43 years. That total may be skewed these days, however, given rising unemployment and the fact that technology has us connected to the office 24 hours a day, 7 days a week. For whatever it's worth, American men, on average, work about an hour longer each day than their female coworkers.

"Crazed Publishers Forced Me to Read Their Drivel"

Strolling into a drugstore in the 1960s and looking at the cover of the National Enquirer *was much like slowing down to look at an auto accident—you knew you shouldn't, but you just couldn't help it. Sensational screaming headlines and gory gross-out photos laid the groundwork for today's celebrity-laden tabloids that shout improbable claims.*

The *National Enquirer* began its life in 1926 as a weekly broadsheet bankrolled by newspaper giant William Randolph Hearst, who was no stranger to sensational journalism. Yet, it was 1954 when an MIT engineering grad named Generoso Pope took over the paper and turned it into a tabloid format. Realizing that magazines such as *Confidential,* with their outrageous and sensational headlines, were a huge success, Pope patterned the *National Enquirer* after them. By the 1960s, newsstands were featuring incredible cover stories:

- "I DRILLED A HOLE IN MY HEAD FOR KICKS!"

- "MOM USES SON'S FACE FOR AN ASHTRAY"

- "MADMAN CUT UP HIS DATE AND PUT HER BODY IN HIS FREEZER"

- "I CUT OUT HER HEART AND STOMPED ON IT!"

- "STABS GIRL 55 TIMES"

- "MOM BOILED HER BABY AND ATE HER!"

- "DIGS UP WIFE'S ROTTING CORPSE AND RIPS IT APART!"

- "I WATCHED A WILD HOG EAT MY BABY!"

- "SON MURDERS DAD FOR $8"

Where Are They Now?
The Goonies

In the 1985 film The Goonies, *Mikey proclaims, "Goonies never say die!" That still seems to be the attitude of the young cast. Their post-Goonies lives are characterized by formidable obstacles, remarkable comebacks, and lots of hard work.*

- **Sean Astin (Mikey)** Astin, the son of actress Patty Duke and stepson of actor John Astin, stuck with the family business. He's appeared in dozens of movies and TV shows, including starring roles in the 1991 action movie *Toy Soldiers* and the 1993 football film *Rudy*. Most notably, he played Samwise Gamgee, Frodo's faithful companion in *The Lord of the Rings* movies. Astin has also dabbled in politics, campaigning for Hillary Clinton in 2008.

- **Josh Brolin (Brand)** Brolin also comes from a Hollywood family (his dad is actor James Brolin), and he has also continued acting. However, through his 20s and 30s, he didn't have much success and turned to stock trading to earn money. Things picked up in 2007 when Brolin starred in *No Country for Old Men,* which won a Best Picture Oscar. In 2008, he played President George W. Bush in Oliver Stone's *W.* That same year, he also appeared in *Milk,* which earned him a Best Supporting Actor nomination. Brolin has had run-ins with the law over the years: a 2004 arrest after a domestic dispute with his wife, actress Diane Lane, and a 2008 arrest following a bar fight while shooting *W.*

- **Jeff Cohen (Chunk)** Cohen, who performed the famous "Truffle Shuffle," gave up acting after *The Goonies.* He earned a business degree from UC Berkeley, where he was elected president of the students' assocation—with the help of "Chunk for President" campaign posters. Today, he's a successful entertainment lawyer, running a Beverly Hills firm.

- **Corey Feldman (Mouth)** After *The Goonies,* Corey Feldman enjoyed life as a teen heartthrob, appearing with Corey Haim in *The Lost Boys, License to Drive,* and *Dream a Little Dream.*

In his 20s, Feldman's career faltered, and he wrestled with drug addiction, but he continued to act. In 2002, he appeared on the reality show *The Surreal Life,* and in 2007, he and Corey Haim reunited for the reality show *The Two Coreys.* Today, Feldman is an actor, a father, an animal rights activist, and the singer for the band Truth Movement.

- **Jonathan Ke Quan (Data)** Ke Quan didn't do much acting after *The Goonies,* but he stuck with filmmaking. After he graduated from the USC School of Dramatic Arts, he jumped to behind-the-scenes work. As a fight choreographer, he helped create the action in *X-Men* and Jet Li's *The One,* among other movies.

- **Kerri Green (Andy)** After *The Goonies,* Green appeared in the hit movie *Lucas,* but then her acting career wound down. She's since taken only occasional supporting acting roles, including appearances in episodes of *ER* and *Mad About You.* She cofounded the production company Independent Women Artists, and in 1999 she produced, cowrote, and directed the movie *Bellyfruit.*

- **Martha Plimpton (Stef)** Plimpton was born into one of Hollywood's preeminent acting familes—her dad is Keith Carradine, John Carradine's son and David Carradine's brother—and she's worked continually as an actress since she was a kid. Since *The Goonies,* she's had roles in some high-profile films, including *Parenthood,* but she's mainly performed on stage and in independent films. She's one of the busiest Broadway actresses today and has been nominated for three Tony awards.

- **John Matuszak (Sloth)** Sadly, the former defensive lineman died in 1989 from an accidental prescription drug overdose.

The Goonies cast, director Richard Donner, and executive producer Steven Spielberg have contemplated making a sequel over the years. The new film, which would likely feature a new generation of young adventurers, seems to have died at this point. Then again, you know how Goonies feel about that word.

The End of the World

Since before Roman times, prophets and doomsday cults have been predicting the end of the world, and fear-mongerers and television preachers continue the tradition today. Fortunately, all of them have been incredibly wrong—so far.

Pre-Christian Doomsday Cults Most people associate doomsday cults with the Rapture or the Second Coming of Jesus, but doomsday prophets were spreading dread even before Christ's birth. In fact, archaeologists discovered an Assyrian tablet dating back to 2800 B.C. lamenting the corruption and degeneracy of the age and stating quite authoritatively that "the world is speedily coming to an end." Care to narrow that down for us?

Millennial Cults Lotharingian (present-day northwest Europe) scholars determined the world would end on March 25, A.D. 970. The prophets' evidence? Their belief that the date represented the anniversary of Jesus' conception and crucifixion, the parting of the Red Sea, and the creation of Adam. That the date was preposterous didn't stop a frenzy of terror from sweeping across Europe as the end of the first millennium approached.

The Millerites One of the first American doomsday cults, the Millerites were a group of Adventists who followed the teachings of William Miller, who prophesied that the Second Coming of Jesus Christ would be some time around 1843. Miller demonstrated little evidence for his predictions, but Millerism spread like wildfire throughout much of the eastern half of the United States nevertheless. Alas, 1843 came and went (throughout the year, Millerites constantly revised the precise end date) with no sign of Jesus. In 1844, the sect definitively established that the end would come on October 22. On that date, a large group of Miller's followers gathered upon hilltops and roofs to wait for Jesus' arrival. They were sorely disappointed.

Heaven's Gate Heaven's Gate, the most famous doomsday cult of the modern era, was founded in the 1970s by Marshall Applewhite. Applewhite and his followers believed that Earth would soon be "recycled" and "spaded under," and that human civilization would be wiped away with it. The harbinger of this end-time came in the form of the Hale-Bopp comet, which blazed across the night sky throughout much of 1997. But as luck would have it, a spaceship traveling along with the comet would whisk cult members away from our doomed planet. In preparation, 39 members of the Heaven's Gate cult dressed in identical black shirts, sweatpants, and running shoes on March 26, 1997, and committed mass suicide in a rented mansion located in a wealthy San Diego suburb. Each was covered by a purple cloth. Nobody has come up with a viable explanation for why they were dressed in such a way, nor is there any explanation for the items cult members were carrying at the time of their deaths—five dollars and a stack of quarters.

Y2K Cults As the year 2000 approached, panic over what would happen when a computer bug went haywire led to countless groups of hysterical survivalists bunkering down with weaponry and canned goods. How common was this irrational—and, in retrospect, unfounded—fear? According to a *TIME* magazine survey taken in 1999, a whopping 9 percent of Americans believed the world was going to end on January 1, 2000.

December 22, 2012 Today there is no shortage of doomsayers proclaiming that the world is going to end in 2012. Their proof for this little prediction? The ancient Mayans said so. Supposedly. According to the Mayan calendar, December 21, 2012, will mark the end of a 5,126-year cycle, and the calendar will reset to zero. Although there's no evidence that the Mayans believed this meant the world was going to end, fear-peddling prophets continue to churn out books about the end-time by the truckload.

End of the World by the Numbers

5,000,000,000	the approximate year astrophysicists believe the sun will burn out
1,200	the minimum number of self-proclaimed doomsday prophets in the United States

Poor Santa!

Everyday life in Santa's Village can be a challenge.

In 2006, Auntie Anne's Pretzel Company conducted a survey of several hundred mall Santas. Here are its findings:

- 34 percent: percentage of Santas who had been peed on by a child
- 60 percent: percentage of Santas coughed or sneezed on more than ten times per day
- 45 percent: Santas who spend much of the day seeing flash spots caused by cameras
- 9 out of 10: number of Santas that have their beards pulled at least once per day by children
- Half of mall Santas have their glasses pulled off more than ten times per day
- 50 percent: average percentage of Santas who said their boots are stomped on by kids at least once per day

Most Resilient Santa

Perhaps the most resilient of all mall Santas was Ken Deever, a Santa from Des Moines, Iowa. In 2005, a few days before Deever's annual Santa visit to a local elementary school, a fire destroyed his family house, incinerating not only all of his personal possessions, but almost 500 wrapped gifts that were meant to be distributed to the schoolchildren. Deever spent the next two days replacing and rewrapping the gifts in time for the school visit.

Don't Tell Mrs. Claus

With all this lap sitting going on in malls across the country each year, improprieties are bound to happen, but this 2007 incident was a little surprising. A Danbury, Conneticut, woman asked to pose with a Santa at the Danbury Fair Mall—a normal enough request. Once on his lap, the woman began fondling him inappropriately. She was charged with fourth-degree sexual assault.

Oddball Beauty Pageants

There are as many kinds of beauty pageants as there are hobbies, sports, and cultural obsessions. If you're a Star Trek *fan, a beach bum with an artistic bent, or the proud owner of a bushy beard or moustache, these are for you.*

Klingon Nation

Every year, Trekkies (or, as some prefer to be called, "Trekkers") gather in Atlanta for a *Star Trek* convention that includes the Miss Klingon Empire Beauty Pageant. Contestants can compete as established female Klingon characters, or, if they prefer, they can invent their own original characters. Contestants are judged on beauty, personality, and talent, but they are warned on the official Web site that the talent portion should not get too wild and crazy: "no flaming bat'leth twirling."

Shell Games

Hermit crabs may not be known for their beauty, but don't tell that to the organizers of the Miss Curvaceous Crustacean Beauty Pageant in Virginia Beach, Virginia. It isn't the crabs so much as their themed habitats that are judged in this annual beachfront event, and there seems to be no end to the unique ideas that contestants dream up as they surround their hermit crabs with elaborate environments. Past winners had such themes as "Hermit the Hulk," "Spider Crab," and "Beauty and the Crab."

It'll Grow on You

At the Annual World Beard and Moustache Championship, held in the past in both the United States and Europe, Germans usually take the top honors, but American contestants are muscling in. There may be other changes coming soon as well: In 2003, a bearded woman became the first female to join the National Beard Registry, an Internet facial hair group, and some feel that it's only a matter of time before a bearded lady will join the men as a winner.

Inside the Belly of the Beast

Some sharks will take a bite out of pretty much anything, as evidenced by the fact that the Navy has discovered shark bite marks on their submarines. But it gets even weirder than that. Check out some wild things that have been discovered inside the bellies of these beasts.

- An entire roll of roof paper was discovered inside one shark's stomach. We can't help wondering whether it stuck to the roof of the shark's mouth on the way down!

- Although the acid in the critter's stomach will burn human skin, it didn't destroy the five-gallon steel bucket found in one shark.

- Shark digestion is slow, but humans are slower. That might explain the bits of surfboard and rubber flipper munchies found in many a shark belly.

- More than one shark, when caught, has regurgitated bits of human. In some cases, shark stomach contents have even been used as forensic evidence to help solve murders.

- Though sharks can't drive, they apparently find cars irresistible: license plates, tires, and other car parts have been discovered in their stomachs.

- While it's normal for a shark to eat fish and seals, other odd things have been discovered on their menu, including entire carcasses of dogs, horses, sheep, and polar bears. One shark was found with a whole side of beef (presumably from a cruise ship) in his innards.

- In the early 1820s, a shark was reportedly found in the West Indies with a cannon ball in his belly.

- A large turtle was found alive inside the stomach of one shark in the early part of the last century. The turtle, revived and named Jonah, became a popular aquarium exhibit in New York.

- Nearly 900 kilos of cocaine was discovered inside frozen shark carcasses in the summer of 2009.

Under a Raging Moon

Does a full moon really influence people's behavior?

Everyone knows that crazy things happen during a full moon. Or do they? Folklore regarding the connection has long, deep roots. In fact, the word *lunatic* derives from the Latin *luna,* or "moon." Recently, studies have been performed to establish a tie between human behavior and the phases of the moon. These tests have focused on such things as homicides, common crimes, even postsurgical crises during lunar phases. Like the full moon itself, the results have proved illuminating.

In one prominent study, University of Miami psychologist Arnold Lieber zeroed in on homicides. During a 15-year period, his team collected murder data from Dade County, Florida. The researchers found that of the 1,887 recorded murders during the period, the incident rate uncannily rose and fell based upon phases of the moon. Simply put, as a full moon or a new moon approached, murders rose sharply. Conversely, homicides dropped off significantly during the moon's first and last quarters.

A previous study performed by the American Institute of Medical Climatology had similar findings. That test revealed a correlation between the full moon and peaks in psychotically oriented crimes such as arson and murder. But criminal impulses aren't the only things mirroring phases of the moon. A study of 1,000 tonsillectomies listed in the *Journal of the Florida Medical Association* revealed that 82 percent of postoperative bleeding crises occurred nearest the full moon, even though *fewer* tonsillectomies were performed during that period.

While such findings certainly *sound* definitive, scientists are reluctant to pronounce a direct connection until a physical model becomes accepted. As for theories that explain *why* the moon might have an influence over human behavior, Dr. Lieber speculates that a human being's water composition may undergo a "biological tide" that wreaks havoc with emotions and body processes. But the fact is that no one can say for certain if the human/lunar connection is real or just so much howling at the moon. Stay tuned.

Ten Memorable Advertising Campaigns

The United States of America... land of the free and home to some of the greatest television commercials of all time!

"Tastes great, less filling" The long-running Miller Lite beer campaign, which started in 1974, featured a plethora of athletes hawking the brewski, including Larry Bird, John Madden, Billy Martin, and George Steinbrenner.

"Mean Joe Greene" Even those who never watched a minute of football were familiar with the Pittsburgh Steelers defensive tackle, thanks to a 1979 Coca-Cola spot. Only a robot could refrain from smiling when Greene tossed his sweat-stained jersey at a kid in exchange for a bottle of Coke.

"1984" Thank you, Apple, for the first Macintosh computer and this crazy, George Orwell–inspired commercial that aired during the Super Bowl.

"Where's the beef?" Rest in peace, Clara Peller.

"Just Do It" Whatever "it" is, Nike encouraged Americans to do it in 1988.

"You deserve a break today" Thank you, McDonald's, for reminding us to take a little "me" time in 1971.

"Energizer Bunny" After 20 years, this campaign still keeps going and going and going....

"Showdown" Larry Bird challenged Michael Jordan to a game of "Horse" in 1993. The prize? A Big Mac. Seriously... these guys can't afford two all-beef patties at Mickey D's?

"Frogs" Who knew amphibians could be so much fun? Three little words: "Bud. Weis. Er." Those talkative little frogs (and their later lizard compadres) were *huge* back in '95!

"Herding Cats" Few knew that this Super Bowl commercial was for Electronic Data Systems, but everyone knew those free-range cats were so dang cute!

Ten Most Common Subjects of Dreams

Dreams have been a source of mystery and study dating back to the ancient Egyptians. Over the centuries, different theories of what dreams are and what they mean have come and gone.
The Greeks thought dreams were messages from the gods, while Freud believed dreams were expressions of sexual urges. Throughout history, though, the major themes of dreams have remained largely unchanged. Here are ten of the most common.

10. Spouse cheating on you

Dream experts say dreaming of spousal affairs doesn't necessarily mean you're afraid of infidelity. Instead, you may feel as though your spouse has too many obligations, such as work.

9. Sex

Sexual dreams aren't just the stuff of adolescence. According

By the Numbers

58% chance that a female will dream about people familiar to her

45% chance that a male will

to dream experts, the most common sexual dream themes include adultery, sex with an acquaintance, sex with a masked lover, and sex in a public place.

8. Snakes

The ancient Egyptians believed snakes were bringers of nightmares. Today, dream analysts equate the appearance of snakes in a dream with hidden psychological and emotional threats in waking life.

7. Car or other mechanical trouble

Dreaming of car trouble often signifies the feeling that your life is out of control.

6. Death

Dreaming of your own death or of loved ones dying doesn't necessarily herald death in real life. Instead, it may just signify that the dreamer is in transition in their waking life—and people and places may be leaving their lives.

5. Missing or failing an exam

Even people who aren't in school anymore report having this common dream. Dreaming that you've missed or failed a test is often seen as an indication that you feel tested or are unprepared for something in your waking life.

4. Teeth falling out

This surprisingly common dream is linked by dream theorists to insecurity about one's personal appearance.

3. Being naked in public

Public nudity in dreams often signifies that the dreamer feels vulnerable or awkward in social situations.

2. Falling/flying

Both falling and flying are representative of feelings of inadequacy and insecurity. But contrary to popular belief, if you don't wake up before hitting the ground in a falling dream, you will not die.

1. Being chased

Dreaming of being chased is by far the most commonly reported dream and is often interpreted as feeling as though you are being pursued by events or unpleasant emotions in your daily life.

Holy Matrimony!

Marriage is a sacred institution. Unfortunately, it's also often described as an expensive, fleeting institution. Here are some statistics about holy matrimony.

Average cost of wedding in 2009, United States: $19,000

Average cost of wedding in 1945, United States: $2,240

Cost of average 1945 wedding, in today's terms: $26,902

Most Expensive Wedding in History $60 million. In 2004, billionaire steel magnate L. N. Mittal dropped $60 million on his daughter's wedding to an investment banker. The wedding included a party at Versailles, a reception at a castle built especially for the occasion, and a $1.5 million wine tab.

Average Age at First Marriage Americans are waiting longer than ever to get married for the first time. Meanwhile, the gap between the average ages of men and women at their first marriage is dwindling (men are listed first; women second):

1900: 25.9, 21.9

1950: 22.8, 20.3

2000: 26.8, 25.1

- Country with highest average age at first marriage for men: **Dominica, 35.4**
- Country with highest average age at first marriage for women: **Jamaica, 33.1**
- Country with lowest average age at first marriage for men: **Nepal, 22.0**
- Country with lowest average age at first marriage for women: **Chad, 18.0**

States that allow same-sex marriage: Massachusetts, Connecticut, Iowa, Vermont, New Hampshire

Divorce rate in Massachusetts, prior to legalizing gay marriage in 2004: 2.2 of every 1,000 total population

Divorce rate in Massachusetts in 2008: 2.0 of every 1,000

Highest and lowest divorce rates, by country: The United States has one of the highest divorce rates in the entire world. Whether this is due to our marriage laws or our quickly shortening attention spans is up for debate. Here are the countries with the highest divorce rates (as of 2007), as a percentage of total marriages:

1. Sweden—54.9

2. United States—54.8

3. Belarus—52.9

And the lowest:

1. India—1.1

2. Sri Lanka—1.5

3. Japan—1.9

Divorce Rates Among Religious Groups According to religious leaders, couples who "pray together, stay together." However, this is not borne out by the facts. Here are the results of a 1999 study of some 4,000 Americans conducted by the Barna Research Group about divorce rates among religious (and nonreligious) folks:

- Nondenominational Evangelical Christians: 34 percent
- Baptists: 29 percent
- Protestants: 25 percent
- Mormons: 24 percent
- Catholics: 21 percent
- Lutherans: 21 percent
- Atheists: 21 percent

Things You Don't Know
(and Didn't Need to Know) About...

Hello Kitty

Wondering about that bow-clad natty catty whose image seems to grace everything these days? Check out these purrrr-fectly true things about Hello Kitty.

- Sanrio, the Japanese company that lays claim to Hello Kitty, was established in 1960. Fourteen years later, artist Ikuko Shimizu was asked to create a character that would appeal to children and adults. He came up with a white kitty with no mouth.

- In late 1974, Sanrio began distributing a vinyl coin purse with that cute cartoon cat on the side. It sold for 240 yen, or roughly 80 cents. The cartoon didn't have a name then but officially became Hello Kitty a year after its debut.

- According to Kitty's "biography," she lives in London with her parents and identical twin sister, Mimmy. You can tell Kitty and Mimmy apart by the location of their hair bows: Kitty wears hers on her left, Mimmy on her right.

- Hello Kitty is in third grade and weighs the same as three apples (hence, Sanrio's charity project, Three Apples).

- These days, you'll find Hello Kitty in Sanriotown. She has many friends there, including a bunny, a puppy, and an owl.

- Hello Kitty has been licensed for nearly every cute (or *kawaii,* which basically means that the cuteness is ubiquitous in the entire culture) product you can think of. She has her own video games, an album, TV shows, and a credit card. There's even a Hello Kitty–themed hospital in Taiwan.

- In fact, according to Sanrio, there are 50,000 branded items available in 12,000 locations in 70 countries. You can stay at a Hello Kitty hotel, sleep on Hello Kitty sheets, work on a Hello Kitty computer, drive a Hello Kitty car, get a Hello Kitty manicure, and basically live your life completely surrounded by Hello Kitty. We bet you think that's the cat's meow.

That's a Crime Too:

Interesting Animal Laws

From pet dogs to bears, animals have been subject to some of the strangest laws out there. Check out our list to make sure you and your pets are living within the law.

- In Alaska, you can't look at a moose from an airplane.
- In Corpus Christi, Texas, you can't raise alligators in your home.
- It's illegal to imitate an animal in Miami.
- Ohioans need a license to keep a bear.
- Utah drivers must beware: Birds have the right of way on all public highways.
- Oftentimes, a homeowner's insurance premiums will increase if they decide to adopt an exotic or unusual pet.
- In Madison, Wisconsin, divorcing couples must be aware that joint custody is not allowed for family pets. Custody is awarded to the party who is in possession of the animal at the time of the divorce.
- Choose your exotic pets well: Zoos will usually refuse to accept pets, and in most places it's against the law to release animals into the wild. Now *what* are you going to do with that pet panther?
- In French Lick Springs, Indiana, there was once a law requiring black cats to wear bells around their necks on Friday the 13th.
- In most villages, towns, and cities, it's illegal to take in a wild animal as a pet.
- In Oregon, you can be fined up to $6,250 and face up to a year in jail if you adopt an endangered animal.
- In most jurisdictions, keeping a deer in your backyard is illegal.
- Many states, including Minnesota, Wyoming, Georgia, California, and Kentucky, ban the private ownership of primates as pets.
- In Florida, it is illegal to have sexual relations with a porcupine.

Death by Stupidity

Death is a fact of life—there's no surprise there. But you might be surprised to learn that throughout history, a surprising number of people have actually invited death through what can only be described as sheer stupidity. Here are some of the more bizarre examples.

Death by Frozen Chicken A true renaissance man, Francis Bacon was a respected statesman, scientist, philosopher, and author whose works include *Novum Organum* and *The New Atlantis*. In March 1626, Bacon came up with the bright idea that meat could be preserved by freezing it. To test his theory, he went to town, bought a gutted chicken, then stood in inclement weather and stuffed the bird with snow. He promptly developed pneumonia and died a few months later.

Death by Martini In 1941, during a party aboard an ocean liner bound for Brazil, author Sherwood Anderson accidentally swallowed a martini olive, toothpick and all. The tiny sliver of wood embedded in Anderson's intestines, leading to peritonitis, which ultimately killed him.

Death by Scarf A groundbreaking and influential dancer in her day, Isadora Duncan was strangled by her own scarf on September 14, 1927, when the long, flowing garment became tangled in the rear wheel of the car in which she was riding.

Death by Light Bulb On March 11, 1978, Claude Francois, a popular French pop singer, was standing in a filled bathtub in his Paris apartment when he noticed a broken light bulb. Obsessed with orderliness, Francois immediately tried to change the bulb, electrocuting himself in the process.

Death by Bottle Cap According to friends and family, Tennessee Williams, the award-winning author of *The Glass Menagerie, A Streetcar Named Desire*, and *Cat on a Hot Tin Roof*, had a habit of opening the cap of his eye-drop bottles with his teeth, then tilting his head backward to moisten his eyes. The system worked until February 25, 1983, when Williams accidentally inhaled the cap and choked to death.

Death by Full Bladder Tycho Brahe, a Danish nobleman and influential astronomer, suffered from recurring bladder problems. In 1601, he attended a formal banquet and was unable to visit the bathroom to relieve himself before the festivities started. Supposedly, he drank heavily over the course of the evening and managed to hold his urine for the duration. This proved to be a fatal mistake—the strain on his bladder resulted in a serious infection, which killed him 11 days later. A more scientific theory, formulated after his body was exhumed in 1996, suggests death by mercury poisoning.

Death by Embrace Considered one of the greatest poets China has ever known, Li Bai was also a raging drunk. Legend holds that one evening in the year 762, while cruising down the Yangtze River, the inebriated writer fell off his boat and drowned when he tried to embrace the moon's reflection on the water. It's a great story, but recent evidence indicates it's more likely that he died from complications of old age and mercury poisoning.

Death by Overcoat A tailor by trade, Franz Reichelt created a garment that was both an overcoat and a parachute. On February 4, 1912, he decided to test his invention by jumping off the Eiffel Tower. He told authorities that he was going to use a mannequin first, but decided at the last minute to try it himself. Confident that his invention would work, Reichelt calmly stepped off a platform and plunged to his death.

Death by Helicopter
Vic Morrow was a well-known actor with scores of screen credits when he signed on to costar as a bigot who learns his lesson the hard way

in a segment of *Twilight Zone: The Movie* (1983). However, things went horribly wrong during the night filming of a combat scene set in Vietnam, and Morrow was decapitated by the blades of a crashing helicopter. Two child actors also perished in the accident.

Not Quite Hotcakes: Product Disasters

It's true that you can't win 'em all, and when you're in the business of making new things, you can pretty much count on a spectacular flop now and then. Here's a sampling of some of the biggest.

New Coke When Coca-Cola CEO Roberto Goizueta introduced a new Coke formula in a 1985 press conference, he proclaimed it, "the boldest single marketing move in the history of the consumer goods business" and the "surest move ever made." The company concocted the new, sweeter formula to compete with Pepsi, and after conducting 200,000 taste tests and spending a whopping $4 million on research and development, executives were convinced they had a hit. But they never gauged how strongly people would react to original Coke being pulled from the shelves. When the new formula debuted, angry customers jammed Coca-Cola's lines with more than 1,000 calls per day, and the press opened up with both barrels. Within three months, the company was selling "Coca-Cola Classic" alongside the new version, and within a year, it decided to scrap New Coke entirely.

Smokeless Cigarettes In the 1980s, R.J. Reynolds spent $325 million to launch Premier, a new cigarette without the smoke and ash that nonsmokers hate. The biggest problem seemed obvious: Nonsmokers don't buy cigarettes. On top of that, the smokeless cigarettes tasted bad, smelled bad, and cost 25 percent more than regular cigarettes. R.J. Reynolds pulled the product from the market quickly but apparently didn't learn its lesson. In the 1990s, R.J. Reynolds dropped $125 million to develop the smokeless Eclipse cigarettes. Nobody liked those either—especially after they learned the filters contained glass fibers.

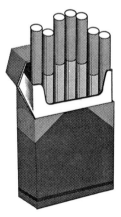

Earring Magic Ken In 1993, Mattel released what they intended to be a cooler, more modern boyfriend for Barbie. But the new Ken—sporting an earring, necklace, mesh shirt, lavender vest, and blonde highlights—suggested something very different to most people. The doll actually sold very well (due in large part to adult collectors), but it was pulled from the shelves in less than a year due to outrage from parents and church groups.

Windows Vista When Microsoft's new operating system launched in 2006—years behind schedule and missing promised features—it was so sluggish, glitchy, and hard to use that PC manufacturers established programs to "downgrade" new PC owners to the previous system, Windows XP. After spending billions to develop what was supposed to be a computing revolution, Microsoft soon found itself soothing customers with promises of a new system, Windows 7.

Gerber Singles In a 1974 push to expand beyond the diaper demographic, Gerber introduced baby-food-style dishes intended for childless adults. Packaged in the same iconic jars as the original baby food, the "Singles" line certainly didn't appeal to real swinging singles.

The Edsel Ho-hum cars are nothing unusual, but the gap between hype and results put the 1958 Edsel in a class by itself. In an effort to compete with General Motors, Ford launched a midpriced division, alongside the budget Ford and the high-end Mercury/Lincoln lines. They spent an unprecedented $400 million in research and development before building a single car. But then they tossed an initial sleek design and sacrificed engineering quality to shrink production costs. They also ignored a year of naming research and opted for "Edsel," the name of Henry Ford's son, even though market research subjects associated it with "weasel." To make the car stand out, they outfitted it with a bizarre grille that one reviewer described as "an Oldsmobile sucking a lemon." In the marketing blitz leading up to the 1957 debut, Ford boasted, "There has never been a car like the Edsel." The company predicted it would sell more than 200,000 cars in the first year—around 5 percent of the U.S. market at the time. In reality, they only sold 64,000 the first year, 44,891 the second, and 2,846 the third before finally halting production.

Are You a Believer?

Faith is a very personal experience, and by definition, it is not based on fact. Over the centuries, people have expressed their faith in a variety of unique philosophies. Perhaps one of these rings true for you?

The Hollow Earth Theory

Hollow Earth believers agree that our planet is a shell between 500 and 800 miles thick, and inside that shell is another world. It may be a gaseous realm, an alien outpost, or home to a utopian society.

Some believers add a spiritual spin. Calling the interior world *Agartha* or *Shambhala,* they use concepts from Eastern religions and point to ancient legends supporting these ideas.

Many Hollow Earth enthusiasts are certain that people from the outer and inner worlds can visit each other by traveling through openings in the outer shell. One such entrance is a hole in the ocean near the North Pole. A November 1968 photo by the ESSA-7 satellite showed a dark, circular area at the North Pole that was surrounded by ice fields.

Another hole supposedly exists in Antarctica. Some Hollow Earth enthusiasts say Hitler believed that Antarctica held the true opening to Earth's core. Leading Hollow Earth researchers such as Dennis Crenshaw suggest that President Roosevelt ordered the 1939 South Pole expedition to find the entrance before the Germans did.

Hollow Earth societies around the world continue to look for proof of this centuries-old legend…and who knows what they might find?

The Raelian Movement

A belief in unidentified flying objects has haunted humanity for generations, with thousands claiming to have had direct contact with alien beings from other worlds. Claude Vorilhon, a French race car driver and onetime musician, asserted that he was visited by an extraterrestrial in 1973. It was a life-altering experience that caused him to change his name to Rael and found the Raelian Church. Rael's religion proclaims that the *Elohim* ("those who came from the sky") created everything on Earth. Although many turn a skeptical eye toward Vorilhon—whose faith also preaches free love—the Raelian Movement is said to include as many as 65,000 members worldwide.

The Vampire Church

With offices located throughout the United States, Canada, and Australia, the Vampire Church provides the initiated and the curious with an opportunity to learn more about vampirism. However, don't expect to find much about the "undead," as vampires have been portrayed in stories since Bram Stoker wrote *Dracula* in 1897. Instead, the church offers insight into vampirism as a physical condition that sometimes requires unusual energy resources, such as blood. In addition, it explains the difference between psychic vampires and elemental vampires. According to the church's Web site, "The Vampire Church continues to grow as more true vampires find the haven they so seek with others of this condition and the knowledge and experience of others here."

The Church of Euthanasia

"Save the Planet—Kill Yourself." These words are the battle cry of the Church of Euthanasia, which was established by Boston resident Chris Korda in 1992. Korda, a musician, had a dream one night about an alien who warned her that Earth was in serious danger. The extraterrestrial, which Korda dubbed "The Being," stressed the importance of protecting the planet's environment through population control. As a result of the encounter, Korda established the Church of Euthanasia, which supports suicide, abortion, and sodomy (defined as any sex act that is not intended for procreation). According to the church's Web site, members are vegetarian, but they "support cannibalism for those who insist on eating flesh." Although it reportedly has only about 100 members in the Boston area, the church claims that thousands worldwide have visited its Web site and been exposed to its message.

Curious Classifieds

This is the model home for your future. It was panned by Better Homes and Gardens.

The hotel has bowling alleys, tennis courts, comfortable beds, and other athletic facilities.

Full-size mattress. Royal Tonic, 20-year warranty. Like new. Slight urine smell. $40.

For a successful affair, it's the Empire Hotel.

Tickle Me Elmo. New in box. Hardly tickled. $700.

Free dinner with any pest control job.

Tired of cleaning yourself? Let me do it.

For sale—Diamonds, $20; microscopes, $15.

Girl wanted to assist magician in cutting-off-head illusion. Blue Cross and salary.

Wanted: chambermaid in rectory. Love in, $200 a month. References required.

The most romantic love songs of the '50s: including "16 Tons" by Tennessee Ernie Ford.

Will swap white satin wedding gown (worn once) for 50 pounds fresh Gravy Train.

Modular sofas. Only $299. For rest or fore play.

Used tombstone, perfect for someone named Homer HendelBergenHeinzel. One only.

Save regularly in our bank. You'll never reget it.

Springmaid sheets are known as America's favorite playground.

Valentine's Day Sale: Ty-D-Bol blue toss-ins.

Wanted: Unmarried girls to pick fruit and produce at night.

Illiterate? Write today for free help.

Used cars: Why go elsewhere to be cheated? Come here first!

Ten Rumors About Fast-Food Restaurants

Cow eyeballs, anyone? How about snakes with your fries? Rumors about fast-food parlors run the gamut from the mundane to the insane.

Kentucky Fried Chicken and the Ku Klux Klan

This one was aimed squarely at KFC's founder, Colonel Harland Sanders. The rumor claimed that Sanders was a racial bigot who siphoned off 10 percent of his profits to the Ku Klux Klan. Intended to under-mine the fast-food chain, the rumor gained little traction. With noses trained to smell a foul, Sanders's customers balked at the allegation, and the fran-chise suffered nary a bit.

Wendy's 25-Cent Hamburgers

More playful than many popular fast-food rumors, this 2008 untruth stated that in honor of Wendy's 60th anniversary, the chain would temporarily revert to founding-era pricing. This would mean that a hamburger would cost a quarter, French fries 15 cents, and so on. There were two problems with the story. First, Wendy's opened in 1969, making it just 39 years old in 2008. Second, the chain had absolutely no intention of altering its prices. Shucks!

McDonald's Uses Cow Eyeballs in Its Patties

A common rumor claims that substandard (read *cheaper*) ingredi-ents are used to produce fast-food favorites. With McDonald's and cow eyeballs, rumor mongers obviously weren't doing their math, since the orbs are actually more expensive than ground beef. It's doubtful that a national chain would spend *more* on production than it had to.

Jack in the Box Serves Up Kangaroo Meat

Did you ever wonder what makes Jack spring up from his box? Could a kangaroo patty, *not* a hamburger, be responsible for Jack's jump? It's rather doubtful since kangaroo meat costs more than beef to produce. Nevertheless, the rumor gained some ground in the 1990s.

Arby's Liquid-Protein Alternative

Are Arby's roast beef sandwiches really made from pastes, gels, or other liquids? No. Well, not really. The truth is each roast beef patty is surrounded by a "self-basting" solution and packed inside an air-tight bag. If viewed by the uninitiated, the product could appear to be completely liquid. One squeeze, however, will dispel such drippy notions.

McDonald's Shakes Are Made from Nonfood Items

Another bit from the seemingly endless mega-chain-cuts-corners rumor mill, this one alleges that McDonald's shakes are *not* made from the real thing. Here's the straight deal: Whole milk, cream, sugar, and corn syrup comprise the principal ingredients in a McDonald's shake. There are also a few food preservatives used in the mix. Bottom line? McDonald's shakes *are* made mostly from food items. Enough said.

Dunkin' Donuts Celebrates 9/11

This nasty rumor tells of Dunkin' Donuts store owners/employees celebrating the 9/11 attacks by burning American flags. The targeted shop-keepers, not too surprisingly, were ethnic, hailing from Pakistan, India, Portugal, and other lands. An investigation found absolutely no merit to the allegations, but the rumors persisted. In an effort to allay fears and stifle prejudices, store owners took to displaying huge American flags on their buildings. Thankfully, things soon calmed down.

Taco Bell Stops Featuring Its Mascot Chihuahua After the Dog Dies

The real reason for ditching the doggie relates to the chain's bottom line, *not* the animal's flatline. Dwindling sales in 2000 prompted an advertising change and a decision to drop the canine. But Gidget (the dog's real name) had a starring role yet to come in *Legally Blonde 2.* The scrappy chihuahua reached 15 years of age in 2009 and then finally broke free of her leash, spiritually speaking. Rest in peace, girl.

In-N-Out Burger's Secret Menu

When is a rumor especially juicy? When it's based in fact and smothered in grease. In-N-Out Burger officially carries just four food items on its menu: a hamburger, a cheeseburger, a double-double, and French fries. But rumors (truths, as it turns out) continue to fly regarding a vast array of other food items. Samplings of these include the Flying Dutchman (two patties, two slices of cheese, nothing else) and Animal Style Fries (fries with special sauce, cheese, and onions). There are many more, but since the meal items are not advertised by name, a hungry patron must track each item down through word of mouth or Internet surfing. Bon appétit.

Burger King Has Snakes in Its Play Pit

This macabre tale tells of a three-year-old boy who was playing inside Burger King's ball pit. Suddenly, the boy started whimpering. Hours later, he was dead. The cause? Baby rattlesnakes had infiltrated the pit and bitten the boy. Is it true? Worry not, moms and dads. This humdinger of a rumor is completely false and was likely cooked up for its shock value.

Worth Repeating

Cringeworthy Baseball Quotes

Rewind the tape! Did he just say what I think he said?

"Four. I don't think I could eat eight."
—Yogi Berra, when asked how many slices he wanted his pizza cut into

"Line up alphabetically according to your height."
—Casey Stengel

"I'm not going to go into the past or talk about my past."
—Mark McGwire, when called before a congressional committee
to talk about his past

*"I have never used steroids. Period. I do not know how to say it
any more clearly than that."*
—Rafael Palmeiro, testifying before Congress five months before
testing positive for steroids

*"I don't want to be a hero. I don't want to be a star.
It just works out that way."*
—Reggie Jackson, on the hardship of being Reggie Jackson

*"There is one word in America that says it all,
and that one word is 'You never know.' "*
—Joaquin Andujar

"My problem's . . . behind me now."
—George Brett, commenting on his hemorrhoid surgery

"The doctors x-rayed my head and found nothing."
—Dizzy Dean, after being struck by a pitch

"Hot as hell, ain't it, Prez?"
—Babe Ruth to President Warren G. Harding

"I'm not in a running mood."
—Rickey Henderson, on why he didn't want to play in
the 2000 New York Mets home opener

"Aw, how could he lose the ball in the sun, he's from Mexico."
—Announcer Harry Caray, critiquing Jorge Orta

"We don't cheat. And even if we did, I'd never tell you."
—Tommy Lasorda

Happy Holidays!

Americans sure do love giving and receiving cards and gifts no matter what the holiday!

Valentine's Day

Ahhh, the day set aside especially for you and that special someone. When it comes to shopping, you needn't worry about not finding something special. There are more than 3,500 confectionery and nut stores in the United States (we eat about 24.5 pounds of candy annually), more than 20,000 florists, and more than 28,000 jewelry stores. What better way to say, "I love you" than to shell out about $14.7 billion on gifts, as Americans did in 2009. A big chunk of change, to be sure, but a 13.5 percent drop from the $17 billion spent in 2008!

Mother's Day

Mom's special day was first observed in 1907, and in 1914 Congress officially declared the second Sunday in May as Mother's Day. Even though our respective moms gave us life—the greatest gift there is—the economic crisis forced Americans to curtail all types of spending, including gifts for mom. According to the National Retail Federation, folks spent about $123.89 on gifts in 2009, a whopping 11 percent drop from the previous year.

Father's Day

Hey Daddy-o, maybe your offspring shopped at one of the 9,000 men's clothing stores or 14,000 hardware stores for that nifty tie and/or hammer. Regardless of the gift, an annual survey by the National Retail Federation found that, on average, $90.89 was spent on dear old dad in 2009, down from $94.54 spent in 2008.

Independence Day

Chances are that the hot dog or sausage you gobbled down over the July 4 holiday originated in Iowa, home to 19.3 million hogs and pigs. And what would the holiday be without the rocket's red glare? The

U.S. Census Bureau reported that China exported $193 million worth of fireworks in 2008, representing most of the $202 million in festive explosives imported to the good old USA.

Halloween

Boo! This holiday generated an estimated 36 million beggars... er, trick-or-treaters... between the ages of 5 and 13 in 2008, according to the U.S. Census Bureau. To satisfy the appetites of those little witches and goblins (and to keep their houses from getting egged), Americans spend about $21 million each year on sweets for the holiday—more than on Valentine's Day or Easter.

Thanksgiving Day

Let's give thanks for all we have by eating some of the 250 million turkeys raised in the United States in 2009. The typical American eats about 14 pounds of the bird each year, with the November holiday accounting for most of that consumption. Let's not forget the 709 million pounds of cranberries produced (thanks, Wisconsin, for taking the lead on this one with your 400-million-pound contribution) or the 1.8 billion pounds of sweet potatoes.

Christmas

The holiday to end all holidays! And we have the stats to prove it. Who doesn't love Christmas... and all the good stuff that goes along with it? According to a National Retail Federation survey of 6,500 consumers, 62.2 percent said they purchase clothing or clothing accessories as holiday gifts, followed by entertainment items such as books, CDs, and DVDs (60.8 percent); gift certificates (50.4 percent); toys (45.4 percent); and beauty items (23.2 percent). Retail department stores reported $28.2 billion in sales in December 2008. However, given the economic situation in 2009, 75.1 percent of consumers planned to shop at discount stores, surpassing online sales. Oh, and according to Hallmark, 192 million Christmas cards are sent to friends and family annually, making it (to no one's surprise) the largest card-sending occasion in the United States.

Weird Fetishes

Although most people give the word fetish *a sexual connotation, the dictionary also describes a fetish as "any object or idea eliciting unquestioning reverence, respect, or devotion." Since that covers a wide range of territory, here are just a few of the more interesting fetishes reported of late.*

- A Tennessee man complained that his home had been burgled; among other things stolen were more than 300 tongue rings.

- A British machinist with bad earaches was found to have a pregnant spider living in his ear. He told a reporter that he had grown fond of the spider and intended to keep it as a pet.

- A 12-year-old Michigan boy has had an obsession with vacuum cleaners since infancy, when, according to his mother, he was mesmerized by the whirring noise. The boy enjoys vacuuming so much that he does the house up to five times a day with one of the 165 vacuum cleaners in his collection. Said a teacher, "It's not that he doesn't like recess, it's just that he prefers to stay in and clean."

- A Canadian woman really likes her daily newspaper. She not only reads it, but she eats it in strips and has done so for the past seven years—because it tastes good. Her only problem occurred when she developed a blockage of her esophagus, whereupon doctors found a ball of paper. After removing it, her doctors said that aside from the obstruction, eating newspaper is not bad for your health.

- In Detroit, a man was arrested for the seventh time—this time for stealing a mannequin outfitted in a French maid's uniform. The arrest came days after he was released for his sixth offense: stealing a mannequin with bobbed hair wearing a pink dress.

- One London woman walks around all day dressed as a beekeeper. She said she must do this because of her "electrical sensitivity." The veil keeps away the incapacitating waves from appliances, including cell phones and refrigerators. Her house windows have silver gauze shades, and the wallpaper has a tinfoil lining.

It Happened in...February

- In 1989, talk show host Geraldo Rivera celebrated Groundhog Day by hosting his show from a nudist colony. He was buck-nekkid and so was the audience.

- The first Super Bowl, called the AFL–NFL World Championship Game, was played in February 1967. The game score, by the way, was Green Bay Packers 35, Kansas City Chiefs 10.

- In February 1972, John Lennon and Yoko Ono cohosted *The Mike Douglas Show* for a full week. Guests included Ralph Nader, Chuck Berry, and Black Panther Bobby Seale.

- When baseball player Jose Canseco was pulled over on a Florida highway in February 1989, he was estimated to be going more than 120 mph. Police gave him a citation for reckless driving, then let him drive away.

- The first toy prizes were inserted in Cracker Jack boxes in February 1913. It made root-root-rooting for the home team way more fun.

- In 1958, "Uncle Walter" Cronkite reported that rock 'n' roll music had just been banned in Iran because many dancers were suffering hip injuries.

- From the "This Gets a Little Complicated" department: In this century, there are four years with five Sundays in February: 2004, 2032, 2060, and 2088. Generally, most centuries have three such occurrences. The next time you'll find this four-of-five calendar phenomena will be in the 25th century.

- Amana rolled out the first compact microwave oven in February 1967. Cooks had two button options—"start" and "light." The newfangled contraption was said to cook a hamburger in 35 seconds.

- Although February is the shortest month, it's big on celebration: February is Return Shopping Carts to the Supermarket Month (you know who you are), Boost Your Self-Esteem Month (give yourself a hand for that one), National Weddings Month (of course), and National Mend a Broken Heart Month.

Bizarre World Records

Fastest plucking of turkey: 1 minute, 30 seconds

Irishman Vincent Pilkington lays claim to the dubious title of world's fastest turkey plucker. In November 1980, Pilkington plucked a turkey in a minute and a half, shattering his previous record by more than a full minute. It's too bad they don't celebrate Thanksgiving in Ireland—he'd have no shortage of dinner invitations.

Most rattlesnakes in shared bathtub: 87

Jackie "The Texas Snake Man" Bibby spent 45 minutes in a bathtub with live, venomous rattlesnakes in November 2007. Incredibly, prior to Bibby's 2007 stunt, he had shared the world record of 75 rattlesnakes with another person, Rosie Reynolds-McCasland. Bibby also holds the world record for holding the most live rattlesnakes in his mouth without assistance. The record is ten—just in case you want to try breaking it.

Longest fingernails: 28 feet, 5 inches

According to *Guinness World Records,* Lee Redmond had the longest fingernails in the world, with a cumulative length of nearly 30 feet. The longest of the nails was the thumb, which measured 2 feet, 11 inches. Redmond, who had not cut her nails since 1979, lost them in a car crash in 2009.

Most people to wear a Groucho Marx disguise at same time: 937

At East Lansing High School in Michigan, nearly 1,000 students and faculty donned a Groucho Marx disguise simultaneously. The disguises consisted of spectacles attached to a large nose, bushy eyebrows, and a mustache. While the record seems unlikely to be broken, you'll be heartened to know that the record for wearing a Karl Marx disguise is still open.

Tallest snowman: 113 feet, 7.5 inches

It took residents of several Maine towns two weeks to construct this enormous snowman in 1999. No word on how long it lasted before the residents' older brother knocked the head off of it.

Loudest belch: 107.1 decibels

The next time your spouse lets loose a postmeal burp, consider this: British man Paul Hunn's ear-splitting burps are louder than a vacuum cleaner (80 dB), a lawn mower (90 dB), and even a jack-hammer at a distance of 10 meters (100 dB).

Dubious Endurance Records

Longest time sitting atop a pole: 39 years

Flagpole sitters, who achieved brief fame in the 1920s, had a long way to go to break the record held by fifth-century monk St. Simeon the Stylite. Simeon was also known to go the entire length of Lent without eating or drinking a single thing.

Longest time spent in an attic: 57 years

Ukrainian Stephan Kovaltchuk went into the attic to hide from Nazi invaders in 1942 . . . and didn't come out until 1999. Kovaltchuk, who was 18 when he disappeared into the attic, was cared for by his sister until she died when he was 75.

Longest lawn mower ride: 14,594.5 miles

Lawn seems endless during Saturday morning chores? Consider Gary Hatter, who chose to ride his lawn mower through all 48 contiguous states during a marathon 260-day expedition.

Who Knew?

Domino Theory

The World Championship Domino Tournament is held annually in Andalusia, Alabama. The two-day event, usually scheduled for early July, has been going strong since 1976. Prize money has been known to total as much as $500,000.

In the Cathedral and on the Court

In 2000, the world-famous Harlem Globetrotters exhibition basketball team visited the Vatican. After a parade in Rome celebrating their 75th anniversary, the team met with Pope John Paul II and named the pontiff an honorary Globetrotter. However, no photos were released of the pope spinning a basketball on his finger.

You've Got to Be in It to Win It

Roberto Madrazo, former presidential candidate in Mexico, was proclaimed the winner of the 2007 Berlin marathon in the 55-and-older category with a time of 2:41:12. But upon closer examination, he appeared to have run 15 kilometers (9.5 miles) in 21 minutes—faster than humanly possible. Madrazo apparently forgot about the microchip he was wearing, which lost track of him at two checkpoints. He was disqualified two weeks later. The politician later said that he'd finished the race after the 21st kilometer and drove to the finish line to get some clothes he had left there.

Take a Bite out of Crime

In 1996, there were 1,102 reports of people being bitten by other people in New York City. If anyone assumes there must have been something in the water in 1996 and that those were isolated incidents, they'd be wrong. Every year in New York, approximately 1,600 people are bitten by other people. Apparently, 1996 was a *slow* year.

Ten Annoying Euphemisms for Being Fired

Reduction in Force In true corporate fashion, the annoying euphemism "reduction in force" has been further modified into an acronym: RIF. As in, "I've been RIFed." Hey, why not just switch the *R* and the *F* and save everybody some irritation?

Synergy-Related Headcount Reduction No, this isn't a made-up term in a David Foster Wallace novel. It was the euphemism used by Nokia Siemens when firing 3,000 employees in 2008.

Downsizing This isn't even a real word, people!

Rightsizing Apparently "downsizing" was too much of a downer for HR departments around the corporate globe. Somehow, someone believes that replacing *down* with *right* will make being fired easier.

Work Force Reduction Notification RadioShack thought the best way to fire 400 employees in 2006 was to send out a mass e-mail stating that "the work force reduction notification had begun." We don't know what it means either.

Made Redundant Of all the euphemisms, this might be the most offensive: Not only is this an annoying euphemism, it's actually an insult!

Special Forces Philosophy Believe it or not, this has nothing to do with the military. It was the actual euphemism employed by Tesla Motors when firing 10 percent of its staff in 2008.

Simplification eBay called its round of 2008 mass firings "employee simplification." If they really wanted to simplify things they would have just said "firings."

Reengineering plan This euphemism has the unintended effect of making fired employees feel as if they are part of a dystopian science-fiction novel: "Sorry, honey, I've been reengineered."

Optimized It's hard to imagine somebody who has just been fired believing that there is anything optimal about it.

Odd Beer Names

You're thirsty, so you decide to stop at your local pub for a drink. The "Menu of Indecision" is literally jam-packed with hundreds of beers. Some are recognizable, but most have names that make you chuckle aloud. Here's a short list of a few oddly named American and Canadian brands.

- Arrogant Bastard Ale
- Oliver's Hot Monkey Love
- Bourbon Barrel Lower da Boom
- Flying Frog Lager
- Satan's Pony Amber Ale
- Butt Monkey Chimp Chiller Ale
- Squatters Emigration Amber Ale
- San Quentin Breakout Stout
- Aroma Borealis Herbal Cream Ale
- Kill Ugly Radio
- Old Knucklehead
- Alley Kat Amber
- Money Shot Cream Ale
- Oatmeal Breakfast Stout
- 3 Stooges Beer

- Moose Drool
- Stone Double Dry Hopped Levitation Ale
- Demon Sweat Imperial Red
- Monk in the Trunk
- Dead Frog Ale
- Tongue Buckler
- Bitter American

I'm Going to Disney World!

With 6 parks, 23 hotels, 5 golf courses, and a 120-acre shopping complex, Walt Disney World is a city unto itself.

- The resort is on 40 square miles of Disney-owned land—enough room for all of San Francisco or two Manhattans. So far, Disney has developed less than 35 percent of that land.

- Disney includes 4,000 acres of maintained landscapes and gardens. To care for 2,000 acres of turf, landscapers log 450,000 mowing miles per year. That's the equivalent of 18 trips around the equator.

- The resort's monorail trains have traveled the equivalent of 30 round-trips to the moon since 1971.

- Spaceship Earth (Epcot's giant sphere) weighs 16 million pounds. The surface comprises 11,324 individual triangles made from an aluminum and plastic alloy.

- The creative team behind the parks, Walt Disney Imagineering, holds more than 100 patents.

- Every year, park guests consume about 10 million hamburgers, 75 million Cokes, 6 million hot dogs, 1.6 million turkey drumsticks, and 9 million pounds of French fries.

- The hotels include nearly 25,000 different rooms. It would take you 68 years to spend a night in all of them.

- With around 62,000 "Cast Members," Walt Disney World is the biggest private single-site employer in the United States. The total payroll is more than $1.3 billion per year.

- Mickey has more than 290 outfits in his closet.

- The complete wardrobe for all cast members includes 2,500 different designs and about 1.8 million separate pieces.

- Every year, the Lost and Found team collects around 3,500 digital cameras, 6,000 cell phones, 18,000 hats, 7,500 autograph books, and 76,000 pairs of sunglasses.

Eight Most Frequent Guest Hosts on *The Tonight Show*

As The Tonight Show's *"permanent guest host" from 1987 to 1992, Jay Leno fronted for Johnny Carson more than 300 times. But before Leno's famous chin graced the small screen, a famous group of eight answered Johnny's call.*

1. Joey Bishop (177 appearances)

A member of the famed "Rat Pack" (which also included Frank Sinatra, Peter Lawford, Sammy Davis Jr., and Dean Martin), Bishop was known for his ultra-dry sense of humor.

2. Joan Rivers (93)

Shocking, abrasive, and occasionally crude, Rivers was everything that "proper" women of the 1960s were taught *not* to be. As a result, the comic was outlandishly funny. Such popularity accounted for her many appearances and a rise to "permanent guest host" status by 1983. In 1986, Rivers fell out of favor with Carson when she abruptly left to head up her own show.

3. John Davidson (87)

Well known as a game show emcee, the good-looking singer/ actor wore many hats. He was said to be personable both on and off camera.

4. Bob Newhart (87)

A self-described "everyman," Newhart's subtle yet biting humor was legendary. Such deft comic skill acted as the perfect counter-point during guest interviews.

5. David Brenner (70)

A hard-working stand-up comedian, Brenner's quick and cocky wit always dazzled.

6. McLean Stevenson (58)

Famous as Lt. Col. Henry Blake of TV's *M*A*S*H*, Stevenson found a second career as Carson's fill-in host.

7. Jerry Lewis (52)

One of the world's most celebrated comics, Lewis knocked 'em dead with his pratfalls and general silliness. If Carson was regarded as King of Late Night, Lewis became his self-appointed court jester.

8. David Letterman (51)

Noted prankster and master of sarcasm, funnyman Letterman would go on to carve out his own nighttime niche. *Late Night* (later renamed *The Late Show with David Letterman*) has run continuously since 1982, proving far and away the cachet of guest hosting *The Tonight Show*.

Life According to Johnny Carson

"Happiness is your dentist telling you it won't hurt and then having him catch his hand in the drill."

"The difference between divorce and legal separation is that a legal separation gives a husband time to hide his money."

"For three days after death, hair and fingernails continue to grow but phone calls taper off."

Danger Around the Next Bend

Don't want your next road trip to be your last? You might want to avoid the following intersections and stretches of road. Oddly, many of America's most dicey intersections exist outside of its largest cities. Strange, too, at least half are of modern design—well regulated by traffic lights and other control devices. High volume and driver error are cited as contributing factors to their deadly status.

∙∙∙∙∙∙∙∙∙∙∙∙∙∙∙∙∙∙∙∙∙∙∙∙∙∙∙∙∙∙∙∙∙∙

Ten Most Dangerous U.S. Intersections

∙∙∙∙∙∙∙∙∙∙∙∙∙∙∙∙∙∙∙∙∙∙∙∙∙∙∙∙∙∙∙∙∙∙

1. Nation's deadliest with 357 accidents measured during January 1999–December 2000 (an average of one accident every other day): Flamingo Road and Pines Boulevard in Pembroke Pines, Florida

2. Red Lion Road and Roosevelt Boulevard, Philadelphia, Pennsylvania

3. Grant Avenue and Roosevelt Avenue, Philadelphia, Pennsylvania

4. Clearview Parkway and Veterans Memorial Boulevard, Metairie, Louisiana

5. 51st Street and Memorial Drive, Tulsa, Oklahoma

6. State Highway 121 and Preston Road, Frisco, Texas

7. 7th Street and Bell Road, Phoenix, Arizona

8. 19th Avenue and Northern Avenue, Phoenix, Arizona

9. Fair Oaks Boulevard and Howe Avenue, Sacramento, California

10. 71st Street and Memorial Drive, Tulsa, Oklahoma

20 Most Dangerous U.S. Roads

1. U.S. Route 19, Florida
The portion stretching from Pasco to Pinellas counties has been dubbed "the most dangerous road in the United States." That's certainly a dubious honor!

2. Highway 21, south of St. Louis, Missouri
This windy, flood-prone roadway makes for some treacherous travel.

3. State Route 138, east of Palmdale, California
No guardrails plus precipitous drop-offs equal disaster.

4. U.S. Route 6, California
Narrow road surface produces mayhem.

5. U.S. Route 6 between Price and Spanish Fork, Utah
Narrow canyon road makes for dicey driving.

6. Southern State Parkway, New York
Dangerous curves and speeding drivers account for its deadly status.

7. Route 110, New York
Heavily traveled stretch produces an inordinate number of accidents.

8. Route 12, New York
Congestion plus driver impatience results in fender benders.

9. Colorado 550, Ouray to Silverton, Colorado
Roadway lies in the path of a major avalanche zone.

10. Los Angeles, 101 to I-405 Interchange
Another dubious honor: This roadway boasts the highest travel time index rating in the nation.

11. I-285 at I-85 Interchange, Atlanta, Georgia
Five-level interchange with frequent stop-and-go conditions spells trouble.

12. I-5, San Diego, California
A DUI hotbed, owing to its intersection with the Mexican border where the drinking age is lower.

13. U.S. Highway 1, Maine
Sharp curves and an abundant moose population add to its treachery.

14. Cross-Bronx Expressway, New York
No shoulders, huge bottlenecks, pothole-ridden surface—the list of undesirable elements goes on and on.

15. I-15, Nevada
Long, straight stretches beckon speedsters to have at it.

16. I-95 at the I-195 interchange, Providence, Rhode Island
Sharp curves and abbreviated on/off ramps cause crashes.

17. I-10, Louisiana
Buckling pavement creates dangerous conditions.

18. Circle Interchange, Chicago
This complex web of single-lane roads can't handle volume.

19. U.S. Route 431 between Seale and Eufaula, Alabama
Abundant hills and curves account for its listing.

20. New York State Thruway between exits 15A and 16, New York
High speeds mixed with inattentive driving secure its status.

Bridal Sweet!

Forget champagne, chocolate-dipped strawberries, and strategically placed mirrors. When booking a suite for their wedding or honeymoon, many modern-day brides and grooms are looking for over-the-top, once-in-a-lifetime luxuries. In fact, their honeymoon will probably be the most expensive and extravagant trip they ever take together as a couple. Here are some of the fabulous bells and whistles found in the world's best hotel suites.

1. **Indian Bridal Suite at Hotel Kura Hulanda Spa & Casino, Curaçao**

   Hand-hammered sterling silver furniture

2. **Over-Water Bungalow at Le Méridien, Bora Bora**

   A glass-bottom floor for watching marine life

3. **Oceanview Rooftop Terrace Junior Suite at Las Ventanas al Paraiso, Los Cabos, Mexico**

   A telescope for stargazing

4. **Champagne Towers by Cleopatra Suite at Caesars Paradise Stream, Mount Pocono, Pennsylvania**

   A seven-foot-tall champagne-glass whirlpool with ladder

5. **Casa del Fiori Suite at Grand Hotel a Villa Feltrinelli, Gargnano, Italy**

   Hand-printed Venetian desk set, including stationery and pencils

6. **Coral Suite at Four Seasons Resort, Punta Mita, Mexico**

   A 92-inch television

7. Longborough Suite at Cotswold House, Chipping Campden, United Kingdom

Acqua di Parma prestige-label bath toiletries

8. Honeymoon Luxury Suite at Sandals Grande St. Lucian Spa & Beach Resort, St. Lucia

A personal butler to draw you a rose-scented bath

9. Bridal Suite at Shade Hotel, Manhattan Beach, California

A Lavazza™ Italian espresso machine

10. Luxury Villa at The Tides, Riviera Maya, Mexico

A love poem on your pillow every night

Nuptials by the Numbers

88:	percentage of Americans who marry at least once
2.4 million:	the average number of weddings performed in the United States each year
44,230:	the average number of weddings performed in the United States each weekend
23 million:	the number of bridesmaids and groomsmen attending brides and grooms each year
16:	percentage of marriages that are destination weddings
Las Vegas:	the leading destination for out-of-town weddings
99:	percentage of all wedding couples who take a honeymoon
3:	percentage of brides who sign a prenuptial agreement

Ten Facts About Jehovah's Witnesses

Study up for your next porch encounter with our handy primer.

1. Jehovah's Witnesses date back to a Pennsylvania Bible study group established in 1872.

2. There are more than 7.1 million Jehovah's Witnesses worldwide, spanning 236 countries and 95,000 congregations.

3. Witnesses believe Jesus Christ is the son of Jehovah (God) but is an inferior spiritual being, not Jehovah incarnate.

4. Witnesses believe the world will soon end in a battle between good and evil. After Satan is defeated, 144,000 resurrected true believers will rule with Christ in heaven. Other believers will enjoy eternal life in an earthly paradise.

5. The church estimates Witnesses dedicate around a billion hours per year to "Bible education"—largely conducted door-to-door. Even world-famous Witnesses like Prince hit the pavement.

6. The church has published *The Watchtower Announcing Jehovah's Kingdom* under various names since 1879. It distributes approximately 37 million copies of each issue, in 174 languages.

7. A 2008 survey on American faith found that only 37 percent of respondents raised as Jehovah's Witnesses still considered themselves Witnesses.

8. Witnesses believe only God is worthy of allegiance and so won't serve in the military, vote, or salute any flag.

9. Witnesses have been involved in 72 Supreme Court cases—more than any other group aside from the government. Among other things, they've won the right for adults to refuse blood transfusions, which Witnesses believe are forbidden in the Bible.

10. Witnesses believe Christmas and Easter are pagan celebrations with no biblical basis. They believe Christ was born in October.

Five Reasons You Won't Survive a Fall from a Cruise Ship

1. Force of Impact

Unless you're an experienced diver, the sheer impact of plunging 70 feet from a cruise ship deck into the ocean will be dangerous. Even if the impact itself isn't enough to kill you or knock you unconscious, the many other dangers of falling into the water unexpectedly—such as slamming into a part of the ship—mean you'll drown before anybody even knows you're gone.

2. Inebriation

An enormous percentage of "overboard incidents" occur due to drunken stupidity. And there is no shortage of drunken stupidity on your average cruise. According to analysts, alcohol sales make up a healthy percentage of the cruise industry's $24.9 billion in gross revenue. It's difficult enough to survive a fully clothed plunge into choppy, cold seawater—but doing it while heavily inebriated is almost impossible.

3. Hypothermia

Hypothermia, a potentially deadly condition in which the body loses heat faster than it can produce it, is the most likely reason you won't last long even if you do survive a trip over the railing. Experts state that the average person can only survive for about 20 minutes in chilly water (about 40 degrees Fahrenheit). And while you'll last longer in the balmy waters of the Caribbean than, say, if you tumbled off a ship during an Antarctic cruise, being submerged for extended periods of time in even warm water can lead to hypothermia.

4. Sharks

Sharks are drawn to human bodily fluids, and even if you manage to stave off drowning and hypothermia, odds are you're going to attract a shark eventually. The Florida Museum of Natural History states that there have been more than 1,000 instances of sharks attacking humans worldwide since 1990. Before leaping into the drink, consider your geography: You'll probably want to avoid diving into the waters off South Africa, which boast three of the world's ten most shark-infested beaches. However, in the Mediterranean, you won't have to be quite as worried. According to a 2008 study, the once plentiful Mediterranean sharks are now "functionally extinct."

5. Dehydration

The human body can only survive for three to five days without water. Sadly, seawater won't help—the high levels of salt and other minerals in seawater will only serve to increase dehydration and hasten your demise.

By the Numbers

122: number of people who fell off cruise ships between 2000 and 2008

30.02: percentage of total falls that occurred from Carnival cruise ships

Five Good Reasons The Weather Channel Should Have Failed

In 2008, The Weather Channel, founded as the brainchild of Chicago weather forecaster John Coleman and media executive Frank Batten, was sold to NBC for the whopping sum of $3.5 billion. That somebody was willing to pay billions for a channel that broadcast nothing but weather information is only slightly less puzzling than the fact that somebody thought a channel devoted to overcast-with-a-chance-of-rain was a good idea to begin with. Here are five of the top reasons why The Weather Channel should have been rained out.

1. Weather is not a commodity

Most television networks make money by providing what no other network can, whether that be through original programming, televised sporting events, or highly paid television personalities. Weather, though, is free to all. What's more, The Weather Channel (TWC) originally got its weather information through the National Weather Service—a government-run organization that was already providing its forecasts free through 24-hour radio broadcasts.

2. Weather is boring

Sure, tornadoes and hurricanes might be exciting, but your average everyday weather isn't exactly a pulse-throttler. Indeed, for most people, weather is a conversation piece of last resort, a signal that you have nothing of substance to say. Sounds like a great idea for a television network.

3. Weather forecasts are notoriously inaccurate

The fallibility of weather forecasts is woven into the fabric of popular culture. In fact, according to ForecastAdvisor.com, a Web site devoted to tracking the accuracy of weather forecasters, The Weather Channel hit the mark a mere 71 percent of the time in 2008—barely a passing grade. We're not sure whether the fact that The Weather Channel's abysmal showing led the weather forecasting pack reflects well on TWC or poorly on everybody else.

4. The Weather Channel didn't provide anything new

The Weather Channel initially provided little more than the average person could get by reading the morning paper, watching the evening news, or sticking their head out the window.

5. It failed everywhere else

Bolstered by their early popularity in the United States, Landmark Communications, the media company behind The Weather Channel, tried to start sister channels in other countries, most notably in the United Kingdom and Europe. These flopped miserably. Evidently Europeans have better things to do than sit around and watch television coverage of the weather!

"Conversation about the weather is the last refuge of the unimaginative."
—Oscar Wilde

Inventors Killed by Their Inventions

The success of history's most famous inventors rested not just upon brilliant ideas but also upon having the dedication and confidence to pursue those ideas in the face of public doubt. Unfortunately, inventors have sometimes been too confident in their work—with disastrous consequences. Here are six inventors whose inventions got the better of them.

Henry Winstanley, Lighthouse Architect

While 17th-century lighthouse-smith Henry Winstanley didn't *invent* lighthouses, he did design a new kind of lighthouse—the Eddystone Lighthouse, an octagonal-shaped structure built to withstand treacherous conditions on tenuous ground. Despite observers' doubts that the lighthouse would stand up to serious meteorological assault, Hank believed in his design—so much so that he insisted on taking shelter in it during a terrible storm in November 1703. It was a poor decision—the lighthouse collapsed, ending Winstanley's life.

Marie Curie, Radiation Pioneer

Marie Curie is known to schoolchildren as the discoverer of the elements radium and polonium, the first woman to win a Nobel Prize, a pioneer in the field of radioactivity, and the inventor of a method for isolating radioactive isotopes. Unfortunately, she is also known as a pioneer in the field of radiation-induced cancer. Curie, who was working with radioactive isotopes well before the dangers of radiation were fully known, contracted leukemia from radiation exposure and died at age 66.

William Bullock, Inventor of the Web Rotary Printing Press

Before the 19th century, the printing press hadn't advanced much beyond Gutenberg's first effort back in the 15th century. In 1863,

William Bullock changed everything by coming up with the idea of a web rotary press—a self-feeding, high-speed press that could print as many as 10,000 pages per hour. Unfortunately, Bullock forgot a basic rule of printing presses: Don't stick your foot into the rotating gears. In 1867, Bullock got tangled up in his invention, severely injuring his foot. Gangrene set in, and he died shortly afterward.

Karel Soucek, Inventor of the "Stunt Capsule"

Soucek shot to fame in 1984 by designing a special stunt capsule that he used to plunge over Niagara Falls. Seeking to capitalize on his newfound popularity, Soucek decided to repeat the stunt in 1985—only this time from an artificial waterfall running from the top of the Houston Astrodome down to a tank of water. It seemed like a bad idea, and it was: The capsule exploded upon impact, and Soucek suffered fatal injuries.

Otto Lilienthal, Inventor of the Hang Glider

Until the late 19th century, human flight was little more than a pipe dream. Otto Lilienthal changed all of that with his hang glider, and his successful glides made him famous the world over. Unfortunately, in 1896, Lilienthal plunged more than 50 feet during one of his test runs. The fall broke his spine, and he died shortly after.

Cowper Phipps Coles, Inventor of the Rotating Ship Turret

The splendidly named Cowper Phipps Coles was a captain in the British navy who invented a "rotating gun turret" for British naval vessels during the Crimean War. After the war, Coles patented his invention and set about building ships equipped with his new turret. Unfortunately, the first ship that he built, the HMS *Captain,* turned into the HMS Capsized. In order to accommodate his turret design, the shipbuilders were forced to make odd adjustments to the rest of the ship, which seriously raised the center of gravity. End result? The ship sank on one of its first voyages, killing Coles and much of his crew.

Sex on TV

It may seem like there's too much sex being shown on TV these days. But sex wasn't always inextricably linked with television. In fact, for most of television history, sex didn't appear to exist at all.

First couple depicted in bed together: *Mary Kay and Johnny*, 1947. Anybody familiar with the golden age of television knows that men and women, even married ones, were never depicted in bed together. Preposterously, scenes shot in the bedroom—when there were any—showed two twin beds sitting primly beside one another. Surprisingly, though, the first couple shown in bed together on television predates the inane twin-bed scenario. According to Snopes.com, the 1940s-era live sitcom *Mary Kay and Johnny,* a sort of precursor to *I Love Lucy,* often depicted the title characters sharing the same bed.

First same-sex kiss, primetime: *Relativity*, 1997. Though same-sex kisses had occurred before on television, the first depiction of homosexual smooching occurred on the short-lived television series *Relativity,* which also has the honor of featuring the first recurring lesbian character in the cast of a television show.

First same-sex kiss, daytime: *As the World Turns*, 2007. Soap operas are known for their steamy romances, but it wasn't until August 2007 that the daytime television world acknowledged that homosexual romance existed. That's when *As the World Turns* characters Noah and Luke shared an onscreen kiss. Perhaps soap opera fans weren't ready for it—in December 2009, producers of the long-running show announced its eminent cancellation.

First gay sex scene, primetime: *Thirtysomething*, 1989. In a post-*Brokeback Mountain* entertainment landscape, the depiction of gay sex during one infamous episode of the hit 1980s drama *Thirtysomething* seems a little tame. In fact, there really wasn't a depiction at all. There was, instead, an intimation—a scene in which two gay male characters did little more than lay in bed after a presumed bout of lovemaking. Still, it was revolutionary for the 1980s. To this day, the episode has never been shown in reruns.

Former Day Jobs

Not everybody started at the top of their profession—in fact, pretty much no one did. Here's what a few people were up to before they became household names.

- Actor Rock Hudson, cartoon tycoon Walt Disney, and crooner Bing Crosby worked for the post office: Hudson as a letter carrier, Disney as an *assistant* letter carrier, and Crosby as a postal clerk.

- Legendary lover Casanova founded the French state lottery.

- Actor/director Clint Eastwood was a firefighter, lumberjack, steel-mill furnace stoker, and lifeguard, so he comes by those craggy, manly good looks honestly.

- Speaking of craggy good looks, actor Robert Mitchum was a heavyweight boxer, and actor Lee Marvin was a plumber and a U.S. Marine.

- Singer Rod Stewart was a grave digger.

- Actor Harrison Ford was, famously, a carpenter who installed kitchens and such for moguls who would later pay him much more handsomely for his theatrical labors.

- Actor/sex symbol Jayne Mansfield was a concert pianist and violinist before she became what some people labeled "the poor man's Marilyn Monroe."

- Actor Dustin Hoffman was once a janitor, but even that had to be easier than his other job—attendant in a mental hospital.

- Actor Greta Garbo toiled as a latherer in a men's barbershop.

- Actor Al Pacino was variously employed as a theater usher, porter, and superintendent of an office building.

- Actor Audrey Hepburn secretly worked with the Dutch Resistance as a youngster during World War II and also performed as a ballet dancer.

Seven Basic Rules of Nudist Camps

What really goes on at a nudist camp? A lot of non-nudists assume it's nothing but sex, ogling, and more sex. The truth is, nudist camps have very well-defined rules about appropriate behavior. And most nudists are really just there to sun, swim, backpack, canoe—even skydive—in their glorious birthday suits. So toss your misconceptions and clothes aside and remember these rules.

1. Take it off.

The most general rule is: "Clothed when practical, nude when appropriate." That means nudity may be optional while dining or at a dance, but it may be "required" in certain designated areas, including the pool.

2. Tote a towel.

Make that two. Proper nudist etiquette deems you carry one towel to sit or lounge on and a second towel for drying off at the pool. It's all about being polite—and sanitary.

3. Don't gawk or stalk.

This is not the place to peep, pry, pick up, or be a paparazzo. Staring is considered a form of aggression.

4. No photos, please.

Along those same lines, be sure to check the resort or facility's photography guidelines before trotting out your camera. Most nudists are rather camera-shy, and it is considered rude to take photos without asking first. After all, no one wants their boss to see photos from their nudist vacation on Facebook!

5. Keep your hands to yourself.

In other words, ixnay the PDA. Any overt sexual behavior that causes others to feel embarrassed, offended, or uncomfortable could get you kicked out.

6. Stick with first names.

Many nudists prefer to keep things on a first-name basis for privacy's sake.

7. Contain your excitement.

Guys, erections are regarded as perfectly normal, but they're not exactly proper in public. If a case of overexcitement overtakes you, turn over, take a quick dip in a cold pool, or bury it in the sand.

The Bare Facts

- Eager to experience the nudist lifestyle? In North America, you'll find more than 250 clubs and resorts where nude vacations are a possibility.

- One in four Americans (about 70 million people) have skinny-dipped or sunbathed in the nude.

- Nude recreation isn't just for aging hippies: 23 percent of EchoBoomers (born since 1979) and 18 percent of Xers (born 1965–1978) are looking for a nude recreation experience.

- A 2006 survey of telecommuters revealed that 12 percent of males and 7 percent of females work from home in the nude.

Munchie Mythology

Food: It's fodder for the best urban legends and old wives' tales. Myths range from complete nutritional nonsense to gluttonous celebrity gossip. Are you one of the gastronomically gullible?

Bad Raps

MYTH: Chocolate causes acne.

TRUTH: No specific food has been scientifically proven to produce pimples—not chocolate, pizza, potato chips, or French fries. Acne's true cause is a buildup of dead skin cells within the pores. This can be triggered by hormones, environment, and heredity, but not by a Mr. Goodbar.

MYTH: Mayonnaise is the major cause of picnic food poisoning outbreaks.

TRUTH: Commercial mayonnaise is pasteurized and—thanks to ingredients like salt and lemon juice—has a high acid content that actually slows the growth of food-borne bacteria. Improperly handled meats and veggies in picnic salads and sandwiches are more likely to be your number one *Salmonella* suspects.

Brown Is Better than White

MYTH: Brown eggs are more nutritious than white eggs.

TRUTH: Brown eggs come from hens with red earlobes, and white eggs come from hens with white earlobes. Crack through the outer shell, and brown eggs offer no better nutritive value, taste, or quality. Why are they more expensive? Brown eggs are usually a smidge larger in size.

MYTH: Brown sugar is healthier than white sugar.

TRUTH: Brown sugar is simply ordinary white table sugar that's turned brown by the addition of molasses. And while molasses does contain certain minerals (calcium, potassium, iron, and magnesium), they're only present in negligible amounts. The real difference is only apparent in the taste and texture of your baked goods.

Lies Your Parents Told

MYTH: Coffee will stunt your growth.

TRUTH: Research does not support the notion that drinking caffeinated coffee will hinder your height. That doesn't mean coffee belongs in a child's diet, however. Some actual adverse effects include bellyaches, nervousness, headaches, rapid heartbeat, and insomnia—all of which make for one crabby kid.

MYTH: You must wait an hour after eating before swimming.

TRUTH: Though swimming strenuously on a full stomach could lead to cramps, the chance of that happening to a recreational swimmer is quite small. One study of drownings in the United States found that less than 1 percent happened after the victim had eaten a meal. What you really need to avoid: eating or chewing gum while in the water. According to the American Red Cross, both activities can lead to choking.

Celebrity Stories

MYTH: Caesar salad was named for Julius Caesar.

TRUTH: The famous salad has no connection with that particular Caesar, or with Rome at all for that matter. Its creation is most often credited to Caesar Cardini, owner and chef of Caesar's Place in Tijuana, Mexico. His original recipe (concocted around 1924) contained romaine lettuce, garlic, croutons, Parmesan cheese, eggs, olive oil, and Worcestershire sauce. No anchovies!

MYTH: Mama Cass died from choking on a ham sandwich.

TRUTH: When Cass Elliot (of The Mamas & The Papas) suddenly died in 1974 at the age of 32, gossip quickly spread that she choked while eating a sandwich in bed. Though a half-eaten ham roll may have been found on her nightstand, an autopsy revealed no food in her trachea. The real cause of death was massive heart failure due to long-term obesity.

Curious Classifieds

Teeth extracted by the latest Methodists.

It takes many ingredients to make our burgers great but... "The secret ingredient is our people."

Stock up and save. Limit: one.

Widows made to order. Send us your specifications.

Tattoos...While you wait.

For you alone! The bridal bed set...

Snowblower for sale...only used on snowy days.

Braille dictionary for sale. Must see to appreciate!

Attorney at law; 10% off free consultation.

"I love you only" Valentine cards: Now available in multipacks.

Dog for sale: eats anything and is fond of children.

For rent: 6-room hated apartment.

Mixing bowl set designed to please a cook with round bottom for efficient beating.

The fact that those we have served return once again, and recommend us to their friends, is a high endorsement of the service we render. Village Funeral Home.

Joining nudist colony, must sell washer and dryer—$300.

MOVING SALE: Wheelchair, hospital bed, deluxe sliding stair glide, and a motorcycle.

LOST DIAPER BAG: With very sentimental items. In Taco Bell parking lot.

A superb and inexpensive restaurant. Fine food expertly served by waitresses in appetizing forms.

We build bodies that last a lifetime.

Christmas tag sale. Handmade gifts for the hard-to-find person.

Our bikinis are exciting. They are simply the tops.

Things You Don't Know (and Didn't Need to Know) About...

The Simpsons

The world's favorite yellow cartoon family, the Simpsons made their television debut as an animated short on The Tracey Ullman Show *on April 19, 1987. The dysfunctional quintet appeared in 48 episodes over three seasons before finally getting their own series. The first episode of* The Simpsons, *a Christmas episode titled "Simpsons Roasting on an Open Fire," aired on December 17, 1989.*

Who Voices Whom?

Dan Castellaneta: Homer Simpson

Nancy Cartwright: Bart Simpson

Julie Kavner: Marge Simpson

Yeardley Smith: Lisa Simpson

Famous Voices

Numerous celebrities have voiced characters on *The Simpsons*, often playing themselves, such as astronaut Buzz Aldrin, actor Mel Gibson, and physicist Stephen Hawking. Others have given voice to various characters within the Simpsons universe. Among them:

Kirk Douglas (Chester J. Lampwick)

Donald Sutherland (Hollis Hurlbut)

Susan Sarandon (ballet teacher)

Rodney Dangerfield (Larry Burns)

Glenn Close (Mother Simpson)

Anne Bancroft (Dr. Zweig)

A Man of Many Hats

Homer Simpson has held numerous jobs over the course of the series. They include: astronaut, boxer, butler, carny, conceptual artist, door-to-door sugar salesman, film producer, food critic, garbage commissioner, Kwik-E-Mart employee, missionary, monorail conductor, nuclear safety inspector, telemarketer, used car salesman, and village oaf.

Not Everyone Loves *The Simpsons*

Over the years, the writers of *The Simpsons* have managed to anger or offend a wide range of individuals, groups, cities, and nations. Among those most ticked off:

1. A principal in Ohio. In 1990, as *The Simpsons* was becoming a national phenomenon, the principal banned students from wearing Simpsons T-shirts declaring "Underachiever."

2. Riotur, the official tourism bureau of Rio de Janeiro, which threatened a civil lawsuit following an episode in which the Simpsons visit Brazil and find it rife with crime, slums, and child-consuming animals.

3. New Orleans, which took umbrage at an all-musical adaptation of *A Streetcar Named Desire* that portrayed the city as the "home of pirates, drunks, and whores." The following week, Bart made amends by writing on the blackboard: "I will not defame New Orleans."

4. Several Jewish groups, which protested the episode "Like Father, Like Clown," a parody of *The Jazz Singer* in which it was revealed that Krusty the Clown is Jewish and estranged from his rabbi dad, voiced by Jackie Mason.

Fun Facts

- In every script, Homer's trademark exclamation—D'oh!—is referred to only as "annoyed grunt."

- Nancy Cartwright, the voice of Bart Simpson, joined the Church of Scientology after reading the works of L. Ron Hubbard.

- Bart Simpson is left-handed.

- Matt Groening, the creator of *The Simpsons,* named the family after his own, except for Bart, which is an anagram for "brat."

5. The families of individuals with Tourette's Syndrome, who flooded the network with complaints following a 1992 episode in which Bart claims to have the condition in order to get out of taking a test. The reference was changed to rabies in reruns.

∙∙∙∙∙∙∙∙∙∙∙∙∙∙∙∙∙∙∙∙∙∙∙∙∙∙∙∙∙∙∙∙∙∙∙∙∙∙

Movie Magic

∙∙∙∙∙∙∙∙∙∙∙∙∙∙∙∙∙∙∙∙∙∙∙∙∙∙∙∙∙∙∙∙∙∙∙∙∙∙

Although any other mega-hit television series would have capitalized on its popularity with a hastily thrown-together motion picture, it took the creators of *The Simpsons* 18 years to come out with a Simpsons movie. Simply titled *The Simpsons Movie* (2007), it grossed more than $183 million in the United States alone.

The Simpsons by the Numbers

58: the number of Emmy Award nominations the series has received

24: the number of Emmy Awards the series has won

1: the number of awards the show has received from the Gay & Lesbian Alliance Against Defamation (GLAAD), for the episode "Homer's Phobia"

21: the number of series staff members who are Harvard University alums

8th: where *The Simpsons* ranked in *TV Guide*'s list of the 50 Greatest TV Shows of All Time

24th: where the "Krusty Gets Kancelled" episode of *The Simpsons* ranked in *TV Guide*'s list of the 100 Greatest Episodes of All Time

2: the number of celebrities who have voiced a character on *The Simpsons* incognito: Michael Jackson (as John Jay Smith) and Dustin Hoffman (as Sam Etic)

Naming Names

Each year, the Social Security Administration of the United States puts out a list of the top 1,000 names given to newborn babies. Where do they get their data? From applications for Social Security cards!

Here are the ten most popular names given to baby boys of the new millennium:

10. Tyler	5. Christopher
9. Daniel	4. Joshua
8. Joseph	3. Matthew
7. Andrew	2. Michael
6. Nicholas	1. Jacob

Number of baby boys named Jacob in 2000: 34,437

Percentage of total baby boys named Jacob in 2000: 1.6514 percent

What About Michael?

Michael was the most popular boy's name for 37 years (1961–1998) before being unseated by Jacob in 1999.

What's in a Name?

Jacob means "he who supplants" or "holder of the heel." Hebrew in origin (Yaakov), the Old Testament Jacob was the grandson of Abraham and the son of Isaac and Rebecca. He was born holding the heel of his twin brother, Esau, and is the traditional ancestor of the people of Israel.

International Forms

Czech: Jakub	Russian: Yakov
Dutch: Jacobus	Spanish: Jacobo
Italian: Giaccobbe	Turkish: Yakup

Endearing Nicknames

Jay

Jake

Jack

Jaco

Cub

Teasing Nicknames

Jacob All Trades

John Jacob Jingleheimer Schmidt

Jake the Snake

Flakey Jake

Jack Off

Jake 'n' Bake

State of Dissent

The most popular boy's name in Texas for the year 2000: Jose

Least Popular Boy's Names of 2000

Dayne

Francesco

Issak

Lionel

Tracy

Famous Jacobs

Jacob Grimm, German linguist and author of Grimms' Fairy Tales *(along with brother Wilhelm).*

Jacob K. Javits, U.S. Senator from New York (1957–1981), who championed civil rights, the ERA, and social welfare.

Jacob "Jake" Gyllenhaal, American actor who portrayed homosexual cowboy Jack Twist in the film Brokeback Mountain.

Jacob Marley, fictional character whose ghost haunts Ebenezer Scrooge in the Charles Dickens novel, A Christmas Carol.

Jacob Black, fictional human shape-shifter/werewolf featured in the Twilight *vampire romance series by Stephenie Meyer.*

Keeping It in the Family

How many famous people can one family produce?
Let's count 'em down.

The Baldwins

This slick-haired band of brothers includes eldest brother Alec (of *30 Rock* and paparazzi-hating fame), Daniel (of rehab fame), William (Mr. Chynna Phillips), and Stephen (minister and D-list celebrity).

The Barrymores

The "Royal Family" of acting includes Maurice Barrymore, Lionel Barrymore, Ethel Barrymore, John Barrymore, and Drew Barrymore. (Numerous spouses and ex-spouses also dabbled in stage and screen work.)

The Fondas

Henry Fonda (not to mention first wife, Margaret Sullavan), his kids Jane and Peter, and grandchildren Bridget Fonda and Troy Garity. 'Nuff said.

The Hemingways

Talent and tragedy followed the Hemingway family, so it seems. Author Ernest Hemingway committed suicide in 1961 after a lifetime of depression. A similar fate awaited his granddaughter, model and actress Margaux Hemingway. Fortunately, granddaughter Mariel Hemingway, an actress and author, has fared better.

The Marx Brothers

An early stage mom, Minnie Marx made sure that all of her boys got a chance in vaudeville. So it came to be that brothers Chico, Harpo, Groucho, Gummo, and Zeppo—the Marx Brothers—carved a niche in history. Gummo ultimately found that he enjoyed life outside the limelight and left the act to become a talent agent.

Whip It:
Roller Derby Names

Roller derby is back on the scene in a big way. Check out this fun list of derby girls' nom de skate.

In 2004, the Women's Flat Track Roller Derby Association was founded, bringing women's competitive roller derby back to the masses. With roots going as far back as the 1930s, derby bouts are rowdy, risky, fun, and imbued with a special brand of gallows humor, as evidenced by the names of the players, referees, and support staff.

There are multiple reasons derby girls skate under an alias. For one, the fake names are a lot of fun, which is basically derby's MO. Alter egos also allow derby girls to show their ferocious sides: Mild-mannered working girls and stay-at-home moms by day can be competitive, outrageous skaters by night. Below is just a sampling of names. Derby girls, referees, and staff members past and present number well over 13,000 worldwide.

Name and League

Tequila Mockingbird—Windy City Rollers

Bone Crawford—Jersey Shore Roller Girls

Gefilte Fists—Philly Roller Girls

Midwife Crisis—Arch Rival Roller Girls

Genghis Connie—Assassination City Roller Derby

Grrrilla—Sonoma County Roller Derby

Graceless Kelly—Maine Roller Derby

Doris Day of the Dead (referee)—Windy City Rollers

Skatie Couric—Boston Derby Dames

Cruisin' B. Anthony—Ithaca Roller Derby

Grudge Judy—Texas Rollergirls

Abbey Rogue—Denver Roller Dolls

Worth Repeating

Memorable Baseball Quotes

They can hit, catch, manage, and sometimes...philosophize.

"It ain't over 'til it's over."
—Yogi Berra

"Because there is always some kid who may be seeing me for
the first or last time, I owe him my best."
—Joe DiMaggio, on why he always played hard

"Show me a good loser and I'll show you an idiot."
—Leo Durocher

"I'm not concerned with your liking or disliking me...All I ask
is that you respect me as a human being."
—Jackie Robinson

"I don't care if the guy is yellow or black or if he has stripes...I'm
the manager of this team and I say he plays."
—Leo Durocher, Jackie Robinson's manager,
upon the latter breaking baseball's color barrier

"Don't look back. Something might be gaining on you."
—Satchel Paige

"Sometimes the best deals are the ones you don't make."
—Bill Veeck

"If I knew I was going to live this long I'd have taken better care of myself."
—Mickey Mantle, on reaching age 46

"Yes sir, I did bet on baseball."
—Pete Rose, admitting what he had long denied

"I had a better year than Hoover."
—Babe Ruth, on earning more than President Herbert Hoover
in 1930 during the Great Depression

"I never could stand losing. Second place didn't interest me."
—Ty Cobb

*"Baseball gives every American boy a chance to excel . . .
This is the nature of man and the name of the game."*
—Ted Williams

It's Probably a Con If...

From shell games to e-mail scams, nearly all con games are played the same way: The "mark" gives up something of value to get a reward that never comes. Here are a few surefire signs that you're being conned.

- You trade money for something with questionable value. "The swap" is the heart of most cons. For example, a con artist might pose as a bank examiner, standing outside a bank. He flashes a badge, "inspects" a customer's withdrawn cash, and seizes the bills, claiming they are evidence in an embezzling case. He gives the customer a receipt and sends him or her back into the bank for replacement bills. When the mark goes back in, the con artist escapes.

- You pay for future money. This basic recipe is a con staple: You hand over your own money to access much more money. For example, in one scam, an e-mail asks you to put up thousands of dollars to pay administrative fees that will unlock millions of dollars held overseas. Of course, after you wire your money, it disappears.

- A stranger trusts you. One way to earn someone's trust is to trust them first. For example, a con man might trust you to hold onto a diamond necklace he "found," if you put up a small fraction of what the necklace is worth (say, $200). A great deal... except the necklace is really a $5 knockoff.

- Someone else trusts the stranger. Many con games involve a "shill," a co-conspirator who pretends to be like the mark. Seeing that someone else believes the con artist, the mark follows suit.

- You're running out of time. Con artists fog a mark's decision making by saying time is limited. The mark doesn't want to miss the opportunity and so throws caution to the wind.

- You're misbehaving. When the mark breaks societal rules, like taking found valuables rather than turning them in, he's less likely to go to the police after figuring out the scam.

Seven Things the Pope Wears in Public

He's got a sweet ride, he lives in a gold-plated mansion, and he performs to billions around the globe. No, he's not a rock star—he's the pope, the nominal head of the Catholic church. Here are seven essential items of papal regalia.

1. **The Ring of the Fisherman** The solid gold Ring of the Fisherman is named after St. Peter, who was a fisherman by trade; it is decorated with a representation of Peter angling from a boat, with the name of the current pope inscribed above it. The pope uses the ring to seal official papal documents.

2. **The Papal Cross** The pope once carried a shepherd's crook to symbolize that he was the head of Christ's flock. Now, though, he wields a cross topped by a figure of the crucified Jesus.

3. **Papal Shoes** Blazing carmine is the color of choice for papal footwear, whether that be the papal slippers worn indoors or the shoes worn outside.

4. **Cope** Have you ever wondered why the pope always looks so bowed and frail? It's probably due to the many layers of capes, robes, and mantles draped over his papal shoulders. The cope is that sweeping, flowing, heavily embroidered cape the pope wears. It's so heavy it requires two assistants (usually deacons) to carry it.

5. **Fanon** The fanon is another capelike garment, made of white silk lined with gold.

6. **Pallium** The pope also sometimes dons a pallium, a scarf-type band worn around the neck and shoulders and weighed down by lead pendants.

7. **Mitre** That pointy hat adorning the papal crown is actually known as a mitre. Pope Benedict XVI is known to be fond of his headgear, often breaking out new mitres for big events.

Ten Highest-Paid CEOs

Sure, 2008 was a lousy year for the economy, but these CEOs still fared pretty well—at least according to a Forbes *report.*

10. Robert W. Lane, Deere & Co.: $61.30 million

The nine-year CEO of the tractor company raked in more than $60 million in 2008. Meanwhile, Deere & Co. stock plunged 57 percent.

9. Hugh Grant, Monsanto: $64.60 million

The head of the agricultural chemical company received almost double his 2007 compensation, while investors were treated to a –36 percent rate of return on their Monsanto stocks.

8. Paul J. Evanson, Allegheny Energy: $67.26 million

Energy prices went up, profits went down, but Paul J. Evanson still took home a cool $67 million.

7. Matthew K. Rose, Burlington Santa Fe: $68.62 million

Who says the railroad is dead? Rose, a University of Missouri grad clocks in at #7 on *Forbes'* list of highest-paid CEOs.

6. William R. Berkley, W.R. Berkley: $87.48 million

The insurance companies may have been the whipping boy for the 2008 fiscal meltdown, but the founder and CEO of insurance titan W.R. Berkley still had a pretty decent year.

5. Mark G. Papa, EOG Resources: $90.47 million

Somehow Mark G. Papa's $90-million compensation package only ranks fourth among CEOs of energy companies.

4. Michael D. Watford, Ultra Petroleum: $116.93 million

The head of oil giant Ultra Petroleum earned an ultra paycheck in 2008.

3. John B. Hess, Hess: $154.58 million

A Harvard graduate and the son of Hess oil company founder Leon Hess, John B. Hess's 2008 salary was about 50 percent more than all of the U.S. senators and representatives—combined.

2. Ray R. Irani, Occidental Petroleum: $222.64 million

Irani's paycheck may seem high, but it's a mere fraction of Occidental Petroleum's $20 billion in revenues in 2008.

1. Lawrence J. Ellison, Oracle: $556.98 million

The lone tech representative on the top ten list, Lawrence J. Ellison's 2008 compensation dwarfs the rest of the competition.

❖ ❖ ❖

"When you innovate, you've got to be prepared for everyone telling you you're nuts."
—Lawrence J. Ellison

That's a Crime Too:
Monster Laws

Planning to bag Bigfoot? Want to capture yourself a Yeti? Or net yourself a sea monster? Better think again. Because believe it or not, there are laws on the books protecting these creatures from harm—even though they may not even exist (the creatures, not the laws). Check it out:

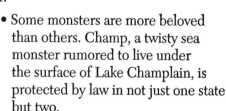

- In 1969, the board of commissioners in Washington state's Skamania County passed an ordinance making it illegal to kill a Bigfoot. The punishments for violating this law are quite severe: a $10,000 fine and a prison sentence of five years.

  The law's text cites the high number of purported Bigfoot sightings in the county as justification. The law also covers its bases by mandating protection not only for creatures called "Bigfoot," but also for those called "Yeti," "Sasquatch," and "Giant Hairy Ape." Of course, it's hard to tell how serious commissioners were about this law: It was originally passed on April 1.

- Some monsters are more beloved than others. Champ, a twisty sea monster rumored to live under the surface of Lake Champlain, is protected by law in not just one state but two.

  In the 1980s, both Vermont and New York passed resolutions that made it illegal to harm Champ in any way. The sea serpent is held in such high esteem in the region that the community of Port Henry, New York, celebrates Champ Day each summer. During this festival, vendors flock to the streets of Port Henry to hawk elephant ears, folk art, and lots of T-shirts with Champ appliqués.

- Champ isn't the only sea monster who's earned protection from hunters and poachers. In 1973, the Arkansas state senate passed a resolution sponsored by Senator Robert Harvey naming certain sections of the White River a safe refuge for a sea monster called Whitey. Whitey is a household name for many Arkansans. Sightings of the creature, described by one witness as a gray-skinned beast as wide as a car and three car lengths long, began in 1915. The creature has been a part of Arkansas folklore ever since.

  In the summer of 1937, inventive monster hunters began building a giant rope net to capture Whitey after a sighting. Whitey escaped capture, though, when hunters ran out of money and materials to build their net.

- U.S. residents aren't the only ones obsessed with protecting undiscovered creatures. In Bhutan (a small Buddhist country bordered by Tibet, India, and China) the government set up the Sakteng Wildlife Sanctuary in 2001 to protect the mythical migoi. The migoi is a version of the United States' Yeti. The beasts are rumored to tower eight feet tall and boast reddish-brown fur. Legends say that the migoi are clever enough to walk backward to mislead trackers. If hunters get too close, the creatures can even render themselves invisible—at least according to legend.

  The Sakteng Wildlife Sanctuary encompasses 253 square miles of land set aside as protected land for the migoi. Again, though, it's difficult to tell just how serious the Bhutan government was when creating the sanctuary. The Sakteng Wildlife Sanctuary also provides a home for snow leopards, tigers, and other wildlife that actually do exist. The "migoi habitat" angle may be a way to attract additional tourists to the region.

❖ ❖ ❖

"I think Bigfoot is blurry, that's the problem. There's a large out-of-focus monster roaming the countryside."
—Mitch Hedberg, comedian

Ten Really Embarrassing Things U.S. Presidents Have Done in Public

Just because you're the leader of the free world doesn't mean you're perfect!

1. Flaunting a mistress: John F. Kennedy

Perhaps booking your alleged mistress, Marilyn Monroe, as a performer at your birthday party is not such a good idea.

2. Mistreatment of an animal: Lyndon B. Johnson

Note to future leaders: Even if you love your beagle *do not* pick him up by the ears in front of the press.

3. Oversharing: Lyndon B. Johnson

LBJ made the list twice! This time he flashed his scar while recovering from gallbladder surgery.

4. Bumbling: Gerald R. Ford

Parodied by *Saturday Night Live* as a bumbler, Ford was actually a football star at the University of Michigan in the 1930s. Yet that didn't stop him from slipping down the steps of Air Force One or shooting his golf ball into a crowd of spectators more than once. News cameras were always there to capture the action.

5. More animal mistreatment: Jimmy Carter

It was supposed to be a private fishing excursion in Georgia. Unfortunately, a nearby cameraman photographed Carter as he battled an attacking swamp rabbit that tried to board his boat.

6. Adultery of the heart: Jimmy Carter

Carter had a run-in with a rabbit of the *Playboy* variety prior to the 1976 election when he admitted to having "committed adultery in [his] heart many times."

7. Illness: George H. W. Bush

What does protocol say about vomiting on the lap of the Japanese prime minister?

8. Infidelity: Bill Clinton

Does an impeachment trial count? And let's not forget that dress!

9. Poor grammar: George W. Bush

There are many "Bush-isms" that would fit this category, but among the best entries was a comment delivered on the 2000 campaign trail: "Rarely is the question asked—Is our children learning?"

10. Trapped: George W. Bush

Another two-time mention. After abruptly ending a press conference in China, the president exited stage right—only to find his escape hampered by a locked door. Despite his tugging at the door and mugging for the cameras, Bush was at a loss until an aide escorted him from the room.

❖ ❖ ❖

"The nine most terrifying words in the English language are: 'I'm from the government and I'm here to help.' "
—Ronald Reagan

In the Mood

Hoping to get lucky tonight? Check out our list of the best-known aphrodisiacs. Some of them might even work!

Rhinoceros Horn A common ingredient in ancient Chinese medicine, ground rhino horn has absolutely no medicinal value. Especially for the rhino.

Chocolate Studies have found that chocolate and sex stimulate the same pleasure sites in the brain. But that doesn't mean a Hershey's bar will make you more enthusiastic between the sheets.

Oysters They may be visually unappealing, but raw oysters are rich in zinc and other compounds necessary for sperm production and a strong libido. They certainly worked for Casanova, who often ate oysters for breakfast.

Exercise Listen up, couch potatoes: Getting in shape can actually make you better in bed. According to physiologists, regular exercise reduces your risk of sex-killing conditions such as obesity and diabetes. Exercise also improves heart function, which will better your endurance.

Music The right tunes can lower inhibitions and put you in the mood for love. (Tip: You can't go wrong with Barry White.)

Fragrances Certain scents can trigger strong desires, so find out which cologne or perfume makes your partner tingly and put on a dab or two.

Coffee Caffeine is a stimulant, so it makes sense that a cup o' joe would get the heart racing and heighten one's sense of awareness. But be careful because too much coffee can also lead to a bad case of the jitters.

Chili Peppers The chemicals that make chilis spicy have long been considered an aphrodisiac, but whether they'll actually put you in the mood for love is questionable.

Ginseng Long considered an aphrodisiac because of its phallic shape, ginseng contains compounds known to improve circulation—never a bad thing when love comes calling.

Strange Celebrity Endorsements

Need shoe polish, mail-order steak, or some dog food? If you can't trust a celebrity, who can you trust?

Muhammad Ali Wanna float like a butterfly and sting like a bee? Try the all-natural "Muhammad Ali Crisp Crunch." Also recommended: "Muhammad Ali Shoe Polish." (Inappropriate and politically incorrect tagline: "The greatest shine.")

Will Ferrell One of America's whitest white men, the comedian not only endorsed but also created a line of sunscreen, including "Sexy Hot Tan" and "Sun Stroke."

NASCAR Talk about brand loyalty! NASCAR romance novels by Harlequin—neither written by nor featuring NASCAR stars!

Old Yeller If you can get past the fact that the lovable Disney pooch became a rabid hound executed by his young owner, then consider giving man's best friend a bowl of "Old Yeller Dog Food." It's the only dog food served in the great beyond!

Jessica Simpson The actress/singer recently announced plans for her own line of luggage. (Dear Reader: Please insert own "Jessica Simpson baggage" joke here.)

Sylvester Stallone "Rocky" traded raw eggs for "Sylvester Stallone's High-Protein Pudding." "You are what you eat," he was quoted as saying. Really. He said that.

Mr. T Pity the fool! His Snickers candy bar ad (aired only in the UK) was pulled for being homophobic. Which begs the question: Why is Mr. T. still popular in Britain?

Donald Trump They're fired...on the grill! Even millionaires have to eat, so why not have them dig into a chunk of Trump Steaks—dubbed "The World's Greatest Steaks." Take that, Kobe beef!

WWF Superstars It was the 1980s, and an ad campaign featured wrestling superstar Jimmy "Mouth-of-the-South" Hart waiting to lick Hulk Hogan (in ice cream bar form). Unnerving, even by 1980s standards.

The Way the Future Wasn't...

Personal Jet Packs

Back in the 1930s, comic book hero Buck Rogers spent a lot of time flying to the rescue via personal jet pack. By the year 2000, we were all supposed to be zipping around with a tube of combustible fuel strapped to our backs. What happened?

The first real-life attempt at developing a personal jet pack was made by German engineers during World War II. Called the Skystormer, it consisted of two simple jet engine tubes, or pulse tubes, attached to a vest. Fortunately—for the Allies, at least—the Skystormers never got far off the ground, probably because pulse tubes small enough to be worn carried too little fuel for extended flight.

After the war, the U.S. military sponsored several jet pack projects. In the early 1950s, Wendell Moore of Bell Labs came up with a "jump belt" that relied on canisters of compressed nitrogen gas for thrust. Within two years, the belt morphed into the Aeropack, a rocket pack strapped to the wearer's back and propelled by hydrogen peroxide.

On April 20, 1961, engineer Harold Graham strapped on the Aeropack and became the world's first genuine rocket man by flying 112 feet in 13 seconds at a height of 20 inches above the ground. Graham made at least 64 demonstrations, including one in front of President Kennedy at Fort Bragg, North Carolina.

Despite, Graham's success, however, the Aeropack never became commercially viable. Expense was one major drawback. Plus, keeping yourself upright while airborne requires a lot of skill—to say nothing of a strong stomach when you find yourself literally flying head over heels.

That doesn't mean jet packs are gone for good. Swiss pilot Yves Rossy gave personal flight enthusiasts a real lift when he flew across the English Channel from Calais, France, to Dover, England, with his winged jet pack on September 26, 2008, covering 21 miles in less than 10 minutes. Things are looking up. The future may be closer than we think.

Who Knew?

The Nitty-Gritty on Baking Soda

Money's tight and you're out of polish, bug killer, and several different household cleaners and health-related items. What's a person to do? Grab the baking soda and get to work!

- A water and baking soda paste will dry out acne. Plus, it's cheaper than any over-the-counter product.

- Keep musty odors from ruining your vacation by sprinkling baking soda in your suitcase between trips.

- Speaking of vacations, don't forget the baking soda! Use it with water to treat sunburn and poison ivy, to brush your teeth, and to take the ouch out of bee stings.

- When you come home, add what's left of your baking soda to dishwashing liquid and water to remove bugs from your car's grille. Baking soda and water can also be used to polish chrome.

- Mix baking soda with confectioner's sugar and feed the cockroaches. Roaches will shun plain old baking soda—which is lethal to them—but they can't resist sugar.

- A pinch or two of baking soda will make milk last longer without affecting its taste.

- Keep baking soda in the tackle box to rid yourself of fishy smells. Put a box in your workshop, too: Baking soda is the main ingredient in fire extinguishers, which means loose baking soda will put out a small fire.

- Keep the kiddos quiet with clay (baking soda, cornstarch, and water) and paint (baking soda, cornstarch, vinegar, food coloring, and light corn syrup). And keep this in mind: Baking soda on a damp cloth will remove crayon from the walls.

- Read this: Get the mustiness out of old books by tying them tight in a plastic bag with a few tablespoons of baking soda. Shake gently and leave them there for a few days. Who knew?

11 People Who Fell from a Great Height and Survived

Don't take this as license to spend your weekends jumping out of windows, but with incredible luck, the human body can survive spectacular plummets. Here are 11 fortunate survivors.

1. In 1960, a boating accident sent seven-year-old Roger Woodward over Niagara Falls (Horseshoe Falls, specifically). Wearing only a bathing suit and a life preserver, he plummeted 161 feet, missed the rocks at the foot of the falls, and emerged unscathed. For 43 years, he was the only person to survive the drop without protective gear.

2. and 3. In 1979, newlyweds Kenneth and Donna Burke fell from a sixth-story balcony while posing for pictures during their wedding reception. They landed on grass 72 feet below, narrowly missing a concrete patio and brick wall.

4. In 2004, a 102-year-old Italian woman toppled over the railing of her fourth-story balcony. A plastic playhouse broke her fall, and apart from an arm fracture, she was fine.

5. In 1999, Joan Murray from Charlotte, North Carolina, couldn't get her parachute to open after jumping from a plane at 14,500 feet (2.7 miles). At 700 feet, her reserve chute opened, but then quickly deflated. She hit the ground at 80 miles per hour, landing directly on a mound of fire ants. Doctors believed the shock of more than 200 ant bites actually kept her heart beating. Less than two years later, she went on her 37th skydive.

6. and 7. When a man in Kuala Lumpur, Malaysia, returned home and caught two burglars in his apartment, they jumped out the window—16 stories up—and landed in a Dumpster. The trash cushioned their fall.

8. John Kevin Hines is one of about two dozen people to survive leaping off the Golden Gate Bridge in San Francisco. He jumped in 2000, when he was 19 and suffering from severe depression. He immediately regretted his decision and turned himself around during the 25-story drop so he could hit feet first, like a diver. He hit the water at about 75 miles per hour, breaking his back and cracking several vertebrae. After he recovered, he launched a speaking campaign calling for the addition of protective barriers on the bridge.

9. In 2007, brothers Alcides and Edgar Moreno were washing the windows on a New York high-rise when the cables holding their support swing failed. Edgar hit a fence below and died instantly. Alcides survived the 47-story fall by holding on to the 16-foot swing. Physicists believe the aluminum platform acted like a giant surfboard, slowed by air currents rising between the buildings.

10. In 1985, mountain climber Joe Simpson broke his leg while he and Simon Yates were descending Siula Grande in Peru. Yates and Simpson tied their ropes together, and Yates steadily lowered Simpson down the mountain. But when Simpson slipped off a cliff, Yates cut the rope to keep from falling himself. Yates assumed Simpson was dead and made his way back to camp. After falling 100 feet into a crevasse, Simpson dragged himself back to base camp. He made the six-mile trek in three days, with no food or water.

11. Serbian flight attendant Vesna Vulovic was the only survivor when Yugoslav Airlines Flight 367 broke up over Czechoslovakia in 1972. An explosion, apparently from a bomb, ripped the DC-9 plane apart when it was 33,333 feet (6.3 miles) in the air. When the wreckage fell to the ground, a villager found Vulovic lying in a piece of fuselage. She made a full recovery, and in 1985 was inducted into *Guinness World Records* for surviving the highest fall without a parachute.

Ten Food Festivals for People with Strong Stomachs

Every year across this great nation people gather to celebrate local food specialties. If you're tired of the same old Rib and Tomato Fests, you might want to check out some of these more, ahem, unusual food festivals.

1. Turkey Testicle Festival, Huntley, IL

Yep, this is pretty much what it sounds like. If you find yourself in the mood for some turkey testicles next November, stop by the Parkside Pub in Huntley, Illinois, for a handful.

2. Rocky Mountain Oyster Festival, Throckmorton, TX

For those of you who didn't get enough animal testicles in Huntley, no need to worry. The good people of Throckmorton, Texas, gather to celebrate bull testicles each May. Enjoy.

3. West Virginia Roadkill Cookoff, Pocahontas County, WV

Only in West Virginia would people flock to a festival promising roadkill delicacies. To be fair, no roadkill is actually used during the "cook-off"—instead, contestants are supposed to only use animals that would normally be found as roadkill. The 2008 winner? "Pothole Possum Stew."

4. WAIKIKI SPAM JAM, Oahu, HI

Like meat in a can? You're in luck! Every April, Hawaiians celebrate SPAM with a street fair sponsored, perhaps not surprisingly, by Hormel.

5. BugFest, Raleigh, NC

This celebration of all things arthropod is hosted by Raleigh's Museum of Natural Sciences. If you go, make sure to stop by Café Insecta for some stir-fried grasshoppers.

6. San Fernando Menudo Festival, San Fernando, CA

A festival to honor the band Menudo would be stomach-turning enough, but this San Fernando Menudo Festival requires an even stronger stomach: Menudo is a Mexican stew made of cow stomachs and pigs' feet.

7. Rattlesnake Hunt, Waurika, OK

For 46 years, celebrants have gathered in Waurika, Oklahoma, to hunt rattlesnakes and partake of a local delicacy: deep-fried rattlesnake meat. Organizers promote this festival as "fangtastic!"

8. Chitlin' Strut, Salley, SC

Events on tap for this year's Chitlin' Strut include a beauty pageant, a Chitlin' Strut Idol contest, and an antique tractor show. Oh, and plenty of pig intestines.

9. RC Cola and Moon Pie Festival, Bell Buckle, TN

Somehow we don't think that too many people interested in an "RC Cola and Moon Pie Festival" will be participating in the festival's opening event: a 10-mile run.

10. National Baby Food Festival, Fremont, MI

If you're an adult who loves to eat baby food, then Fremont, Michigan, is the town for you. Every summer, baby-food aficionados convene on this Midwestern town to participate in baby-food cook-offs, bingo, and its main event: the Adult Baby Food Eating Contest.

Most Unusual Museums

A list of every hyper-specific museum in the world could fill (and no doubt has filled) a book of its own, but perhaps this random sampling might fuel some interesting vacation ideas.

Beatles for Sale

Anyplace with even the slightest Beatles connection has tried to cash in on the fame of the Fab Four, and although the most authentic sites are naturally in Liverpool, American fans need not despair. The Hard Day's Nite [sic] B&B & Beatles Mini-Museum in Benton, Illinois, is a house once owned by George Harrison's sister Louise and boasts a room used by George himself. Louise answered thousands of fan letters from here. Off the mainland, the Kauai Country Inn, the only Beatles museum in Hawaii, is also an organic farm with an "extensive 40-year collection...including a Mini Cooper 'S' car registered by [manager] Brian Epstein...and many other interesting items." It's also conveniently located near the Waialua River's "Fern Grotto," used as a location in Elvis Presley's *Blue Hawaii.*

Elvis Has Left the Building

Speaking of the King, aside from the obvious tour of Graceland and a visit to the Tupelo, Mississippi, shotgun shack (complete with gift shop and chapel) where he and his twin, Jesse Garon, were born, there's the "world's largest private collection of Elvis memorabilia" in Pigeon Forge, Tennessee. Where else can you see items such as EP's 1967 "Honeymoon" Cadillac, the headboard from his Hollywood bedroom, and artifacts from his last tour, including Prell shampoo and Crest toothpaste?

The Peanut Gallery

Elvis's favorite sandwich was fried peanut butter, bacon, and banana; and while we couldn't divine a shrine to pork, there is a First Peanut Museum (in Waverly, Virginia) with myriad peanut memorabilia. It competes against the Agrirama Peanut Museum in Tifton, Georgia, which depicts "the dramatic transition from the horse and mule days to mechanized farming." Neither of these should be confused with the Charles M. Schulz Museum and Research Center in California devoted to the man who created the comic strip *Peanuts*.

Gone Bananas

Top this off by visiting the International Banana Club Museum in Hesperia, California. *Guinness World Records* declared that this was the world's largest collection devoted to a single fruit. Established in 1976, the museum spent 32 years in Altadena, California, before moving to its present location. You'll find banana lamps, gold-plated bananas, banana trees, banana body spray, and even a Banana Club golf putter.

There's No Such Thing as Too Much Cheese

Still peckish? Consider the Netherlands' Kaasmuseum (Cheese Museum), located in Alkmaar in a 14th-century chapel. No buxom maids a-churning, just mechanisms for making and weighing the finished product; visit the outdoor cheese market Fridays from 10:00 A.M. to noon. (Alkmaar also has its own Fab Four museum.) Then there is the chocolate museum in Barcelona (which features entire dioramas, including bullfights, sculpted out of the sweet stuff) and one in Cologne (the 13,000-square-foot Schokoladenmuseum has its own greenhouse to support cacao plants). But don't forget the Burlingame, California, Pez Museum, which has every dispenser ever made—including a rare counterfeit one of Adolf Hitler.

Medical Mayhem

If that's not enough to kill an appetite, there's New York's Burns Archive, which houses photos of people with nightmarish medical conditions, and the Lizzie Borden B&B in Falls River, Massachusetts, site of the grisly ax murders, complete with obligatory gift shop. Or there's the possibility of Philadelphia's Mütter's Museum, "home to a plethora of what were once quaintly referred to as freaks," including a full-body cast of Chang and Eng, the original Siamese twins.

People Who Deserve to Be a Lot More Famous

Sadly, inheriting a fortune can make you a superstar while saving countless lives may not. These folks deserved better.

- **Philo T. Farnsworth** You can hardly blame him for reality shows, but you should credit this self-taught Utah inventor with the first fully electronic television system.

- **Stanislav Petrov** On September, 26, 1983, Soviet Lieutenant Colonel Petrov likely saved 100 million Americans when he recognized an apparent U.S. missile attack as a satellite error and stopped an all-out counterstrike.

- **The Funk Brothers** The house band at Motown Records played on more number one singles than The Beatles, The Rolling Stones, The Beach Boys, and Elvis combined.

- **Sam Philips** Speaking of Elvis, we have producer Philips to thank for launching his career. He also recorded early records for Johnny Cash, Roy Orbison, and Jerry Lee Lewis, among others.

- **Norman Borlaug** This Nobel Peace Prize winner developed high-yield varieties of grain crops that averted mass famine in developing nations, saving hundreds of millions of lives.

- **Joseph Rochefort** In World War II, Rochefort cracked the Japanese Navy's JN25 code and intercepted plans for an assault on Midway Atoll. Because of this, the Allies won a crucial victory that shortened the war, saving countless lives.

- **Alan Turing** Speaking of codebreakers, Turing deserves credit for cracking the infamous Nazi Enigma code, which saved many lives as well. He also came up with the concept of modern computer hardware and software.

- **Edith Wilson** After President Woodrow Wilson suffered a stroke in 1919, First Lady Edith took over many duties, effectively functioning as co-president.

- **George Mason** In 1776, the "Forgotten Founding Father" wrote the Virginia Declaration of Rights, which inspired parts of the Declaration of Independence. Mason also helped draft the Constitution but ultimately opposed it because it lacked a Bill of Rights and made compromises to defend slavery.

- **Shigeru Miyamoto** Dubbed "the Walt Disney of the digital generation," he's the designer behind Nintendo's *Mario, Legend of Zelda, Donkey Kong*, and *Metroid* games, among many others.

- **Roy Sullivan** Between 1942 and 1977, park ranger Sullivan survived seven direct lightning strikes—certainly worthy of fame.

- **Stan Musial** Between 1942 and 1963, the St. Louis pitcher racked up 3,630 hits, played in 24 All-Star games, led the league in doubles eight times, and had 6,134 total bases—more than anybody but Hank Aaron.

- **Harold Ramis** Ramis deserves kudos for his impressive contributions to comedy. He directed *National Lampoon's Vacation*; directed and cowrote *Caddyshack, Groundhog Day,* and *Analyze This*; cowrote *Animal House*; and cowrote and costarred in *Stripes* and *Ghostbusters*.

- **Ben Hecht** Even Ramis had nothing on Hecht, who worked on the screenplays for more than 100 movies, including beloved films from Alfred Hitchcock, John Ford, and Howard Hawks.

- **William Tyndale** In the 16th century, Tyndale crafted the first widely published English translation of the Bible, introducing phrases like "sign of the times" and "salt of the earth" in the process. His reward? Being burned at the stake as a heretic. But in the 17th century, his work made it into the King James Bible, the most popular book of all time.

- **Steve Ditko** Stan Lee often gets sole credit for creating Spider-Man, but the reclusive Ditko was the artist who actually came up with the outfit and web shooters, among other details.

- **Leif Eriksson** The Norse explorer was the first European on record to set foot in North America, beating Columbus by 500 years.

How Does It Really End?

Think you know everything about your favorite films? Think again. Movie studios often preview new movies with test audiences who can help producers and directors predict whether or not they've got a hit on their hands. After getting feedback, changes to the film are made—anything from small tweaks to total overhauls. Read on for some cases of big changes that were made at the eleventh hour. Consider this your official spoiler alert.

Little Shop of Horrors

The Broadway version of this story goes something like this: Boy meets girl, boy and girl fall in love, boy and girl get eaten by carnivorous plant. Audiences were traumatized by Frank Oz's movie version of *Little Shop*, however, so the boy and girl live happily ever after on the big screen.

Fatal Attraction

Crazy Alex Forrest, the jilted lover brilliantly played by Glenn Close, was originally supposed to commit suicide and frame Michael Douglas's character for it. Test audiences didn't want the nasty lady to get off so easy, though; instead, Close's character was shot by Douglas's wife.

E.T.: The Extra-Terrestrial

In the original script, the lovable alien E.T. dies. This didn't sit well with children, so director Steven Spielberg gave in and allowed the little guy to make it home.

I Am Legend

This film adaptation, starring Will Smith in Richard Matheson's classic horror novella, is all about role reversals. Well, that and vampires. In the book, the mean, nasty vampires are actually revealed to be compassionate creatures only out to protect their own. It becomes clear that Smith's character is *their* enemy, just as much as they seem to be *his*. Well, this cautionary tale didn't fly with test audiences, so the main theme of Matheson's book was scrapped. Instead, Smith's character in the movie just blows everybody up.

The Wizard of Oz

The first audiences for this ultra-classic film thought Dorothy's classic "Over the Rainbow" number slowed down the story. It was kept in at the last minute.

Blade Runner

Ridley Scott, the Oscar-winning director who adapted Philip K. Dick's sci-fi classic to film, loved the dark tone of the story. The studio, however, didn't love it as much. In the original version of the film, the intense protagonist (played by heartthrob Harrison Ford) decides to harbor the renegade android he loves, even though she's doomed to short-circuit any second. Throughout the film, there are also allusions to the notion that Ford's character himself might be an android. The studio thought all this was a little too bleak, though, and decided to let the man and his android live happily ever after.

Pretty Woman

In the original version, Vivian, the prostitute with a heart of gold and legs for miles (played by Julia Roberts), rejects Richard Gere's character and goes on to seek her fortune. Test audiences cried foul, and the film ends with the couple together.

Butch Cassidy and the Sundance Kid

At the end of this timeless Western, Butch and Sundance are surrounded by what seems to be the entire Bolivian army. The film ends before the final gunfight, a clever way to leave it up to the audience to decide if the duo dies or manages to survive. The original version of the film showed their death, but test audiences preferred the alternate—more ambiguous (and less bloody)—ending.

The President of the United States: Also Known As...

Can you guess what your favorite president was called by the Secret Service?

1. The Secret Service promoted him to General but the men he served in the Army with just called him Captain. Who was the General?

    a. Jimmy Carter   c. Gerald Ford

    b. John F. Kennedy   d. Harry Truman

Answer: d. Harry Truman was a captain during World War I and left the service as a colonel in the Army Reserves. Carter, Ford, and Kennedy were all in the Navy.

2. Rawhide owned a ranch, and horseback riding was one of his favorite hobbies—he did a lot of it on the job in his younger years. Who was he?

    a. George W. Bush   c. Ronald Reagan

    b. Lyndon B. Johnson   d. Dwight Eisenhower

Answer: c. Ronald Reagan owned Rancho del Cielo, or Ranch of the Sky, in California. He also rode plenty of horses in cowboy movies during his acting career—never on the TV series *Rawhide*, however.

3. This president didn't "Volunteer" for the job as his code name suggests. Who was the surprised Volunteer who had the presidency suddenly thrust upon him?

    a. Richard Nixon   c. Lyndon B. Johnson

    b. John F. Kennedy   d. Franklin D. Roosevelt

Answer: c. Lyndon B. Johnson is the Volunteer who found himself suddenly bumped from vice president to president when JFK was assassinated.

4. Which two presidents had code names that started with the same letter because of a characteristic they shared?

     a. Barack Obama and John F. Kennedy

     b. George W. Bush and George H. W. Bush

     c. Bill Clinton and Jimmy Carter

     d. Gerald Ford and Lyndon B. Johnson

Answer: b. What they had in common was the same last name. Traditionally a president, his wife, and children have code names that begin with the same letter.

5. His name of Renegade matches his children's names of Radiance and Rosebud. Who is he?

     a. Barack Obama   c. George W. Bush

     b. Lyndon B. Johnson   d. John F. Kennedy

Answer: a. Barack Obama is Renegade while his daughters Malia and Sasha are Radiance and Rosebud. Michelle rounds out the R family as Renaissance.

6. Who was the first president to have a Secret Service code name?

     a. Harry Truman   c. Franklin D. Roosevelt

     b. Woodrow Wilson   d. George Washington

Answer: a. Presidents have had plenty of nicknames—both naughty and nice—over the years, but Truman was the first to have an official Secret Service "nickname."

The Secret Service does not choose the code names. The names are actually assigned by the White House Communications Agency.

7. Maybe Searchlight used his nickname to look for the truth. It was a tough thing to find during an administration that ended in scandal.

    a. Bill Clinton   c. Jimmy Carter

    b. Richard Nixon   d. Dwight Eisenhower

Answer: b. Richard Nixon was Searchlight until he resigned amid a scandal of lies called Watergate.

8. The Deacon was scandal-free when he got his code name. Of course that was before we all found out he had "lust in his heart" thanks to a *Playboy* interview. So who was this lusty fellow?

    a. George W. Bush   c. Bill Clinton

    b. Jimmy Carter   d. John F. Kennedy

Answer: b. In November 1976, Carter told *Playboy* "…anyone who looks on a woman with lust in his heart has already committed adultery. I've looked on a lot of women with lust." Who knew Jimmy was so randy?

9. What bird served as Bill Clinton's code name?

    a. eagle   c. falcon

    b. mockingbird   d. robin

Answer: a. Although the mockingbird was the official state bird of his home state of Arkansas, Clinton was the Eagle.

10. Dwight Eisenhower shares his code name with the capital of the state where he had his summer White House. So where did Ike work on his tan?

    a. Kansas   c. Pennsylvania

    b. Rhode Island   d. Texas

Answer: b. Ike was born in Kansas, raised in Texas, and retired to Pennsylvania. But his summer White House was in Rhode Island, and his code name was Providence.

Misheard Lyrics

Beck, "Loser"
Correct: "In the time of chimpanzees I was a monkey"
Wrong: "In the time of ham and cheese I was bologna"

Duran Duran, "Hungry Like the Wolf"
Correct: "Smell like I sound, I'm lost in a crowd"
Wrong: "Smell like a clown, I'm lost and I'm found"

Barry Manilow, "Mandy"
Correct: "Oh Mandy, well you kissed me and stopped me from shaking"
Wrong: "Oh Mandy, will you get me a pizza from Shakey's?"

'Til Tuesday, "Voices Carry"
Correct: "Hush, hush, keep it down now. Voices carry"
Wrong: "Oh John, keep it on now, you're so hairy"

R.E.M., "Losing My Religion"
Correct: "That's me in the corner, that's me in the spotlight"
Wrong: "Let's pee in the corner, let's pee in the spotlight"

Creedence Clearwater Revival, "Bad Moon Rising"
Correct: "There's a bad moon on the rise"
Wrong: "There's a bathroom on the right"

The Beatles, "Get Back"
Correct: "Jo Jo was a man who thought he was a loner"
Wrong: "Jo Jo was a man before he was a woman"

Madonna, "Like a Virgin"
Correct: "Like a virgin, touched for the very first time"
Wrong: "Like a virgin, touched for the thirty-first time"

Jimi Hendrix, "Purple Haze"
Correct: " 'Scuse me, while I kiss the sky"
Wrong: " 'Scuse me, while I kiss this guy"

That's a Crime Too

- Kissing a woman while she's asleep is a crime in Logan County, Colorado.

- Men with mustaches are not allowed to kiss women in Eureka, Nevada.

- Any man who comes face-to-face with a cow has to remove his hat in Fruithill, Kentucky.

- Flirting in public is against the law in Little Rock, Arkansas.

- Michigan law states that a woman's hair is technically owned by her husband.

- It's illegal for kids under the age of seven to attend college in Winston-Salem, North Carolina (sorry, Doogie).

- Talking on the phone without a parent on the line is a crime in Blue Earth, Minnesota.

- You can't buy a lollipop without a doctor's note while church services are in session if you live in Kalispell, Montana.

- It's illegal to eat chicken with a fork in Gainesville, Georgia.

- You could go to jail for making an ugly face at a dog in the state of Oklahoma.

- A frog—yes, a frog—can be arrested for keeping a person awake with its "ribbit" noises in Memphis, Tennessee.

- Eating nuts on a city bus in Charleston, South Carolina, could cost you a $500 fine or even 60 days in jail.

- Don't get too friendly at happy hour in Nyala, Nevada—buying drinks for more than three people in a single round is against the law.

- North Dakota has outlawed the serving of beer with pretzels at public restaurants and bars.

Ten Euphemisms for Infidelity

Birds do it, bees do it, even educated fleas do it...just don't let your significant other catch you doing it.

1. **Affair** The term is straight to the point...but boring as can be!

2. **Cooking for Someone Else** It's probably better to leave your utensils in your own drawer and out of someone else's pots and pans.

3. **Extracurricular Activities** Or simply "activities" as Kate Gosselin (of the reality TV series *Jon & Kate Plus 8*) once referred to her husband's weekend plans.

4. **Having Someone on the Side** Yeah, that's one way to do it.

5. **Hiking the Appalachian Trail** Thank you very much, South Carolina Governor Mark Sanford, for taking that excursion to Argentina and adding this priceless idiom to our vernacular in 2009!

6. **Open Marriage** Welcome back to the 1970s! A popular phrase during the era of disco balls and leisure suits, the term does not "technically" describe infidelity, as both sides agree to have extramarital relations. Good luck dodging that frying pan, however, when one side "technically" has a change of heart.

7. **Parking the Car in Someone Else's Garage** No further explanation necessary.

8. **Parallel Relationship** Hand it to the Finns to come up with such a blasé term for something so tawdry.

9. **Pinch the Cat in the Dark** We have no idea what this means, but supposedly if you're Dutch, you're winking and laughing hysterically right now.

10. **Seven-Year Itch** We can thank playwright George Axelrod for his 1952 play (and Marilyn Monroe for her 1955 film performance)—both of which led to this familiar phrase for infidelity. Statistically speaking, by the way, the U.S. Census Bureau maintains that most first marriages that fail do so after eight years. A case of life imitating art?

19 Strange Illnesses and Disorders that Almost Nobody Gets

1. Progeria
It might *seem* like you're getting old fast, but for people who suffer from progeria—a disease for which there were only eight certified cases in the United States as of 2004—premature aging is a reality. This condition, which speeds up the aging process, causes people to grow old and die within just a few years.

2. Foreign Accent Syndrome
People afflicted with FAS wake up one day suddenly speaking with a completely different accent—often from countries they've never even been to. Doctors think the odd disorder is caused by brain injury, though they aren't sure exactly what kind.

3. Harlequin Ichthyosis
Children with this extremely rare disorder are born with thick, scaly patches of skin covering their face, like a suit of armor. Unfortunately, the armor harms more than protects, and most afflicted with harlequin ichthyosis die in childhood.

4. Kuru
Kuru is a rare neuromuscular disease, but you probably don't need to worry about catching it—unless you're a cannibal. That's because the disease is only transmitted by eating infected human brain tissue. The only known cases of Kuru occurred among the Fore tribes-people of New Guinea who practiced cannibalistic funeral rites until the 1950s.

5. Pantothenate Kinase-Associated Neurodegeneration
PKAN is a rare degenerative brain disease that causes spasms, tremors, loss of speech, and blindness. It commonly strikes children before the age of 10, making it both terrifying and heartbreaking. Luckily, doctors estimate that only one in a million individuals are affected.

6. Sleeping Beauty Syndrome

For people suffering from Sleeping Beauty syndrome—more officially known as Kleine-Levin syndrome—it's no fairy tale. Sufferers of this rare hypersomniac condition go through long stretches of their life sleeping. Worse, when they're awake they're spaced out and nonfunctional.

7. Mermaid Syndrome

Officially known as *sirenomelia*, "mermaid syndrome" is a birth defect in which an infant is born with its legs fused together. The syndrome only strikes about 1 in 100,000 births, and to date only one child born with the disease has been known to survive longer than ten years.

8. Cold Urticaria

Nobody likes cold weather, but imagine being allergic to it. People suffering from cold urticaria develop rashes and hives when exposed to cold weather.

9. Hyperthymesic Syndrome

People with hyperthymesic syndrome never forget what day their anniversary falls on—or anything else, for that matter. People suffering from this extremely rare disorder (only three cases have been identified worldwide) remember every detail of every day for most of their lives.

10. Reduplicative Paramnesia

People with this unusual and rare mental disorder believe that they are in a place different from where they actually are. For example, mental patients with this disorder often believe the room they are in is their house or that the hospital is in another part of the country.

11. Capgras Syndrome

This rare psychological disorder makes sufferers suspicious of their loved ones or even their own reflections.

12. Fregoli Delusion

People with Fregoli delusion have the opposite problem of those with Capgras syndrome—they believe they're being followed by someone and that everybody they see is that person dressed up in disguise.

13. Fields Condition

This neuromuscular condition is so rare that there are only two known cases in the history of recorded medical science. The disease is named after British identical twins Catherine and Kirstie Fields, the only two people known to have the affliction.

14. Cotard Delusion

People suffering from the little-seen mental disorder known as the Cotard delusion take low self-esteem to its limits. At the extreme, patients believe they do not exist. Others believe that organs are putrefying, limbs have vanished, or blood is disappearing from the body.

15. Landau Kleffner Syndrome

In this rare childhood neurological disorder, children suddenly lose the ability to comprehend and express language. Even more strangely, sufferers of this condition sometimes completely regain speech within a few years.

16. Craniopagus Parasiticus

One of the rarest of all conditions, *craniopagus parasiticus* describes a birth defect in which a "parasitic" twin head is attached to a newborn's head. Only ten cases of this condition have been reported in the history of medical literature.

17. Subjective-Double Syndrome

Don't tell a person suffering from subjective-double syndrome that you saw somebody who looked like him or her on the street. He or she already believes that they have one or more doppelgängers.

18. Dancing Eyes-Dancing Feet Syndrome

Dancing eyes-dancing feet syndrome isn't nearly as fun as it sounds. Symptoms of this obscure condition include irregular, rapidly twitching eyes and random muscle spasms that make sitting and standing nearly impossible.

19. Alien Hand Syndrome

This unusual condition is pretty much what it sounds like—the sensation that a force completely beyond your control is manipulating your hands.

How to Survive a Winter Night Alone in the Woods

You may not need to worry about lions and tigers and bears (well, maybe bears), but that's no reason to think you're home free. Cold weather can be just as deadly as wild animals.

- **Make a Shelter** The chief danger when you're stuck in the cold is hypothermia, a potentially deadly drop in your core body temperature. The most important factors in preventing hypothermia are staying dry and blocking the wind. To make a shelter, prop a large branch against a stump or rock, leaving enough room to lie underneath. Make a bed of sticks, leaves, and moss under the branch. This will insulate you from the cold, wet ground. Prop smaller branches along each side of the large branch to make a simple tent. Fill the tent with leaves and climb inside. The leaves will help retain your body heat, block the wind, and keep moisture away from your body.

- **Signal for Help** While you're in your shelter, tie a piece of clothing in a visible spot. When you're lost, periodically yell for help—but without expending so much energy that you wear yourself out.

- **Don't Eat Mysterious Plants** Only a fraction of the tens of thousands of North American plant species are edible. It's best not to roll the dice; you can survive for weeks without food.

- **Don't Drink Dirty Water** You need two to four quarts of water per day for optimum health, but drinking potentially contaminated water in rivers and streams can do more harm than good. If you don't have a way to purify water, like iodine tablets, it's safer not to drink anything, even if you're without water all night.

- **Stay Put** If you figure out you're lost and don't know how to get back to civilization, your best bet is to stay in one place. This will make it easier for rescuers to find you.

World's Most Toxic Places

Environmentalists have tracked down the ten most toxic sites on the planet, and what they've found paints a startling picture of problems left unsolved. Experts say living in one of these cities is like "living under a death sentence." The statement, as you can see, is no exaggeration.

Sumgayit, Azerbaijan

This former Soviet industrial center is now home to countless contaminants. Untreated sewage and mercury-laden sludge are among the chief concerns, leading to unusually high cancer and death rates. Scientists have also found a large number of premature births or babies born with defects as extreme as clubbed feet and extra fingers.

Linfen, China

More than three million people are at risk in Linfen, a city in the Shanxi province known for its place as a leader in Chinese coal production. Families say they actually choke from the thick dust in the air. Bronchitis, pneumonia, and lung cancer are common diseases.

La Oroya, Peru

In this city, toxic emissions from mining result in food filled with high levels of lead. In fact, inspectors found only 1 percent of children have normal amounts of lead in their blood. Hospitals say many babies are never even born because of prenatal damage.

Tianying, China

Lead production leaves this region with approximately ten times more air pollution than national health standards allow. Even worse, crops at local farms have been found to have almost 25 times the recommended maximum levels of lead. Children suffer the worst effects, with rampant learning disabilities, low IQ, and other physical ailments.

Sukinda, India

Chromium is the issue in this mine-heavy region of India. Untreated water has been found to have more than twice the amount national and international standards allow. Side effects range from internal bleeding to widespread tuberculosis and infertility.

Vapi, India

In this town in southern India, chemical manufacturing plants produce pesticides, pharmaceuticals, and fertilizers. With no safe disposal system, the waste runs right into the groundwater. The pollution is so severe that some areas are now devoid of biological life.

Dzerzhinsk, Russia

Pollution in Dzerzhinsk dates back to the Cold War era when the city was named by *Guinness World Records* as the most chemically polluted in the world. Average life expectancy here is only 44 years.

Norilsk, Russia

Norilsk is home to metal mining and processing plants that have polluted the air with hundreds of tons of copper and nickel oxides. Life expectancy is low, and the rate of illness among children is alarming.

Chernobyl, Ukraine

More than 20 years after the world's worst nuclear disaster, much of Chernobyl is still unlivable. The meltdown of a nuclear plant reactor's core sent unfathomable amounts of radiation into the city. Thousands of cases of cancer have been detected in young adults, and millions still suffer from various health-related problems.

Kabwe, Zambia

Children bathe in contaminated water in this African nation, once home to intensive lead mining operations. Lead saturates the city's water and soil, and there are no health restrictions to keep the community safe. Many children have blood-lead levels just barely under the amount considered deadly.

Presidentially Speaking

"Mankind, when left to themselves, are unfit for their own government."
—George Washington

"In my many years I have come to a conclusion that one useless man is a shame, two is a law firm, and three or more is a congress."
—John Adams

"When you reach the end of your rope, tie a knot in it and hang on."
—Thomas Jefferson

"The man who reads nothing at all is better educated than the man who reads nothing but newspapers."
—Thomas Jefferson

"Better to remain silent and be thought a fool than to speak out and remove all doubt."
—Abraham Lincoln

"Philosophy is common sense with big words."
—James Madison

"A little flattery will support a man through great fatigue."
—James Monroe

"There is no pleasure in having nothing to do; the fun is having lots to do and not doing it."
—Andrew Jackson

"As to the presidency, the two happiest days of my life were those of my entrance upon the office and my surrender of it."
—Martin Van Buren

"All the measures of the Government are directed to the purpose of making the rich richer and the poor poorer."
—William Henry Harrison

"I like the job. That's what I'll miss most . . . I'm not sure anybody ever liked this as much as I've liked it."
—William Jefferson Clinton

"I'm a Ford, not a Lincoln."
—Gerald R. Ford

"I am not one who—who flamboyantly believes in throwing a lot of words around."
—George H. W. Bush

That's the Way the Cookie Crumbles:

Fortune Cookie Facts

Perhaps it's fitting that a cookie that foretells the future has such a murky past. Who invented the fortune cookie? There's a debate over that. But here are some interesting facts about fortune cookies that can't be disputed. (Well, maybe just a little.) Confucius recommends that you read on; it will bring you health and prosperity.

- According to author Jennifer 8. Lee, more than three billion fortune cookies are made each year, the vast majority of them in the United States. Lee should know; she's the author of *The Fortune Cookie Chronicles,* a 2008 book that traces the history of Chinese food in the United States.

- Fortune cookies are a mainstay in the United States, but they are also served in Britain, Italy, France, and Mexico. Surprisingly, it's extremely difficult to find fortune cookies in China. This is because the fortune cookie actually traces its origins back to Japan, not China.

- No one knows for sure who introduced the fortune cookie to the United States, but two entrepreneurs are given credit for it. One legend says that Japanese immigrant Makoto Hagiwara introduced the first U.S. fortune cookie in 1914 in San Francisco. A second legend credits David Jung, a founder of the Hong Kong Noodle Co. Legend says that Jung introduced the cookie in 1918 in Los Angeles. According to the story, Jung was concerned about the number of poor people living on the streets, so he passed out free fortune cookies to them. Each cookie contained an inspirational verse written by a Presbyterian minister.

- In 1983, San Francisco's Court of Historical Review held a mock trial to determine whether

Hagiwara or Jung should get credit for bringing fortune cookies to U.S. diners. Not surprisingly, the judge ruled for San Francisco and Hagiwara. A piece of evidence that surfaced during the trial was a fortune saying, "S.F. judge who rules for L.A. not very smart cookie."

- Wonton Food, Inc., in Long Island City, New York, is the largest producer of fortune cookies in the United States. The factory churns out 4.5 million cookies per day. The company also boasts a database of 10,000 possible fortunes. Company officials say that only about 25 percent of these fortunes are used at any given time.

- The recipe for fortune cookies is surprisingly simple. The batter used to make fortune cookies is a mix of flour, sugar, and vanilla or citrus flavoring.

- Fortune cookies have proven fertile ground for jokes. One of the oldest and most popular? A diner cracks open a fortune cookie to find the following fortune: "Help! I'm trapped in a fortune cookie factory."

- Fortune cookies today come in a wide variety of flavors. Diners can munch on fortune cookies that are covered in chocolate or caramel. Many bakeries also sell fortune cookies decorated for Christmas, Valentine's Day, and other holidays.

- Some fortune cookies don't contain fortunes at all. Crack one open, and you'll often find lucky lottery numbers or a philosophical message: "No one is richer than he who has many friends." Some fortune cookies even contain riddles or jokes.

- Unless you really love them, you won't gain too much weight eating fortune cookies. The average fortune cookie contains about 30 calories and no fat. So eat away!

Audacious Prison Escapes

When you have nothing to lose, you have everything to gain. Such appears to be the mind-set behind these wild and woolly escapes.

Alcatraz, San Francisco Bay, California

In the movie *Escape from Alcatraz* (1979) a determined Clint Eastwood (playing Frank Morris) escapes from the famously "escape-proof" penitentiary. In reality, Morris and two accomplices rode a makeshift raft off the "the Rock" on June 11, 1962. The three were never seen again. The facility closed in 1963.

Libby Prison, Virginia

After digging a 50-foot tunnel, 109 Union soldiers broke free on February 9 and 10, 1864. Over half made it to safety behind northern lines.

Brushy Mountain State Prison, Tennessee

The convicted killer of Martin Luther King Jr., James Earl Ray used a makeshift ladder to scale the prison's 14-foot-high walls in 1977. He eluded authorities for 54 hours in what's been described as "one of the greatest manhunts in modern memory."

Colditz P.O.W. Camp, Germany

During World War II, British inmates built a glider to escape from this Nazi P.O.W. camp. Before they could use it, they were liberated. Tests later proved that the contraption could indeed fly.

Pascal Payet, French prisoner

Payet pulled off not one but two daring prison escapes, both times with the use of accomplices flying hijacked helicopters. After a 2007 escape from France's Grasse Prison, the fugitive underwent cosmetic surgery. Despite his proactive attempt at alluding authorities, Payet was soon recaptured.

Salag Luft III, Germany

Immortalized in *The Great Escape* (1963), the March 24, 1944, escape from the Nazi P.O.W. camp featured three tunnels (Tom, Dick, and Harry) that reached beyond the prison's fences. In all, 76 men crawled to freedom. Sadly, only three evaded recapture.

Henry "Box" Brown, North Carolina

Brown escaped the "prison" of slavery by entering a box and having it mailed to Pennsylvania on March 23, 1849. He arrived the following day, disoriented but free.

Prison by the Numbers

2,424,279: number of prisoners incarcerated in the United States at the end of 2008; this amounts to 1 person out of 133

93%: the percentage of prisoners who are male

Texas: state holding the largest number of detainees at the end of 2008 (8,695)

That's a Crime Too

- In Chicago, serving whiskey to a dog is against the law.

- Fishing tackle isn't allowed in cemeteries in Muncie, Indiana.

- Shooting rabbits from motorboats is illegal in Kansas.

- You can't take your French poodle to the opera in Chicago.

- Hartford, Connecticut, has made it illegal for dogs to go to school.

- Cats and dogs can't fight in the town of Barber, North Carolina.

- A dentist who pulls the wrong tooth from a patient in South Foster, Rhode Island, can be required to have the same tooth removed from his own mouth by a blacksmith.

- Mannequins can only be dressed behind closed shades in Atlanta.

- Any woman weighing 200 pounds or more is forbidden from riding a horse while wearing shorts in the town of Gurnee, Illinois.

- Putting a skunk in a boss's desk is a crime in Michigan.

- It's illegal to fall asleep during a haircut in Erie, Pennsylvania.

- In Florida, snoozing under the hair dryer is prohibited.

- Sleeping in the fridge is illegal in Pittsburgh.

- Any man shaving his chest is breaking the law in Omaha, Nebraska.

- Mispronouncing the city name is illegal in Joliet, Illinois.

- Snoring so loudly that your neighbors can hear you is illegal in Dunn, North Carolina.

- Throwing a knife at anyone wearing a striped suit is illegal in Natoma, Kansas.

- Oxford and Cleveland, Ohio, made it illegal for women to wear leather shoes at voting polls.

Live from New York...
It's that Guy (Again)

It's not just your imagination—Steve Martin does host Saturday Night Live *a lot! Following are the top ten most frequent hosts of* SNL. *Any surprises in the bunch?*

Steve Martin The winner and still champion! This wild and crazy guy (now turned sedate actor) has hosted 15 times, including 3 separate occasions in 1978.

Alec Baldwin Tied with Martin is one of the Baldwin brothers, who has also delivered the opening monologue 15 times (including one appearance with his now ex-wife, Kim Basinger).

John Goodman The rotund star chalked up a dozen appearances—once per season between 1989 and 2001, with the exception of 1991.

SNL by the Numbers

2: times the show has aired on a seven-second delay (when Richard Pryor hosted on December 13, 1975, and when Andrew Dice Clay hosted on May 12, 1990)

21: number of primetime Emmy Awards *SNL* players have won

11: *SNL* players who have appeared on an episode of *Seinfeld*

1: presidents who have opened the show with "Live from New York..." (Gerald Ford on April 17, 1976)

4,484: complaints received after Sinead O'Connor tore up a photo of the pope on air; O'Connor was banned from ever appearing on *SNL* again

Buck Henry His last appearance was in 1980, but he hosted twice a year for the first five seasons (traditionally taking the helm of the last broadcast of the year).

Chevy Chase Sometimes former cast members can't stay away. Chase, one of the original "Not Ready for Prime-Time Players," is an eight-time host and the first former star to host five times. In 1997, he was banned from ever again hosting the late-night program after verbally abusing the cast and crew. Despite the ban, Chase has made cameo appearances and starred in the 25th anniversary special in 1999.

Tom Hanks When he's not making Academy Award–winning films with Ron Howard, the good-natured Hanks has managed to fit *SNL* into his schedule a total of eight times.

Christopher Walken He's hosted seven times, but most people probably only remember one skit involving a sincere desire for "more cowbell."

Drew Barrymore A six-time host, she also holds the distinction of being *SNL's* youngest host (she hosted the show for the first time at age 7).

Elliott Gould He struck while the iron was hot, making six appearances between 1976 and 1980.

Danny DeVito Another six-timer, though he hasn't hosted since 1999.

Fast Facts

Saturday Night Live *premiered October 11, 1975. As its name suggests, the show is broadcast live.*

Proving that you can be funny and successful too, Tina Fey has distinguished herself by becoming the show's first female head writer.

Live from New York!: Darrell Hammond has delivered this opening line 69 times—more often than anyone else in the show's history.

Ten Lowest-Paid CEOs

CEOs take a pasting in the popular mind, depicted as well-fed fat cats who bring home eight- and nine-figure paychecks while their employees struggle to make ends meet. But not all CEOs earn enormous salaries. Here's a list of the ten lowest-paid CEOs of Fortune 500 companies for 2008, according to Forbes *magazine.*

10. Richard H. Anderson, Delta Air Lines: $600,000

With Delta Airlines spending most of the past few years in bankruptcy, it's no wonder that its CEO earned a fraction of his contemporaries' salaries.

9. Michael S. Dunlap, Nelnet: $510,000

The founder and CEO of this student-loan servicing company made about a half-million in 2008—or about how much it costs to send three kids through Harvard.

8. Eric E. Schmidt, Google: $510,000

The CEO of Internet search giant Google earned a mere $1 in base salary in 2008, though he earned $510,000 in "other" compensation. Don't feel too bad for him though—he owns about $3.5 billion worth of Google stock.

7. Charles A. Schrock, Integrys Energy Group: $460,000

Schrock is the lowest-paid of all the utility company CEOs. He makes less than 1 percent of the salary of the best-paid CEO in the utility field, William R. Berkley of W.R. Berkley.

6. Joseph W. Brown, MBIA: $440,000

Brown earned less than a half-million in 2008, a far cry from the $22.8 million he brought home the previous year.

5. Leland E. Tollett, Tyson Foods: $130,000

Tollett may have only made $130k last year, but on the bright side he probably didn't have a very high grocery bill.

4. Warren E. Buffett, Berkshire Hathaway: $100,000

Buffett's salary is merely a token—he's worth an estimated $37 billion.

3. Herbert M. Allison Jr., Fannie Mae: $60,000

Perhaps no other entity received more public scorn during the fiscal meltdown of 2008 than Fannie Mae. Not surprisingly, the CEO position wasn't the most lucrative of jobs during that time.

1. Steven P. Jobs, Apple: $1

Jobs, the founder and CEO of uber-hip computer firm Apple, earned just $1 in salary last year. Of course, you can afford to do that when you raked in $660 million the previous five years.

1. Edward M. Liddy, AIG: $1

For many, insurance company AIG became the symbol of the 2008 recession, and though its CEO only made $1 in 2008, it was a dollar more than many Americans thought he deserved.

More Odd Beer Names

Here's another helping of some of those oddly named American and Canadian brands.

- Polygamy Porter
- Flying Dog In-Heat Wheat Hefeweizen
- Ruination
- Dead Guy Ale (with a label that glows in the dark)
- White Dog Cafe Leg Lifter Lager
- Cave Creek Chili Beer
- Doggy Style Classic Pale Ale
- Cold Cock Winter Porter
- Dixie Crimson Voodoo Ale
- Sweaty Betty Blonde Wheat

- Stinky Hippie
- Blood of 1,000 Corpses
- Horse You Rode in On
- Hoppin' to Heaven India Pale Ale
- Otay Buckwheat Ale
- Crop Circle Extraterrestri-Ale Amber Ale
- Kilt Lifter Scotch Ale
- Tire Biter Ale
- Bard's Tale Beer
- Mothership Wit

Countries with the Highest Beer Consumption

Country	Gallons per Person per Year
1. Ireland	41.0
2. Germany	32.0
3. Austria	28.0
4. Belgium (tied)	26.0
4. Denmark (tied)	26.0

If the Moon Were Made of Green Cheese...

Ever wonder how many sandwich-size slices of cheese the moon would make if the moon were made of green cheese? Of course you have!

21,900,000,000 km³: volume of moon

0.0002835 km³: volume of one Kraft single

74,074,074,100,000: number of Kraft singles that could be produced with moon-size wheel of cheese

3,741: number of years the population of American students—from kindergarten through high school—could be fed grilled cheese sandwiches made from this cheese for school lunch

The idea of the moon being made of green cheese dates back to John Heywood's 1546 *Proverbes.* But when Heywood wrote "The moon is made of a greene cheese," he was not referring to the color green, but green in the sense of "new" or "unaged." However, there are several cheeses that are actually green in hue. Here are five of the more popular ones:

1. **Basiron Pesto** A bright green Dutch gouda-style cheese with a strong pesto flavor.

2. **Sage Derby** The practice of adding sage to this cheese to impart a green color dates back to the 17th century.

3. **Green Thunder** This Welsh cheese is infused with garlic and green herbs.

4. **Vermont Sage** This Vermont classic is flavored with bits of sage that give the cheese a greenish hue.

5. **Schabziger** Produced only in one canton of Switzerland for more than a millennium, the practice of adding fenugreek to this Swiss cheese dates back to at least the eighth century.

12 Useful Rules of Etiquette that Most People Seem to Have Forgotten

Emily Post spent her life sorting out the vagaries of where to seat royalty at a dinner party, what was acceptable attire for a semiformal wedding, and how much to tip the chambermaid. She would be appalled to learn that most of us have abandoned even the basic tenets of manners. But it isn't too late. Make Emily proud!

1. **Use the Magic Words** *Please, thank you, excuse me, sorry.* For things big and small, friends, family, coworkers, and even strangers deserve a sprinkling of the magic words.

2. **Write the Official Thank You** Some things deserve "the H"—a handwritten note. Thank yous—they aren't just for weddings.

3. **Learn Your French** "Répondez s'il vous plaît," aka RSVP, sounds confusing but it isn't. It means "Pick up the phone and tell me if you're coming or not. No changing your mind at the last minute. No assuming I know you're coming (or not coming). Call!"

4. **Make Introductions** Instead of letting a person lurk behind you, mute and uncomfortable, say: "Friend A, I'd like you to meet Friend B. Friend B this is Friend A."

5. **Outlaw the Manners Police** Emily Post, the Queen of Manners, would never look down her nose at someone who used the wrong fork at dinner or (perish the thought) actually point out a manners gaffe. Why should you?

6. **Get Off Your Butt** We may all be equal but that doesn't absolve you from offering some people your seat on the bus: pregnant women, people with small children, the elderly, or a person with a medical condition that might make standing difficult. (Hint: crutches? Yes. Mechanical arm? No.)

7. **Don't Hijack Host Duties** Hosts specify on invitations who is invited. Anyone not mentioned—children, houseguests, teenager's boyfriend—isn't going. And don't *ask* if you can bring extra guests. Your host will say yes but will secretly complain that you were impolite enough to ask. There may be some wiggle room on this one though. An extra at an informal BBQ isn't as problematic as an extra at a formal affair like a wedding.

8. **Learn to Tell Time** No one thinks your perpetual lateness is cute. Plan ahead for traffic jams, phone calls, and wardrobe malfunctions.

9. **Forget Money Exists** Stop talking about money! Don't offer or ask for info about salary, purchases, or market losses.

10. **Remember Life Is Not Jerry Springer** Celebs and reality stars may routinely blab about their personal lives, but it isn't polite. "Did you have in vitro?" is not a conversation opener for a stranger in the elevator or your cousin Elaine! Neither is marriage, divorce, or sex.

11. **Stop Asking for Gifts** Nowhere on an invitation should gifts be mentioned—a move that indicates guests are being invited, not for their charming personalities, but for their gift potential. A few friends should have info about registry, preferences, or charities to tell guests *only* if they ask.

12. **Do Not be Disruptive** In public, your every action should be measured against this motto. Drunk at the office party? Cell phone ringing at the movies? 30 items in the 10 items or less aisle at the grocery store? Insisting on a special lo-carb, vegan-organic meal at a dinner party? All disruptions. All bad manners.

"Good manners can replace morals. It may be years before anyone knows if what you are doing is right. But if what you are doing is nice, it will be immediately evident."
— P. J. O'Rourke

Who Knew?

"Taking the Odds" Doesn't Mean You Always Win

The car used as a time machine in the *Back to the Future* movies was a De Lorean. Its inventor, John De Lorean, manufactured 9,000 cars in 1981. On the verge of success, the entrepreneur appeared in an ad for Cutty Sark alcohol that same year. Its tagline read, "One out of every 100 new businesses succeeds. Here's to those who take the odds." The De Lorean plant closed in 1982. Ouch!

Reach Out and Touch Someone

On December 11, 2004, more than five million people joined hands to form a human chain 652.4 miles (1,050 kilometers) long. It snaked from Teknaf to Tentulia in Bangladesh. Organizers, who billed the event as a human wall, were protesting against the ruling political party at the time. The chain averaged 7,664 people per mile.

Free-falling

Are there any bungee jumpers out there who enjoy the experience but find it's over far too quickly? They should visit the Sky Jump at the Macau Tower Convention and Entertainment Center in Macau, off the east coast of China. The ride starts on the 61st floor of the building—764 feet above the ground—and drops riders in a controlled descent for 17 to 20 seconds. Not a pure bungee jump, the Sky Jump offers a "decelerator descent" ride, which features a second cable to guide the direction of the fall rather than simply a free-swinging bungee cord.

He's Got a Basketball Jones

Despite standing at the petite height of around 5'2" (minus the heels), artist extraordinaire Prince Rogers Nelson, or just simply Prince, is an excellent basketball player. In fact, he was well-known for his exceptional ball-handling ability and speed in high school.

Dumb Things that Some Americans Are Apt to Believe

Let's face it: Some Americans (not you, of course!) believe some pretty silly things. Here are a few.

Barack Obama Is Not an American Citizen

Despite the fact that in order to even run for public office in this country one needs to be an American citizen, a dismayingly large percentage of Americans seem to believe that Barack Obama is not. According to a recent Public Policy Poll, a mere 62 percent of Americans believe that Obama was born in the United States. Of the doubters:

10 percent believe he was born in Indonesia.

7 percent believe he was born in Kenya.

1 percent think he was born in the Philippines.

6 percent correctly believe Obama was born in Hawaii, but incorrectly believe Hawaii is a foreign country.

Meanwhile, Web sites and articles abound detailing the supposed conspiracy to falsify birth records and plant a Muslim jihadist in the White House. Here are the facts, conspiracy theorists: Barack Obama was born on August 4, 1961, in Honolulu, Hawaii, making him a U.S. citizen. That's right: Hawaii is a part of the United States!

Humans and Dinosaurs Coexisted

When blog posts falsely reported that vice presidential candidate Sarah Palin believed that humans and dinosaurs walked the earth at the same time, it made her fodder for plenty of late-night comedy. But this bewildering assertion—one that flies in the face of everything we know about the world—is made by plenty of Americans.

Most of these Americans are fundamentalist Christians who believe the Bible to be literal truth. According to the Bible, Earth is only about 6,000 years old, so it would make sense that dinosaurs and humans would *have* to have lived at the same time. Meanwhile, scientists continue to believe that dinosaurs existed 60–65 million years before the first humans appeared.

Christopher Columbus Discovered America

"In 1492," American schoolchildren recite every October, "Columbus sailed the ocean blue." Uh, wrong. Despite hundreds of years of mythology to the contrary—and an entire holiday devoted to the man—Christopher Columbus most definitely did not discover America. For starters, the land he "discovered" (if by *discovering* you mean getting completely lost and thinking he was on the opposite side of the globe) was Hispaniola, a Caribbean island, not what would become the United States.

Actually, Columbus wasn't even the first European to make it to North America. Back in the early 11th century, the Viking explorer Leif Erikson made it all the way to the rocky coasts of present-day New England and Newfoundland, where he planted a few grapevines and then promptly returned to Iceland.

The Sun Revolves Around the Earth

According to a Gallup poll, 18 percent of Americans believe that the sun revolves around the Earth. Really.

The Government Is Hiding Aliens in New Mexico

On July 8, 1947, something crashed in Roswell, New Mexico. The government maintained that it was an experimental weather balloon from a secret project. Americans, of course, knew otherwise. No, what crashed in Roswell was clearly an extraterrestrial spaceship. And even though the government has gone to great pains to issue report after report detailing what really happened in Roswell, it's just not quite good enough for us conspiracy-loving Americans.

Ben Franklin Discovered Electricity

Saying that Ben Franklin discovered electricity is like saying that the Wright Brothers discovered air. What Ben Franklin actually did with his kite and key was conduct experiments about the nature of lightning.

Illegal Immigration Is a Recent Problem

Back in the good old days, some believe, we didn't have any illegal immigration problems. That this was partially because for much of American history, you didn't need to do anything other than show up to get into the country is conveniently ignored by these people— many of whom are here because of immigrants who, at various times in American history, wouldn't qualify for visas.

At any rate, the problem of illegal immigration started way before America even began—just ask the Native Americans for their thoughts on the matter.

"What Washington needs is adult supervision."
—Barack Obama

ER Weirdness!

The doctors and nurses who staff emergency rooms in the United States see it all—and then some! Following are some bizarre-but-true reasons why people have visited their local ERs, straight from the medical professionals who took care of them.

- Man assaulted by his wife—with a bucket of fried chicken.
- Man high on methamphetamine ate a pile of rocks.
- Man accidentally set his nether regions on fire with a candle after shaving himself from his navel to his knees then dousing himself with rubbing alcohol. This one leads to more questions than it answers!
- A homeless alcoholic who hadn't bathed in quite a while removed his glass eye, put it in his mouth, then placed it back in his eye socket, causing an infection.
- Man inserted a tampon into his nose to stop a nose bleed and was unable to get it out.

ER Visits by the Numbers

3.2 hours: the average length of an ER visit

227: the number of ER visits per *minute* in 2006

Washington, D.C.: most ER visits per year

$1,038: the average cost of a typical ER visit (based on 2007 data)

Strange Twitter Trending Topics

Often, Twitter captures trends before any other social media space. Here's a look at some of the more unusual hash-tagged trending topics the site has seen.

#oneletteroffmovies

Movie titles with, you guessed it, one letter off. So these include such classics as *When Harry Wet Sally, The Princess Bribe, Winding Nemo, The Green Male, Bleepless in Seattle, Germs of Endearment,* and *Where the Wild Thongs Are.* These are especially fun when cross-listed with . . .

#cowfilms

. . . when you get titles like *Die Herd, Udder Siege, Fiddler on the Herd,* and *Apocalypse Cow.*

#unseenprequels

And one more for movie lovers. This time around? The pre-quels. Like this, from @kyriabeingbanal: *The Alien Who Couldn't Take Care of His Pet (The Cat from Outer Space).* Or this, from @nahbois: *Close Encounters of the First Kind.*

#videogamesIregretbuying

This collection of posts includes some real games, like *Pokemon Crystal,* but lots of made-up ones too. For instance: Wii Staring Contest, PETA Rodeo, MSNBC's Morning Joe Challenge, Madden Hand Jive 6, and Popemania.

#margesimpson

This hit the Twitter airwaves when Marge Simpson ended up on the cover of *Playboy.* 'Nuff said.

#badhalloweencostumes

How about these: "A pirate with all of his limbs and two perfectly good eyes," from @DrZibbs, or "Sexy Al Gore," from @dorsalstream.

#badimprovscenarios

So, for instance, from @McSweeneysBooks: "You are a strip of bacon, your partner is a jar of peanut butter, and here comes Elvis." You get the idea.

#getoffmylawn

This is the Twitter topic for grumpy neighbors. So you get posts like this one from @leia: "Hey hipster: Crossing the street in skinny jeans while playing a ukulele doesn't exempt you from traffic signals." Or this philosophical inquiry from @sarahdcady: "Does yelling at the law-breaking smokers in the courtyard make me a neighborhood grump or concerned citizen?"

Twitter by the Numbers

140: maximum number of characters allowed in a single tweet

55 million: number of tweets per day

41%: percentage of individuals who have not tweeted since they created their Twitter account

106 million: total number of Twitter accounts

❖ ❖ ❖

"For the uninitiated, here's how Twitter works—I have no. .idea. I have no idea how it works—or why it is."
—Jon Stewart, host of *The Daily Show*

Billboard Bucks

We may be some time away from David Foster Wallace's dystopic vision of ad-sponsored calendar years, but it's virtually impossible to think of our day-to-day lives without advertising saturating them. It's like that old advertising koan: If there were no billboards, would Times Square exist? We may never know.

Most expensive billboard location, One Times Square, New York City: The building at One Times Square rents out 19 billboards, which rake in more than $20 million dollars annually. It's perhaps not surprising that with that kind of income generated by the exterior of the building, the building's owners aren't too concerned with tenants. Until a Walgreens pharmacy moved into the digs in 2007, the building had been vacant for six years.

Total revenue generated by billboards in Times Square, which has more ads per square foot than anywhere else in America: $69 million per year

Cost for a permit to use space in Times Square, minimum: $25,000. According to *The New York Times*, advertisers must pay a minimum of $25,000 to use space in Times Square for advertising purposes—though many types of permits start at $50,000 per day.

Largest billboard company in the world: Clear Channel Outdoor. In 2008, Clear Channel, which controls the majority of American billboards, raked in more than $7 billion in revenue.

Most elaborate billboards in the world (tie):

- **The BMW billboard, Moscow:** In 2008, BMW unveiled a massive, 1.5-acre billboard in downtown Moscow featuring a depiction of an expressway. The elaborate part? Attached to the billboard are several real, full-size BMWs, which appear to be zooming along.

- **Adidas billboard, Tokyo:** What's more interesting than a billboard depicting soccer players? How about a billboard featuring *living* soccer players. In 2003, Adidas erected a billboard in Tokyo's Shibuya district featuring two live human beings playing "vertical soccer." The soccer players were suspended from the billboard with bungee cords, as was the soccer ball.

Nitroglycerin and Other Unlikely Medicines

Alfred Nobel quite literally rocked the scientific world in 1866 when he combined nitroglycerin with diatomaceous earth and sodium carbonate to invent dynamite. Only slightly less explosive was the discovery decades later that nitroglycerin could be used for medicinal purposes. But while dynamite might seem like an unlikely medicine, it's downright commonplace compared with some of the other ingredients being used in contemporary medical research.

Snake Venom While snake oil was once the unlikeliest—and most fraudulent—of medicines, snake venom is drawing increased attention in the medical community as a possible cancer fighter. According to scientists, natural compounds in snake venom may prevent the growth of cancerous tumors by acting as a targeted tissue killer, as opposed to current cancer treatments such as chemotherapy, which attack cells indiscriminately.

Blue M&M's Millions of people around the world are fully aware that M&M's provide a soothing emotional balm—not to mention a foolproof cure for a trim waistline. But doctors recently made the surprising discovery that the blue dye used in blue M&M's (and Gatorade, incidentally) could help cure patients with spinal cord injuries. Researchers at the University of Rochester Medical Center found that an injection of the dye Brilliant Blue G halted the chemical reaction that destroyed spinal tissue after an injury. Better yet, when the dye was injected into rats paralyzed from spinal cord injuries, they were able to walk again. The only side effect? They temporarily turned blue.

Nicotine Everybody knows smoking is bad for you, right? Believe it or not, some studies have shown that nicotine may have neuro-protective traits that guard smokers against developing brain diseases such as Alzheimer's and Parkinson's in their golden years. But that doesn't mean you should go light up—cigarette smokers still have a far shorter lifespan than nonsmokers, which means you probably won't live long enough to enjoy your Alzheimer's-free old age.

Walt Disney: The Man Behind the Mouse

Walt Disney is arguably the most famous moviemaker in the world—an icon adored by millions. But how much do you really know about him? Maybe less than you think.

- As a youngster, Disney made extra spending money by selling drawings to his neighbors.

- Disney tried to join the military in 1918 but was rejected as being too young (he was 16). He joined the Red Cross instead. He was sent to France, where he drove an ambulance.

- Walt Disney grew his trademark mustache at the age of 25.

- The first commercially released Mickey Mouse cartoon, *Steamboat Willie,* was also the first Disney cartoon to feature synchronized sound. It premiered in New York City on November 18, 1928.

- Disney provided the voice for both Mickey and Minnie Mouse for nearly 20 years.

- Disney's first animated feature film, *Snow White and the Seven Dwarfs,* cost nearly $1.5 million to produce. It was a huge gamble for the Disney studio but went on to tremendous financial success and critical acclaim.

- Following the success of *Snow White and the Seven Dwarfs,* Disney and his brother, Roy, gifted their parents with a new house close to their studios. A month later, their mother died from asphyxiation caused by a broken furnace in the new home. It was a tragedy from which Disney never recovered.

- Disney won more Academy Awards than any other individual: 32 total.

- Although television made him world-famous, Disney experienced terrible stage fright every time he had to step in front of the camera.

Show-and-Tell Hell

*What did you take to show-and-tell when you were in kindergarten?
Well, things have gotten a lot wilder since then. If nothing else, this
list should convince you that it's a good idea to check your child's
backpack before sending him or her off to school!*

Perhaps a good rule of thumb is to restrict kids to something they
can *fit* in a backpack. A **five-foot alligator** certainly wouldn't have
made it to school in that case! Or maybe it would have since the
gator was actually brought in by dear old dad—a wildlife officer. But
it gets better: The alligator escaped from the father's vehicle, sending Panama City, Florida, officials on a wild chase to capture the
class's show-and-tell!

Of course, **crack cocaine** does fit in a backpack. Believe it or not,
a first grader from Louisiana brought the narcotic as his show-and-
tell item, prompting officials to arrest the boy's mother for improper
child supervision.

Continuing in that same vein, a six-year-old brought **marijuana** to
school for show-and-tell, along with a pipe so he could demonstrate
the drug's use for his classmates. Needless to say, his teacher wasn't
chill with it, and the boy's father was arrested for child endangerment.

A second grader from Texas looking for an explosive show-and-tell
item hit the mark when he brought a **hand grenade** into school,
prompting a school-wide evacuation. The grenade later turned out
to be inactive, but it sure *looked* real! No word on whether or not the
second-grade teacher had the courage to continue with show-and-
tell after that incident.

Not to be outdone, a student in Des Moines, Iowa, brought in an
entire bag of **shell casings,** which she had taken as souvenirs during
a trip to a South Dakota ranch. The casings had the word "blank"
imprinted on them, but the 12-year-old was suspended anyway for
violation of the school's weapons policy. Needless to say, her parents
were not pleased.

We're pretty sure teachers aren't paid nearly enough. We'll stick
to publishing, thank you very much!

Least Religious of the United States

They say God is everywhere... but residents in New England and the Pacific Northwest aren't so sure.

According to a 2008 Gallup poll, 65 percent of 350,000 U.S. citizens age 18 and older said that religion is an important part of their lives. Not surprisingly, the highest concentrations were found in the "Bible Belt" of the southern states (with 85 percent of Mississippi residents offering a "hell yeah" when asked if religion was important). New Englanders—who receive a daily dose of flora and fauna of nearly every kind—weren't quite so certain.

In Vermont, only 42 percent of those questioned responded that religion was an important part of their daily lives. The trend continued from respondents in neighboring New Hampshire (46 percent), Maine, and Massachusetts (48 percent). This lack of faith then took a turn to the Pacific Northwest, with the number-five spot held by, of all places, Alaska (51 percent), followed closely by Washington (52 percent) and Oregon, tied with itty bitty Rhode Island, with 53 percent. Rounding out the list was Nevada (54 percent—perhaps those praying to hit it big in Las Vegas were too busy to reply) and another East Coast favorite, Connecticut (55 percent).

A similar study conducted by the Pew Forum on Religion and Public Life, a Washington, D.C., organization, revealed that 16.1 percent of people surveyed said that they were not affiliated with any religion, with a scant 1.6 percent of that number maintaining that they were atheists.

Of course, all this begs the question of whether Canadian secularism is seeping into American culture. A 2008 study showed that approximately one in four Canadians (23 percent of those surveyed) said that they do not believe in any god. (Check a map: New England and Alaska are eerily close to Canada, whereas Mississippi is *very* far away.)

The Name Game

Why is every kid at the park named Isabella? Baby names, just like hairstyles and hemlines, spike or fall in popularity according to the times. The new millennium gave parents a great chance to play around with more modern monikers, but many chose girl names with timeless biblical ties. And those that got a little more creative? They simply turned stuffy old surnames into rather androgynous first names.

Ten Most Popular Girl Names of 2000

10. Elizabeth	5. Sarah
9. Taylor	4. Ashley
8. Jessica	3. Madison
7. Samantha	2. Hannah
6. Alexis	1. Emily

Number of baby girls named Emily in 2000: 25,941

What's in a Name?

Emily means "industrious" or "eager." Latin in origin, it's derived from the old Roman surname "Aemilius." Emily did not become a common first name in the English-speaking world until after the

Songs About Emily

- "Emily," created by Johnny Mandel and Johnny Mercer for the 1964 film, *The Americanization of Emily*

- "For Emily, Whenever I May Find Her," recorded live by Simon & Garfunkel in 1969 (just before the duo split)

- "See Emily Play," made famous on Pink Floyd's 1971 album *Relics* and also recorded by David Bowie for his 1973 album, *Pin Ups*

German House of Hanover had taken the British throne in the 18th century. King George II had a daughter named Amelia Sophia Eleanor, more fondly known as "Princess Emily."

Endearing Nicknames

Emmy

Millie

Em

Teasing Nicknames

Emmie Whemmie

Em-A-Flea

Embolism

Famous Emilys

Emily Brontë, English poet and novelist who penned the doomed love story of Catherine and Heathcliff in Wuthering Heights.

Emily Dickinson, American lyric poet famous for writing nearly 1,800 poems during her lifetime of brilliant seclusion.

Emily Post, the American authority on etiquette and good taste.

Auntie Em, fictional aunt of Dorothy Gale, portrayed by actress Clara Blandick in 1939's tornado tale, The Wizard of Oz.

Hurricane Emily, a Category 5 storm that brought death and destruction to Grenada, Quintana Roo, and Tamaulipas when it struck in July 2005.

That's a Crime Too

- It's illegal to smoke a pipe after sunset in Newport, Rhode Island.

- Arresting a dead man for debt is a crime in the state of New York.

- Swearing around dead people is illegal at funeral homes in Nevada.

- Hitting a baseball out of the park is a crime in Muskogee, Oklahoma.

- Playing baseball in any public place is against the law in Wentachee, Washington.

- In Alabama, you can't play dominos on Sunday.

- In Kansas, you can't sell cherry pie with ice cream on a Sunday.

- Providence, Rhode Island, doesn't allow stores to sell toothpaste on Sunday.

- Columbus, Ohio, made it illegal to sell corn flakes on a Sunday.

- You can't even cross the street on Sunday in Marblehead, Massachusetts.

- Selling suntan oil after noon on Sunday is a crime in Provincetown, Massachusetts.

- Humming on the street on Sunday is illegal in Cicero, Illinois.

- Hunting is illegal in Virginia on Sundays. That is, except for raccoons—you can hunt them until 2 A.M.

- Kissing your wife is a Sunday no-no in Hartford, Connecticut.

- In Houston, it's illegal to sell Limburger cheese on Sundays.

- Playing hopscotch on a sidewalk is forbidden on Sundays in Missouri.

- In 1845, there was a British law that made attempting suicide punishable by hanging. One can only wonder what the penalty would have been for succeeding.

- It is illegal to fish for whales on land in Oklahoma but legal to hunt them off the "coast."

You Live Where?

Ever hear of Boring, Maryland? How about Nimrod, Minnesota, or Boogertown, North Carolina? Many of the small towns that dot the United States have interesting stories (true or not) behind the oddball names. Here are a few stops to put on your next cross-country road trip.

- **Peculiar, Missouri** As the story goes, 30 miles south of Kansas City was a small community needing a name. The folks put off naming their town—they didn't want to name it until their post office actually required it. The postmaster wrote the U.S. government requesting the regal-sounding "Excelsior." Unfortunately, the name was already taken. The postmaster wrote time and time again for permission, using different names each time. Finally, in his exasperation he told them, "We'll take any name you have available as long as it's peculiar." Apparently it stuck!

- **Wide Awake, Colorado** One night when a group of miners were sitting around a campfire, they were trying to come up with a good name for their new settlement. After passing a bottle around late into the night, someone finally said, "Let's just turn in and talk about it more when we're wide awake." "That's it!" shouted one of the miners. "Let's call it Wide Awake!"

- **Toad Suck, Arkansas** Before the Army Corps of Engineers completed a highway bridge over the Arkansas River in 1973, the most reliable way over the river was by barge. Next to the river stood an old tavern where many of the bargemen would pull over to drink rum and moonshine. As one version of the story has it, it was at this tavern that they would "suck on bottles until they swelled up like toads."

- **Accident, Maryland** The town of Accident traces its history to 1750 when a local named George Deakins accepted 600 acres from King George II of England in relief of a debt. Deakins sent out two independent surveying parties to find the best 600 acres in the county—neither of which was aware of the other. By coincidence, they both surveyed the same plot, beginning at the same tree. Confident that no one else owned the property, Deakins named the tract the "Accident Tract."

- **Hell, Michigan** There are several competing stories as to how Hell got its name. One story suggests that two traveling Germans stepped out of a stagecoach and remarked, *"So schön und hell!"* which loosely translates to "So beautiful and bright!" Hearing this, the neighbors focused on the latter part of the statement. Another story is that one of the early settlers, George Reeves, was asked what they should call the town. Ever the eloquent gentleman, Reeves replied, "For all I care, you can name it Hell!"

- **Ding Dong, Texas** Despite evidence to the contrary, the town of Ding Dong was not named because it's located in Bell County. Nor was it named after Peter Hansborough Bell, the third governor of Texas, nor for the Hostess snack cake. Back in the 1930s, Zulis and Bert Bell owned a country store, and they hired a creative sign painter named C. C. Hoover to put up a new sign. Hoover suggested that he dress up the sign by painting two bells on it with the words, "Ding Dong." The surrounding community quickly took to the name.

- **Tightwad, Missouri** During the town's early days, a local store owner cheated a customer (who just happened to be a postman) by charging him an extra 50 cents for a watermelon. To get back at the proprietor, the postman started delivering mail to the newly dubbed town of Tightwad, Missouri.

Other Oddball Town Names:
- Hot Coffee, Missouri
- Truth or Consequences, New Mexico
- Embarrass, Wisconsin *and* Minnesota
- Knockenstiff, Ohio
- What Cheer, Iowa

Strangest Baseball Injuries

Athletes are famous for sustaining injuries, but baseball players seem to have a knack for scoring some of the strangest afflictions of all.

Lingerie Laceration

Former Giants manager Roger Craig actually cut his hand while trying to unhook a bra. No word on what kind of emotional damage was done to the lady.

Eating Exertion

First baseman Ryan Klesko pulled a muscle while with the Braves—by lifting his lunch tray.

Chili Power

Former second baseman Bret Barberie had to sit out during a Marlins game after accidentally rubbing some chili juice in his eye.

Butter Slip

Another dinner winner, former Rangers outfielder Oddibe McDowell ended up slicing his hand open while trying to butter a roll at a celebration luncheon.

Belly Achin'

A knife nearly caused then-Padres player Adam Eaton to pass out. Eaton was using a blade in an attempt to get a DVD out of its wrapper when he slipped and stabbed himself in the abdomen.

Food Force

Former Mets and Giants outfielder Kevin Mitchell may take the cake when it comes to food flaps. He once made the disabled list by straining his rib muscles while vomiting. Mitchell also missed the first four days of spring training after hurting himself while scarfing down a microwaved donut. He is also rumored to have injured himself eating a cupcake at some point.

Given the Boot

Hall of Fame third baseman Wade Boggs got a little too excited putting on cowboy boots and was injured as a result. Boggs ended up missing seven games because of the back strain he incurred.

Protection Problems

Outfielder Ken Griffey Jr. found his protection to be his problem: Griffey had to miss a Mariners game after his protective cup apparently slipped and pinched the goods in a not-so-good way.

Virtual Spiders

One-time Blue Jays outfielder Glenallen Hill smashed a glass table while asleep. He dreamt that spiders were attacking him.

Not-So-Cool Moves

Former Orioles pitcher Mark Smith hurt his hand when he reached into an air-conditioning unit. He said he wanted to find out why it wasn't working.

Iron Man

Braves pitcher John Smoltz smoldered when he tried to iron a shirt—while he was wearing it. Smoltz ended up burning his chest.

Operator Error

Former pitcher Steve Sparks wanted to show off his Brewers strength by tearing a phone book in half. Instead, he had to show off a dislocated shoulder.

Stressful Sneezes

Former outfielder Sammy Sosa suffered more than a stuffy nose when two sneezes struck him right before a Cubs game. The powerful projections caused Sosa to have back spasms, and he spent the rest of the afternoon getting treatment.

Worst-Case Scenarios:

The All-Time Deadliest Disasters

Dino-B-Gone

The deadliest disaster in Earth's history may have struck long before humans even existed. According to leading scientific theory, the dinosaurs (and many others) checked out when a massive asteroid slammed into Earth about 65 million years ago. The resulting destruction dwarfs anything that's happened since:

- Scientists estimate the asteroid was about six miles wide—bigger than Mount Everest.

- The energy of the impact was likely equal to hundreds of millions of megatons. That's about a million times more powerful than the explosion you would get if you detonated all the nuclear bombs in the world at once.

- The asteroid hit in what is now the Gulf of Mexico, blasting massive amounts of scorching steam and molten rock into the sky and creating tsunamis that were hundreds of yards high and that moved 600 miles per hour.

- The resulting shock wave rocked the entire planet and killed everything for hundreds of miles around.

- Molten rock fell back to Earth for thousands of miles around the impact, setting much of the planet on fire.

- The kicked up material darkened the atmosphere everywhere and generated nitric acid rain.

- All told, the asteroid wiped out as much as 75 percent of all life on the planet.

King of Plagues

The worst disaster on record in terms of human death toll was the Black Death—a pandemic thought to be bubonic plague, pneumonic plague, and septicemic plague, all caused by bacteria carried by fleas:

- The plague infected the lymphatic system, resulting in high fever, vomiting, enlarged glands, and—in the case of pneumonic plague—coughing up bloody phlegm.

- Bubonic plague was fatal in 30–75 percent of cases; pneumonic plague was fatal in 75 percent of cases; and septicemic plague was always fatal.

- Between 1347 and 1350, the plague spread across Europe and killed approximately 75 million people—nearly half the European population.

- Improvements in sanitation helped bring the Black Death to an end, but the plague still pops up now and then in isolated outbreaks.

An Extra Large Shake

The deadliest earthquake and string of aftershocks in recorded history rocked Egypt, Syria, and surrounding areas in 1201:

- Of course, nobody was measuring such things back then, but experts believe the initial quake ranked as a magnitude 9.

- As luck would have it, Egypt was already experiencing a major drought, and damage from the quake exacerbated the problem, leading to mass starvation (and a bit of cannibalism to boot).

- Historians put the total death toll at about 1.1 million.

The Storm of Several Centuries

The deadliest storm on record was the Bhola Cyclone, which hit East Pakistan (now Bangladesh) on November 13, 1970:

- The storm's winds were in excess of 120 miles per hour when it finally hit land.

- It generated an astonishing storm surge of 12 to 20 feet, which flooded densely populated coastal areas.
- Parts of the Ganges River actually turned red with blood.
- According to official records, 500,000 people died (mainly due to drowning). Some sources put the total at closer to one million.

Blast from the Past

The deadliest known volcano eruption occurred in Indonesia in 1815:

- When the 13,000-foot Mount Tambora erupted, it blew two million tons of debris 28 miles into the air and continued to burn for three months.
- The seismic energy generated massive tsunamis, leading to widespread flooding.
- Three feet of ash covered much of the surrounding area, killing all vegetation and resulting in a devastating famine.
- The debris in the atmosphere darkened skies all around the world and continued to block sunlight for years afterward.
- In 1816, parts of the United States saw snow in June and July, thanks to the persistent cold caused by the eruption on the other side of the world.
- All told, the eruption claimed more than 70,000 lives.

Four TV Series Saved from Cancellation

*Don't change that channel...unless you plan on mounting
a campaign to save your favorite television series from cancellation.
Good old-fashioned petitions, phone calls, and letter-writing
campaigns saved these shows from the dustbins.*

Star Trek

The granddaddy of them all! Trekkies were up in arms in 1968 when
NBC threatened to pull the plug on the five-year mission of the USS
Enterprise after only two seasons. The show was officially canceled
in 1969, but it wasn't gone forever—as evidenced by four television
spin-offs and eleven motion pictures.

Cagney & Lacey

Initially canned in 1983 due to poor ratings, this CBS drama about
two female New York City police detectives was saved from extinction by a plea from its producer, which led to an outpouring of
fan support. The critically acclaimed program went on to receive
36 Emmy nominations.

Quantum Leap

It wasn't time travel but rather a strong fan base that saved this NBC
series following its third season, which ended in 1991. Time finally
caught up with the program in 1993, when it was canceled.

Dr. Quinn, Medicine Woman

A fan campaign to save the good doctor succeeded—depending on
your point of view. Although CBS refused to reinstate the series following its cancellation in 1998, outraged viewers persuaded network
executives to give the go-ahead to a made-for-TV movie that aired
in 1999. Although the movie generated poor ratings, CBS officials
agreed to a second television movie in 2001.

Misheard Lyrics

Elton John, "Tiny Dancer"
Correct: "Hold me closer tiny dancer"
Wrong: "Hold me closer Tony Danza"

Britney Spears, "Oops!...I Did It Again"
Correct: "Oops, I did it again"
Wrong: "Oops, I dated a pen"

Outkast, "Hey Ya"
Correct: "Shake it like a Polaroid picture"
Wrong: "Shake it like a polar bear ninja"

Justin Timberlake, "Sexy Back"
Correct: "Get your sexy on"
Wrong: "Who's a sexy goat?"

Eurythmics, "Sweet Dreams (Are Made of This)"
Correct: "Sweet dreams are made of these"
Wrong: "Sweet cream is made of cheese"

Johnny Rivers, "Secret Agent Man"
Correct: "Secret Agent Man"
Wrong: "Seasick Asian man"

Pat Benatar, "Hit Me With Your Best Shot"
Correct: "Hit me with your best shot"
Wrong: "Hit me with your pet shark"

Eddie Money, "Two Tickets to Paradise"
Correct: "I've got two tickets to paradise"
Wrong: I've got flu, rickets, and parasites"

Ramones, "I Want to Be Sedated"
Correct: "I want to be sedated"
Wrong: "I want a piece of bacon"

Broken by Drudge

The Web site known as The Drudge Report *started in 1996 as the gossipy brainchild of CBS gift shop employee Matt Drudge but quickly became a political juggernaut, breaking—and often blowing—major stories about America's most important people.*

Three Drudge Got Right

1996: that Jack Kemp would be the running mate for Republican presidential candidate Bob Dole. This kind of story's not momentous, but it showed how tapped in Drudge was.

1998: that President Bill Clinton had been having an affair with intern Monica Lewinsky. Drudge didn't actually get this one first, but he was the first to print it, and that's what counts. A *Newsweek* reporter had it first, but when *Newsweek* spiked the story—on the old-fashioned grounds that it wasn't the public's business—the reporter gave it to Drudge, who happily ran with it.

2008: printed the news that Britain's Prince Harry was serving in the war in Iraq—a sensitive bit of information that other news organizations had suppressed in the belief that, if divulged, it would put his fellow troops in grave danger of a suicide attack.

Three Drudge Got Wrong

1997: that then-White House aide Sidney Blumenthal had violently abused his wife. Drudge retracted the piece and apologized. Blumenthal sued.

1999: claimed that a former prostitute had made a videotaped "confession" that Bill Clinton was her son's father. The confession turned out to be a hoax.

2004: claimed that General Wesley Clark had said that John Kerry's presidential campaign would "implode" over an alleged affair. Drudge later removed the story.

Familiar Numbers and the Logic Behind Them

• •

ZIP Codes

For most Americans, ZIP codes are as synonymous with the U.S. Post Office as the annual price increase on postage. But it wasn't always that way. ZIP ("Zoning Improvement Plan") codes were only introduced in 1963 as a way to help ease the massive burden on the post office. According to the USPS, this is what your five-digit ZIP code means:

- The first digit represents the geographic area of the country (the higher the number, the farther west).

- The next two digits represent the "sectional facility"—one of several hundred major distribution centers maintained by the post office.

- The last two digits represent the individual post office or zoning area.

Social Security Numbers

The social security number may seem like a random string of nine digits, but there is actually logic behind it.

- The first three digits are called the "area number" and were originally supposed to represent the state in which the card was issued, though now they are based on the ZIP code of the applicant.

- The two digits that follow the area number are known as the "group number." These numbers are issued based on a convoluted odd/even numbering sequence. The logic of the group number defies explanation.

- The last four digits are known as a "serial number." These numbers are issued consecutively from 0000 to 9999 within each group.

666

Any fan of horror movies can tell you that there's nothing good about the number 666. But they might be less certain about the reason why the number is associated with the Devil. The number 666—also known as the Number of the Beast—gets its evil connotation from the Book of Revelation in the New Testament, specifically in chapter 13, verse 18: "Wisdom is needed here; one who understands can calculate the number of the beast, for it is a number that stands for a person. His number is six hundred and sixty-six." Thus, the number of both the Devil and the Antichrist is revealed to be 666.

Many people have noted that this is unusually specific for a book that otherwise deals with what are presumably symbols, such as dragons coming out of the earth and fire shooting from the sky. As with the interpretation of the Book of Revelation in general, there has been a lot of debate about the precise meaning of this number.

On one side, there is the lunatic fringe, which ascribes the sign of the beast to whichever public figure has raised its ire. In the 1980s, for example, some malcontents pointed out that President Reagan's full name—Ronald Wilson Reagan—is composed of three six-letter groupings.

A more sane theory attributes the number 666 to the Roman emperor Nero. Nero blamed the Christians for the infamous burning of Rome in the first century A.D., and consequently started a brutal campaign of persecution against the fledgling religion. It is believed that the author of the Book of Revelation, John the Apostle, was attempting to send a coded message to his fellow Christians to give them hope that Nero's tyranny would soon come to an end.

To ensure that only other Christians would understand his message, John used Hebrew numerology. John chose Hebrew because it is the language of Judaism, the religion that Christianity grew out of after the arrival of Christ. In Hebrew, each letter corresponds with a number. The letters/numbers from Nero's full name in Hebrew, Neron Qeisar, add up to—you guessed it—666.

11 Stupid Legal Warnings

Our lawsuit-obsessed society has forced product manufacturers to cover their you-know-whats by writing warning labels to protect us from ourselves. Some are funny, some are absolutely ridiculous, but all are guaranteed to stand up in court.

- Child-size Superman and Batman costumes come with this warning label: "Wearing of this garment does not enable you to fly."

- A clothes iron comes with this caution: "Warning: Never iron clothes on the body." Ouch!

- The instructions for a medical thermometer advise: "Do not use orally after using rectally."

- The side of a Slush Puppy cup warns: "This ice may be cold." The only thing dumber than this would be a disclaimer stating: "No puppies were harmed in the making of this product."

- The box of a 500-piece puzzle reads: "Some assembly required."

- A Powerpuff Girls costume discourages: "You cannot save the world!"

- A box of PMS relief tablets has this advice: "Warning: Do not use if you have prostate problems."

- Cans of Easy Cheese contain this instruction: "For best results, remove cap."

- A warning label on a nighttime sleep aid reads: "Warning: May cause drowsiness."

- Cans of self-defense pepper spray caution: "May irritate eyes."

- Boys and girls should read the label on the Harry Potter toy broom: "This broom does not actually fly."

I Scream, You Scream for Asian Ice Cream!

Ever have the taste for red bean ice cream? How about black sesame? These flavors—and many others that Westerners might find odd—are popular in Asian countries. But you don't have to travel overseas to find them. Many Asian ice cream parlors, especially in bigger cities, now serve everything from taro- to ginger-flavored ice creams.

Here are some of the more popular, and not-so-popular, Asian ice cream flavors:

- **Red Bean** It shouldn't come as a surprise to see beans used to flavor ice cream. After all, vanilla is a bean, right? Asian red bean ice cream is a bit different, though, mainly because this ice cream has real red beans inside it that you can actually touch. Red beans are a common ingredient in Asian sweets. Ever have sweet red bean soup in a Chinese restaurant for dessert? Consider red bean ice cream part of the same family of Asian sweets.

- **Taro** The taro plant, in its raw form, is considered toxic. Once it's cooked, though, the plant is perfectly safe to eat. That's a good thing, considering that taro-flavored ice cream is a popular treat in Asian countries. Taro ice cream actually uses the plant's root for its flavor. This root is colored lavender and has the texture of a potato. Taro ice cream itself, which is usually purple in color, boasts a nutty flavor.

- **Durian** In Southeast Asia, the durian fruit is known as the "king of fruit." That's because it's so large and tasty. The durian fruit, though, does have a drawback: It stinks. The fruit's odor is so overpowering, in fact, that some hotels in Asia have a strict policy forbidding the durian fruit on their premises. The taste is another story, though. Durian fruit has a rich custardlike flavor.

- **Horse Meat** Even the most adventurous of Westerners might shy away from basashi ice cream. You can find this strange treat at the Ice Cream City ice cream shop in Tokyo. What is it? It's vanilla ice cream made with shreds of raw horse flesh. What would John Wayne say?

The ABCs of SCRABBLE™

It's fortunate for word junkies that Alfred Mosher Butts was out of work in the late 1930s. The Poughkeepsie, New York, architect had lost his job, giving him enough free time to create his own board game. That game, which Butts invented in 1938, eventually became known as SCRABBLE. Today, millions of SCRABBLE sets are sold each year in North America. How much do you know about SCRABBLE?

- When Butts first invented SCRABBLE, he called it LEXIKO. Later, the game was named CRISS CROSS WORDS. Obviously, neither name took, and the game was christened SCRABBLE in 1948.

- According to legend, SCRABBLE struggled to find an audience in its first two years. It wasn't until the early 1950s that SCRABBLE sales started to boom, thanks to an assist from the president of Macy's department store in New York City. The story goes that the business tycoon discovered a SCRABBLE game when he was on vacation and was so taken with it that he ordered several sets for his store. Suddenly, everyone had to have a SCRABBLE game. The game has been extremely popular ever since.

- How popular is SCRABBLE today? More than 150 million sets have been sold worldwide.

- Businessman James Brunot bought the rights to Butts's game in 1948. Brunot renamed the game SCRABBLE, a word that means "to grope frantically."

- Determining how many *W*s, *T*s, *P*s, or other letters to include in the game was no easy task. Butts

pored over the front pages of *The New York Times* to figure out how often each letter of the alphabet showed up. That determined how many tiles each letter would get. There was one exception: Butts only included four *S* tiles. He didn't want players to simply make words plural.

- The secret to success in playing SCRABBLE is to rely on sometimes unusual words to get out of jams. For instance, there are 121 SCRABBLE words that contain no vowels. Unfortunately, if you don't have a *Y*, you'll only be able to use 20 of them. Some of these vowel-free words include *crypt, cysts, dry, fly, fry, nymph,* and *myth.* Some of the 20 *Y*-free, no-vowel words include *tsk, brr, psst,* and *crwth.* A *crwth,* by the way, is an archaic stringed musical instrument. It's usually associated with Welsh music.

- You may also need to use a word that has a *Q* but no *U*. These are rare. In fact, *The Official SCRABBLE Players Dictionary* only features 24 of these words. Some of them include *qadi,* which is an Islamic judge; *faqir,* a Muslim or Hindu monk; *sheqel,* an ancient unit of weight; and *qindar,* an Arabian currency.

- Two-letter words are also vitally important in championship-level SCRABBLE play. These words don't generally give you a lot of points, but they do help players out of tough spots. *The Official SCRABBLE Players Dictionary* lists 102 two-letter words. Some are common like *am, an, be,* and *ox.* Others, though, are quite unusual. Do you know what a *za* is? It's slang for "pizza," as in "Let's order a za tonight." How about *qi?* That's the ancient Chinese term for the vital energy that supposedly flows through our bodies.

- *The Official SCRABBLE Players Dictionary* is usually updated once every five years. For the fourth edition, which was updated in 2006, more than 3,300 new words were added. Thanks to the words *za* and *qi,* the dictionary now, for the first time ever, contains two-letter words that use the Z and Q tiles. This is important for tournament players, because these two tiles boast ten points each—the highest number of points for any letters in the game.

Things You Don't Know
(and Didn't Need to Know) About...
Donald Duck

Why does Donald Duck wear a shirt but no pants? We don't have the answer to that one, but we've covered just about everything else!

- Donald Duck made his 1934 film debut in a cartoon about hens. You might not recognize him, though; he had a skinny neck, a longer bill, overexaggerated feet, and a thicker body. A makeover in 1940 made him the duck he is today.

- Donald's middle name is Fauntleroy. His official birthday is June 9, 1934.

- Walt Disney discovered Clarence "Ducky" Nash (who created Donald's voice) on the radio. Nash was using that distinctive voice to act as a spokesman for a local business.

- Donna Duck was Donald's first girlfriend (1937). Ever the romantic, Donald's suave pick-up line was "Hiya, Toots!" He dumped Donna for Daisy Duck in 1940.

- Daisy is obviously very patient. She and Donald have been an item for 60 years but have never married...although they came close in 1954's *Donald's Diary*.

- Donald's uncle, Scrooge McDuck, was once listed in *Forbes* as the second wealthiest fictional character, with a net worth of just over $29 billion.

- It's easy to tell Donald Duck's nephews apart. Starting with *Duck Tales*, Huey wore red, Dewey wore blue, and Louie wore green.

- In some cartoon panels, Donald has *four* nephews, Huey, Dewey, Louie, and the one most widely called Phooey. Cartoon conspiracy theorists admit that the duckling's presence may have been a mistake or a misunderstanding.

- Though Donald is always basically a good-intentioned guy, he is known for his occasional outbursts. At least once, he was accused of profanity, causing a cartoon video to be pulled from shelves. Ain't that just ducky?

Washington, D.C.: The Official Story

First, let's put a myth to rest: The District of Columbia was not wrested from swampland back in the 1790s. It only feels that way. The temperature, officially designated as "sub-tropical," averages 86 degrees during the summer, and it rains approximately 115 days per year. (The record high, by the way, was 106 degrees on July 20, 1930.)

The city itself was built mostly on farm and forestland on the north bank of the Potomac River and encompasses 68.3 square miles, including 6.9 square miles of water and 13.25 square miles of parkland, making Washington one of the greenest cities in America. That's good news for the 591,833 residents who are packed in at a density of 9,639 people per square mile. Washington is currently the 27th most populous city in the United States, slightly behind Nashville and a little ahead of Las Vegas.

Approximately one-fifth of D.C.'s population is younger than 18. More than a quarter of the population is between ages 18 and 34, and a little more than a tenth is older than 65.

Nearly half of the city's adults, or about 243,000 people, work for the federal government. And they're a well-educated bunch. Almost 40 percent have a bachelor's degree or higher, compared to 24 percent of all Americans. As of 2008, their annual median income hovered around a whopping $50,000.

What will that salary get you, though? A home in Georgetown, D.C.'s priciest neighborhood, will set you back an average of $3 million. Condos in trendy Dupont Circle go for around $1 million and a *pied-a-terre* in bohemian Adams Morgan costs a "mere" $650,000.

Of course, Washingtonians don't always stay home even when they can afford one. The city's culture-vultures and socialites help keep the 106.3-mile Metro Rail subway system one of the busiest in the nation, carrying 215 million passengers per year.

If they're not going to work, Washingtonians might be headed to one of the capital's 30+ professional theaters, 40 museums, or going out to eat, perhaps at Citronelle on fashionable M Street. Welcome to Washington, D.C., and bon appétit!

The USPS: The Check Is in the Mail

What is now known as the United States Postal Service was established in 1775 by the Continental Congress, which also appointed Benjamin Franklin the first postmaster general. It was a job with which Franklin had some experience—he worked as postmaster of Philadelphia under the British Parliamentary Post and later as one of two deputy postmasters of North America. (The other was a less famous guy named William Hunter.)

Through Rain and Sleet...

There are 32,741 post offices throughout the United States. Combined, they employ 656,000 career employees and manage 221,000 vehicles—the largest civilian fleet in the world. Here's more:

46 million: the number of address changes processed each year

8.5 million: the number of passport applications accepted in 2008

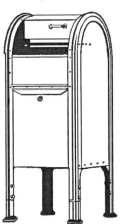

597,000: the average number of postal service money orders issued daily

300: the number of "employee heroes" recognized by the postal service in 2008 for saving the lives of customers on their routes

For Your Protection

- The Postal Inspection Service is one of the oldest federal law enforcement agencies and was the first to offer federal agent careers to women.

- More than 9,000 suspects were arrested in 2008 for crimes involving the mail or for crimes against the postal service.

- Postal inspectors prevented 800,000 fake checks—worth an estimated $2.7 billion—from entering the United States in 2008.

Mail by the Numbers

203 billion: pieces of mail processed in 2008

667 million: the approximate number of mail pieces processed each day

28 million: pieces of mail processed each hour (on average)

463,000: pieces of mail processed each minute (on average)

36.6 million: the number of stamps printed in 2008

$62 million: the amount of money raised for breast cancer research since July 1998 through the sale of the Breast Cancer Research Semi-Postal Stamp

1963: the year the Zoning Improvement Plan (ZIP) Code was launched

❖ ❖ ❖

"Neither snow, nor rain, nor heat, nor gloom of night stays these couriers from the swift completion of their appointed rounds."
—The motto of the U.S. Postal Service

How to Beat a Lie Detector Test

If you've been told that you'll need to take a polygraph test before accepting a job or to be cleared of a crime, watch out—you're about to be duped. The polygraph or "lie detector" test is one of the most misunderstood tests used in law enforcement.

Many experts will tell you that lie detector tests are based on fallible data. Regardless of how scientific the equipment appears, there's no sure way a person can tell whether or not someone is lying. Since the test is so imperfect, be suspicious of anyone who makes your fate contingent upon the results of a polygraph test. Still, here are a few suggestions on how to beat one:

- Unless you're applying for a job that requires it, refuse to take the polygraph test. There are no laws that can compel anyone to take one.

- Keep your answers short and to the point. Most questions can be answered with a "yes" or "no." Keep it simple.

- During the polygraph test, you'll be asked three types of questions: irrelevant, relevant, and control questions. Irrelevant questions generally take the form of "Is the color of this room white?" Relevant questions are the areas that get you into trouble. Control questions are designed to "calibrate" your responses during the test. See the next point.

- Control questions establish information known to be true, such as your name or your age. They are asked so that the technician can compare correct responses to questions against a known entity. The easiest way to beat a lie detector test is to invalidate the control questions. Try these simple techniques when asked a control question: Change your breathing rate and depth from the normal 15 to 30 breaths per minute to anything faster or slower. Solve a math problem in your head, or count backward from 100 by 7s. Bite the sides of your tongue until it begins to hurt.

Five Unpleasant But True Facts About Bats

Long associated with vampires, bats have gotten a bad rap. But the truth is that bats are our friends. They keep down the insect population, pollinate flowers, and are a vital part of many ecosystems. Of course, this doesn't change the fact that they're kind of creepy.

1. They *do* carry rabies.

Okay, not all of them. But some of them. About .5 percent of bats have rabies. And bat bites cause about 71 percent of rabies cases in the United States. They might not, as old wives' tales have it, purposefully tangle themselves in your hair, but they do bite. It's not a bad idea to stay away from them.

2. They have razor-sharp teeth.

Sure, these teeth are tiny, but they're still, very, very sharp. And scary.

3. Some of them have strangely long tongues.

One species of nectar bat, the *Anoura fistulata,* has a longer tongue relative to the length of its body than any other mammal. It uses this long tongue to reach inside flowers and get pollen. When the bat is not using its tongue, the appendage curls up in the bat's rib cage like a little garden hose.

4. One bat can eat 1,000 insects in an hour.

This might be less unpleasant if you consider that bats mean fewer insects flying around and bothering you.

5. Bloodsucking

Some species of bats suck the blood from the backs of cattle or the feet of chicken. They use their sharp toenails to slit the skin of these animals and then lap up the blood.

Bragging Rights

Over the Hill: The World's Oldest Things

- Biologists believe that *turritopsis nutricula,* a type of hydrozoan, has the longest lifespan of any animal. Like some other hydrozoans, it begins life as a polyp and later changes into a jellyfish. But it can also turn back into a polyp, rebooting its life cycle. It seems to be able to do this indefinitely, which means its lifespan is essentially infinite. Nobody knows how old any specific *turritopsis nutricula* is, however.

- In 2007, a 405-year-old quahog clam claimed the title for oldest specific animal. The scientists who found it off the coast of Iceland determined its age by counting its growth rings.

- The oldest known living tree is a spruce on Fulu Mountain in Sweden, discovered in 2004. According to carbon dating, the tree is 9,550 years old, which means it took root soon after the last ice age.

- The oldest known building site is an arrangement of ten post holes on a hill near Tokyo. Archeologists believe the holes were the foundation for two huts, half a million years old, built by the extinct human species *Homo erectus.*

- The oldest structure built by modern humans is Gobekli Tepe, a temple of elaborately carved pillars unearthed in Turkey. Archeologists believe the temple is 11,500 years old, which predates Stonehenge by about 7,000 years.

- Some Wyoming residents claim the oldest structure is their own Fossil Cabin. It wasn't built until 1933, but the construction material—a collection of dinosaur fossils—is between 100 million and 200 million years old.

- The oldest known object on Earth is a microscopic zircon crystal, found in western Australia. Through chemical analysis, scientists have determined the crystal is 4.4 billion years old—only 100 to 200 million years younger than Earth itself.

Five Reasons People Think Nixon Was a Great President

Believe it or not, Nixon was once very popular. In his 1972 reelection bid, he carried 49 states and 60.7 percent of the popular vote— one of the widest margins in history. And his greatest hits are nothing to sneeze at either.

1. **China** In the 1940s, Nixon made his political mark as an anti-communist crusader. So, it surprised many when he became the first U.S. president to go to China—after years of hostility between the nations—in February 1972. Nixon met with Chinese Premier Chou En-lai and Communist Party Chairman Mao Zedong, laying the groundwork for the establishment of full diplomatic relations with China in 1979.

2. **Détente** Only three months after his visit to China, Nixon accepted Soviet Premier Leonid Brezhnev's invitation to meet in Russia. During the visit, Nixon and Brezhnev signed the Strategic Arms Limitation Treaty and the Anti-Ballistic Missile Treaty. This ushered in a period of reduced Cold War tensions called *détente,* which lasted until the early 1980s.

3. **Ecology** Nixon had a spotty environmental record, but he did establish the Environmental Protection Agency in 1970. He also signed the Marine Mammal Protection Act in 1972, the Endangered Species Act in 1973, the Safe Drinking Water Act in 1974, and enacted amendments to the Clean Air Act in 1970 that set the course for curbing auto emissions.

4. **OSHA** In 1970, Nixon established the Occupational Safety and Health Administration, a government agency dedicated to making workers safer.

5. **School Desegregation** In 1970, Nixon committed to enforcing the Supreme Court's 1954 ruling against school segregation. His landmark discussions with leaders from seven holdout Southern states led to peaceful integration of the last segregated schools.

Not Coming to a Theater Near You

Given some of the duds that do make it to the screen, it may seem odd that so many promising movie ideas end up on the shelf. But Hollywood lore is full of intriguing projects that never were.

Don Quixote *Citizen Kane* director Orson Welles abandoned more movies than he actually made, including a film version of Adolf Hitler's *Mein Kampf* and the story of Jesus Christ (with Welles as Jesus). But his most infamous unfinished film was an adaptation of the 16th-century classic *Don Quixote,* about an old dreamer who imagines adventure everywhere. Welles dropped Don Quixote in 20th-century Spain and cast himself as a character making a Don Quixote movie. He started the project in 1954 and continued working on it off and on until his death in 1985, funding it out of his own pocket. In 1993, Welles associates assembled and released salvaged scratchy footage, but audiences saw it more as an epic home movie than a completed Welles film.

The Man Who Killed Don Quixote *12 Monkeys* director Terry Gilliam has also spent years on Don Quixote. In 2000, a decade after he conceived the idea, Gilliam finally started shooting his adaptation, in which an ad executive time travels back to the 1600s. But after six days of shooting and a series of catastrophes, including a flash flood, the production ground to a halt. Insurers backed out, the movie was canceled, and Gilliam lost control of the screenplay. He's been trying to get back to the project ever since, finally regaining the script rights in 2009.

Roger Rabbit 2 After *Who Framed Roger Rabbit* raked in $325 million, a sequel was a no-brainer. Disney initially developed a prequel script that put Roger in the middle of World War II. But Steven

Spielberg, who partially controls the rights to the characters, was approaching the war on a more serious note with *Schindler's List* and didn't want to cast Nazis as cartoonish villains. Eventually, Disney came up with a second script, set in the Great Depression, and produced some test footage. Disney CEO Michael Eisner liked what he saw but didn't like

the projected budget, which topped $100 million. He canceled the project in 1999.

A Day at the United Nations In 1960, *Some Like It Hot* director Billy Wilder decided to make the first new Marx Brothers film in a decade. In his film, the Marx Brothers would play jewel thieves who are mistaken for Latvian delegates to the United Nations. The Marx Brothers were interested, but when Harpo had a heart attack, Wilder decided it was too risky to proceed.

Up Against It In 1967, avant-garde playwright Joe Orton wrote a screenplay for a third Beatles movie. In the film, John, Paul, George, and Ringo would have been revolutionaries battling an oppressive government run entirely by women. But the material was awfully dark for The Beatles (in the story, the fab four assassinate a female prime minister) and they opted not to do it.

Alternative Supermans Between 1987's *Superman IV: The Quest for Peace* and 2006's *Superman Returns,* the man of steel had several failed takeoffs. In the biggest misfire, *Superman Lives,* which began development in 1994, Superman is killed but then resurrected by a cyborg. Oddly enough, producer Jon Peters dictated Superman should wear a black suit in the movie and should never be shown flying. *Clerks* writer/director Kevin Smith wrote the screenplay, Tim Burton signed on to direct, and Nicholas Cage got fitted for the cape. But after racking up millions in preproduction costs, the project fell apart. Later, the studio's attention turned to *Batman vs. Superman*, which would have featured the two heroes battling each other. Ultimately, Warner Bros. decided separate Batman and Superman movies were a better bet (more ticket sales), so it killed the project.

Surfing: The Stats

The Internet began life in the United States in 1969 as a network of computers designed to connect government and defense installations in the event of a telecommunications failure. Even with the 1991 introduction of the World Wide Web, the Internet initially had limited uses and few users. These days, you can practically live your life online—and some people do. Here's a snapshot of the ever-evolving Internet world.

- By 2008, Google had identified one trillion individual Web pages. The Microsoft Bing team estimates it would take six million years to read everything available online.

- According to Internet World Stats, there were more than 1.59 billion people online as of 2009. Seems like a big number, but that's actually only 23.8 percent of the world's population.

- Around 18 percent (298 million) of Web users live in China.

- In China, 99 percent of all digital music files were downloaded illegally. Oops!

- A 2009 study concluded that the average download speed in the United States is 5.1 megabits per second. That puts the United States in 28th place worldwide.

- South Korea is at the top of the list, with an average speed of 20.4 megabits per second.

- In 2007, a 75-year-old Swedish woman got the world's fastest home Internet connection. Her son, an optical Internet expert, set up a 40-gigabits-per-second connection to demonstrate fiber-optic technology. Her setup could download an entire movie in two seconds, but she mainly used it to dry laundry. (The routing system would get very hot.)

- Between 2004 and 2009, the online population of American kids grew by 18 percent. Their time online grew 63 percent, to an average of 11 hours per month.

- As of March 2010, Wikipedia boasted 14 million articles in 262 languages, including 3.2 million articles in English.

- In July 2009, Americans racked up 21.4 billion online video views.

It Happened in...March

- It's a veritable food free-for-all: Ray Kroc formed the McDonald's franchise company in March (1955). "Rambo" candy was introduced in March (1985). The first cooking school was opened in Great Britain in March (1784). And the creator of the Eskimo Pie died in March (1992).

- On March 19, 1957, Elvis did not leave the building but instead purchased it. He bought Graceland for just over $100,000. Nearly one year later to the day, he was sworn into the U.S. Army. Two years later, almost exactly, he was discharged.

- A horse-drawn public bus was introduced in Paris in 1662. Meant for the poor, the vehicles quickly became a fad of the city's wealthy. Unimpressed, the poor shunned the buses, making the experiment short-lived.

- You can see where this is going: In 1954, it was announced that the first cornea-size plastic contact lenses had been developed.

- The Academy Awards show included costume design for the first time in March 1949 (for movies made in 1948). At that time, separate awards were given for black-and-white movie costumes versus color movie costumes.

- Also in 1949, South Carolina became the last state to allow divorce.

- The U.S. Patent Office gave young Chester Greenwood the patent for earmuffs in March 1877. Other notable March patents: the cotton gin, false teeth, the escalator, and the pencil with eraser.

- March is Women's History Month, Optimism Month, National Umbrella Month, Employee Spirit Month, and—just so you can stay awake for it—National Caffeine Awareness Month.

World's Least Healthy Foods

Dining out too often is never good for the waistline, but these restaurant menu items ranked among the absolute worst, according to Men's Health.

Awesome Blossom, Chili's:

2,710 calories, 203g fat, 6,360mg sodium

This "appetizer" delivers almost three times the amount of sodium needed in an entire day. That *is* awesome!

Aussie Cheese Fries with Ranch Dressing, Outback Steakhouse:

2,900 calories, 182g fat

Eating this snack from the Land Down Under too often will put you six feet under.

Stacked Border Nachos, On the Border:

2,740 calories, 166g fat

In terms of fat content, eating these nachos is the equivalent of downing five Big Macs. Olé!

Spaghetti and Meatballs with Meat Sauce, Macaroni Grill:

2,430 calories, 128g fat

Mamma Mia! Italians are known for their health and longevity. That's probably because they don't eat at Macaroni Grill.

Chicago Classic Deep Dish Pizza, Uno Chicago Grill:

2,310 calories, 162g fat

Would 18 slices of normal pizza seem like a reasonable lunch? No? Well, this deep-dish gut bomb is roughly equal to that.

Caramel Banana Pecan Cream Stacked and Stuffed Hotcakes, Bob Evans:

1,540 calories, 109g sugar

Nothing like starting the day with 250 percent of your maximum recommended sugar intake.

Bella Turkey Burger, Ruby Tuesday's:

1,145 calories, 71g fat

The worst thing about this entry is that turkey burgers are supposed to be healthy.

Grande Taco Salad with Taco Beef, On the Border:

1,450 calories, 2,410mg sodium

Make sure you order nonfat dressing with that.

Classic Italian Sandwich, Quizno's:

1,510 calories, 3,750mg sodium

This one sandwich is the caloric equivalent of about four PB&Js.

20 oz T-Bone Steak, Lonestar Steakhouse:

1,540 calories, 124g fat

That's not even counting the sides that come with it!

Five Least Healthy Fast-Food Restaurants in America

1. Pizza Hut   3. Domino's Pizza   5. Arby's

2. Panera Bread   4. Burger King

By the Numbers

33%: percentage of American middle and high schools with fast-food restaurants within walking distance

16.3%: percentage of American children considered obese

Celebrities Who Influenced Baby-Name Trends

- Shirley Temple, child star of the 1930s, may have kick-started the trend of naming children after movie stars. Her name was the second most popular for girls in 1935 and remained in the top ten until 1941.

- Judy Garland's fame in the 1940s no doubt helped her name remain in the top 20 between 1940 and 1949.

- Gary Cooper's role as an all-American cowboy kept his name in the top 20 for boys for nearly two decades, from 1940 to 1959.

- If you're a female baby boomer named Deborah you probably have actress Debbie Reynolds to thank for your name. Deborah was among the top ten girls' names from 1950 to 1962.

- Scottish actor Sean Connery's on-screen role as Agent 007 put his name in the top 100 for boys. It ranked 79th in 1965. Actor Sean Penn helped keep the name popular in the 21st century. Sean ranked 83rd among boys' names in 2008.

- Pop star Miley Cyrus's first name didn't even rank in the top 1,000 until 2007. It ranked 279th that year and jumped to 127th in 2008.

- After Leonardo di Caprio starred in the film *Titanic,* his name jumped from 357th in 1997 to 257th in 1998. It ranked 170th among all boys' names in 2008.

- Not all celebrities are actors—former First Lady Jackie Kennedy inspired many parents to call their little girls Jacqueline. The name ranked 37th in 1961 and remained in the top 100 for more than 40 years. It ranked 152 as of 2008.

- President Theodore (Teddy) Roosevelt's name ranked in the top 50 for boys during his two terms in office (1901 to 1908).

Does this mean we'll soon be welcoming a generation of Baracks, Michelles, Malias, and Sashas? We'll just have to wait and see.

Cigarette Trivia

Cigarettes—we think we know everything there is to know. The Surgeon General's warning, the Marlboro Man, smoking bans, nicotine patches. But cigarettes have been around for more than 1,000 years, and quite a lot of weird and surprising things have happened in that time.

- The earliest forms of cigarettes weren't found at coffee breaks but at religious ceremonies. They were used by Mayan priests in Central America and Aztec priests in South America in the ninth century.

- In 1854, Philip Morris, a London tobacco seller, was the first to manufacture cigarettes. Forty cigarettes could be hand-rolled in one minute. By 1880, the first cigarette-rolling machine could produce 120,000 in ten hours.

- Although most people associate sports collector cards with gum, the cards were first found in cigarette packs (they helped protect cigarettes from being crushed). The most valuable baseball card—a 1909 Honus Wagner—was found in American Tobacco Company packs. The Wagner card sold for $2.35 million because only around 50 still exist. Wagner worried that children would begin smoking after buying the cigarettes to get his card so he had it pulled from circulation.

- Smoking was initially considered "unladylike," but tobacco companies defeated the ban on public smoking by women by appealing to women's rights groups. They invited debutantes to light up their "torches of freedom" at the 1929 Easter Parade in New York City. And they did!

- Joe Camel and the Marlboro Man weren't the only ones touting cigarettes. Ads have featured dentists, doctors, babies, and even Santa enjoying a puff. In the 1940s, Madison Avenue highlighted health benefits: calming nerves, soothing throats, boosting energy, and maintaining a healthy weight.

- According to the Department of Health and Human Services, the 1994 tobacco blend of cigarettes lists some 600 ingredients. When lit, they create more than 4,000 chemical compounds, of which 43 cause cancer. For a short time in the 1950s Kent's "Micronite" filter was even made of asbestos!

- The constantly puffing characters on the TV series *Mad Men* aren't exaggerating. Cigarette consumption peaked in the United States in 1965 at 4,259 smokers per capita. At the time, 50 percent of men and 33 percent of women were smokers.

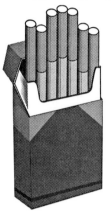

- President Richard Nixon signed the Public Health Cigarette Smoking Act of 1969, banning cigarette ads on television and radio in the United States starting on January 2, 1971. Why not January 1? Advertisers were given a one-day reprieve to take advantage of ad time during the New Year's Day football games!

- Get around the smoking bans with an e-cig, or electronic cigarette. A plastic e-cig looks like a regular cigarette (the tip even glows red when you're "smoking") but holds a cartridge of flavored liquid (with or without nicotine) and is run with a lithium battery. Smokers can inhale, but the exhaled vapor instantly disappears and has no odor.

- According the American Cancer Society, 6.3 trillion cigarettes will be consumed in 2010.

- Check your entrée for ashes! A study by the U.S. Substance Abuse and Mental Health Services Administration found that the occupations with the highest rates of smoking (45 percent) were food-preparation and serving-related occupations.

- Cigarette taxes range from $1.08 per pack in South Carolina to $3.76 in New York. Globally, taxes range from 0 percent to 80 percent of retail price. Because of these wild fluctuations, cigarette smuggling is huge. In some states (We're talking to you, Delaware!), as many as 82 percent of all cigarettes purchased are smuggled.

Out to Lunch

Human beings are social creatures, and what brings us together most often is food. Our early ancestors shared their kill around a fire, but when we don't feel like cooking, we just run out for a bite. Here a few nuggets of knowledge on restaurants and restaurant culture.

Oldest Restaurant: Casa Botin. Situated on Calle de Cuchilleros in the heart of Madrid, Spain, Casa Botin was founded in 1725 and still cooks up such famous foods as roast pig, baby eels, and caramel custard in its 18th-century stove.

Most Expensive Sandwich: A McDonald's. No, not that McDonald's. This sandwich, named after its creator, Scott McDonald, was available for a brief time in 2006 at Selfridges in London. At a cost of $175, this was no grilled cheese. Its ingredients included Kobe beef, foie gras, black truffle mayonnaise, Brie, mustard confit, and aged sourdough bread.

Most Expensive Restaurant: Aragawa. Admission to this tiny steak house in Tokyo, Japan, is by invitation only. The succulent, locally raised Kobe beef is presented simply (with pepper and mustard only) at a price of nearly $400 per person.

Most Popular Occasion for Dining Out: A birthday. Mother's Day follows close behind and Valentine's Day takes third place.

By the Numbers

935,000: number of restaurants in the United States in 2007

$537 billion: sales projections for U.S. restaurants in 2007

24%: percentage of an individual's meals eaten in restaurants

12.5 million: number of restaurant employees in the United States—only the government employs more people

Real Names You Probably Wouldn't Want to Have

Whether by chance or by choice, the following people were saddled with some truly heinous monikers. Read on to see just how bad the name game can get.

Dick Pole Professional baseball player/pitching coach.

Talula Does the Hula from Hawaii An actual name given to a New Zealand girl. Considered a social handicap by the girl and authorities, the name was later blocked by a judge's ruling.

Rusty Kuntz Professional baseball player/first base coach.

Tu Morrow Daughter of American actor Rob Morrow.

Peter Bonerz American actor.

Fred Fuchs Television and film producer.

Will Power Australian race car driver, *Indycar* series.

Jaime Sin A Roman Catholic archbishop who went by the improbable title Cardinal Sin.

Argélico Fucks Brazilian soccer player. A memorable sports headline once declared: "Argel Fucks off to Benfica."

Dick Trickle American race car driver, NASCAR series.

Spontaniouse Grant Aspiring American model. Named for her "spontaneous" birth on the way to the hospital.

Ima Hogg Daughter of Texas Governor James Stephen Hogg.

Notwithstanding Griswold Name given to a girl in Connecticut during the 1700s.

Lucious Pusey The unlikely birth name of the current Lucious Seymour. To avoid continued taunts, he had his name legally changed.

Mai Phat Sau Nghin Ruoi Boy named in protest after his father was fined 6,500 dong for ignoring Vietnam's two-child policy. It translates to "Fined Six Thousand Five Hundred." The boy's name was eventually changed to Mai Hoang Long (Golden Dragon).

Dick Seaman British race car driver, Grand Prix series.

Trout Fishing in America As a testament to his love of Richard Brautigan's novel of the same name, teenager Peter Eastman Jr. legally adopted the name as his own in 1994. His friends reportedly call him Trout.

Legal Tender Coxey Son of American social reformer Jacob Coxey.

Thursday October Christian Son of mutineer Fletcher Christian. Name was given so Fletcher would have "no name that reminded me of England."

Dick Assman Canadian service station owner. In 1995, his funky name brought him much fame via the *Late Show with David Letterman*.

Celebrities' Real Names

Many celebrities have catchy names that strike your interest and imagination. But you didn't think they were born with them, did you?

Anna Nicole Smith—Vickie Lynn Hogan

Whoopi Goldberg—Caryn Johnson

Winona Ryder—Winona Laura Horowitz

Brigitte Bardot—Camille Javal

Charlton Heston—John Charles Carter

Woody Allen—Allen Stewart Konigsberg

Elle Macpherson—Eleanor Gow

Harry Houdini—Ehrich Weiss

Jennifer Aniston—Jennifer Anastassakis

Natalie Portman—Natalie Hershlag

Nicolas Cage—Nicolas Coppola

Ralph Lauren—Ralph Lipschitz

Ten Unusual or Unexpected Hobbies of U.S. Presidents

From skinny-dipping to tenor saxophone, these chief executives had to do something when life in Washington, D.C., got boring.

Thomas Jefferson A noted statesman and, of course, the third U.S. president, Jefferson was also an architect. His designs included his famed home, Monticello, and the Virginia State Capitol building. Word has it he was a pretty good cook too.

John Quincy Adams Adams liked to swim naked in the Potomac River. Apparently when you're age 60-something and the sixth president, you can get away with such things. Just don't get caught. According to political legend, a reporter found Adams during a skinny-dipping jaunt and refused to let him out until the president granted him an interview.

Andrew Jackson The former military man and seventh U.S. president enjoyed passing his free time by drinking heavily, brawling, and—according to legend—gambling and partying in the Executive Mansion.

Theodore Roosevelt Many historians agree that the 26th president had more hobbies than any president before or since. "TR" enjoyed the outdoors and relished hunting and exploring. Roosevelt also enjoyed reading, writing, and ornithology...when he wasn't speaking softly and carrying a big stick, that is.

Calvin Coolidge America's 30th president, "Silent Cal" lived up to his reputation as a quiet individual. His favorite pastime: napping. He purportedly justified snoozing on the job by arguing that he couldn't initiate any costly federal programs while sleeping.

Franklin Delano Roosevelt Whenever FDR needed to take his mind off the events of the day—such as the Great Depression or World War II—he turned to his stamp collection. The 32nd president, who took up the hobby during his childhood, was so passionate about those gum-backed pieces of paper that during his four terms in office, he helped oversee the design and promotion of about 200 stamps.

Dwight D. Eisenhower Okay, it really isn't shocking that someone like Ike—a former U.S. Army general and the 34th U.S. president—might want to unwind with a game of golf. It's a very presidential thing to do. And Ike probably thought that rank had its privilege when he requested (in 1956) that a tree at Augusta National be removed because it was interfering with a few of his drives. Nature won out, and the so-called "Eisenhower Tree"—a pine on the 17th hole—still stands.

Lyndon Baines Johnson Driving. Specifically, drunken driving, especially on his Texas ranch... in a specially designed convertible that had been converted for amphibious use. (Maybe to forget about the war in Vietnam for a while, the 36th chief exec would feign brake failure and plunge his magic car into the nearest body of water, taking his unsuspecting passengers with him.) Kind of brings new meaning to "All the way with LBJ!"

Bill Clinton From his days as a kid growing up in Hope, Arkansas, William Jefferson Clinton always enjoyed sax. He couldn't get enough sax. Even after he became a married politician and eventually the 42nd president of the United States, he still found time for sax... even if it occasionally got him into trouble. He also enjoyed doing crossword puzzles and contributed clues to one of *The New York Times* crossword puzzles.

Barack Obama He may not be Michael Jordan, but this chief executive *loves* his basketball! Having watched tapes of Obama's high school playing career, sports writers admitted the kid wasn't half-bad—definitely deserving of the nickname "Barry O'Bomber."

The Human Body

Estimated size of human brain capacity, in terabytes:
   between 1 and 1,000

Total size of collections in Library of Congress, in terabytes:
   approximately 50

Average Human Brain Size:
   1350 cc

Average Neanderthal Brain Size:
   1600 cc

Homo neanderthalensis, better known to modern humans as the Neanderthal, has long existed in the popular imagination as an apelike primitive ancestor of modern man. Yet recent anthropological and genomic studies have indicated that Neanderthals were remarkably similar to modern humans and may, in fact, have coexisted with our ancestors. According to DNA studies, Neanderthals not only had physical and cultural traits similar to their human contemporaries, but they actually had larger brains as well.

The Speed of Human

Speed at which fingernails grow:
   .004 millimeter per hour

Speed of a human sneeze:
   around 100 mph

Speed of hair growth:
   .16 millimeter per hour

Speed of blood:
   about 2 miles per hour

Human top foot speed:
   28 mph

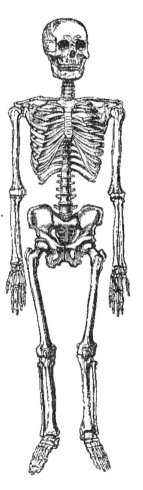

Human Hands

Percentage of population identified as left-handed:
10 percent

Percentage of presidents since 1974 who have been left-handed:
71 percent

Handedness is still something of a mystery to scientists. Some evolutionary biologists suggest that left-handedness is so rare due to persecution of lefties dating back to ancient prejudices—the Latin word for left, *sinistre,* is the root of the English term "sinister"—that prevented left-handers from passing on their genetic material. It is equally unclear why such a disproportionate number of history's greatest leaders and thinkers have been left-handed. Besides five of the past seven American presidents (Obama, Clinton, George H. W. Bush, Reagan, and Ford), other famous historical lefties include Alexander the Great, Newton, Picasso, da Vinci, Michelangelo, and of course, Jimi Hendrix.

Technical Terms for Bodily Functions

1. Eructation = Burp

2. Sternutation = Sneeze

3. Singultus = Hiccup

4. Lachrimation = Crying

5. Pandiculation = Yawning while stretching

Term for the indentation above the upper lip: philtrum

The word *philtrum* derives from the ancient Greek term *philtron,* which means "love potion." Although the philtrum may seem pointless to modern humans, the ancient Greeks believed it to be one of the most erogenous parts of the human body.

Things You Don't Know (and Didn't Need to Know) About...

Bugs Bunny

Shhhhhh. Be vewy, vewy quiet. We're hunting wabbit twivia. We know it's awound here somewhewh.

- The Oscar-winning rabbit made his unofficial debut in 1938 in *Porky's Hare Hunt,* a Porky Pig cartoon. He was eventually named by accident: Because the director of that cartoon, Ben Hardaway, was nicknamed "Bugs," preliminary sketches were identified as "Bugs' bunny."

- Had director Fred "Tex" Avery (who is widely given credit for creating the Bugs we know) had his way, Bugs would've been called Jack E. Rabbit.

- The familiar "What's Up, Doc?" came from Avery, who'd spent his teen years hearing the question from neighbors and high school classmates. Since 1940, almost every Bugs Bunny cartoon has included those three words (or a variation thereof).

- There was a Mrs. Bugs Bunny—at least for a few minutes. The little, uh, woman appeared in 1942's *Hold the Lion, Please!* Later comic books gave Bugs a girlfriend named Honey Bunny.

- Broccoli and celery growers once begged Warner Bros. (Bugs's studio) to allow the Wascally Wabbit to replace the carrot by sampling their crops too. The studio said no. Mel Blanc, the voice behind Bugs Bunny, was *not* allergic to carrots, by the way. He reportedly just didn't like them.

- Blanc was also the voice of Barney Rubble, Daffy Duck, Mr. Spacely on *The Jetsons,* Twiki on *Buck Rogers in the 25th Century,* and some 400 other characters.

- Bugs Bunny has his own star on Hollywood's Walk of Fame. He appeared on a U.S. postage stamp in 1998. And yes, he really did win an Oscar in 1958.

Th-th-th-th-th-that's all, folks!

Ten Particularly Germy Places in Hotel Rooms

If you want your hotel stay to be a healthy one, be ever vigilant. Nasty microscopic critters are present and waiting to pounce.

Bedspreads We've all heard that bedspreads at hotels are washed less frequently than sheets. Is it true? You bet your *E. coli.* Bottom line? Ditch the bedspread.

Carpets With gravity acting as it does, some pretty nasty germs work their way into carpets. Proper footwear acts as a guard.

Whirlpool Tubs A veritable breeding ground for germs, hotel whirlpools are rarely serviced with the same frequency as private baths. In one study, 100 percent of whirlpool water samples tested came up positive for agents that can cause urinary tract infections, rashes, and pneumonia.

Shower Can you say athlete's foot? Shower floors are rife with the bacteria that cause this condition. Wear flip-flops.

Mattress If germ-laden bodies never come in direct contact with a mattress, what's the risk? Bedbugs. To see if such nasties are present, aim a hair dryer at the mattress and observe closely. Bedbugs are attracted to heat and if present will likely make an appearance.

Sink Common sense dictates that a basin used for frequent hand washing and tooth brushing contains an abundance of germs.

Faucets Think of the number of people who touch these. Then wipe down accordingly.

Toilet Seat This one is almost too obvious. The best defense is a complete wipe down with an antibacterial wipe.

Remote Control Cold viruses and other nasty bugs can live on this surface for a day or more.

Telephone A trap for more airborne germs than perhaps anything else in a hotel room, the telephone can and does make people sick. Wipe it down with an antibacterial cloth.

Walking on the Moon

On July 20, 1969, at 10:56 P.M., Neil Armstrong accomplished the seemingly impossible by climbing down a short aluminum ladder and placing the first human footprints on the moon. Millions worldwide watched on television as Armstrong, followed by lunar module pilot Edwin "Buzz" Aldrin, took that "one giant leap for mankind," then explored the lunar surface. When they departed, Armstrong and Aldrin left behind a plaque reading, "Here men from the planet Earth first set foot upon the moon July 1969 A.D. We came in peace for all mankind."

Apollo 11: Facts and Figures

- **Crew:** Neil A. Armstrong, commander; Michael Collins, command module pilot; Edwin Aldrin, lunar module pilot
- **Launched:** July 16, 1969, from Kennedy Space Center Launch Complex 39A
- **Landed on the moon:** July 20, 1969, at 4:17 P.M.
- **Landing site:** Mare Tranquillitatis (Sea of Tranquility)
- **Time spent on the lunar surface:** 21 hours, 38 minutes, 21 seconds
- **Time spent exploring the lunar surface:** 2 hours, 31 minutes
- **Moon rocks collected:** 21.7 kilograms
- **Departed the lunar surface:** July 21, 1969, at 1:54 P.M.
- **Returned to Earth:** July 24, 1969, at 12:50 P.M.
- **Retrieval ship:** USS *Hornet*

A Not-So-Easy Landing

Despite hundreds of hours of practice on Earth, Armstrong and Aldrin found landing on the moon's surface a little tricky. As they approached the designated site, they realized it was covered with huge boulders, which meant they had to find another location quickly or abort the mission. They had just 30 seconds of fuel left

Moon Landing by the Numbers

6: the number of Apollo missions to successfully land on the moon: *Apollo 11*, *Apollo 12*, *Apollo 14*, *Apollo 15*, *Apollo 16*, and *Apollo 17*

12: the number of human beings who have walked on the surface of the moon: Neil Armstrong and Edwin Aldrin (*Apollo 11*), Charles Conrad and Alan Bean (*Apollo 12*), Alan Shepard and Edgar Mitchell (*Apollo 14*), David Scott and James Irwin (*Apollo 15*), John Young and Charles Duke (*Apollo 16*), Eugene Cernan and Harrison Schmitt (*Apollo 17*)

1: the number of *Apollo* moon missions unable to make a successful lunar landing (*Apollo 13* was forced to abort its mission following a catastrophic explosion in one of its oxygen tanks. The three astronauts—James Lovell, John Swigert, and Fred Haise—returned to Earth safely.)

2,415: the number of moon rocks and soil samples collected during the six successful *Apollo* moon missions; total weight: 842 pounds

4: the number of Lunar Rovers constructed

3: the number of Lunar Rovers actually used on the moon, for *Apollo 15*, *Apollo 16*, and *Apollo 17*

$38 million: the cost to design and construct four Lunar Rovers

2: the number of golf balls hit on the moon's surface by *Apollo 14* astronaut Alan Shepard

when they spotted an area free of debris and successfully brought down the module. Armstrong was unflappable on the communicator, but his heart rate, which jumped to 156 beats a minute during the final seconds of the landing, clearly illustrated the stress he was feeling.

What Did Armstrong Really Say?

Debate has raged for decades over Neil Armstrong's first words as he stepped out of the lunar lander and onto the moon's surface. Armstrong has long maintained that he said, "That's one small step for a man. One giant leap for mankind." However, forensic linguist John Olsson recently analyzed the original magnetic tape recordings made at Johnson Space Center and has concluded that Armstrong, who understandably was under a lot of pressure at that moment, left out the "a" as he spoke those famous first words. Regardless, Armstrong's inspiring observation will be a part of human history forever.

· ·

Match the Lunar Mission with the Name of its Command Module

· ·

1. *Apollo 11*	a. *Odyssey*
2. *Apollo 12*	b. *Endeavor*
3. *Apollo 13*	c. *Casper*
4. *Apollo 14*	d. *America*
5. *Apollo 15*	e. *Yankee Clipper*
6. *Apollo 16*	f. *Kitty Hawk*
7. *Apollo 17*	g. *Columbia*

(**Key:** 1-g; 2-e; 3-a; 4-f; 5-b; 6-c; 7-d)

How the Birds and the Bees *Really* Do It

Humans can get pretty kinky in the bedroom, but we don't hold a candle to some of the other critters on this planet. Here are just a few of nature's more bizarre mating habits.

- It's no fun being a male honeybee. Those "lucky" enough to engage in a mating flight with a virgin queen usually die after their genitalia snap off inside her.

- Flatworms are hermaphrodites, which means they have both male and female sex organs. During mating, two worms will "fence" with their penises until one is pierced and impregnated.

- Size matters—at least it does if you're a frigate bird. During mating season, males inflate their throat sacs while engaging in a wild dance. The females usually hook up with the males possessing the largest, brightest sacs.

- Size is also a consideration among Galapagos giant tortoises. When it comes time to mate, males rise on their legs and extend their necks; the male with the longest neck gets the girl.

- Orgies are all the rage among red-sided garter snakes. When a female awakens from hibernation, she releases a scent that attracts every male in the area. The result: a huge, writhing "mating ball."

- Male giraffes will not mate until they know a female is in estrus. To find out, they nudge a prospective mate's rump until she urinates—then taste her urine. If estrus is guaranteed, the male will follow the female around until she finally gives in to his advances.

- Male dolphins have very strong libidos. In fact, they enjoy sex so much that they've been known to mate with inanimate objects and even with other sea creatures, such as turtles.

- Percula clownfish live in families consisting of a mating male and female and several nonbreeding males. If the female dies, the mating male changes sex to become the female, and one of the nonbreeding males gets a promotion to hubby.

Big American Cities with the Worst Infrastructures

Year by year, our nation's infrastructure falls into deeper disrepair. Once viewed as the model of modernity, America's vital network of roads, bridges, utilities, and waterways has reached an alarming state. Limited funding and continued backbiting add to the dilemma. One thing seems certain: If you live in one of the following cities, you may want to be extra careful.

Minneapolis, Minnesota

The August 1, 2007, collapse of the I-35 bridge signaled a growing infrastructure crisis in the United States. When the span suddenly gave way, it swept away the lives of 13 people. Previous and subsequent checks have turned up problems with many of the city's spans. As is often the case with infrastructure in need of repair, funding stands as a near-immovable roadblock.

Atlanta, Georgia

When a drought hit Atlanta in 2007, the city's aging plumbing added to the crisis. Leaky pipes buried below the streets hemorrhaged as much as 18 percent of the city's water. But rotting municipal pipes aren't exclusive to this bustling Southern city. Sadly, the situation plays out clear across the United States.

New Orleans, Louisiana

Each year, 20 million tons of cargo move through the city's Industrial Canal Lock, a passage that leads to the Gulf Intracoastal Waterway. This vital commercial link is critical to the nation's economy, yet its 1921 design has rendered it nearly obsolete. At certain times, the undersized lock detains ships for up to 36 hours. Congress authorized the lock's replacement in 1956, but a mountain of red tape, including plan changes and community concerns, placed the project on indefinite hold. Work finally commenced in 2002 but was slowed when a judge ruled that the Army Corps of Engineers had failed to prepare a proper environmental study. No completion date has been issued, but the project is expected to cost nearly $1.3 billion.

New York, New York

The Brooklyn Bridge is among a growing number of crumbling spans and rotting roadways. With rusting structural steel and rotting road decks bearing testament to its neglect, the 1883 icon has been listed as "structurally deficient" by America's federal rating system. Repairs are slated to begin in 2010.

Nashville, Tennessee

In addition to its own infrastructure concerns, Nashville has another worry. A big one. If Kentucky's 55-year-old Wolf Creek Dam should burst—a very real possibility given its current horrendous state—the country music giant could be playing a sad tune. The mile-long structure impounds the largest artificial reservoir east of the Mississippi. When seepage holes were discovered along the reservoir's foundation, engineers dropped the dam's water level. The action offered a quick fix for a looming problem. If the dam should break, many cities along the Cumberland River, including Nashville, would be inundated. Thankfully, a $309 million upgrade is currently under way.

Sacramento, California

In 2007, the Army Corps of Engineers cited 122 American levees that were "at risk of failure." A disproportionate 19 were located along the Sacramento River. The Natomas Levee, in particular, poses an ominous threat. If it were to fail, its surging waters would place 70,000 area residents in deadly peril and would put the ARCO Arena and Sacramento International Airport under an estimated 20 feet of water.

Seattle, Washington

Like far too many American cities, Seattle is dogged by decaying infrastructure. Unlike most, however, the city is situated in an active earthquake zone. In 2001, an earthquake did serious damage to the Alaskan Way Viaduct—a major artery that runs through the city. Inspectors discovered earth subsidence of as much as five inches beneath the structure, a situation that foretells disaster if left unchecked. Options for repair remain mired in red tape. In the meantime, the seismic clock keeps ticking.

Chicago, Illinois

Traffic woes add mightily to Chicago's infrastructure headache. Considered the nation's third most congested, the Circle Interchange slows traffic to a crawl due to its outdated, tightly curved ramps. This produces an estimated 25 million hours of delays per year. The problem has yet to be addressed.

"Stadiums rise with tax dollars; schools and clinics crumble, in the same city. Grotesque!"
—Ralph Nader

Novel High School Team Names

Choosing team names is never an easy task—heck, even the professionals swing and miss every once in a while (the Utah Jazz, anyone?). When it comes to true mascot ingenuity, nothing beats some of the offerings of our great nation's high school athletic programs. Here are some of the most—how shall we put it—"creative" high school team names in the United States.

Arkansas School for the Deaf Leopards (Little Rock, AR) One can only imagine the "hysteria" that sweeps through the crowd when the Arkansas School for the Deaf's football team "brings on the heartbreak" to the opposition.

Hoopeston Area Cornjerkers (Hoopeston, IL) Hoopeston is located in central Illinois, one of the major corn-growing regions of the world. Still, that does not excuse a logo consisting of a maniacally grinning ear of corn that vaguely resembles Danny Bonaduce.

Hesston Swathers (Hesston, KS) Only in Kansas would a high school name its athletic teams after an obscure farming implement.

Poca Dots (Poca, WV) The Poca high school team mascot gets points for creativity, but that's about all the points it gets—the football team won a feeble two games in 2008.

Watersmeet Nimrods (Watersmeet, MI) No, Watersmeet Nimrods isn't the name of a made-up athletic team in a Monty Python sketch. Instead, the team is the terror of the equally whimsically named "Porcupine Mountain Conference" in upstate Michigan.

Sutherland Sailors (Sutherland, NE) Sure, "Sailors" doesn't seem like such an odd nickname—except that it's the team name for schools in Sutherland, Nebraska, a town whose nearest body of water, Lake McConaughy, is more than an hour away.

Fairbury Jeffs (Fairbury, NE) If the mascot is anything to go by, a Jeff is apparently a guy dressed in a top hat, red tuxedo coat, and yellow-striped pants. Oddly, not one member of the 2009 football roster is named Jeff.

Presidentially Speaking

*"If this is coffee, please bring me some tea;
but if this is tea, please bring me some coffee."*
—Abraham Lincoln

*"I can think of nothing more boring for the American people than to
have to sit in their living rooms for a whole half hour looking at my
face on their television screens."*
—Dwight D. Eisenhower

*"You know nothing for sure . . . except the fact that you
know nothing for sure."*
—John F. Kennedy

*"It's a damn poor mind that can only think of one way
to spell a word."*
—Andrew Johnson

*"I only know two tunes. One of them is 'Yankee Doodle,'
and the other isn't."*
—Ulysses S. Grant

"Man cannot live by bread alone; he must have peanut butter."
—James Garfield

*"Sensible and responsible women do not want to vote.
The relative positions to be assumed by man and woman in
the working out of our civilization were assigned long ago
by a higher intelligence than ours."*
—Grover Cleveland

*"I am only an average man but, by George, I work harder
at it than the average man."*
—Theodore Roosevelt

*"By 'radical,' I understand one who goes too far;
by 'conservative,' one who does not go far enough;
by 'reactionary,' one who won't go at all."*
—Woodrow Wilson

*"I have long enjoyed the friendship and companionship
of Republicans because I am by instinct a teacher and
I would like to teach them something."*
—Woodrow Wilson

*"I don't know much about Americanism, but it's a damn
good word with which to carry an election."*
—Warren G. Harding

*"When a great many people are unable to find work,
unemployment results."*
—Calvin Coolidge

20 Winning Wheaties Box Athletes

"Stone Cold" Steve Austin Remember when professional wrestling was fun and entertaining? Anyone? This Wheaties box may be the only chance Austin has to be mentioned in the same list as Olympians and Hall of Famers.

Glenn Davis This halfback and Heisman Trophy winner spent two years with the Los Angeles Rams.

Babe Didrikson Zaharias In 1935, the golf legend became the first female athlete to appear on the box, albeit on the back. (She also achieved success in basketball and track and field...did a breakfast cereal have anything to do with that talent?)

Tom Dolan This swimmer captured both an Olympic gold medal and placement on a Wheaties box.

Stacy Dragila This pole-vaulter won an Olympic gold medal and a Wheaties box cover. We wonder which she prized more?

Chris Evert She's got 18 tennis Grand Slam singles titles to her name and bragging rights as one of only seven official Wheaties spokespeople.

Doug Flutie Did Wheaties give him a taste for Flutie Flakes cereal? Is that who we hold responsible?

Hank Greenberg Not well remembered as a Wheaties box athlete, perhaps, but diehard baseball fans know of his refusal to play on Yom Kippur (the Jewish day of atonement) in 1934.

Joe Horlen Okay, everyone. Finish your bowl of cereal and pitch a no-hitter (as Horlen did for the Chicago White Sox in 1967), and the good people at Wheaties may come knocking at your door.

Bruce Jenner Hey kids! Before he became dad to *Hills* star Brody and stepdad to those Kardashian kids, Jenner was famous for winning the Olympic gold medal in the decathlon in 1976 (as well as for being an official Wheaties spokesman).

Bobby Layne This hard-playing and hard-drinking football Hall of Famer took his place on a Wheaties box in 1956.

Johnny Lujack The 1947 Heisman Trophy winner may not be remembered for his cereal connection, but in certain circles the guy is still revered for his days at the University of Notre Dame—not to mention his time with the Chicago Bears.

Tom Matte Baltimore fans may still warmly recall Matte, who earned a championship ring as a member of the Colts during Super Bowl V.

Billy Mills A Sioux Native American, Mills captured a gold medal as a runner in the 1964 Olympic games in Tokyo and fame as a featured Wheaties athlete. Oh, and Mills was a commissioned first lieutenant in the U.S. Marine Corps at the time too.

Rob Richards The "Vaulting Vicar" was an ordained minister, a two-time Olympic pole-vault champion, and the first Wheaties spokesman who also holds the honor of being the first athlete to appear on the *front* of the familiar orange box (1958).

Preacher Roe A great nickname for a pitcher with a great arm.

Jim Thorpe Why remember Jim Thorpe? After all, he was only one of the most versatile athletes of the 20th century, earning gold medals in the 1912 Olympics and playing semiprofessional and professional baseball, football, and basketball.

Lee Trevino The first golfer to appear on the front of a box (in 1969) before that Tiger kid came along and everyone forgot the name of anyone else who had ever played golf.

Bob Waterfield Another Wheaties footballer who (coincidentally) also earned enshrinement in the Pro Football Hall of Fame.

Esther Williams Wheaties officials seemed to have had a fondness for splashing swimmers on their cereal boxes, and it may have all started with this actress and former Olympian (she was also the ex-wife of actor Fernando Lamas).

Ancient Egyptian Pyramids and Burial Chambers

The Great Pyramid

- The Great Pyramid is the only one of the original Seven Wonders of the Ancient World still standing.

- The Great Pyramid held the title of world's tallest artificial structure for approximately 3,800 years.

- Number of limestone blocks used to build the Great Pyramid: 2 million

- Average weight of each block: 2.5 tons

- Number of years it took roughly 100,000 workers to build the pyramid: 20

Total number of Egyptian pyramids discovered as of 2008: 138

Estimated total percentage of Egyptian monuments still undiscovered by archaeologists: 70

The Curse of King Tut's Tomb

Mummies' curses have been the fodder of horror stories since the turn of the 18th century, but none has captured the popular imagination more than the Curse of King Tut's Tomb. The tomb was discovered in 1922 by a group led by British archaeologists Howard Carter

and Lord George Carnarvon, with eerie coincidences and untimely deaths supposedly following shortly after. Is there any credence to this curse? Here's a list of five events often offered as proof of the "Curse of King Tut."

1. Lord Carnarvon, one of the tomb's discoverers, fell ill and died shortly after the tomb opening: TRUE

2. Lord Carter's pet canary was eaten by a cobra—the symbol of the ancient pharaohs—on the day of the tomb's discovery: FALSE

3. An inscription above the door to the tomb read "Death shall come on swift wings to him that toucheth the tomb of the Pharaoh": FALSE

4. At the moment of Lord Carnarvon's death, the lights went out in Cairo: TRUE

5. Most or all of the people present at the opening of the tomb met tragic ends: FALSE

Seven Steps to Mummification

1. Wash and ritually purify body

2. Remove intestines, liver, stomach, and lungs; embalm them with natron (soda ash) and place in jars

3. Stuff body cavity with natron

4. Remove brain through nose using a hook; throw brain away

5. Cover body with natron and place on embalming table for 40 days

6. Wrap 20 layers of linen around body, gluing linen strips together with resin

7. Place mummy in protective sarcophagus, and add another layer of wrapping

World's Healthiest Foods

Four Best Brain Foods

1. **Blueberries** Blueberries are rich in antioxidants, which may help fend off the degenerative effects of conditions such as Alzheimer's disease.

2. **Wild Salmon** Salmon is loaded with omega-3 fatty acids—the kind of fat that helps create and strengthen brain tissue.

3. **Spinach** Eating a can of spinach may not make your muscles bulge like Popeye's, but it will increase serotonin and dopamine levels in the brain.

4. **Flaxseed** Sharpen your senses with a tablespoon of flaxseed oil per day. High levels of alpha-linolenic acid help improve cerebral cortex functioning.

Four Unexpectedly Healthy Foods

1. **Red Wine** *Vive la France!* A substance found in red wine known as *resveratrol* has anti-inflammatory properties and also helps to protect against heart disease.

2. **Chocolate** Chocolate has been shown to lower blood pressure, fight heart disease, and defend against cancer. Only dark chocolate or cocoa powder, though—so put down that Snickers bar.

3. **Blue M&M's** Okay, so M&M's aren't really *good* for you, but the dye found in blue M&M's has been shown to slow paralysis in rats with spinal cord injuries.

4. Coffee Coffee has been proven to markedly improve memory and cognition.

The Spice of Life

Four spices have been shown to have powerful health properties.

1. **Cinnamon** Recent studies indicate that this common spice helps control blood sugar levels, making it a good choice for Type 2 diabetes sufferers.

2. **Ginger** For centuries, ginger has been used to treat stomach ailments.

3. **Cayenne Pepper** Here's good news for those who like spicy food: Cayenne pepper has been shown to alleviate circulatory problems and to help the body fight infections.

4. **Turmeric** Since ancient times, turmeric has been used to treat conditions ranging from diarrhea to skin disease.

Lowest Rates of Heart Disease Deaths, by Country

The typical American diet isn't particularly heart-healthy, as illustrated by the fact that Americans suffer more than 106 heart disease deaths annually per every 100,000 people. Folks at risk for heart disease might want to check out the diets of the people in these countries.

1. Japan, 30 per 100,000

2. France, 39.8 per 100,000

3. Spain 53.8 per 100,000

4. Portugal 55.9 per 100,000

5. Belgium 64.6 per 100,000

Seven Scandalous Cults

Groups like these give cults a bad name.

Aum Shinrikyo The Japanese religious movement earned two strikes against it—as both a cult and a terrorist group—after members carried out a sarin gas attack on the Tokyo subway system in 1995. Japanese police began raiding Aum Shinrikyo locations days later.

Branch Davidians Followers of David Koresh looked upon him as one of God's messengers. Koresh thought of himself the same way. The U.S. government, however, had a different point of view (including allegations of polygamy, child abuse, and rape). Koresh and many followers of his religious sect were killed in 1993 when federal agents attempted to raid the group's compound near Waco, Texas. The ensuing 51-day standoff ended on April 19 when the Branch Davidian compound burned to the ground. The fallout wasn't limited to Koresh and company—the federal government was highly criticized for its handling of the situation.

Heaven's Gate UFOs and Comet Hale-Bopp were the basis of this cult, which was led by Marshall Applewhite. Members believed that Earth was about to be "recycled" and instead opted to commit mass suicide. Thirty-nine members of the cult (including Applewhite as well as the brother of *Star Trek* actress Nichelle Nichols) were found dead in a San Diego mansion in 1997.

Manson Family More than 40 years after his followers murdered Leno and Rosemary LaBianca and actress Sharon Tate, the name "Charles Manson" still sends a chill down the spines of many people. Manson was charged with murder and conspiracy and has been serving a life sentence. Among the members of the Manson family was Lynette "Squeaky" Fromme, who attempted to assassinate President Gerald R. Ford in 1975.

Order of the Solar Temple Cultists do like their space-aged names... even secret societies headquartered in Europe. Started in 1984 and based on the ideals of the Knights Templar, leaders sought to unify many different beliefs before the end of the world. Things went bad for the members in 1994 after one of its founders, Joseph Di Mambro, ordered the murder of the three-month-old child of another member. The reason? The child was the antichrist (at least according to Di Mambro). A few days later, members in Canada and Switzerland are believed to have killed other followers before committing suicide.

The People's Temple About 900 followers of a quasi-religious group led by Reverend Jim Jones drank cyanide as part of a mass suicide in Jonestown, Guyana, in 1978. Many experts view the event as one of the largest mass suicides in recorded history. For the record, Jones chose not to imbibe of the poisonous drink he offered the others. He shot himself in the head instead. Oh, but the story isn't over. Before things fell apart at his headquarters, Jones ordered a group of his followers to a nearby Georgetown airstrip to stop the departure of some People's Temple followers who had lost the faith. The armed men opened fire on the group as they were departing. Among those killed was U.S. Representative Leo Ryan of California, who had traveled to Guyana to investigate the cult on the behalf of concerned family members.

Unification Church Led by the Reverend Sun Myung Moon, the controversial church has faced allegations of fraud by some elderly members as well as highly publicized allegations of brainwashing, though these claims have never been proven.

"A cult is a religion with no political power."
—Thomas Wolfe

"The only difference between a cult and a religion is the amount of real estate they own."
—Frank Zappa

A Witch Doctor's Daily To-Do List

Once upon a time, a witch doctor was somebody who actually treated ailments that were thought to be a result of witchcraft. Over time, though, the term began to be applied—usually disparagingly—to traditional healers in societies seen as primitive by colonial powers. There are traditional healers in societies all over the world, but the Sangoma of southern Africa are the most prominent. Here's a typical day for your average South African witch doctor.

1. **Color-code your medicines** Black-colored medicine is used to detoxify the patient. White is used to purify, and red is for strengthening.

2. **Find your goat gallbladder, and tie it in your hair** Part of the witch doctor's initiation ceremony includes the slaughter of a goat; this goat's gallbladder, tied into the witch doctor's hair, is an important part of the wardrobe.

3. **Fill your goat horns, and grab your whisk** Goat horns filled with powders and medicines and a whisk made of a cow tail are two other important accoutrements for the Sangoma.

4. **See your patient** A recent survey indicated that 84 percent of southern African residents visit a witch doctor at least three times per year. Patients may seek cures for physical ailments, respite from bad dreams, or help finding lost objects.

5. **Get in a trance** The trance state is necessary for healing. Accomplishing the trance state can be done through the use of tobacco or other herbs, by beating on drums, or through meditation.

6. **Call your ancestors and throw your bones** Once in a trance, the witch doctor calls upon the ancestors for the solution to the patient's problem. Once the spirit of the ancestors enters the body of the Sangoma, the doctor scatters bones upon the skin of an impala and reads their arrangement for guidance.

It Happened in...April

- Ukulele player Tiny Tim believed that New Yorkers needed a musical mayor. New Yorkers obviously begged to differ. Tim withdrew his candidacy in April 1989.

- New Coke. 'Nuff said. (1985)

- April 15 isn't just the day your taxes are due. Also on April 15: The *Titanic* sank. Rand McNally debuted its first road atlas. Jackie Robinson broke the color barrier in Major League Baseball. Abraham Lincoln died. And Leona Helmsley was sent to jail for—go figure—tax evasion. Of course, all of these things didn't happen in the same year!

- Important big-time news flash! In April 1967, Davy Jones won the Most Popular Monkee Poll with 63 percent of the votes.

- In April 1956, Elvis made his Vegas debut with the Freddy Martin Orchestra and popular Las Vegas comedian Shecky Greene. The show was canceled after just one week due to poor audience attendance.

- America's first Washateria (aka Laundromat) opened in April 1934 in Ft. Worth, Texas, proving once again that everything—even personal cleanliness—is big in the Lone Star State.

- Wonder if they're trying to tell us something: Both the safety pin and the zipper were patented in April (of different years).

- A New Orleans businessman, Oliver Pollock, officially created the dollar sign ($) by drawing one line through an "S" in 1778. A few years later, Pollock lost his $ through poor financing.

- April is National Card & Letter-Writing Month (e-mail your friends and tell them!), National Kite Month, National Humor Month (too funny!), and Workplace Conflict Awareness Month.

Brazen Armored Car Heists

From Butch Cassidy to John Dillinger, bank robbers have captured the imagination of the American public. Here are some of the most brazen heists of armored cars in American history.

The Great Vault Robbery,
Jacksonville, Florida: $22 million

In March 1997, 33-year-old Philip Johnson, who made $7 an hour as a driver for armored-car company Loomis Fargo, took off with one of the cars he was supposed to be guarding. Johnson pulled off the caper by waiting until the end of the night, when the armored cars returned to the Loomis Fargo vaults. Johnson tied up the two vault employees, loaded an armored car with about $22 million in cash, and took off.

He remained on the lam for more than four months, despite a half-million-dollar reward for his arrest. He was finally arrested crossing into the United States from Mexico in August 1997.

The majority of the money—which had been stashed in a rental storage unit in rural North Carolina—was recovered shortly afterward.

Dunbar Armored,
Los Angeles, California: $18.9 million

Though not *technically* an armored-car robbery, the 1997 heist of $18.9 million dollars from the Dunbar Armored vaults in Los Angeles, is noteworthy for its meticulous planning and the fact that it is considered the largest armed cash robbery in American history.

The mastermind behind the theft was Dunbar Armored employee Allen Pace III, who used his knowledge of the vault's security system, along with his company keys, to gain access to the loot. Pace and his gang were eventually brought down when one of his cohorts, Eugene Hill, paid for something with a stack of bills banded in a

Dunbar wrapper. That, plus a shard of taillight that had been the only piece of evidence left at the scene, was enough for investigators to crack the case. Despite the arrest of Pace and several coconspirators, nearly $10 million of the haul still remains unaccounted for.

Armored Motor Service of America,
Rochester, New York: $10.8 million

In June 1990, a driver for the Armored Motor Service of America (AMSA) and his female partner stopped for breakfast at a convenience store near Rochester. While the female guard went into the store, a band of armed thieves attacked the driver, waited for the female guard to return, then ordered them to drive the truck to an unnamed location, where the thieves transferred the money to a waiting van, tied up the two guards, and escaped with the money. The total haul of $10.8 million ranked as one the largest heists in history. The robbery was also noteworthy for the fact that it remained unsolved for more than a decade. In 2002, though, the driver of the robbed AMSA truck, Albert Ranieri, admitted to masterminding the scheme.

Express Teller Services,
Columbia, South Carolina: $9.8 million

In 2007, two young men overpowered an Express Teller Services armored car driver when he and his partners stopped to fuel up. They drove the car to a remote area, where two accomplices waited with another vehicle to transfer the cash. The theft of $9.8 million was one of the biggest in American history, but it wasn't particularly well executed. First, the thieves didn't bring a large enough vehicle or enough bags to take the nearly $20 million that was in the truck. Next, the bandits savagely beat one of the guards, while leaving the other one—who was later arrested as the mastermind—untouched. But the gang really did themselves in by going on a weeklong spending spree involving strippers, tattoos, and Mother's Day gifts. Not surprisingly, just about the entire gang was arrested less than a week later.

What Is that Written on Your Dollar Bill?

Money is hard to come by these days. But that hasn't stopped artists from drawing, writing, and painting on dollar bills. Just ask all those poor George Washingtons wearing hats, fake mustaches, and glasses as they pass through drive-through windows and dollar-store cash registers.

Where's George?

Hank Eskin may be responsible, at least indirectly, for defacing more dollar bills than any one person. Eskin is the founder of the Where's George Web site, which since 1998, has allowed visitors to enter their local zip code along with the serial number of their dollar bills to track where those bills have traveled. As of June 2010, the site was actively tracking more than 173 million bills (not just $1 bills) with a total value of more than $937 million.

Where's George used to sell rubber stamps advertising the Web site, which people then used  to stamp their dollars. It's not unusual to find dollar bills today with some form of www.wheresgeorge.com stamped on them. However, the Web site stopped selling the stamps in 2000 following an investigation by the U.S. Secret Service. The agency informed the site's administrators that the stamps constituted a form of advertising on U.S. currency—something that is illegal.

Defacing Currency with Joe D

Who is Joe D? He's one of the busiest dollar-bill—any bill, actually—defacers today. The mysterious Joe D runs his own Flickr site, which catalogues his currency artwork. Some of his most famous work includes an extremely politically incorrect $5 bill that's been altered to show the left side of Lincoln's head being blown out by a gunshot and a $1 bill in which George Washington has been turned into Darth Vader—all with the skillful use of a ballpoint pen. Joe D's site also features George Washingtons that have been turned into red devils and green-haired Jokers of Batman fame, as well as a rather cute Abraham Lincoln who has been turned into a dead ringer for Mario of Nintendo video game fame.

Making a Statement

Some money doodlers seem to have a sense of humor. Several Web sites feature a dollar bill with the timeless question "Do you like root beer?" while another recommends simply if inelegantly "Write anything on more bills." Finally, if you ever end up with the dollar bill advising "If you see any writing on this bill call 1–800–5187," don't bother picking up the phone. There are three numbers missing from that phone number. And for the animal lovers out there, you have to appreciate the sentiment behind "Free the werewolves," another message printed on yet another dollar bill.

Money on the Wall

Some bar and restaurant owners have the right idea: They encourage their patrons to write silly messages on dollar bills and then stick them to the walls of their establishments. The messages may not always be clever, but it's not a bad way for a bar owner to make a few extra bucks.

The average dollar bill lasts a little less than two years before it's worn out and pulled from circulation.

An individual dollar-bill weighs a gram, as does a five-dollar bill. A 10-, 20-, 50-, and a 100-dollar bill are likewise one gram in weight.

Bragging Rights

Highest Scores Ever Racked Up on Popular Video Arcade Games

The days of begging your parents for quarters to use in the arcade are over. Now, video games are big business, raking in an estimated $35 billion annually and spawning professional leagues around the globe. Here are some high scores racked up by the world's best players.

Pac Man:
Billy Mitchell, Ft. Lauderdale, Florida, 3,333,360 points

In 1999, video game legend Billy Mitchell (yes, there are video game legends) took more than six hours to become the first person to get a "perfect" score on *Pac Man*—the most famous arcade game of all time—completing 256 boards while eating every dot, power pellet, ghost, and piece of fruit. Mitchell achieved his score at the Funspot Family Fun Center in Weirs Beach, New Hampshire, the unofficial proving ground for world-record–seeking gamers. According to Twin Galaxies, the official record-keeping institution of arcade gaming, it was the first perfect score in more than ten billion attempts world-wide since the game's invention.

Donkey Kong:
Billy Mitchell, Ft. Lauderdale, Florida, 1,050,200

Not content with the world's only perfect *Pac Man* score, Mitchell has been in a heated battle with rival Steve Wiebe for the *Donkey Kong* crown. (Wiebe has the second highest total ever at 1,049,100.) The rivalry has been so intense and has sparked such interest that an award-winning documentary, *The King of Kong*, was made about the pair in 2007.

Ms. Pac Man:
Abdner Ashman, Queens, New York, 933,580

Ashman is no Billy Mitchell, but he holds the world records for *Ms. Pac Man, Jr. Pac Man,* and *Robotron: 2084.*

Space Invaders:
Donald Hayes, Windham, New Hampshire, 55,160

Donald Hayes not only has the world record for *Space Invaders,* he also ranks in the top ten for dozens of other arcade games, including the classics *Galaga, Centipede, Dig Dug,* and *Q-bert.*

Other High-Scores Heroes

Tapper:	9,437,400	Kelly Tharp
Asteroids:	41,336,440	Scott Safran
Centipede:	16,389,547	Jim Schneider
Pole Position:	67,310	Les Lagier

Arcade Games by the Numbers

2: number of documentaries released in 2007 about the arcade gaming subculture

120,000: number of people who turned out to watch the 2005 finals of the SKY Pro League, a professional gaming league in South Korea

78,000: number of people who watched the Super Bowl in Alltel Stadium in the same year

$24,000: average annual salary of pro gamers

Gang Nation

Everybody knows about the Bloods and the Crips, but over the past century there have been thousands of street gangs prowling city neighborhoods around the world. And while most of these haven't had the success or notoriety of today's largest street gangs, it wasn't for a lack of good names.

Classic Chicago Street Gangs

From Al Capone's reign in the 1920s up until the 1980s, Chicago was America's undisputed "Gangland USA." For many gang historians, the "golden age" of street gangs occurred in Chicago in the 1960s and 1970s, when gangs sprang up in nearly every neighborhood. Some of the more unique gang names included:

The Almighty Bishops

The Stooge Bros.

Casanova Stones

Old Hatchet

Little Loafers

Mumchecks

Party Masters

Surprisingly, many of these gangs—sometimes little more than a few guys from the block—even came up with their own business cards, complete with a roster of gang members and hand-drawn logos.

Global Gangs

Street gangs are not limited to the United States. Here is a list of some street gangs around the world including their country of residence.

Mongrel Mob (New Zealand)

The Yardies (Jamaica)

First Command of the Capital (Brazil)

The Numbers (South Africa)

Cheetham Hill Hillbillies (England)

Bosozoku (Japan)

Indian Posse (Canada)

Least Intimidating Gang Names

Chaplains (Chicago)

Clovers (Chicago)

Young Asian Boys (Los Angeles)

Sane (Chicago)

Happy Gentlemen (Chicago)

Hawaiian Gardens (Los Angeles)

United Bamboo (Taiwan)

The South Side Winos (Los Angeles)

East Side Peckerwoods (Los Angeles)

Why You Buy

Supermarkets have gone to great lengths to make you think that "impulse" buy really was an impulse.

End Caps

The "end caps"—the shelves at the outer ends of each aisle—are the equivalent of beach-front property. Studies have shown that placing items on end caps can boost their sales by as much as a third. By giving items their own little plot of land, supermarkets convey the impression that they are special or that they are a good deal. Not necessarily. Just because something is on the end cap doesn't mean it's on sale. Worse, supermarkets sometimes use the end caps to move product that hasn't been selling that well—meaning those Little Debbie snack cakes you just threw into your cart might be expiring any day now.

Ambience

Mood lighting. Sample counters. Espresso bars. These days, high-end grocery stores like Whole Foods more closely resemble Macy's or Nordstrom than a traditional supermarket. That's because retailers know that the more welcoming you can make an environment—and the longer people spend in a store—the more people will buy (this is also the theory behind Wal-Mart's greeters).

But it's not just lighting and music. Supermarkets also use aromas to get you in the mood to shop. That's why you'll find the rotisserie chicken roasting near the entrance to many grocery stores.

Changing Locations of Items

For many people, the grocery store becomes routine—they purchase the same staples each week, and after a while, shoppers on autopilot begin to ignore the other items in the store. To combat this, grocery stores will constantly rotate stock. By shifting items—even within the same aisle—supermarkets can force shoppers to consider new—and hopefully more expensive—items.

Product Placement on Shelves

It's one of the fundamentals of marketing: People are lazy. But just how lazy is surprising. Study after study has shown that the average grocery shopper can't even be bothered to look at anything beyond eye level. Some supermarkets take advantage of this by putting the most expensive items on eye-level shelves in the aisles, while others charge suppliers a hefty fee for a spot there. Consumer experts suggest better deals can be found by simply checking out the items on the bottom or top shelves.

Putting Promotional Displays or Nonfood Items at the Entrance

When's the last time you walked into a grocery story and saw what you needed at the entrance? Probably never. Consumer psychologists have found that shoppers need a little time to get into the shopping mind-set. As a result, the entrance of grocery stores are known as something of a dead zone, sales-wise. That's why you'll often find magazines, books, and the flower department near the front of the store—anything to get the shopper into a more relaxed state of mind.

Advertising Nonsale Items in the Sale Flyers

Savvy grocery shoppers in search of the best deal head straight for the flyer rack when they enter a supermarket. Little do they know that those "sale flyers" are littered with nonsale items. Advertising items at their regular price alongside items that are actually on sale creates the illusion that the regularly priced items are a great buy.

By the Numbers

$820 billion: total annual U.S. sales of grocery industry (approximate)

$328 billion: total spent by shoppers on unintended grocery purchases, according to a 2008 survey

$98 billion: total spent by shoppers on groceries that go to waste, average year

Things You Don't Know
(and Didn't Need to Know) About...

The Penny

We collect them in jars, make them appear magically behind people's ears, and long for the days when a handful would get us a candy bar at the corner store. We handle thousands of them every year, but how much do we really know about the familiar penny?

- Since they were introduced in 1787, more than 300 billion pennies have been produced. Today, there are about 150 billion pennies in circulation—enough to circle Earth 137 times.

- Since 1909, Abraham Lincoln has been the star of the penny, but it wasn't always that way. There have been 11 different designs, including the popular Indian Head penny, which was introduced in 1859.

- The princess on the Indian Head penny was neither a Native American nor a princess. She was, in fact, the sculptor's daughter, Sarah Longacre.

- On the 200th anniversary of Lincoln's birth, the U.S. Mint introduced pennies that depicted four different representations of Lincoln's life. These replaced the Lincoln Memorial on the penny.

- Examine the faces on a penny, an original Jefferson nickel, a dime, and a quarter. All the presidents except Lincoln are facing left. People have long imagined a secret meaning behind this, but Victor David Brenner, the sculptor of the Lincoln penny, explained that he had worked from an image of Lincoln facing to the right.

- If you have a strong magnifying glass, you can see the initials of the sculptors who designed the pennies. Since 1959, the initials of Frank Gasparro have been near the shrubbery to the right of the Lincoln Memorial. Pennies dated 1918 to 1958 have the initials VDB (Victor David Brenner) under Lincoln's shoulder.

- Pennies haven't been made of pure copper since 1864. During World War II, the U.S. Mint helped the war effort by recycling:

It melted shell casings to make pennies. To conserve further, it considered creating plastic pennies but settled on zinc-covered steel. After the war, the Mint returned to a zinc-and-copper combination.

- Pennies have become popular souvenirs thanks to the penny-press machines at museums, amusement parks, and family vacation spots. These machines, introduced at Chicago's World Fair in 1893, flatten and elongate a penny between two rollers and imprint a new image—anything from an octopus to the Liberty Bell to Mickey Mouse. Each year, these machines roll out more than 12 million pennies into fun oval shapes.

- Money is shrinking—and not just in value. When the penny was introduced in 1787, it was about twice the size of today's version. The penny didn't shrink to its current size until 1857.

- See a penny, pick it up. There are about forty 1943 copper pennies in existence. One sold in 1999 for $112,500.

- You can't use pennies to pay your fare at tollbooths—unless you're in Illinois. Lincoln's home state has a soft spot for pennies.

- A coin toss isn't a game of luck if you use a penny and call heads. The penny is the only coin with the face of the same person on both sides. A magnifying glass will reveal Lincoln sitting inside the Lincoln Memorial.

- Could the penny be relegated to the endangered-coin list? Because the price of metals is rising, it now costs more than a cent to make a penny. It costs only about four cents to make a $100 bill.

- Pennies got their reputation as being lucky from the Victorian wedding saying "Something old, something new, something borrowed, something blue, and a silver sixpence in your shoe." In the United States, the penny replaced the sixpence as a guard against want for the newlywed couple.

- In 1839, the nickname for a U.S. cent was "Silly Head" because people thought the image of Miss Liberty on the front looked strange.

Biggest Soccer Riots of All Time

Despite its lack of popularity in the United States, soccer is by far the most popular sport worldwide. Only slightly less popular, though, is the less skilled sport of "soccer rioting"—also known as hooliganism. Here are some of the biggest riots in soccer history.

Lima, Peru: May 24, 1964

This one was a doozy. During an Olympic qualifying match between Peru and Argentina, frenzied Peruvian fans grew irate when referees disallowed a goal for the home team. The resulting riot left 300 people dead and 500 injured.

Calcutta, India: August 16, 1980

Tensions were already high in post-partition India when an official's call sparked rioting during a soccer match in Calcutta. The result: 16 dead, 100 injured.

Brussels, Belgium: May 29, 1985

Nobody does soccer riots like the British, who are so good they can cause riots in other countries. Take the case of the "Heysel Disaster"—a match in Brussels between British team Liverpool and Italian club Juventus. The game hadn't even begun when a crowd of drunk Liverpool supporters charged toward a group of Juventus fans. The stampede caused a stadium wall to collapse, resulting in 39 deaths and a five-year ban on all British soccer teams in Europe.

Zagreb, Croatia: May 13, 1990

In a grim harbinger of the ethnic violence that would ensnare the region over the next few years, Serbs and Croats fought each other before, during, and after a match between the Dinamo Zagreb and the Red Star Belgrade soccer teams, leaving hundreds wounded and throwing the city into a state of chaos.

Orkney, South Africa: January 13, 1991

Fights broke out in the grandstand during a game between the Kaizer Chiefs and Orlando Pirates after a disputed goal. In the ensuing rush of panicked fans trying to flee the fights, more than 40 people were killed and another 50 were injured. Ironically, most of the deaths were a result of being crushed against riot-control fencing. Fans of these two teams would combine for another riot in 2001, in which 43 people were killed.

Accra, Ghana: May 9, 2001

Unruly fans throwing bottles and chairs onto the field during a Ghanaian soccer match were bad enough, but to make it worse, police responded by firing tear gas into the jammed grandstands. The resulting panic killed more than 100 people.

Moscow, Russia: June 9, 2002

When Russia lost to Japan in the 2002 World Cup, Russian fans decided to express their disappointment by setting fire to Moscow. The ensuing riots left one dead and more than two dozen injured, including a group of Japanese tourists.

Basel, Switzerland: May 13, 2006

The Swiss might be neutral when it comes to wars, but they certainly are passionate about their football. Never was this more apparent than when FC Basel lost their chance to win the Swiss League title when FC Zurich scored a late goal in their match. The resulting riot—which included fans storming the field and attacking FC Zurich's players—resulted in more than 100 injuries and became known as the "Disgrace of Basel."

Manchester, England: May 2008

Observers knew there was going to be trouble when hooligans began fighting the day *before* the 2008 UEFA Cup Final. But the rioters kicked it up on a notch on game day, attacking police officers and lighting things on fire in a sad display that became known as the "Battle of Piccadilly." The impetus? Failure of a large television screen erected to give fans without tickets a view of the game.

Fill-Ins for the D-Word

How often have you gone to a funeral and heard one of the D-words? Chances are never. Instead we get creative and say everything but dead, death, *or* die. *If you think about it, most of the euphemisms don't even make sense and raise some interesting questions to chat about at the wake—after you've had a few drinks.*

Biting the Big One/the Dust Does she even have her dentures in?

Buying a One-Way Ticket To where? How much does this ticket cost? Can I get one from a scalper?

Buying the Farm If he was going to buy anything, it wouldn't be a farm. Bought the Porsche, maybe?

End One's Earthly Career Death and retirement are not the same thing—even though it sometimes feels like it.

Falling Asleep in the Lord First, if anything's going to give you insomnia, this phrase will. Second, "in the Lord"? Are we saying "the Lord" is a huge bed?

Giving up the Ghost Weird, isn't death taking *on* the ghost?

Going Toward the Light Wouldn't all the lights in his hospital room confuse him about which light was *the* light?

Gone to Her Just Reward She was mean and cranky. Doesn't bode well for how she'll be spending eternity, does it?

In a Better Place Are you sure? It could be a worse place.

No Longer with Us She isn't in Cincinnati or in the next room.

Passed Over Over what? Is this like jumping hurdles? If so, she was in no shape to pass over.

Pushing Up Daisies Truthfully, he was known for chopping down daisies with his lawn mower. Would he really want to spend eternity growing them?

Shuffle Off this Mortal Coil Does anyone know what a mortal coil is? The last person to use it in conversation was...Shakespeare!

SkyMall: The United States' Oddest Shopping Mall

Need a butler robot? (Who doesn't?!) How about an indoor doggie bathroom or a singing Christmas tree? Everything you ever wanted but totally don't need can be found in the SkyMall *catalog. Here's a sampling of what you've been missing.*

Interior Dog Restroom This rather disturbing product looks like a rectangular patch of grass. But when you lift the grass covering, you realize that this green isn't for putting: There's a collecting tray underneath. Yes, dogs are supposed to "use" the grass indoors when their owners just can't get them outside.

Kitty Washroom Cabinet The people at *SkyMall* don't discriminate against cats, either. The washroom cabinet resembles a big white box covered in wainscoting. This rather pleasant-looking piece of furniture, though, hides a stinky secret: Inside, owners can discretely hide their kitty's litter box.

Branding Irons Want to make sure that everyone knows it was you who barbecued that steak or charbroiled that burger? Purchase your own set of personalized branding irons to scorch your initials in the chicken thigh you just burned.

Richard the Lionhearted Throne The folks at *SkyMall* seem to be obsessed with the bathroom. If your plain toilet seat just isn't exciting enough, you can order the Richard the Lionhearted toilet seat. This commode capper comes inlaid with three regal lions against a rich blue background. Unfortunately, once you buy this throne, you're stuck with it. *SkyMall* won't accept returns "due to the nature of this product."

Batman Sword Letter Opener On the heels of the recent Batman movies comes the Batman sword letter opener. This seven-inch, stainless-steel blade is perfect for the business executive who wants to murder a rival while opening the morning mail.

17 Unusual Book Titles

1. *How to Avoid Huge Ships* by John W. Trimmer

2. *Scouts in Bondage* by Michael Bell

3. *Be Bold with Bananas* by Crescent Books

4. *Fancy Coffins to Make Yourself* by Dale L. Power

5. *The Flat-Footed Flies of Europe* by Peter J. Chandler

6. *101 Uses for an Old Farm Tractor* by Michael Dregni

7. *Across Europe by Kangaroo* by Joseph R. Barry

8. *101 Super Uses for Tampon Applicators* by Lori Katz and Barbara Meyer

9. *Suture Self* by Mary Daheim

10. *The Making of a Moron* by Niall Brennan

11. *How to Make Love While Conscious* by Guy Kettelhack

12. *Underwater Acoustics Handbook* by Vernon Martin Albers

13. *Superfluous Hair and Its Removal* by A. F. Niemoeller

14. *Lightweight Sandwich Construction* by J. M. Davies

15. *The Devil's Cloth: A History of Stripes* by Michel Pastoureaut

16. *How to Be a Pope: What to Do and Where to Go Once You're in the Vatican* by Piers Marchant

17. *How to Read a Book* by Mortimer J. Adler and Charles Van Doren

Some Registered Tax-Exempt Religions You've Never Heard Of

Perhaps you've read about Pastafarians who worship the Flying Spaghetti Monster. This so-called faith may inspire a few chuckles, but it's not a bona fide religion in the eyes of the U.S. government. But there are some surprising faith-based organizations that do qualify for federal tax-exempt status.

Take the **Ordo Templi Orientis** (OTO), aka Order of Oriental Templars, for instance. Founded in 1904 by British mystic Aleister Crowley, the group currently has 44 lodges in 26 states, including the Leaping Laughter Lodge of Minneapolis and the Subtlety of Force Encampment of Albuquerque. Based on a system of beliefs called Thelema, the OTO claims to promote the acquisition of "light, wisdom, understanding, knowledge, and power through beauty, courage, and wit." A fairly tall order for any faith.

Speaking of tall orders, **Eckankar** teaches that people can connect with other realities through out-of-body experiences. This faith has its roots in the Age of Aquarius and was founded in 1965 by American spiritualist Paul Twitchel. Followers call themselves Ecckists, and their leaders are referred to as Living Eck Masters.

The **Raelians,** by contrast, focus their attention on the future. Founded by French race-car enthusiast Claude Vorilhon in 1974, the Raelian Movement believes humans were created by extraterrestrials called *Elohim* who will one day return to Earth as foretold in Vorilhon's book *Let's Welcome Our Fathers from Outer Space.*

And finally, the **Monks of New Skete,** an offshoot of Eastern Orthodox Christianity, engage in a highly unorthodox practice. They train dogs, both as a source of income and as a spiritual pursuit. The monks have authored several popular books, including *How to Be Your Dog's Best Friend* and *I & Dog*. They even manufacture their own dog biscuits—a sure way to make a believer out of your pooch, if not out of you.

Five Obvious TV Cast Changes Maybe No One Will Notice

Ill health, educational pursuits, and a dislike for the job are just some of the reasons an actor may choose to depart a series. But do TV execs really think viewers are too stupid to notice the difference?

Batman Holy cast changes! Let's see...two Riddlers (John Astin and Frank Gorshin), three Mr. Freezes (Otto Preminger, Eli Wallach, and George Sanders), and two Catwomen (Julie Newmar and Eartha Kitt—three if you count Lee Meriwether in the *Batman* movie). The man behind the cowl, however, was always Adam West.

Bewitched The "original" Darrin—Dick York—left the comedy in 1969 due to back problems. He was replaced by the "new" Darrin—Dick Sargent. And no one ever said a word. (The series actually had multiple actor/character changes, though none as notable as the two Darrins.)

Cagney & Lacey Chris Cagney's badge was passed around a lot before landing in the hands of Sharon Gless. It started with Loretta Swit (of *M*A*S*H* fame) in the made-for-TV movie, then was passed to Meg Foster, who was dismissed for being too "aggressive," before being turned over to Gless.

Roseanne Oldest daughter Becky (Alicia Gorenson, who left to attend college) became oldest daughter Becky (Sarah Chalke) who became oldest daughter Becky (again, Gorenson). A few passing references to the switch were made, most notably in the series' final episode. The series also poked fun at the switch in one version of the opening credits.

The Munsters Beverley Owen never liked the role of "Marilyn Munster" on *The Munsters*, so few people (including the actress herself) were upset when the character was replaced after 15 episodes by Pat Priest. Priest became a part of TV history; Owen...did not.

It's Not You, It's Me

Fraternal twins come from two different eggs that have fertilized separately but implant in the womb together. Identical twins started out as the same fertilized egg, but that egg splits and each develops into two separate babies. With that in mind, here are a few famous twins of both kinds.

- Perhaps the most famous twins in history are Romulus and Remus. According to mythology, these identical boys were the victims of political jealousy and rage and were ordered to be killed, along with their mother. Abandoned rather than murdered outright, they were raised by wolves until a kind-hearted shepherd brought them into his home.

- The lovelorn and those in despair had two different advice columnists from which to choose: Ann Landers (real name, Eppie Friedman Lederer) began dispensing advice when she took over for a deceased columnist, using the same pen name, in 1955. A few months later, her identical twin sister (Pauline Friedman Phillips) created advice rival Abigail Van Buren (Dear Abby).

- While Chang and Eng Bunker were certainly not the first conjoined (therefore, identical) twins, they were arguably the most famous. Born in 1811 in Siam, they spent many years traveling as a sideshow exhibit with P. T. Barnum's circus. In their later years, they became gentlemen farmers, married, moved to North Carolina, and raised separate families. Other famous conjoined twins were vaudevillians Daisy and Violet Hilton and former slaves Millie-Christine, usually referred to by one hyphenated name.

- White House watchers had lots to watch when fraternal twins Jenna and Barbara Bush lived on Pennsylvania Avenue.

- If your household members are divided in their NFL loyalties, imagine what it's like at the Barber house. Identical twins Ronde and Tiki Barber play for different NFL teams.

- Other famous twins: Actresses Mary-Kate and Ashley Olsen (they're fraternal twins, believe it or not); country singers Jim and Jon Hager; and Ross and Norris McWhirter, creators of *Guinness*

Presidentially Speaking

*"About the time we think we can make ends meet,
somebody moves the ends."*
—Herbert Hoover

"A radical is a man with both feet firmly planted in the air."
—Franklin Delano Roosevelt

*"Do you realize the responsibility I carry? I'm the only person
standing between Richard Nixon and the White House."*
—John F. Kennedy

*"If one morning I walked on top of the water across
the Potomac River, the headline that afternoon would read:
'President Can't Swim.' "*
—Lyndon Baines Johnson

*"An atheist is a man who watches a Notre Dame–Southern
Methodist University game and doesn't care who wins."*
—Dwight D. Eisenhower

"If you can't convince them, confuse them."
—Harry Truman

*"When a man is asked to make a speech,
the first thing he has to decide is what to say."*
—Gerald Ford

*"Being president is like running a cemetery:
You've got a lot of people under you and nobody's listening."*
—William Jefferson Clinton

*"No matter how much cats fight, there always seem
to be plenty of kittens."*
—Abraham Lincoln

*"Leadership to me means duty, honor, country. It means character,
and it means listening from time to time."*
—George W. Bush

*"Free nations are peaceful nations. Free nations don't attack each
other. Free nations don't develop weapons of mass destruction."*
—George W. Bush

*"The fact that my 15 minutes of fame has extended a little longer
than 15 minutes is somewhat surprising to me and completely
baffling to my wife."*
—Barack Obama

15 Great Sports Upsets

Keep the faith! Because as Yogi Berra said, "It ain't over 'til it's over."

1. 1906 World Series

The Chicago White Sox defeat the crosstown Chicago Cubs. So what if the Cubbies won a record 116 regular season games that year?

2. 1919: Man O' War

Whoa, big fella! The horseracing legend loses his only race to a 100–1 long shot named Upset.

3. 1951 New York Giants

One swing of the bat was all it took Bobby Thomson of the New York Giants to launch the "Shot Heard 'Round the World." The walk-off home run enabled the Giants to take the National League pennant from the Brooklyn Dodgers with a 5–4 win as announcer Russ Hodges screamed, "THE GIANTS WIN THE PENNANT!" (The Giants fell to the New York Yankees in the World Series, by the way.)

4. 1959 Patterson–Johansson

Looking at the old photos, even Ingemar Johansson seemed shocked that he knocked down Floyd Patterson to claim boxing's heavyweight title in 1959. Patterson returned the favor the following year.

5. 1969 Super Bowl III

Joe Namath and the New York Jets weren't supposed to get past the domineering Baltimore Colts. Everyone said so. Everyone was wrong as the Jets toppled the Colts 16–7.

6. 1969 "Miracle Mets"

The New York Mets had never finished better than ninth place prior to 1969—the year they won the National League division and championship playoffs, not to mention the World Series. Truly "Amazin' " stuff.

7. 1974 Ali-Foreman

In 1974's "Rumble in the Jungle," George Foreman and Muhammad Ali squared off in Zaire for the World Heavyweight Championship. The bout was stopped in the eighth round, with Ali handing Foreman his first defeat.

8. 1980 "Miracle on Ice"

Who can forget the 1980 U.S. Olympic hockey team—a squad of collegiate athletes who defied the odds with a suspenseful 4–3 victory over their Soviet Union opponents. Broadcaster Al Michaels' cry of "*Do you believe in miracles?*" still resonates. Oh, and for good measure, Team USA then captured a 4–2 victory over Finland in the gold-medal round.

9. 1990 Douglas–Tyson

Mike Tyson was the undefeated heavyweight boxing champion in 1990. Then Buster Douglas delivered a punishing (and truly unexpected) defeat to the ill-prepared champ.

10. 1990 World Series

The Oakland A's had won 103 games in the regular season, so it made sense that they would easily take the World Series crown. No one told the Cincinnati Reds that as they swept Oakland in four games.

11. 1991 Final Four

Vegas odds-makers are still trying to explain Duke University's 79–77 win over top-ranked UNLV in the NCAA Final Four.

12. 2000 Olympic Games

American wrestler Rulon Gardner defeated Russian Alexander Karelin, who had been undefeated for more than a decade.

13. 2004 Boston Red Sox

The Red Sox win the World Series? Unlikely, since they were cursed by Babe Ruth. To make matters worse, they were down three games to none in the best-of-seven American League Championship Series (against the Yankees) and were trailing 4–3 in the bottom of the ninth. The rest is history as the BoSox later shocked the St. Louis Cardinals with a four-game sweep in the Fall Classic.

14. 2005 Chicago White Sox

Perhaps inspired by the Red Sox, the White Sox took baseball's crown in 2005, snapping their 88-year drought.

15. 2008 Super Bowl XLII

Poor Tom Brady. All he had left were good looks, a hot girl-friend, and lots of money after his New England Patriots fell to Eli Manning and the New York Giants. So much for the Pats' perfect season.

❖ ❖ ❖

"If you're in professional sports, buddy, and you don't care whether you win or lose, you are going to finish last. Because that's where those guys finish, they finish last."
—Leo Durocher, *Nice Guys Finish Last*

Surviving Life Behind Bars, Part 2

Headed to the Big House? No matter the length of your sentence, your time might be easier to serve if you know what to avoid once you get to prison. Here are a few no-nos..

- Don't borrow anything from anyone. It makes you indebted, and payback's a... Likewise, don't gamble, for the same reasons.

- Don't show weakness. Don't cry or whine.

- Don't discuss your crime, particularly if it involved anything of a sexual nature. Not only is it nobody's business, but that information gets around quickly.

- Don't try to smuggle anything into prison. You're not as smart as you think; the guards have seen it all.

- Don't trust anyone with your belongings; likewise, don't "watch" someone else's things. Petty disputes and forcing others to take sides are good ways to draw unwanted attention to yourself.

- Don't take sexual violence lightly. If a group of inmates threatens you, make it clear that you *will* retaliate. If you fight back, don't do so with lethal intent; a murder rap added to your sentence is the last thing you need.

- Don't ask for protective custody (PC) unless it's an absolute last resort. Being in PC brands you as a punk or a snitch, both of which will make it difficult (at best) to go back into the general population.

- Don't snitch. Just. Don't.

- No matter how comfortable you get while in prison, never let down your guard.

- Don't assume you'll have free access to just anyone on the outside. Phone usage is often restricted, and mail—both incoming and outgoing—may be censored.

- Don't cave in or freak out. You did the crime, and you *can* do the time.

Unusual World Customs

Table Manners

- In Italy, eat spaghetti as the Romans do: with a fork only. Using a spoon to help collect the pasta is considered uncouth.

- It is considered improper and impolite to use silverware to eat chicken in Turkey.

- Keep your right elbow off the table when eating in Chile. (Just be sure not to elbow your neighbor.)

- In the United States, one should never butter an entire piece of bread before eating it. The proper, if impractical, way to eat bread is to pull off a small bit from your larger piece and butter it before popping it into your mouth.

- In China, slurping one's food and belching at the end of the meal are considered acceptable and even polite.

- Tipping is uncommon, and even considered rude, in many Asian countries.

Personal Care

- Up until the 19th century, long fingernails were considered a symbol of gentility and wealth among the Chinese aristocracy. Wealthy Chinese often sported fingernails several inches in length and protected them by wearing special coverings made of gold.

- In ancient Rome, urine was commonly used as a tooth whitener.

- In many countries, toilet paper is unheard of. Instead, people wash themselves after using the bathroom, using their left hand. For this reason it is considered rude to use the left hand in many social situations.

Body Language

- In Chile, pounding your left palm with your right fist is considered vulgar.

- In Thailand, feet are considered unclean. Using one's foot to move an object or gesture toward somebody is considered the height of rudeness. Similarly, one should never cross their legs when in the presence of elders.

- When conversing in Quebec, keep your hands where they can be seen. Talking with your hands in your pockets is considered rude.

- Make sure to get enough sleep when traveling through Ecuador. Yawning in public is considered gauche.

Holidays

- The people of Ottery St. Mary, England, celebrate Guy Fawkes Day by racing through the streets of their town with barrels of flaming tar strapped to their backs.

- In many Latin American cultures, a girl's 15th birthday is considered one of the most important days of her life. Known as the *quinceanera,* the celebration can be as elaborate as a wedding.

- In Sweden, the Christmas season begins on Santa Lucia's Day (December 13), when the eldest daughter of a household, clad in white and wearing a wreath holding seven lit candles on her head, serves her family breakfast in bed.

Rituals and Traditions

- Until being banned in 1912, foot binding was common in China. The practice, which involved breaking girls' toes and wrapping them tightly in cloth, prevented women's feet from growing normally. Small, dainty feet were considered a symbol of status.

- In parts of India, some women still perform *sati,* an ancient custom in which a widow throws herself on the funeral pyre of her deceased husband to commit suicide.

- For almost 500 years, a form of conflict resolution known as "dueling" took place in western Europe and the United States. The highly ritualistic tradition began with the offended party throwing down his glove at the foot of another and ended with a sword or pistol fight—often to the death.

- In parts of Tibet, some people practice a funeral ritual known as a "sky burial." In this ceremony, the body of the deceased is dissected and placed atop a mountain as an offering to the elements and birds of prey.

It Happened in... May

- *Sesame Street* was banned in Mississippi in May 1970 because of the show's integration. The ruling was reversed later in the month.

- The first recorded auto accident happened in May 1896 in New York City when a man driving his car collided with a man on a bike.

- At the end of May 1964, almost a dozen boys were suspended from a school in Coventry, England, for sporting a Mick Jagger–like hair style.

- In 1907, Anna Jarvis, who loved her mother very much, began a letter-writing campaign to establish a nationwide annual Mother's Day. In May 1913, the U.S. House of Representatives unanimously agreed that mothers should have their own official day. The holiday didn't end up being what Anna Jarvis had in mind, but Hallmark is a fan.

- May 25 is Flitting Day in Scotland, the traditional day to move households or change residences. Scottish landlords usually learn early in February if tenants will "sit or flit," giving everybody plenty of notice to relax, pack up, or find new tenants.

- Big change occurred in May 1866: The U.S. Treasury Department added the five-cent piece to its lineup of coins. The first nickel had a shield on one side and the number "5" on the other.

- May is National Hamburger Month, National Moving Month (maybe the Scots are on to something), and—lucky you!—it's Get Caught Reading Month.

You Are What You Eat

When you enjoy your favorite Italian pasta dish, what exactly are you eating? Match pastas to their Italian translations so next time you can order Bridegrooms with Marinara Sauce or Worms and Pesto. On second thought... maybe you'd better stick to the Italian names.

1. Tortellini
2. Vermicelli
3. Spaghetti
4. Farfalle
5. Fettuccine
6. Fusilli
7. Linguine
8. Manicotti
9. Mostaccioli
10. Penne
11. Rotelle
12. Ziti

A. Springs
B. Butterflies
C. Mustaches
D. Worms
E. Ribbons
F. Wheels
G. Pens or Quills
H. Bridegrooms
I. Strings
J. Tongues
K. Twists
L. Muffs

Answers:

1-K; 2-D; 3-I; 4-B; 5-E; 6-A; 7-J; 8-L; 9-C; 10-G; 11-F; 12-H

Mall of America: Consumer's Delight

For fans of "retail therapy," Mall of America in Bloomington, Minnesota, is a little slice of heaven. Boasting 2.5 million square feet of retail space and more than 520 stores, it's the largest enclosed mall in the United States and the second largest mall in North America, after the West Edmonton Mall in Edmonton, Canada. Here are a few more fascinating fun facts:

- More than 40 million people visit Mall of America each year—that's more than the populations of North Dakota, South Dakota, Iowa, and Canada combined.
- Mall of America is so large it could hold 258 Statues of Liberty, 7 Yankee Stadiums, or 32 Boeing 747s.
- If Mount Rushmore were carved into four parts, a president would fit in each of the mall's four courts.
- The walking distance around one level of the mall is .57 miles.
- Regardless of season, the temperature inside the mall is always a balmy 70 degrees.
- More than 5,000 weddings have been performed at Mall of America since it opened in 1992.
- The mall generates nearly $2 billion in economic activity each year for the state of Minnesota.
- On any given day, four out of ten visitors to the mall are tourists.
- Mall of America employs 11,000 year-round workers—13,000 during peak periods.
- The mall's roof contains eight acres of skylights.
- More than 32,000 tons of trash are recycled by the mall each year.
- The mall's 100-member security force includes three bomb-sniffing dogs.

Masks Only a Robber Could Love

Do bank robbers actually wear Richard Nixon masks? Or is that just something we see in the movies? You might be surprised.

Laughing on the Inside

Hollywood gave us *Quick Change* in 1990, in which Bill Murray dresses as a clown to rob a bank. In 2008's Batman movie *The Dark Knight,* the Joker and his gang dress in clown masks to rob a bank of their own.

In real life, a gang of six thieves, some of whom dressed in clown costumes, robbed a jewelry store in the Mexican city of Guadalajara in July 2009. They got away with at least 1.2 million pesos worth— about $900,000 USD—of stolen goods. Police, though, might get the last laugh: In October, prosecutors filed robbery charges against two alleged members of the gang.

I'm Not a Crook. Well...

Patrick Swayze and company robbed a bank while wearing the masks of former presidents in *Point Break* (1991). One of the robbers wore a Richard Nixon mask, while the others wore masks of Jimmy Carter, Lyndon Johnson, and Ronald Reagan.

In October 2009, a robber wearing his own Richard Nixon mask held up a Dunn County, Wisconsin, bank at gunpoint. No word on whether he declared "I am not a crook," before he fled the scene.

He's Not Really Going Skiing

Countless bank robbers in movies and television shows have worn ski masks. In January 2009, a robber in Stow, Ohio, followed suit. Obviously having been taught the value of good manners, Feliks Goldshtein waited in line at the National City Bank branch behind several other customers. When he finally reached a teller, though, his good manners disappeared. He refused to take off his mask when asked and instead pointed a gun at the teller. The police caught Goldshtein after a short chase.

Who Knew?

Plastic Bottles

Okay, so you know you should recycle them. But every now and then, those plastic bottles come in handy for all kinds of projects around the house. Who knew?

- Tired feet love this one: Fill a two-liter soda bottle with hot water, cap it and roll it under your feet to warm your tootsies. Or fill the bottle with cold water and freeze to cool hot, burning feet after a long day.

- Keep your pantry neat with a two-liter plastic soda bottle. Cut the bottom off, turn the bottle upside down, hang it, and stuff plastic bags inside. The small opening acts as a dispenser. This works for storing string, too.

- Fill clean one-liter bottles with juice and freeze them. They'll keep items cold until lunchtime; by then, the juice will be thawed enough to drink.

- Speaking of freezing, fill a one-liter bottle two-thirds full of water and freeze it. Makes a great spill-proof ice pack for little boo-boos.

- The top half of a one-liter soda bottle makes a great water balloon filler. Just slip the balloon over the small opening and fill.

- Milk jugs aren't just for milk! Cut an empty jug at an angle to make a handy scoop. Slice the jug in half and make a funnel from the top part; use the bottom half as a disposable tray for a small paint job. A bottomless jug works great as a protector for delicate seedlings. Fill jugs with water for use as anchors or weights. Fill with sand for use as free weights in your home gym.

- Clean squeeze bottles from mustard or catsup make great summertime outdoor toys. Fill with water, hand them to the kids, and watch the fun. They are also great for bath time.

- Empty laundry detergent bottles make great portable carriers. Cut a medium-size hole opposite the handle and use for hauling whatever you need in and out of the garden, including small produce. Who knew?

Overdue

Just how long have you had the library's copy of War and Peace? *And when exactly are you planning to pay that $5.00 fine you've accrued? Read on to see how your library misdeeds stack up.*

The most overdue library book in U.S. history was never officially checked out. What's more, the man who took it thought it belonged to another library entirely. That's the story that emerged in February 2009 when book collector Mike Dau of Wake Forest, Illinois, showed up at the Washington & Lee University Library with volume one of W.F.P. Napier's *History of the War in the Peninsula and in the South of France.* According to a handwritten note on one of the pages, the book was taken on June 11, 1864, by Union soldier C. S. Gates during a raid on the area. Gates wrote that the volume came from the nearby Virginia Military Institute, which had been burned by the Union army.

The book passed to Gates's descendents and eventually ended with Dau, who noticed that the title page clearly indicated it had originally belonged to Washington & Lee—at that time known as Washington University. He decided to do a good deed and returned the book to the university's Leyburn Library 52,858 days after Gates had removed it. Librarian Laura Turner graciously waived the fine.

If you've accrued a hefty library fine and think you can ignore it, you might be in for a rude surprise. Rabbi Avrohom Sebrow of Queens, New York, found out the hard way when he applied for a mortgage and discovered an overdue library fine made him ineligible for the loan. The Queens Public Library had turned to a collection agency, Unique Management, to pursue lapsed fines. The agency reported Rabbi Sebrow's fine of $295.40 plus $66 in late fees to credit agencies. The embarrassed rabbi returned the overdue materials and cleared his record. He's still welcome at the library.

Perhaps we should all take a page from the book of 91-year-old Louise Brown of Stranraer, Great Britain. As of July 2009 she had borrowed (and returned) nearly 25,000 books from her local library. And she's never had to pay an overdue fine.

The Face of the Future?

Are you on Facebook? Odds are pretty good that your coworkers, your mom or dad, your kids, or your best friends from grade school are.

Harvard University is well known for its innovators. Adding his name to that esteemed number, Mark Zuckerberg (class of 2006) put together a Web site on February 4, 2004, that afforded students an opportunity to communicate en masse. Buzz about the Web site spread across the campus as quickly as talk of a free keg party. (Well, maybe not *that* fast!) Soon, Stanford and Yale universities joined the new, funky site. Realizing that he had tapped into something big, Zuckerberg dropped out of college (sorry, mom and dad; I'll make you proud regardless) and took the idea to the national level. Facebook was on its way.

Although it is considered one of the more user-friendly social networking sites, Facebook is actually staggeringly complex. But what else would you expect from a Web site featuring more than 300 million users in total, half of whom log on to the site every day? Of course, these figures only scratch the surface of Facebook's story. Behind each number is a person, and behind each person, a face. Get it?

Surprisingly, the fastest growing demographic on Facebook does *not* include teens or those in their 20s—even though these age groups are renowned for their keen interest in technology. In fact, it is the over-35 crowd (backhandedly referred to as "dinosaurs" by cyber-snobs) who are logging on in unprecedented numbers. Can you possibly believe it?

As is plain to see, there is nothing trivial about Facebook. Nevertheless, the Web site does harbor its quirky facts. According to *Forbes* magazine, founder Mark Zuckerberg is America's youngest billionaire (the Harvard dropout turned a ripe 26 in 2010), and his Web site ranks as the third largest in the world—bettered only by Google.com and Yahoo.com. Facebook also features its share of controversy. In 2008, Zuckerberg dished out $65 million as a final settlement to a long-running legal battle. The claim? That it was Zuckerberg's former roommate who actually invented the Facebook concept. Yikes!

Facebook sustains itself with U.S. offices in Atlanta, Chicago, Dallas, Detroit, New York, Venice Beach, and Palo Alto. Its international offices are located in Toronto, Sydney, Dublin, London, and Paris. The average Facebook user is said to have 130 friends in their personal network. More than 70 language translations are available on site. This is especially handy since 70 percent of Facebook users are located outside of the United States. Who knew?

Finally, what self-respecting Web giant would be complete without a bona-fide behavioral disorder named after it? Facebook Addiction Disorder (FAD) is said to be a legitimate problem that can strike anyone who doesn't use Facebook judiciously. No, we're not kidding. Actually, this isn't too surprising. In a world where 130 cyber friends are as accessible as one's fingertips, the Facebook-driven disorder was bound to gain ground. Particularly in those trendy coffee shops.

Facebook by the Numbers

3 billion: the number of photos uploaded to Facebook each month

14 million: the number of videos uploaded each month

35 million: the number of status updates posted each day

6 billion: the collective number of minutes Facebook users spend (waste?) on the site each day

Most Dangerous Toys

"You'll shoot your eye out, kid!" Anyone who has seen A Christmas Story *is familiar with this line from the movie, which follows (more or less) the story of a kid who wants a BB gun for Christmas. The familiar refrain from adult after adult: "You'll shoot your eye out, kid!" Yes, some toys are clearly dangerous. But it might surprise you to learn which toys are the most dangerous.*

You'll Want to Stay Away from These...

Over the years, numerous toys have been recalled because they posed a danger to users. Here are a few of the most hazardous:

1. **Gilbert U-238 Atomic Energy Lab** This one dates back to the 1950s, but it's a doozy. For $50, kids received three radioactive (yep, that's right—*radioactive*) compounds, a Geiger-Mueller radiation counter, and a Wilson Cloud Chamber. Perfect for the mad scientist in every family!

2. **Lawn Darts** Perhaps the most dangerous game ever created, steel-tipped lawn darts were responsible for an estimated 6,700 injuries and 4 deaths before they were finally taken off store shelves in the 1980s.

Toys by the Numbers

18: the number of toy-related deaths among children younger than age 15 reported nationally in 2007 (Most common causes of death: riding toys, including nonmotorized scooters, and small toy balls.)

232,900: the estimated number of toy-related injuries, among all ages, treated in U.S. hospital emergency departments in 2007

34: percentage of toy-related injuries involving children younger than five years of age

This Little Piggy Went Kaboom!

Japanese parents, like most, encourage their children to save money. But they're not on board with a quirky piggy bank introduced by TOMY toys in 2007. If the money-hungry porker isn't fed with coins on a regular basis, it explodes, showering those around it with loose change.

3. Easy-Bake Oven An oven door that trapped little fingers and a painfully hot light bulb led to this toy being recalled in 2007.

4. Clackers Two acrylic spheres connected by a cord, Clackers were popular among kids in the 1970s. Unfortunately, the spheres had a nasty habit of smacking users in the face or un-expectedly shattering on impact.

5. Aqua Dots These Chinese-made craft sets featured tiny beads that could be sprayed with water to create a sculpture. On the downside, the dots metabolized into the date-rape drug gamma hydroxybutyrate (GHB) when swallowed. Good thing little kids don't put stuff in their mouths—oh, wait a minute...

6. Snacktime Cabbage Patch Dolls Designed to teach kids how to feed their younger siblings, the dolls' mechanized jaws munched on anything placed inside them—including children's hands.

7. Creepy Crawler Thingmaker The idea was simple: Pour plastic goop into a mold then cook at 310 degrees. The result? For many, a trip to the ER.

Things You Don't Know (and Didn't Need to Know) About...

GI Joe

GI Joe is not a doll. No way. He's an action figure. A "fighting man from head to toe." Who cares that he once said "Let's go shopping" in a high, sweet voice?

- Joe was said to have been based on a 1963 television show called *The Lieutenant* and named after a movie, *The Story of G.I. Joe.*

- Brainstorming developers, seeing the popularity of Barbie, thought that a similar toy for boys would be a good idea and marched forward with the concept. At the beginning, Joe had 75 different products at his disposal, all relating to the U.S. military.

- Because the original 1964 Joe had 21 movable parts (including his waist), his twist-n-turn ability predated Mattel's Barbie (who got her twist-n-turn ability in 1967).

- Though GI Joe was a he-man through and through, he had a female counterpart: GI Nurse (GI Jane to collectors), who in 1967 came with all sorts of medical accoutrements for her own M*A*S*H. She only lasted a year before her enlistment was up; boys didn't want a girl doll, and girls avoided anything to do with GI Joe.

- Current events shaped GI Joe considerably: When controversy over the Vietnam War began to hurt sales, Hasbro (makers of GI Joe) reassigned his platoon to an Adventure Team.

- Every baby boomer boy remembers his GI Joe as being 12″ tall, but Joe shrunk to 8½″ when he became Super Joe in 1977. Shortly thereafter—partly because smaller *Star Wars* action figures became so wildly popular—Joe retired from toy stores. But old soldiers never die: Joe made a comeback, reenlisting in 1982 as a 3″ action figure and later, as a limited-time, larger "Classic" collectible.

- Joe was never officially called a "doll." He had a brush with doll-dom in 1993, though, when social pranksters switched his voice with Barbie's and replaced both toys on store shelves.

Candy Bars that No Longer Exist

The first candy bar was manufactured in Norway in 1906. Within a few decades, candy lovers on both sides of the Atlantic had more than 5,000 different bars to choose from. Some, such as Baby Ruth (introduced in 1921) and Mr. Goodbar (1925), are still around. Others have not been so fortunate.

- The Seven Up Bar, manufactured by the Pearson's Candy Company of Minnesota from 1951 to 1979, had seven individual sections, each with a different creamy filling covered in milk or dark chocolate.

- Chicken Dinner certainly wins the award for the candy bar with the strangest name. A chocolate-covered caramel peanut roll, it was made by the Sperry Company of Milwaukee from around 1920 until the company was sold in 1962. Sperry also produced a bar named Cold Turkey, but the ingredients are, alas, unknown.

- Powerhouse, a quarter-pound bar of peanuts, caramel, and fudge, even had its own comic strip superhero, Roger Wilco, who offered kids prizes in return for a wrapper and 15¢. He always reminded his fans that "Candy is delicious food." The bar, originally manufactured by Walter Johnson Candy, sold from the 1920s until 1988.

- The Marathon Bar introduced by the Mars Company in 1974 also had its own cartoon spokesmen—Marathon Mike and the Pirates. The eight-inch-long braided roll of caramel-covered chocolate was discontinued in 1981.

- Nestle's Triple-Decker—three layers of dark, milk, and white chocolate in one bar—sold from the 1940s to the 1970s. The company reportedly stopped making it because the cost was too high.

- Last but not least, the Good News bar was saved in the nick of time by loyal fans in Hawaii. Introduced in the late 1930s, this combination of chocolate, peanuts, and caramel really caught on in the islands. When the company tried to discontinue it, the natives rose up in protest. Thanks to them, it is still sold today, but only in Hawaii.

Olympic Disasters

After years of training, even Olympic-caliber athletes are vulnerable to last-minute injuries that dash their hopes. Athletes are sidelined by everything from the common pulled muscle or cold to more unexpected ailments. For instance, in 1912 Sweden's cyclist Carl Landsberg was hit by a motor wagon during a road race and was dragged down the road. The performance of runners Pekka Vasala (Finland) and Silvio Leonard (Cuba) suffered in 1968 and 1976 when Vasala got Montezuma's Revenge and Leonard cut his foot on a cologne bottle. Perhaps the most memorable Olympic disaster was when Janos Baranyai of Hungary dislocated his elbow while lifting 148 kg during the 2008 Beijing Olympics. Who knew the Olympics could be so dangerous?

- The U.S. track-and-field team for the 1900 Paris games was weakened because the French unexpectedly held events on the Sabbath. Several universities forbade their collegiate athletes to compete.

- Runner Harvey Cohn was almost swept overboard, and six athletes required medical treatment, when the SS *Barbarossa* was hit by a large wave enroute to Athens in 1906. Several favored U.S. athletes did poorly or dropped out because of their "ocean adventure."

- Francisco Lazaro of Portugal collapsed during the 1912 marathon and died the next day from sunstroke.

- After losing his opening round at the Berlin 1936 Olympics, Thomas Hamilton-Brown, a lightweight boxer from South Africa, drowned his sorrows with food. But the competitors' scores had accidentally been switched. Sadly, the damage was done—a five-pound weight gain kept Hamilton-Brown from the final round.

- Shortly after arriving in London for the 1948 Olympics, Czech gymnast Eliska Misakova was hospitalized. She died of infantile paralysis the day her team competed and won the gold. At the award ceremony, the Czech flag was bordered in black.

- During the 1960 cycling road race in Rome, Dane Knut Jensen suffered sunstroke, fractured his skull in a fall, and died.

- In 1960, Wym Essajas, Suriname's sole athlete, misunderstood the schedule and missed his 800-meter race. Suriname couldn't send another athlete to the Olympics until 1972.

- Australian skier Ross Milne died during a practice run for the men's downhill at Innsbruck in 1964 after smashing into a tree.

- Mexico City's altitude of 7,347 feet slowed the times of endurance events in the 1968 games. Three men running the 10,000-meter were unable to finish while others fell unconscious at the finish line.

- The Munich Massacre of 1972 resulted in the deaths of eleven Israeli athletes, five Palestinian terrorists, and one German policeman after the kidnapping of the athletes.

- In 1972, U.S. runners Eddie Hart, Rey Robinson, and Robert Taylor, supplied with an outdated schedule, rushed to the 100-meter semifinals at the last minute. Hart and Robinson, both winners in the quarterfinals, missed their heats. Taylor ran and won the silver medal.

- Sixteen-year-old swimmer Rick DeMont took two Marex pills for an asthma attack the day before his 400-meter freestyle race. His gold medal was revoked when he failed the drug test. The 1972 team physicians never checked to see whether his prescription contained banned substances. The same thing happened to Romanian gymnast Andreea Raducan in 2000. She was stripped of her gold medal for the all-around competition when she tested positive for the banned substance pseudoephedrine—an ingredient in the cold medicine provided by team doctors.

- In 1996, two people were killed and 111 were injured when American Eric Robert Rudolph detonated a bomb at the Atlanta Olympics.

- During the 2010 Winter Olympics in Vancouver, Georgian luger Nodar Kumaritashvili died during a training run on the luge track, losing control of his sled in a tight turn and crashing headlong into a steel support pole. Kumaritashvili's death prompted officials to alter the luge course in an attempt to make it less dangerous. Sadly, the modifications came too late for Nodar.

The A to Z of IM-ing

Interpersonal communication keeps getting faster. Writing letters took too long, so people became adept at the quick phone call, which was largely replaced by e-mail. Instant messaging offers the speediest way to express yourself, but only if you know the lingo.

AFK: Away from keyboard

ADN: Any day now

AYTMTB: And you're telling me this because?

BRB: Be right back

BTA: But then again

BTDT: Been there, done that

CRBT: Crying really big tears

CU: See you

CUL8R: See you later

DEGT: Don't even go there!

DIKU: Do I know you?

DQMOT: Don't quote me on this

EG: Evil grin

EOM: End of message

FICCL: Frankly, I couldn't care less

FWIW: For what it's worth

FYEO: For your eyes only

GD/R: Grinning, ducking, and running

GGOH: Gotta get outta here

GMTA: Great minds think alike

HB: Hurry back

H&K: Hugs and kisses

H2CUS: Hope to see you soon

IB: I'm back

IDTS: I don't think so

IMHO: In my humble opinion

JIC: Just in case

J/K: Just kidding

JMO: Just my opinion

KIT: Keep in touch

KOTL: Kiss on the lips

KWIM: Know what I mean?

LOL: Laughing out loud

LTNS: Long time no see

MOS: Mother over shoulder

MTFBWU: May the Force be with you

NM: Never mind

NMU: Not much, you?

NOYB: None of your business

OMG: Oh my God

OTH: Off the hook

OTTOMH: Off the top of my head

P911: My parents are in the room

PRW: Parents are watching

PU: That stinks!

QIK: Quick

QT: Cutie

RME: Rolling my eyes

ROTFLUTS: Rolling on the floor laughing, unable to speak

SH: Same here

SMHID: Scratching my head in disbelief

SSIF: So stupid it's funny

TIC: Tongue-in-cheek

TMI: Too much info

TNSTAAFL: There's no such thing as a free lunch

UCMU: You crack me up!

UV: Unpleasant visual

VEG: Very evil grin

VSF: Very sad face

WH5: Who, what, where, when, why?

WOMBAT: Waste of money, brains, and time

X: Kiss

XLNT: Excellent

YG2BKM: You've got to be kidding me

YKWYCD: You know what you can do

ZUP: What's up?

Zzzz: Bored

16 Unusual Facts About the Human Body

1. Don't stick out your tongue if you want to hide your identity. Similar to fingerprints, everyone also has a unique tongue print!

2. Your pet isn't the only one in the house with a shedding problem. Humans shed about 600,000 particles of skin every hour. That works out to about 1.5 pounds each year, so the average person will lose around 105 pounds of skin by age 70.

3. An adult has fewer bones than a baby. We start off life with 350 bones, but because bones fuse together during growth, we end up with only 206 as adults.

4. Did you know that you get a new stomach lining every three to four days? If you didn't, the strong acids your stomach uses to digest food would also digest your stomach.

5. Your nose is not as sensitive as a dog's, but it can remember 50,000 different scents.

6. The small intestine is about four times as long as the average adult is tall. If it weren't looped back and forth upon itself, its length of 18 to 23 feet wouldn't fit into the abdominal cavity, making things rather messy.

7. This will really make your skin crawl: Every square inch of skin on the human body has approximately 32 million bacteria on it, but fortunately, the vast majority of them are harmless.

8. The source of smelly feet, like smelly armpits, is sweat. And people sweat buckets from their feet. A pair of feet have 500,000 sweat glands and can produce more than a pint of sweat per day.

9. The air from a human sneeze can travel at speeds of 100 miles per hour or more—another good reason to cover your nose and mouth when you sneeze or to duck when you hear one coming.

10. Blood has a long road to travel: Laid end to end, there are about 60,000 miles of blood vessels in the human body. And the hard-working heart pumps the equivalent of 2,000 gallons of blood through those vessels every day.

11. You may not want to swim in your spit, but if you saved it all up, you could. In a lifetime, the average person produces about 25,000 quarts of saliva—enough to fill two swimming pools!

12. By 60 years of age, 60 percent of men and 40 percent of women will snore. But the sound of a snore can seem deafening. While snores average around 60 decibels (the noise level of normal speech), they can reach more than 80 decibels. Eighty decibels is as loud as the sound of a pneumatic drill breaking up concrete. Noise levels over 85 decibels are considered hazardous to the human ear.

13. Blondes may or may not have more fun, but they definitely have more hair. Hair color helps determine how dense the hair on your head is, and blondes (only natural ones, of course) top the list. The average human head has 100,000 hair follicles, each of which is capable of producing 20 individual hairs during a person's lifetime. Blondes average 146,000 follicles. People with black hair tend to have about 110,000 follicles, while those with brown hair are right on target with 100,000 follicles. Redheads have the least dense hair, averaging about 86,000 follicles.

14. If you're clipping your fingernails more often than your toenails, that's only natural. The nails that get the most exposure and are used most frequently grow the fastest. Fingernails grow fastest on the hand that you write with and on the longest fingers. On average, nails grow about one-tenth of an inch each month.

15. No wonder babies have such a hard time holding up their heads: The human head is one-quarter of our total length at birth but only one-eighth of our total length by the time we reach adulthood.

16. If you say that you're dying to get a good night's sleep, you could mean that literally. You can go without eating for weeks without succumbing, but ten days is tops for going without sleep. After ten days, you'll be asleep—forever!

Three-Ring Tragedies

For more than 200 years, various circuses have brought smiles to the faces of American children of all ages. They're popular attractions, but they've also been the scene of horrendous disasters. Here are five of the most memorable.

The Wallace Brothers Circus Train Disaster

On August 6, 1903, two trains owned by the Wallace Brothers Shows were involved in a calamitous rear-end collision at the Grand Trunk Railroad Yard in Durand, Michigan. Twenty-three people were killed instantly, and several others died shortly after; nearly 100 individuals were injured. Numerous animals also perished in the crash, including three camels, an Arabian horse, a Great Dane, and an elephant named Maud.

The *Owosso Argus Press* described the aftermath this way: "The scene that followed is indescribable, the cries and groans from the injured persons and frightened passengers, the roars from the terrified animals and the escaping steam aroused the whole city, and hundreds rushed to the scene to assist in every way in the sad task of caring for the dead and wounded."

The Hagenbeck-Wallace Circus Train Disaster

In the early morning hours of June 22, 1918, the Hagenbeck-Wallace Circus train was struck by an empty troop train just outside Hammond, Indiana. Of the 300 passengers asleep in the circus train, 86 were killed and more than 127 were injured. As a result of the ensuing fire, fed by the wood-constructed Pullman cars, many of the dead were burned beyond recognition.

Thanks to assistance from its competitors, including Ringling Brothers and Barnum & Bailey, which loaned equipment and performers, the Hagenbeck-Wallace Circus had to cancel only two performances.

The Hartford Circus Fire

Perhaps the nation's best-known circus disaster is the devastating fire that broke out during an afternoon performance of the Ringling Brothers and Barnum & Bailey Circus on July 6, 1944, in Hartford, Connecticut. An estimated 167 people—most of them children—died in the blaze and the ensuing mayhem, and several hundred were injured (exact totals vary depending on the source). The cause of the fire remains a mystery, but investigators blame the speed with which the fire spread on the fact that the massive circus tent had been waterproofed by coating it with gasoline and paraffin.

The Death of Jumbo the Elephant

Standing 11 feet tall, Jumbo was one of the star attractions of the Barnum & Bailey Circus when the celebrated pachyderm was struck and killed by a train at a marshaling yard in St. Thomas, Ontario, Canada, on September 15, 1885. Ever the showman, Barnum told the press at the time that Jumbo had managed to toss a younger elephant to safety right before the train struck, though eyewitness accounts suggest the story isn't true.

Barnum had acquired Jumbo from the London Zoological Gardens for $10,000 in 1882. After Jumbo's death, his skeleton was donated to the American Museum of Natural History in New York City; his heart was sold to Cornell University; and his hide was stuffed and mounted. Barnum continued to exhibit Jumbo's remains until 1889, at which time he donated the stuffed behemoth to Tufts University, where it was displayed until destroyed by a fire in 1975.

The Death of Karl Wallenda

The "Flying Wallendas" were one of the most publicized tightrope acts in modern circus history, dazzling audiences with amazing stunts such as the seven-person chair pyramid. But on March 22, 1978, Karl Wallenda, the family's 73-year-old patriarch, fell to his death during a promotional tightrope walk in San Juan, Puerto Rico. His was not the first family tragedy—Karl's sister-in-law Rietta Wallenda fell to her death in 1963, and his son-in-law, Richard Guzman, was killed in 1972 when he accidentally touched a live wire while holding part of the metal rigging.

The Way the Future Wasn't...

Cities Under Glass

*The vision of cities flourishing under glass domes dates back
to the science fiction of the late 19th century. During the early
20th century, futuristic pictures of urban life frequently depicted
gigantic overturned bowls protecting people and buildings
from the elements. But it was little Winooski, Vermont, that
almost became the world's first real domed city.*

In 1979, rising fuel oil prices had given Winooski residents a chill.
One fateful night, Mark Tisan, a 32-year-old community development planner, came up with a novel idea. Why not enclose the entire
city under a glass dome?

Though it seems incredible in retrospect, city officials encouraged
Tisan to pursue federal funding for the newly christened Winooski
Dome Project. Tisan called a press conference. Within a few days
the story had gone viral, and he began to receive a flood of mail from
people all over the world eager to help.

Tisan didn't even know what the dome would look like, so he
hired conceptual architect John Anderson, who quickly whipped
up a design for a clear vinyl structure supported by a web of metal
struts. Shaped rather like a hamburger bun with a wide, flat top, the
dome would measure 250 feet high and encompass an area of one
square mile—most of the residential city. Of course there were still a
few kinks in the plan—like how to get rid of auto exhaust and other
fumes. Tisan remained undeterred. He assured skeptics that electric
cars and similar innovations would solve any potential problems.

All systems were go for Winooski to become the city of the future.
Engineer Buckminster Fuller, designer of the geodesic dome,
endorsed the project, as did President Jimmy Carter. Carter, however,
lost his bid for reelection to conservative Ronald Reagan. In 1980,
the government turned down Tisan's request for funds, and the dome
disappeared into the mists of history as if it had never happened.

Things You Don't Know (and Didn't Need to Know) About...

Pop-Tarts

Since the 1970s, rumors have been circulating about exploding Strawberry Pop-Tarts. In 1994, computer scientist Patrick Michaud performed an experiment called "Strawberry Pop-Tart Blow-Torches." The study confirmed that the tarts were a potential fire hazard capable of causing flames of up to three feet high to shoot from the toaster if the Pop-Tart was left in too long. Read on to find out more than you ever wanted to know about Pop-Tarts.

- After examining sales data in the wake of Hurricane Charley in 2004, Wal-Mart executives discovered that Strawberry Pop-Tarts sold at seven times their normal rate in the days leading up to the hurricane.

- Even without hurricanes, Americans devour about two billion Pop-Tarts each year—enough to stretch halfway to the moon.

- Some lucky celebrities get to have a tart named after them. Back in 2005, Barbie had her very own flavor, Barbie Sparkleberry, with her picture stamped on the frosting. Other celebrity-themed tarts have included Indiana Jones Brown Sugar Cinnamon, American Idol Blue Raspberry, and Disney Princess Jewelberry.

- Kellogg's is always introducing new flavors. Over the years, the company has marketed Wild Watermelon, Guava Mango, and Chocolate Chip Cookie Dough.

- Frosted Strawberry is the favorite flavor of Bill Post of Glen Arbor, Michigan, the plant manager who invented Pop-Tarts back in 1963. He has "Pop-Tarts" engraved on his personalized license plate and sometimes drives over to the local supermarket just to hang out in the Pop-Tarts aisle. "I like to stand there and watch customers take them off the shelves," he told a reporter from Michigan's *Northern Express* on the tarts' 40th anniversary in 2003. Do his tarts ever catch fire in the toaster? No. He says he prefers to eat them raw.

Deadly Jobs

Looking for a new job? The U.S. Bureau of Labor Statistics has compiled a list of occupations you might want to avoid if your safety is a big concern.

According to the bureau's Census of Fatal Occupational Injuries, a total of 5,488 workers died from injuries they suffered on the job in 2007 (the most recent year for which such stats are available). The most dangerous occupations in the United States are:

1. **Commercial Fishing** Fishers had the highest rate of fatalities for any occupation in 2007, with nearly 112 of every 100,000 of them dying. Most of these deaths took place on fishing boats working off the sometimes frozen coasts of Alaska and Maine.

2. **Loggers** Commercial loggers also work in a dangerous profession. Nearly 87 out of every 100,000 loggers died from work-related injuries in 2007. The dangers are obvious in this profession: Loggers often work from great heights; they are in constant danger of having large tree limbs fall on them; and they often work in remote locations—far from medical help.

3. **Commercial Pilots** Flying may be a dream career for many, but it's also a dangerous one. The Census of Fatal Occupational Injuries reports that pilots died at a rate of 67 out of every 100,000 in 2007.

4. **Iron and Steel Workers** Despite manufacturing declines, iron and steel are still big industries in much of the country. But working in a steel mill, with heavy machinery and blazing-hot temperatures, can be deadly. Steelworkers died at a rate of 45 for every 100,000 in 2007 because of workplace injuries.

5. **Farmers and Ranchers** It may be a surprise to some, but farming and ranching can be a dangerous profession too. According to the Bureau of Labor Statistics, farmers and ranchers died at a rate of about 38 for every 100,000 from job-related injuries in 2007.

Things You Don't Know (and Didn't Need to Know) About...

Barbie

"Born" in 1959 and sold worldwide, Barbara Millicent Roberts is one of the most popular dolls ever. The average American girl has ten of them. But what do you really know about Barbie? Read on...

- Barbie is a Leo. Her parents' names are George and Margaret. She grew up in Willows, Wisconsin, and graduated from Willows High School. While there is no mention of higher education, she has had more than 100 different careers. "Model" seems to be the main one.

- Barbie sported a ponytail for the first two years of her career. She got her first new 'do in 1961, when she started wearing a bubble cut. Two years later, she got wigs. She decided to grow her hair out in 1967 and has kept it long ever since.

- While Barbie was meant, in part, as a toy to inspire little girls to "do anything," Barbie had self-esteem issues of her own. Until Malibu Barbie hit the scene in 1971 (with her forward-friendly eye contact), Barbie could only manage demure, sidelong glances.

- Maybe the problem stemmed from her dieting habits. Included with the outfit for Barbie Baby Sits was a book called *How to Lose Weight* with the advice "Don't eat." To underscore that, Barbie Slumber Party included a scale that only went up to 110 pounds.

- Barbie got her first house in 1962. Perhaps because it was mostly cardboard (as was the furniture), Barbie and her many pals continued to live half-naked beneath countless little girls' beds.

- Barbie was blissfully single until 1961, when Ken Carson came into her life. They broke up on Valentine's Day 2004. She kept the house. They're still friends.

- When Twist 'N Turn Barbie was introduced in 1967, Mattel offered the new doll at reduced prices with the trade-in of an older Barbie. The old dolls—undoubtedly worth a lot now—were donated to charity. That Barbie! She's such a doll!

Last Meal Requests

U.S. prisoners on death row traditionally have the chance to order a special last meal on the night before they are to be executed. Last meals over the years have been a bizarre mix of ice creams, cigarettes, fried chicken, and—in one case—a single olive with a pit in it. Here are some of the more memorable last meals ordered by prisoners.

Velma Barfield, who killed five people, made history when she was executed by lethal injection at Central Prison in Raleigh, North Carolina, in 1984. She was the first woman in the United States to be executed after capital punishment was reinstated in 1977. Barfield, who became a devoted Christian while in prison, had simple tastes: She ordered a bag of Cheez Doodles and a can of Coca-Cola for her last meal.

Timothy McVeigh, a veteran of the U.S. Army, was responsible for 168 deaths when he bombed the Alfred P. Murrah Building in Oklahoma City. Prior to September 11, 2001, the Oklahoma City bombing ranked as the deadliest terrorist attack in the United States. McVeigh was executed on June 11, 2001. He ordered two pints of mint chocolate chip ice cream as his last meal.

No one knows exactly how many victims serial killer **Ted Bundy** claimed, but the estimates range from 26 to 100. Bundy did not request a last meal before he was executed on January 24, 1989, in Florida. Instead, he was given the traditional last meal of steak, eggs over easy, hash browns, toast, milk, coffee, juice, butter, and jelly.

The crimes of **John Wayne Gacy** shocked the nation. Gacy was arrested in 1978 and was ultimately convicted of murdering 33 boys and young men in Illinois. He was executed on May 10, 1994, at Stateville Correctional Center in Crest Hill, Illinois. Before the execution, Gacy ate a last meal of a dozen deep-fried shrimp, a bucket of Kentucky Fried Chicken, French fries, and a pound of strawberries.

Serial killer **William Bonin** was known as the Freeway Killer and is thought to have killed as many as 36 young men and boys. He was convicted for 14 of those killings. Bonin, who was put to death on February 23, 1996, in San Quentin State Prison, was the first person executed by lethal injection in California. For his last meal, he ordered two sausage-and-pepperoni pizzas, three servings of chocolate ice cream, and 15 cans of Coca-Cola.

Victor Feguer killed a doctor in 1960 in Illinois, after picking him at random from the phone book. He was arrested in Montgomery, Alabama, after trying to sell the doctor's car. On March 15, 1963, Feguer was hanged at the Fort Madison Penitentiary in Iowa. Feguer requested one of the more unusual last meals—a solitary olive with a pit in it. Feguer was buried with the olive pit in his suit pocket.

Philip Workman was convicted in 1982 of murdering a police officer during a failed robbery of a fast-food restaurant in Memphis. Workman's conviction was controversial, with many doubting that he was the man who fired the shot that killed the officer. Before he was executed on May 9, 2007, Workman made an unusual request for a last meal: He asked that a large vegetarian pizza be donated to a homeless person in Nashville. Prison officials denied this request, and Workman subsequently ate nothing for his last meal. However, many other people across the country donated vegetarian pizzas to homeless shelters in the state on the day Workman was executed, honoring his final request.

Ice cream dates back to first-century Romans, specifically Emperor Nero, who ordered runners to pass buckets of snow from the northern mountains down the Appian Way to the city, where it was flavored with fruit toppings before being served.

15 Waterfalls that Will Blow Your Mind

Majestic beyond compare, the world's greatest waterfalls are frothy-white wonders of nature. Featuring wispy cascades, gushing troughs, and dizzying drops, each "chute" is a variation on a theme with its own unique charm and character.

1. Niagara Falls, New York/Canada

When it comes to waterfalls, none gush more famous than Niagara Falls. From the look of abject terror on the face of 63-year-old Annie Edson Taylor—the first daredevil to ride over the falls in a barrel (1901)—to Marilyn Monroe's suggestive sway as she walked beside the spray in *Niagara* (1953), the Niagara cataract has captivated like no other. Comprised of two separate falls (American and Horseshoe) Niagara's notoriety comes not only from its height (176 feet and 167 feet, respectively) but from its combined  width of nearly three-quarters of a mile. Today, a thriving tourist industry replete with casinos and amusements lures visitors in droves, and the azure-blue water of the falls never fails to mesmerize.

2. Angel Falls, Venezuela

When American aviator Jimmie Angel flew over this 3,212-foot wonder in 1933, he probably didn't know that he was gazing at the world's tallest waterfall or that someday the falls would be named for his "discovery." A narrow ribbon by Niagara's standard, Angel Falls drops so far that its waters actually atomize into mist before reaching the ground.

3. Yosemite Falls, California

Located in Yosemite National Park, this lofty spigot is the United States' answer to Angel Falls. At 2,425 feet, the waterfall is America's tallest and the sixth tallest in the world.

4. Victoria Falls, Zambia/Zimbabwe

Africa's giant, this 360-foot waterfall doubles Niagara in height and easily surpasses it in width (Victoria Falls is one mile wide). Victoria's flow is generally about one-half that of Niagara, but during the annual rainy season, the waterfall can flow twice as hard as its North American rival.

5. Multnomah Falls, Oregon

With a total drop of 620 feet, this waterfall runs mid-pack in the height wars, but its true claim to fame lies in its approachability and stunning beauty. It ranks as Oregon's tallest.

6. Iguacú Falls, Argentina/Brazil

Comprised of some 275 separate channels, this famous waterfall's signature element is its massive volume. Reaching 269 feet at its tallest point, Iguacú Falls currently flaunts the greatest average annual flow worldwide.

7. Lower Yellowstone Falls, Wyoming

At 308 feet in height and 70 feet in width, this majestic waterfall caps off any visit to Yellowstone National Park. It's considered the largest volume major waterfall in the U.S. Rocky Mountains.

8. Cumberland Falls, Kentucky

To the uninitiated, Cumberland Falls seems somewhat ordinary. At 68 feet tall and 125 feet wide, the curtain of water, while undeniably scenic, is almost minuscule by world standards. But during times of full moon, a lunar rainbow or *moonbow* appears before the falling sheet. This prompts sighting parties to visit the falls well *after* sundown, a strange occurrence indeed.

9. Gavarnie Falls, France

France's tallest at 1,384 feet, the *grande cascade* spills into a huge natural amphitheater of uncommon beauty.

10. Gocta Catarata, Peru

This well-hidden 2,531-foot (estimated) sliver was only recently "discovered" by Peruvian officials in 2002. If the fall's true height comes near this estimate, it will easily knock Yosemite Falls out of its sixth-tallest berth.

11. Kaieteur Falls, Guyana

At 741 feet tall and 370 feet wide, this waterfall features great height *and* great width. Its resultant hydro power ranks it among the most forceful on Earth.

12. Langfoss, Norway

A cascading waterfall of incomparable grandeur, Langfoss slides down 2,008 feet of bare rock before splashing into Akra fjord.

13. Sutherland Falls, New Zealand

The 1,904-foot waterfall is powered by Lake Quill, a glacial-fed body of water that produces many of its own waterfalls. It is one of New Zealand's most celebrated spillways.

14. Depot Creek Falls, Washington

Water appears to rush down this frenetic waterfall. That's because the 967-foot waterfall veils down a smooth granite headwall at a comparatively shallow angle. This promotes a gushing torrent that kicks up an impressive cloud of spray.

15. Montmorency Falls, Quebec, Canada

A natural waterfall seemingly created for tourists, 272-foot *Chute Montmorency* is a sight to behold. A suspension bridge above and decks below bring people frightfully close to the action, while a tramline spanning the gorge fills in the remaining visual gaps.

Nine Really Odd Things Insured by Lloyd's of London

Average people insure average things such as cars, houses, and maybe even a boat. Celebrities insure legs, voices, and some things you might not want to examine if you're a claims adjuster. Here are a few unusual things insured by the famous Lloyd's of London over the years.

1. In 1957, world-famous food critic Egon Ronay wrote and published the first edition of the *Egon Ronay Guide to British Eateries.* Because his endorsement could make or break a restaurant, Ronay insured his taste buds for $400,000.

2. In the 1940s, executives at 20th Century Fox had the legs of actress Betty Grable insured for $1 million each. After taking out the policies, Grable probably wished she had added a rider to protect her from injury while the insurance agents fought over who would inspect her when making a claim.

3. While playing on Australia's national cricket team from 1985 to 1994, Merv Hughes took out an estimated $370,000 policy on his trademark walrus mustache, which, combined with his 6'4" physique and outstanding playing ability, made him one of the most recognized cricketers in the world.

4. Representing the Cheerio Yo-Yo Company of Canada, 13-year-old Harvey Lowe won the 1932 World Yo-Yo Championships in London and toured Europe from 1932 to 1935. He even taught Edward VIII, then Prince of Wales, how to yo-yo. Lowe was so valuable to Cheerio that the company insured his hands for $150,000!

5. From 1967 to 1992, British comedian and singer Ken Dodd was in the *Guinness World Records* for the world's longest joke-telling session—1,500 jokes in three and a half hours. Dodd has

sold more than 100 million comedy records and is famous for his frizzy hair, ever-present feather duster, and extremely large buck-teeth. His teeth are so important to his act that Dodd had them insured for $7.4 million, surely making his insurance agent grin.

6. During the height of his career, Michael Flatley—star of *Riverdance* and *Lord of the Dance*—insured his legs for an unbelievable $47 million. Before becoming the world's most famous Irish step dancer, the Chicago native trained as a boxer and won the Golden Gloves Championship in 1975, undoubtedly dazzling his opponents with some extremely fast and fancy footwork.

7. The famous comedy team of Bud Abbott and Lou Costello seemed to work extremely well together, especially in their famous "Who's on First?" routine. But to protect against a career-ending argument, they took out a $250,000 insurance policy over a five-year period. After more than 20 years together, the team split up in 1957—not due to a disagreement, but because the Internal Revenue Service got them for back taxes, which forced them to sell many of their assets, including the rights to their many films.

8. Rock and Roll Hall of Famer Bruce Springsteen is known to his fans as The Boss, but Springsteen knows that he could be demoted to part-time status with one case of laryngitis. That's why in the 1980s he insured his famous gravelly voice for $6 million. Rod Stewart has also insured his throat, and Bob Dylan has a policy to protect his vocal cords for that inevitable day when they stop blowin' in the wind.

9. Before rock 'n' roll, a popular type of music in England in the 1950s was skiffle, a type of folk music with a jazz and blues influence played on washboards, jugs, kazoos, and cigar-box fiddles. It was so big at the time that a washboard player named Chas McDevitt tried to protect his career by insuring his fingers for $9,300. It didn't do him much good because skiffle was replaced by rock 'n' roll, washboards by washing machines, and McDevitt by McCartney.

Criminals Behaving Nicely

The following mixture of life's flotsam proves far and away that, like books, people can't always be judged by their covers.

John Dillinger

Seen as a modern-day Robin Hood by many cash-strapped, Depression-era citizens, bank robber Dillinger took what he wanted when he wanted it. The public, angry at banks and the government for doing little to help them, cheered for the antihero's escape, but they weren't looking at the full picture. Dillinger and his gang were responsible for at least ten murders. And unlike Robin Hood, Dillinger didn't share his ill-gotten booty with those in need. Nevertheless, his charm carried him along until one fateful day when he agreed to meet the now-infamous "Lady in Red" (Ana Cumpanas) at Chicago's Biograph Theater. Unbeknownst to the gangster, Miss Cumpanas had sold him out to federal agents who had come to apprehend him. In the end, the popular gangster was cut down by a hail of bullets—a fitting end for a not-so-nice criminal.

John Gotti

It's amazing what a quick smile and a few block parties can do for one's popularity. Labeled the "Teflon Don" for his uncanny knack at evading prosecution, the Gambino family crime boss was beloved by his Queens, New York, neighbors. Each year, the cheerful don would stage an elaborate Fourth of July celebration, free of charge, solely for their benefit. When the Teflon finally wore off in 1992 and Gotti was convicted on murder and racketeering charges, no one defended him more passionately than his neighbors. But their faith was misplaced. In 2009, informant Charles Carneglia testified that Gotti had neighbor John Favara "dissolved in a barrel of acid" after the man accidentally killed Gotti's 12-year-old son in a car accident. So much for Gotti's good neighbor policy.

Theodore "Ted" Bundy

If a polite, good-looking law student on crutches asked for your assistance lifting heavy objects into his car, would you help him? For those obliging young women smitten by Bundy's boyish charm, such kindness equated to a death sentence. Bundy would be tried and convicted for the murder of Kimberly Leach, just one of more than 30 women he'd eventually admit to killing. Even Dade County Circuit Court Judge Edward D. Cowart appeared impressed by Bundy as he sentenced him to death. "You're a bright young man. You'd have made a good lawyer, and I would have loved to have you practice in front of me," said the judge in a fatherly tone. "But you went another way, partner." On January 24, 1989, 2,000 searing volts of electricity ensured that Bundy's "charm" could seduce no more.

John Wayne Gacy

Serial killer Gacy often donned a clown outfit to amuse children at local hospitals. He was seen as a pillar of society, working closely with the Jaycees and other groups for community improvement. But Gacy had a dark side that could repel even the most hardened criminals. His modus operandi was to drug, torture, and rape young men before killing and burying them under his house. Gacy died at the Stateville Correctional Center in Illinois on May 10, 1994, when a lethal injection shut his circus down permanently.

Charles Manson

As revolting as he now seems, there's no denying that Charles Manson once had a magnetic personality. Much like Svengali, the charismatic man had a knack for placing people under his spell. After this was accomplished, the rest was elementary. Such a talent could be used for good or evil purposes. Manson ran with the latter. In 1969, a group of faithful followers performed unthinkable acts on Manson's direct orders. The Tate/LaBianca murders rocked America for their unusual viciousness and revealed Manson as a deranged puppet master, bent on the death and destruction of humankind. Manson has spent the past four decades behind bars and by most accounts has lost all of his charm. A classic case of too little, too late.

Notable Attempts to Prove the Existence of an Afterlife

When you're investigating the afterlife, ridicule from skeptics comes with the territory. But for many researchers, inventors, and weekend mad scientists, the potential payoff of proving there's life after death is well worth any taunting. Here are some highlights from a century of prodding into the great hereafter.

- In 1901, surgeon Duncan Macdougall attempted to weigh the human soul. He laid dying tuberculosis patients on massive scales and noted any changes at the moment of death. Based on six weigh-ins, he determined that body weight drops about ¾ ounce (21 grams) when a person dies—presumably because the immortal soul exits the premises. There's no record of anyone re-creating these results.

- In 2000, an Oregon rancher named Lewis Hollander Jr. tried his hand at soul-weighing, enlisting eight sheep, three lambs, and a goat as his subjects (the animals were already at death's door). No animals lost weight as they passed on, but all of the sheep gained weight for one to six seconds after death. One sheep put on almost two pounds.

- In the 1920s, two Dutch physicists claimed a disembodied spirit had explained to them, via séance, how to build a soul-detecting machine. The spirit said the human soul lives on as a gaseous body, which could interact with the physical world by expanding and contracting. The physicists built an elaborate pressure detector and reported that the spirit did indeed alter gas pressure on demand.

- At the time of his death in 1931, Thomas Edison was reportedly working on a type of megaphone to allow, in his words, "personalities which have left this earth to communicate with us." No one has ever turned up any "Spirit Phone" prototypes or technical specs, however.

- In order to stop fake mediums from capitalizing on his fame when he died, escape artist and enthusiastic spiritualist debunker Harry Houdini vowed that if he could communicate from beyond the grave, he would relay a ten-word code, known only to his wife. For ten years, Houdini's wife held séances on the anniversary of his death (Halloween), but the code never came through.

- Beginning in the 1960s, Latvian writer Konstantin Raudive made 70,000 recordings of electronic voice phenomena (EVP), the supposed voices of ghosts captured on audio tape.

- In the 1970s, two Icelandic scientists spent four years examining accounts from 1,000 doctors and nurses of what American and Indian patients experienced as they approached death. With the help of computer analysis, they noted persistent common details in the accounts, which covered experiences of people of all ages, with highly varied cultural backgrounds. The most common general themes were a bright light, an overpowering feeling of peace, and a sense of an otherworldly realm.

- Michael Persinger, a professor of neuroscience at Laurentian University, has found that when subjects place their heads in strong electromagnetic fields, most sense a ghostly presence. His theory is that intense electromagnetic fields either cause hallucinations or enable people to sense ghosts that are there all the time.

- In order to test the validity of near-death, out-of-body experience reports, psychiatry professor Bruce Greyson displays distinctive images while patients undergoing implanted defibrillator testing are briefly brain dead. So far, no one has recalled seeing the pictures.

- In 2008, the English physician Sam Parnia launched a similar experiment designed to gauge the validity of out-of-body experiences in heart attack survivors. He outfitted an operating room with shelves showing pictures that are only visible from the top of the room. He hopes, over three years, to analyze the near-death recollections of 1,500 patients.

Unfortunate Product Names

Ever take a slurp of Pee Cola? Ever wash your clothes with Barf detergent? You can. These two products are just two of the many unfortunately named consumer goods that you can find as you travel around the world.

SARS Soda By 2003, the SARS respiratory disease, short for Severe Acute Respiratory Syndrome, had infected more than 8,000 people and caused 774 deaths. The SARS soft drink manufactured by Australian food company Golden Circle has done nothing similar. That doesn't change the fact that SARS is an unfortunate name for a soft drink.

There's a method behind Golden Circle's naming madness. SARS is short for sarsaparilla, a vine plant found mostly in Central America, Mexico, and South America. The soft drink has been around longer than the syndrome. Hopefully, it will outlast it, too.

Ayds If you were trying to lose weight in the late 1970s or early 1980s, you might have given Ayds diet candies a try. Unfortunately, the candy's name sounds exactly like AIDS. As the public became more aware of this disease in the early to mid-1980s, sales of the candies dropped. In 1988, the chairman of Dep Corporation, which was then distributing the dietary candies, announced that the product's name was changing to Diet Ayds. This didn't help, and the product soon disappeared.

You can still find the commercials for the candy scattered about the Internet. Some of the now regrettable taglines include "Thank goodness for Ayds" and "Ayds helps you lose weight."

Pee Cola If you're ever traveling in Ghana, you can take a swig of ice-cold Pee Cola. Of course, it's not what it sounds like; Pee, it turns out, is a rather common last name in the West African country of Ghana. Maybe you can use Pee Cola to wash down some Shitto, also available in Ghana. Shitto is canned gravy that includes as its ingredients dried pepper, dried shrimp powder, garlic, tomatoes, and dried fish. Nothing goes with a Shitto quite as well as a Pee Cola.

Potty Talk

Studies show that you spend an average of 30 minutes a day in the bathroom. Seems to us you could stand to know a little more about bathroom-related topics.

- Antacids have been around for more than 5,000 years. Ancient stomach remedies included chalk, which can still be found in some over-the-counter heartburn remedies today.

- Bathtubs, too, have been around for centuries, but earlier ones were made of clay, marble, and even wood. Claw-foot tubs were invented in Great Britain in the mid-1800s. In 1911, the  bathtub as we know it was invented, in part because a claw-foot tub is difficult to clean under.

- Prior to World War II, the average American bathed just once a week.

- In Elizabethan times, the smell of sweat was considered to be an aphrodisiac, but about 100 years ago Americans decided otherwise. The first deodorant made its appearance in 1888, and the first antiperspirant was available in 1902. Yes, by the way, there is a difference between antiperspirants (which can be used on the feet and other body sites) and deodorants (used mostly on the underarms).

- Ancient people kept their toothsome smiles by chewing a stick shredded at one end. About 1,000 years ago, the Chinese plucked hog bristles and inserted them into a wooden handle to clean their teeth. While hog bristles worked well enough, most people preferred the softness of horsehair brushes (though the cleaning power wasn't as good) until soft nylon was invented in the 1950s.

- Cotton swabs were invented in the 1920s by an American father who had a "Eureka!" moment as he watched his wife wrap cotton around a toothpick to better clean their baby's ears, fingers, and toes. After trial and error, he perfected his new product and named it "Baby Gays." The name was later changed to Q-Tips.

- Over the centuries, many products have been used as shampoos, including vinegar, eggs, rainwater, lemon juice, and fermented beverages. Soft detergents (basically shampoo) were invented by the Germans during World War I. They were searching for an effective, cheap cleanser to get them through the war. In the process, they really got into our hair.

- Though many of the world's population thought at one time that filth was healthy, soap has been around for thousands of years. An old recipe—still used in some places—adds animal fat, ashes, and water to make lye soap, which cleans but is hard on the skin. In the mid-to-late 1800s, mass-produced (soft) soap replaced the caustic, home-made stuff in most homes.

- Did you know that you have the remains of an animal in your bathroom? If you've got a natural sponge, you do. Natural sponges are, basically, the skeletons of sea creatures.

- What does your garage have in common with your bathroom? Both contain lacquer, one on your car's body and one on yours—on your fingernails! While nail decoration has been around for more than 3,000 years, modern women didn't really know what to make of liquid, synthetic polish when it first became available. By the 1920s, though, they were happy to dig their fingernails into the new, popular cosmetic. Red polish—so much a staple in many women's beauty routines even today—wasn't popular until a decade later.

- For centuries, doctors have believed that a lack of, um, elimination was the root of all ills. Ancient Egyptian physicians offered their patients a variety of laxatives, including goose fat, figs, old books, and castor oil. Chinese medicine used gingerroot and licorice root, while other remedies included aloe vera, honey, and rhubarb. Though "modern" doctors preach colon health and seem at times to be obsessed with it, laxatives as we know them were created only 100 years ago.

Random Records

What does it take to somersault the entire length of Paul Revere's 12-mile ride from Boston to Concord, Massachusetts? Ask Ashrita Furman. In April 1986, he accomplished this amazing feat—only one of many that have landed him in Guinness World Records. *Born in 1954, the mild-mannered store manager from Queens, New York, has jumped a record 23.11 miles on a pogo stick (1997), raced the fastest mile hula-hooping while balancing a milk bottle on his head (11 minutes, 29 seconds in 2007), and duct taped himself to a wall in record time (8 minutes, 7 seconds in 2008). In fact, Furman has the record for the most records in Guinness: 225 since 1979. Furman's accomplishments may be exceptional, but he's not the only one trying to shine.*

- According to the *Book of Alternative Records,* New Zealander Mem Bourke glued a record 31,680 rhinestones to the body of her friend Alastair Galpin in 2006.

- American magician Todd Robins ate a total of 4,000 lightbulbs during his nearly 30-year career, which ran from 1980 to 2009.

- On October 25, 2008, 4,179 people from ten nations, who were joined by video feed, simultaneously performed Michael Jackson's "Thriller" routine.

- A record 552 children danced the Macarena together at Britain's Plumcroft Primary School in 2009.

- Some kids are born record-breakers. On November 30, 1998, triplets Peyton, Jackson, and Blake Coffey came into the world with a collective weight of 3 pounds, 8 ounces, making them the smallest threesome ever born. On February 9, 2003, Tomasso Cipriani of Italy became the world's largest newborn when he weighed in at 28 pounds, 4 ounces.

- But what's really the strangest record ever? Consider this: Between September 21 and October 6, 1984, Rob Gordon of Shropshire, England, sat in a bathtub filled with cold spaghetti for a total of 360 hours while working as a disc jockey at a local radio station. Try to top that one, Ashrita Furman!

Top Five Ferocious Prehistoric Creatures

Think that Tyrannosaurus rex *was the most fearsome creature to roam the earth? Think again. Eons ago, the planet was literally teeming with toothsome, terrifying monsters. Here are five of the most ferocious.*

1. *Giganotosaurus* Averaging 47 feet in length and weighing 8 tons, *Giganotosaurus* would have made *T. rex* run home to its mama. Luckily, these monstrous behemoths lived millions of years apart. What made *Giganotosaurus* so menacing? Well, its eight-inch-long serrated teeth didn't hurt.

2. *Spinosaurus* According to paleontologists, *Spinosaurus* is the largest carnivorous dinosaur known to have existed. It measured a whopping 55 feet in length, weighed almost 10 tons, and had long, crocodilian jaws that sparked terror in anything foolish enough to cross its path. It also sported a sail on its back that was more than six feet tall.

3. Megalodon Sharks are some of the oldest creatures on the planet, and Megalodon was the granddaddy of them all. It measured nearly 60 feet in length—longer than a city bus—and weighed more than 75 tons. To survive, Megalodon had to consume an estimated 2,500 pounds of food every day. That's a lot of sashimi.

4. *Tylosaurus* Equal to Megalodon in ferocity, *Tylosaurus* was one of the most vicious creatures ever to swim the oceans. It measured more than 45 feet in length, and its jaws were lined on each side with two rows of cone-shaped teeth. What did *Tylosaurus* eat? Anything it wanted to, including other *Tylosauruses*.

5. Saber-Tooth Tiger Known scientifically as *Smilodon*, the saber-tooth tiger was a dominant carnivore during the early days of humans. Though smaller than today's large cats, it was twice as heavy and sported 11-inch-long canine teeth. Luckily, *Smilodon* went extinct about 10,000 years ago.

Memorable Sideshow Personalities

In a decidedly less sensitive era, deformed humans were often relegated to working in sideshows. The following represent the crème de la crème of nature's cruelties.

The Siamese Twins

Chang and Eng Bunker (1811–1874) were born conjoined twins but were determined to live as normal people. They married two sisters—a joint union that produced 21 children. When Chang died, Eng refused surgical separation. He followed his brother to the grave just three hours later.

The Elephant Man

Englishman Joseph Merrick (1862–1890) suffered from Proteus syndrome, a condition that can turn the face and body into a lumpy, amorphous mass. Mistreated by a sideshow manager until his rescue by a sympathetic London doctor, Merrick henceforth drew the favor of Victorian high society.

Schlitzie the Pinhead

The breakout character in the cult movie *Freaks* (1932), the huggable Schlitzie Surtees (1901–1971) helped to soften people's attitudes toward those born different. Suffering from microcephalus, the "pin-headed" 31-year-old possessed the intelligence of a 3-year-old. When he died in 1971, the penniless actor was buried in an unmarked grave. In 2008, Hollywood historian Scott Michaels and a small army of fans bought Schlitzie a proper stone.

General Tom Thumb

Sideshow personalities weren't always grotesque. In fact, some were downright adorable. Three-foot, four-inch Tom Thumb (1838–1883) could sing and dance with aplomb. As a result, he became P. T. Barnum's star attraction. Big news was made in 1863 when the "general" married Livinia Warren, a woman even shorter than he was.

The World's Tallest Man

At a confirmed height of 8'11.1", Robert Pershing Wadlow (1818–1940) was easily the tallest man in the world. To this day, he remains the tallest man in recorded history.

The World's Heaviest Man

Tipping the scales at a breathtaking 1,041 pounds, Robert Earl Hughes (1926–1958) equaled the combined weight of *seven* average men. Suffering from a malfunctioning pituitary gland, Hughes actually had a modest appetite. He was buried in a huge coffin sometimes mistakenly called a piano case.

The Lobster Boy

Afflicted with a condition called *ectrodactyly,* Grady Stiles (1937–1992) had clawlike hands and feet. Though he couldn't walk, he was ambulatory, moving about on very strong arms. An abusive alcoholic, Stiles shot and killed his daughter's fiancé in 1978. Stiles himself was shot and killed in 1992 by a hit man hired by his irate second wife.

Half Boy

Johnny Eck (1911–1991) was another member of the *Freaks* ensemble. Born without legs, he stood only one foot, six inches tall. Eck performed one-armed handstands, among other skills, as part of his act.

Half Lady

Mademoiselle Gabrielle of Switzerland was a beautiful woman whose body ended smoothly just below the hip. She traveled with the Ringling Brothers Circus in the 1900s and married multiple times. Gabrielle believed that she was "no less a woman" despite her lack of legs and lived her life accordingly.

The Lion-Faced Boy

Stephan BiBrowski (1891–1932) was a classic case of "more than meets the eye." With six-inch-long hair covering his entire head and body, most thought him animallike. Not true. In fact, BiBrowski was personable, intelligent, and capable of speaking five different languages.

The Four-Legged Lady

Josephine Corbin (1868–1930) was born with a *dipygus* twin sister dangling between her legs. The twin was smallish and formed only from the waist down. Records show that Corbin and her attached twin had fully developed sexual organs. Corbin married and produced five children. It's unclear which parts were used for conception and delivery.

The Human Owl

Martin Laurello (1885–?) looked, walked, and talked just like everyone else. But his veneer of normality was deceiving. Laurello could rotate his head a complete 180 degrees so he could look directly behind him. His owllike skill earned him a coveted slot in the Ringling Brothers Circus.

The Mule-Faced Woman

A degenerative, genetic condition known as Sturge–Weber syndrome was likely to blame for Grace McDaniels's lot in life. Born in 1888, Grace's face grew and twisted into an alarming balloonlike mass of tissue and discolored skin as she got older. She joined F. W. Miller's freak show in 1935 after winning an "ugly woman" contest, though she much preferred to be known as "The Mule-Faced Woman."

15 Tips for Surviving a Bear Encounter

In North America, there are two species of bears—black and brown (which includes subspecies grizzly and Kodiak bears)—but it is often difficult to distinguish between the two. Both types are known to attack humans, and in the past century, approximately 100 people have died in North America due to bear attacks. In the interest of not becoming part of that "grizzly" statistic, the following list offers a few tips on how to avoid or survive a bear attack.

1. Why Are You Here?

Avoid investigating dark, unknown caves or hollow logs, where bears make their dens, and avoid areas identified by scavengers, such as raccoons, as there may be a feeding bear nearby.

2. You're Kidding with the Camera, Right?

Leave pictures of bears to professional wildlife photographers. Many attacks have occurred because someone decided to try to snap a photo in bear territory. Bears don't like you, and they don't want their picture taken.

3. Whoa, Mama!

If you see a bear with a cub, leave quickly. A mother bear with her cubs is not open to negotiation. She will attack if she thinks she or her cubs are in danger.

4. Leave No Trace

If you're camping, pick up all garbage, cooking supplies, and other materials. Clean up thoroughly after meals, and secure food overnight high above the ground (by hanging it from a tree branch) to prevent it from attracting bears. Not only do sloppy campers damage the area's ecosystem, they're also more likely to come face-to-face with a bear that has followed their gravy train.

5. Keep a Lookout

As you hike through bear country, keep an eye out for claw marks or droppings, and note any scratched up trees or fresh kills, such as deer.

6. Raise a Ruckus, Ring a Bell

Some experts recommend tying a bell to your foot or backpack to make noise as you travel. You can also sing or holler at your hiking buddies. Just don't be a ninja. Bears don't like to be surprised.

7. Freeze! Stick 'Em Up!

Okay, so you've spotted a bear, and the bear has spotted you. Stop right there, and don't move. Speak to the bear in a low, calm voice, and slowly raise your arms up above your head. This makes you appear larger.

8. Back Off

Clearly, you should try to leave now. Do it slowly and go back from whence you came. Don't cross the path of the bear (or any cubs, if present). Just rewind, slowly, and don't come back.

9. Don't Run!

The worst thing you could do at this point would be to get out your camera or try to feed the bear a snack. The second worst thing you could do would be to run. Bears run faster than humans, and they think chasing prey is fun.

10. Hello, Tree

"But bears can climb trees," you say. You're right: Some bears, like black bears, can climb trees. But others, like grizzly bears, cannot. Either way, if you can get more than 12 feet up into a tree, you should be okay. That's pretty far up, so this is not your best option.

11. Grizzly Bear? Play Dead!

If a bear is charging you, you've got a couple of less-than-desirable options. The first thing you might try is going into the fetal position and playing dead. This might make you seem vulnerable to the grizzly bear, and he or she will sniff you, growl at you, and hopefully leave you alone. Being in the fetal position will also protect your vital organs. IMPORTANT: If you're dealing with a black bear, do NOT play dead. They'll be thrilled that the work's been done for them and will commence lunch. If you can't tell what kind of bear you're dealing with, don't try it!

12. Go Undercover

While you're in the fetal position, try to pull your backpack on top of you for an extra layer of protection.

13. Bang, Bang

If a bear is charging you and you've got a gun, now might be the time to use it. Make sure you've got a clean shot because it usually takes more than one bullet to kill a bear and bad aim will only make it angrier. This should only be used as a last resort—wrongful killing of a bear in the United States incurs a hefty fine of up to $20,000.

14. Spray, Spray

Many camping and national park areas don't allow firearms, so some recommend bear spray or pepper spray. But beware: If you spray halfheartedly, it will only make the bear angrier.

15. The Fight of Your Life

Your last option is to fight back with everything you've got. There's really no need to tell you that, at this point, you're in big trouble. Kick, scream, flail your arms, go for the eyes—do whatever you can because you're in for the fight of your life.

Famous People Who Rarely Left Their Houses

Not all celebrities enjoy the spotlight.

Howard Hughes

Perhaps the world's most famous recluse, this hermit's hermit has grown to symbolize that subgroup of people who, for various reasons, prefer to navigate life in the singular, apart and aside from others. A true Renaissance man, Hughes was an aviator, industrialist, film producer, and director; he also ranked as one of the world's wealthiest men. Hughes began to show subtle signs of mental illness in his 30s. Idiosyncrasies followed him from that point forth, but many chalked this up to the eccentricity of the well-coddled. It wasn't. On Thanksgiving Day in 1966, Hughes moved into a suite at Las Vegas's Desert Inn and dug in deep, rarely emerging from that point forward. When hotel staff finally asked him to leave, he countered by buying the hotel. Hughes would dwell reclusively in the penthouses of many more hotels until his death in 1976, remaining incognito throughout. At the time of his death, Hughes's beard, hair, toenails, and fingernails were freakishly long—a situation that suggested that personal hygiene no longer carried much weight with the billionaire.

Elizabeth Barrett Browning

The Victorian-era poet renowned for such poems as "How Do I Love Thee? Let Me Count the Ways" and "The Cry of the Children" fell into a deep depression after the drowning death of her brother in 1840. She isolated herself from the outside world and communicated, when necessary, by letter. In 1845, the poet Robert Browning sent her a telegraph: "I love your verses with all my heart, dear Miss Barrett ... and I love you too." Love may not conquer all, but in this case, it came pretty close. The two met, fell for each other, and eloped a year later. Elizabeth Barrett Browning lived from that day forth blessedly unencumbered by the melancholy that had once held her hostage.

Brian Wilson

The leader and chief songwriter of The Beach Boys, Wilson fought mental illness and drug addiction for much of his life. In the early 1970s, the artist retreated to his home in an effort to dodge his problems. He would seldom leave its protective cocoon. This pattern would continue for nearly three decades until Wilson, now in better charge of his demons, emerged, returning to the studio and stage with renewed vigor. Perhaps Wilson discovered that a life lived "In My Room" isn't all that it's cracked up to be.

H. P. Lovecraft

Famed writer of horror and science-fiction novels, Lovecraft (1890–1937) was troubled from the onset by psychosomatic illnesses. When the loss of his family home nearly pushed the budding writer over the brink, Lovecraft became depressed and reclusive. He lived the life of a hermit from the age of 18 to 23, making human contact only with his mother. When a letter to a magazine drew the attention of the president of the United Amateur Press Association, Lovecraft contributed a number of poems and essays to the organization. With his confidence now at a peak, Lovecraft was able to hold his demons at bay and rejoin the world.

J. D. Salinger

When *The Catcher in the Rye* was released in 1951, a firestorm of attention, negative and positive, drove Salinger into deep retreat. He produced books and articles only sporadically from that point on and fell completely out of the public eye. His last published work, *Hapworth 16, 1924*, appeared in *The New Yorker* in 1965. Many wonder whether Salinger's sudden reclusiveness was due to the uproar surrounding the book or if his shyness stemmed from personal fears. The jury is still out on Salinger's motives, but one thing is certain: Seldom has a writer reached this level of success only to simply walk off the stage.

It Happened in...June

- An Idaho pilot spots nine objects hovering in the sky over the mountains while flying to Oregon. Although officials pooh-pooh his observation—and that of dozens of people who saw the same disc-shaped object in the sky over 30 different states—the phrase "unidentified flying object," or UFO, is coined in June 1947.

- In June 1989, when several thousand people claimed to have won the Dodge Caravan in a Philip Morris/Kraft contest, officials were red-faced. Since there was only supposed to be one winner, the mistake in promotional printing cost the company millions of dollars in goodwill compensation.

- McDonald's made parents happy and kids happier when they rolled out their Happy Meal (complete with toy) in June 1979.

- Shopping carts were invented by a supermarket owner in Oklahoma City in June 1937. Before that, shoppers had baskets to carry. Baskets on wheels meant customers could spend more money.

- One of the most beloved Christmas movie classics premiered in theatres in June 1947. *Miracle on 34th Street* starred Maureen O'Hara and a very young Natalie Wood. We're not sure why it premiered in June rather than, say, December.

- You say "potato," I say it's spelled wrong: It was in 1992 that Dan Quayle erroneously told a grade-school student that a spud should be spelled *potatoe.*

- June is Accordion Awareness Month (are you aware now?), Potty Training Awareness Month (you've *got* to be aware of that!), and—mmmmm—National Candy Month, among others.

Weird Collections

Some people collect baseball cards. Others collect belly button lint.
Yes, you read that correctly—belly button lint. Now that's
a collection that brings a whole new meaning to the phrase
"one person's trash is another person's treasure"!

In 1984, Graham Barker's navel gazing led to an interesting hobby.
You can see the results online at his Incredible World of Navel Fluff,
where samples of his personal lint are neatly displayed in labeled
jars. But maybe you'd prefer to visit the Museum of Burnt Food?
Or take a gander at Becky Martz's array of banana stickers (she has
more than 7,000, though not all are online)? Or view New Zealand
artist Maurice Bennett's Toast Portraits of Famous People?

Some collections that might be classified as "weird" actually
have a serious purpose. Dr. Bindeshwar Pathak created the Sulabh
Museum of Toilets in New Delhi, India, to educate people about the
need for sanitation. The Trash Museum in Harford, Connecticut,
will surely boost your commitment to recycling. And after visiting
the Museum of Hoaxes in San Diego you're not likely to be hooked
by tales of fur-bearing trout or swallow any stories about Italian
spaghetti trees. Here's something to keep in mind if you ever drop
by the Icelandic Phallological Museum: Most of the 245 embalmed
penises on display are from real Icelandic animals, but curator
Sigurur Hjartarson has mixed in a few from "elves" and "trolls" just
to keep natural historians on their toes.

A passion for collecting goes way back in human history. The
Egyptian pharaohs of the Ptolemaic dynasty (332–30 B.C.) collected
enough papyrus scrolls to establish the world's first library. A few
centuries later, around A.D. 10, Roman Emperor Augustus scoured
his empire for unusual objects, including the bones of sea monsters
(which we would now recognize as whales).

Collecting really took off during the Renaissance, however, when
wealthy merchants used *Wunderkammers,* known in English as
Wonder Cabinets, to display their collections of antiques and oddi-
ties. Today, thanks to the wonders of the Internet, almost anyone
can have a Wonder Cabinet in cyberspace. In addition to those

mentioned above, here are a few of our top picks when it comes to the weirdest of the weird:

- Jef Beck's collection of vintage Ken dolls, among them the rare "Business Ken" and "Coca Cola" Ken, which was produced as a promotional gimmick along with "Coca Cola" Barbie.

- Chocolate freak Martin Mihál's collection of 38,579 chocolate bar wrappers, including 8,700 from his native Germany. One question: Did he eat all the contents himself?

- A must-see for office mavens is the Acme Staple Company's collection of antique staplers. The Early Office Museum has a collection of staples to fit those machines.

- The Air Sickness Bag Virtual Museum displays more than 2,000 barf bags from around the world. Curator Steven J. Silberberg insists he's never been out of North America. Perhaps the instructions on Virgin Australia airline's "Fully Sick" bag are one good reason why.

- It's natural to move from the barf bag museum to the gallery of moist towelettes. Michael Lewis's Web site, Modern Moist Towelette Collecting, even gives awards in categories such as "Humor," "Most Original Use for a Towelette," and "Strangest Place to Find a Towelette." (The World of Oz on Ice, in case you were wondering.)

- Hygiene does seem to fuel many collectors' obsessions. Carol Vaughn of England has more than 5,000 bars of soap and Dr. Val Kolpakov of Saginaw, Michigan, displays 1,407 different brands of toothpaste at his Toothpaste World online. In Malaysia, they brush with DawnMist, in Russia with Splat, and in the United States with something called Warheads, in three flavors, no less.

- Finally, if you want to know the future of collecting, consult the Museum of Talking Boards, a collection devoted to the art and history of Ouija boards. Or try the Weird Fortune Cookie Collection. Still no answer? Shake a Magic 8-Ball. According to antique dealer Deanna Dahlsad, there are plenty of these little "spheres of influence" floating around out there just waiting for someone to collect them. Which gives us an idea...

Funky Flavors of Jones Soda

For Seattle-based Jones Soda Co., if it's not innovative, it's not worth drinking. At least, that's how it seems when you take a gander at some of the flavors they've created over the years. Go on—try a Roadkill-flavored soda! Dare ya!

- Antacid
- Bananaberry
- Black cat licorice
- Broccoli casserole
- Brussels sprout with prosciutto
- Bug juice
- Candy corn
- Christmas ham
- Christmas tree
- Dirt
- Fruit cake
- Green bean casserole
- Invisible
- Jelly doughnut
- Latke
- Lemon meringue pie
- Mashed potatoes and butter
- Natural field turf
- Pecan pie
- Perspiration
- Pumpkin pie
- Roadkill
- Salmon pâté
- Sugar plum
- Turkey and gravy
- Wild herb stuffing

Curious Creatures Among Us

- When some types of frogs vomit, their entire stomach comes out. The frog then cleans out the contents and swallows the empty stomach.

- Pacific Island robber crabs love coconuts so much that they have developed the ability to climb trees to satisfy their cravings.

- The water-holding frog is the greatest survivor in the animal kingdom. When it rains, the frog absorbs water through its skin. It then burrows into the sand, where it can live as long as two years off its water reserve.

- The praying mantis is the only insect that can turn its head 360 degrees.

- A chameleon can focus its eyes separately to watch two objects at once. This lizard also has a tongue that is longer than its body.

- The electric eel can produce 350 to 550 volts of electricity as often as 150 times per hour without any apparent fatigue.

- Spider silk is five times stronger than steel, but it is also highly elastic—a rare combination in a material. Silk stretches 30 percent farther than the most elastic nylon.

- A large parrot's beak can exert 500 pounds of pressure per square inch, enabling the bird to feast on such delicacies as Brazil nuts with a simple crunch.

- The extinct Madagascan elephant bird laid eggs as large as 13 inches in length and 9 inches in diameter. Today, ostriches lay the largest eggs, up to 8 inches in length and 6 inches in diameter.

- Wasps can make paper by mixing wood pulp with saliva to form a paste, which dries stiff.

- The bald eagle is larger at the age of two than it is when fully grown.

- The eggs of some species of the mayfly take three years to hatch, and then the flies live only six hours.

It Happened in...July

- The first annual National Baby Food Festival was held in July 1990 in Fremont, Michigan, the hometown of Gerber Products Company.

- In 1981, the courts ordered a wife (Neva Rockefeller) to pay her ex-husband alimony for the first time ever.

- In July 1935, 150 parking meters were installed in downtown Oklahoma City, making them the first in the United States. Depending on their location within the city, it would cost drivers as much as a nickel to park for as long as an hour.

- In 1958, fuel company Esso warned motorists that listening to rock 'n' roll in their cars might cause a money drain. The company's researchers claimed that the beat of the music gave drivers a lead foot, thereby wasting gas.

- Nineteen-year-old Elvis Presley signed a contract with Sun Records in July 1954. He hoped to become a professional singer.

- Two things to write home about: In July 1919, the price of first-class postage actually went down due, in part, to the end of World War I. The ZIP code went into effect in July 1963.

- P. T. Barnum is supposed to have said "There's a sucker born every minute." That was true sometime on July 5, 1810—the day Barnum came into the world.

- Man O' War, considered by some to be the greatest racehorse in history, ran the Dwyer Stakes in July 1920. He finished in well under two minutes, defeating the horse John P. Grier.

- July is National Doghouse Repairs Month, National Horseradish Month (that's so hot!), and Wheelchair Beautification Month.

The Many Deaths of Wile E. Coyote

Come on, admit it: After all these years, wouldn't it be nice to see Wile E. Coyote succeed in his futile quest to capture the Road Runner—even just one time?

Created by Warner Bros. animation director Chuck Jones, cartoon character Wile E. Coyote is renowned for the outlandish inventions—all of them purchased from the shady Acme company—he uses in his vain attempts at capturing the Road Runner. These contraptions, which run the gamut from dehydrated boulders to jet-propelled skis, inevitably cause nothing but insult and injury to Wile E., yet he refuses to give up, turning to Acme again and again.

Wile E. Coyote made his debut in the 1949 cartoon "Fast and Furry-ous" (written by Michael Maltese, who would go on to script another 15 stories depicting the creative coyote). Although Wile E. tried desperately to catch the Road Runner with an electric motor and a super outfit, such tools were no match against his fleet-footed nemesis. The coyote had tasted defeat—and not for the last time.

Over the years, Wile E. Coyote has appeared in a total of 45 shorts, a short film, and—more recently—in three brief shorts that aired only on the Internet. He has also appeared in a handful of television shows—primarily compilations of earlier cartoons—and in the motion pictures *Space Jam* (1996) and *Looney Tunes: Back in Action* (2003).

Wile E. Coyote has assumed a variety of personas and has encountered many different foes over the course of his career. In a separate set of cartoons, he is known as Ralph Wolf and spends his time trying to steal sheep from a laconic but very effective sheep dog. And in a few cartoons, his foil is Bugs Bunny instead of the Road Runner. At the end of the day, however, the results of his actions are the same: abject failure and an empty stomach.

Creator Chuck Jones and the cartoons' animators conceived a series of strict rules governing Wile E. Coyote's behavior and his relationship with the Road Runner. Among them: The Road Runner cannot harm the coyote except by saying "beep beep." Also, no outside force can harm the coyote—only his own ineptitude or the failure of the various Acme products can derail the animal. In several cartoons, Wile E. is also thwarted by the unexpected arrival of various trucks and trains.

Over the decades, Wile E. Coyote has suffered tremendously at the hands of the Acme devices he places his trust in time and again. Following are some of the outlandish ways that the long-suffering desert dog has dispatched himself, along with the cartoons in which they were featured:

- Anvil, "Gee Whiz-z-z," 1956
- Axle grease (guaranteed slippery), "Zip N Snort," 1961
- Bumble bees (one-fifth), "Zoom and Bored," 1957
- Do-It-Yourself Tornado Kit, "Whoa Be Gone," 1958
- Earthquake pills, "Hopalong Casualty," 1960
- Explosive tennis balls, "Soup or Sonic," 1980
- Giant mousetrap, "Chariots of Fur," 1994
- Giant rubber band, "Gee Whiz-z-z," 1956
- High-speed tonic, "Hip Hip Hurry," 1958
- Instant icicle maker, "Zoom at the Top," 1962
- Jet-propelled pogo stick, "Hot Rod & Reel," 1959
- Lightning bolts (rubber gloves included), "Chariots of Fur," 1994
- Little Giant Do-It-Yourself Rocket-Sled Kit, "Beep Prepared," 1961
- Mouse snare, "Hip Hip Hurry," 1958
- Nitroglycerin, "Beep Beep," 1952
- Road Runner lasso, "Freeze Frame," 1979
- Rocket-powered roller skates, "Beep Beep," 1952
- Triple-strength battleship steel armor plate, "Gee Whiz-z-z," 1956
- Triple-strength fortified leg muscle vitamins, "Stop! Look! and Hasten!," 1954
- Water pistol, "Whoa Be Gone," 1958

Peculiar Presidential Facts

- President William Taft had a new bathtub installed in the White House that could hold four grown men. Why? His 300-pound frame wouldn't fit in the original presidential tub.

- Grover Cleveland was the first and only president to marry in the White House itself. He wed Frances Folsom in 1886.

- With 15 children from 2 marriages, President John Tyler was the most prolific chief executive.

- President George Washington never shook hands with visitors, choosing to bow instead.

- The only president never to have won a national election was Gerald Ford, who took office after President Richard Nixon resigned in 1974.

- President Jimmy Carter is said to be able to speed-read at the rate of 2,000 words per minute.

- Franklin Delano Roosevelt was related to 11 other presidents, either directly or through marriage.

- There hasn't been a bearded president since Benjamin Harrison, who left office in 1893.

- President James Garfield could write Latin with one hand and Greek with the other—at the same time.

- George W. Bush's brother Neil was scheduled to dine with John Hinckley's brother, Scott, the day after Hinckley tried to kill President Ronald Reagan.

- John Adams and Thomas Jefferson both died on July 4, 1826, 50 years to the day after the official signing of the Declaration of Independence.

- Edwin Booth, the brother of Abraham Lincoln's assassin, John Wilkes Booth, once saved the life of President Lincoln's son, Robert. He kept the boy from falling off a train platform.

Ten Most Popular Boys' Names, 1950

Happy 60th birthday. Here's who shared your moniker in 1950.

James Congratulations! You not only have the most popular boys' name for 1950, but according to data culled from U.S. government Web sites and Social Security card applications, you also bear the most popular name of that decade!

Robert Another popular name throughout the 1950s, "Robert" began a slide in popularity in the 1960s, with its sharpest decline occurring in the 1970s.

John Noteworthy "Johns" born that year include Candy, Hughes, and Landis. This simple moniker remained popular through much of the 20th century, but like Robert, the name has seen a steady decline since the 1970s.

Michael This top ten name actually gained in popularity and held steady through much of the mid-20th century before dropping off in the 1990s.

David *The Partridge Family* heartthrob David Cassidy premiered in 1950.

William Both William Hurt and William H. Macy were born in 1950. So was comedian Bill Murray.

Richard 1950 was the lucky year that gave us Richard Dean Anderson, aka "MacGyver."

Thomas Director Tommy Schlamme, owner of one of the greatest names in Hollywood, turned 60 in 2010.

Charles The early 1950s saw the peak of popularity for this name, conceivably due to the 1948 birth of Charles, the prince of Wales. Since 1880, the name has been given to more than two million boys.

Gary We would've loved to include Gary Sinise, but he wasn't born until 1955, so we went with Gary Graham, star of *Alien Nation* and *Star Trek: Enterprise*.

The Capital(s) of the United States

Washington, D.C., wasn't always our nation's capital. Since America's inception, no less than nine cities have served in that illustrious capacity. Looks like Congress has always had trouble making up its mind.

Philadelphia, Pennsylvania
(1774–76, 1777, 1778–83, 1790–1800)

Carpenters' Hall served as the original meeting spot for America's First Continental Congress. Now-famous delegates like George Washington, John Adams, and Patrick Henry hammered out policy in an attempt to assuage difficulties cast upon them by England, their ruling country. But a war for independence was on the horizon.

Baltimore, Maryland
(December 20, 1776–February 27, 1777)

In an attempt to evade hostile British forces then massing in Philadelphia, Baltimore's Henry Fite House was tapped as America's next headquarters. However, expensive living costs and distasteful conditions would quickly drive Congress back to Philadelphia's Independence Hall.

Lancaster, Pennsylvania
(September 27, 1777)

Sensing a continued British threat, Congress resolved to meet in Lancaster, Pennsylvania. Only one session was convened at Lancaster's Court House before Congress issued another headquarters resolution. The group would next meet across the Susquehanna River in the town of York.

York, Pennsylvania
(September 30, 1777–June 27, 1778)

The York Court House served as America's next base. Nine months later, Congress learned that the British Army had evacuated Philadelphia, so they decided to return to Independence Hall. But Congress' short stay in York had been a productive one. While there, the assembled throng passed the Articles of Confederation and signed a treaty of alliance with France.

Princeton, New Jersey
(June 30, 1783–November 4, 1783)

During the final days of the Revolutionary War, negotiations to sign a peace treaty with England were under way, but many battle-weary soldiers thought that an end would never come. As a result, some turned mutinous. On June 20, 1783, a group of these disgruntled soldiers surrounded Philadelphia's Independence Hall. While violence was ultimately averted, Congress felt that Pennsylvania had failed to provide them with proper protection. The group passed another resolution naming Nassau Hall in Princeton, New Jersey, as command center. In well-practiced fashion, Congress would only stay at its new home a few short months before relocating to Annapolis, Maryland.

Annapolis, Maryland
(November 26, 1783–August 19, 1784)

For the brief period that the Annapolis State House acted as America's headquarters, two key incidents took place: A definitive peace treaty was ratified with Great Britain, and General George Washington resigned as commander in chief of the Continental Army. Next, it was on to Trenton.

Trenton, New Jersey
(November 1, 1784–December 24, 1784)

If the French Arms Tavern sounds like an unlikely spot to house Congress, a closer look suggests otherwise. Formerly a personal residence, the ornate tavern was considered Trenton's most beautiful home. The dwelling was leased by the New Jersey legislature for use by Congress, but few actions were taken under its roof during their tenure. Congress would spend just two months at its New Jersey home before relocating to New York.

Manhattan, New York
(January 11, 1785–Autumn 1788;
March 4, 1789–August 12, 1790)

Taking a cue from the French Arms Tavern before it, New York's Fraunces Tavern became the second of four Manhattan venues to host Congress (City Hall and two locations on Broadway rounded out the roster). The delegates would remain at these transitory sites for five years before making their final move to Washington, D.C.

Washington, D.C.
(1800–present)

The Congressional Act of July 16, 1790, provided that Washington, D.C., would serve as America's permanent seat of government beginning in December 1800. Since then, the president, Congress, and many branches of government have been based in this agreeable location beside the Potomac River.

"If people see the Capitol going on, it is a sign we intend the Union shall go on."
—Abraham Lincoln

Successful Dropouts!

Parents commonly tell their children, "You'll never become successful without a college education!" Sound advice to be sure, but it's not always true. Consider these 17 extremely wealthy individuals who turned their backs on higher education.

1. **S. Daniel Abraham** Made billions by founding Slim-Fast. Never attended college.

2. **Christina Aguilera** One of the most successful pop singers in the world. Dropped out of high school.

3. **Paul Allen** Made billions as one of the cofounders of Microsoft. Dropped out of Washington State.

4. **Bill Bartman** Made billions as a successful businessman. Dropped out of high school.

5. **Richard Branson** Billionaire founder of Virgin Music and Virgin Atlantic Airways. Dropped out of high school.

6. **Andrew Carnegie** One of America's first multibillionaires. Dropped out of elementary school.

7. **Jack Kent Cooke** Billionaire owner of the Washington Redskins. Dropped out of high school.

8. **Ron Popeil** Multimillionaire inventor and television pitchman. Dropped out of college.

9. **Kjell Inge Rokke** Billionaire Norwegian businessman. Dropped out of high school.

10. **J. K. Rowling** Billionaire author of the *Harry Potter* series and one of the richest women in Great Britain. Never attended college.

11. **Frederick Henry Royce** Made millions as the cofounder of Rolls-Royce. Dropped out of elementary school.

12. **Vidal Sassoon** Made millions as the founder of Vidal Sassoon hairstyling salons and hair care products. Dropped out of high school.

Ten Cool Things Available for Rent from 20th Century Props

The harsh economic climate of 2009 took its toll on numerous businesses, including Hollywood's 20th Century Props. Owner Harvey Schwartz was forced to sell his more than 93,000-item warehouse collection at auction. Among the items once available:

1. ***Austin Powers* Escape Pod** This cryogenic chamber was used by Dr. Evil in *Austin Powers: International Man of Mystery* (1997).

2. **Cleopatra's Throne** No, this chair didn't belong to *the* Cleopatra. More accurately, this is the silver-and-gold chair that Claudette Colbert sat on in the 1934 film *Cleopatra*.

3. **Dragon Armchair** This hand-carved chair was used in Nicole Kidman's boudoir in *Moulin Rouge* (2001).

4. **Egyptian Mummies** Individually wrapped for freshness.

5. **Howard Hughes's Desk** Actually used by the moneymaking genius and also employed as a prop in the Hughes biopic, *The Aviator* (2004).

6. **J. R. Ewing's Desk** Oil and *Dallas* theme music not included.

7. **Life-sized Alien** Taken from *The X-Files* morgue.

8. **Life-sized *Tyrannosaurus Rex* Skeleton** The perfect Halloween decoration, often called into service for *Jurassic Park*–themed soirees and once used in an episode of *CSI:NY*.

9. **Marilyn Monroe Armchair** It may not have belonged to her, but she sat on it, so it still counts.

10. **Pirate Ship** This vessel was 15 feet long and probably not seaworthy, yet still fun at boarding parties.

Ten Wild Animal Stories

Talk a walk on the wild side with these unpredictable creatures.

1. Mooo!

The lure of Nashua, New Hampshire, proved to be too much for two Massachusetts cows. In June 2009, the animals wandered away from their farm and walked five miles across the state line. One cow was captured—but only after it got stuck up to its neck in the mud. The other, it seems, made it to greener pastures.

2. Dolphin Dilemma

If there's one thing New Jersey is famous for, it's dolphins. Well, at least for a little while in 2009 when a few dolphins found their way into the Shrewsbury River, searching for food. After the water froze, the good people of New Jersey feared the worst, but witnesses at a seafood restaurant later claimed they saw our flippered friends headed into the open waters of Sandy Hook Bay, apparently none the worse for wear.

3. Grin and "Bear" It

The sedate atmosphere of a Denver suburb was broken in October 2009 when a bear cub found itself trapped inside a car. There was no word on how the bear made its way into the vehicle. Rather than eat his rescuers, the cub simply ran from the car once an officer (who presumably drew the short straw) opened the door.

4. Oh Deer!

A Winston-Salem deli must have some of the best sandwiches in town. Why else would a pet deer break free from its owner (who happened to be taking the animal for a walk), crash through the eatery's window, and run through the establishment? As for the question of why a person would have a deer for a pet in the first place, we don't have an answer.

5. Eat Me

An Angus steer was none too happy to learn that it was on the menu. When the 1,000-pound animal arrived at a suburban Cincinnati meat-packing business, it spotted an open gate and made a mad dash for freedom. A market spokesman was quoted as saying, "It's not a mean animal…it's running, not even knowing where it's headed."

6. Don't Ask, Don't Baaaaaa

There's nothing wrong with being a gay sheep. Researchers at Oregon Health & Science University learned that the hard way after they killed dozens of homosexual sheep in order to dissect their brains to uncover a cause for their behavior. Several groups, among them PETA, were not amused. (Incidentally, scientists believe that 8 percent of all rams prefer same-sex partners.)

7. What About the Butter?

When you're stuck in a tank at the supermarket, what else are you going to do but plot your escape? In 2007, a group of lobsters took advantage of a loose lid to depart their cages and exit the store via the front door, where they were later apprehended.

8. Last Call for Alcohol

Dogs just don't know when to say when. Case in point: In 2008, a pooch was taken to the vet reeking of booze and unable to stand. Seems the hound ate a pound of yeast dough, which then fermented in the animal's tummy.

9. Bad Dog

So what's a dog that's chasing a car going to do when it catches the vehicle? Why, rip off the bumper with its teeth, of course! That's what two pit bulls did in October 2009 in Arkansas, when a resident called police to report that the pups were attacking her parked car. Part of the vehicle's bumper and fender were torn off by the pooches, which bloodied their mouths before they fled the scene.

10. Gobble Gobble BITE

After years of being the main course, turkeys in Davis, California, seem to have mounted a counterattack. Sort of. A pack of wild turkeys—the kind of ne'er-do-wells who hang out in cemeteries—began attacks on residents in 2007. The three-foot-tall birds were especially fond of bicyclists.

- *Just as humans favor their right or left hand, elephants favor their right or left tusk.*
- *Zebras are black with white stripes (not white with black stripes) and have black skin.*

Weasel Words

Advertisers, politicians, and corporations are infamous for using doublespeak and euphemisms to either hide or neutralize what they're trying to sell or say. Weasel words drain the meaning from a thought or action, just as a weasel sucks the contents from an egg. Here are a few weaselly words and phrases we hear every day.

bad patient outcome

between jobs

chemically tested

companion animal

complexity resolution

control technique

core strength

critical matrix

destination icon

dysfunctional family

empowerment

exit strategy

extraordinary rendition

fixer-upper

headcount reduction

human resources

immersive experience

inclusion support facilitator

lifestyle destination

limited mobility

mainstreaming

network-centric

new and improved

ongoing value creation

outside the box

partner (as a verb)

positive birth experience

pre-owned vehicle

productivity gains

quality face time

retail landscape

self-harm incident

self-regulation

touch base

vacation specialist

voluntary termination

Nine Ridiculous "Fans on the Field" Incidents

For these misguided fans, "Take Me out to the Ball Game" could just as easily have turned into "Jailhouse Rock."

1. Ten-Cent Beer Night

In the planning stages, selling beer for a dime probably seemed like a good promotion back in 1974. But things got a little dicey after approximately 60,000 brews were sold. Fans at Cleveland Municipal Stadium stormed the field as the Indians played the Texas Rangers. Punches were thrown, chairs were used as weapons, and the Rangers were awarded the game.

2. Hank Aaron Breaks Babe Ruth's Record

Considering that Hank Aaron had received numerous death threats as he closed in on Babe Ruth's all-time home run record in 1974, it may have been ill-advised for fans to take to the field and run toward the future Hall of Famer—even if they only wanted to give him a congratulatory pat on the back.

3. Morganna

One baseball constant during the 1970s and 1980s was Morganna the Kissing Bandit. The top-heavy blonde became famous for running onto various ball fields to steal a kiss from a player. Among those puckered: George Brett, Pete Rose, and Nolan Ryan (the Ryan kiss resulted in her arrest).

4. Flag-Burning Rescue

Chicago Cubs center fielder Rick Monday wasn't amused when a pair of fans ran onto the field at Dodger Stadium on April 25, 1976. He was even less amused when the spectators prepared to set an American flag on fire. Monday swooped in and snatched the flag while police arrested the scofflaws. The stadium gave Monday a standing ovation.

5. Disco Demolition Night

A simple promotion—blowing up disco records—featuring popular Chicago radio disc jockey Steve Dahl turned into a mob scene on July 12, 1979, at Comiskey Park. Between games of a Chicago White Sox–Detroit Tigers doubleheader, Dahl exploded a collection of records. Within minutes, thousands of fans descended upon the field, forcing the ChiSox to forfeit Game 2.

6. A Pitcher's Duel

Fans are accustomed to booing pitchers when they give up key runs. One fan took it to the next level in 1995 after Cubs reliever Randy Myers gave up a home run to give the Houston Astros the lead. The man rushed the pitcher's mound, perhaps to give Myers some advice on what to throw next. Instead, Myers floored him with his forearm.

7. Attacking Fans

Houston right fielder Bill Spiers was on the receiving end of such an attack in 1999 as the team was playing the Milwaukee Brewers. He ended up with a welt under his left eye, a bloody nose, and whiplash. The fan ended up with a beating from pitcher Mike Hampton.

8. Attacking Fans—a Different Approach

Chad Kreuter and several members of the Los Angeles Dodgers put a little twist on this category when they chased a fan into the Wrigley Field seats after the man grabbed Kreuter's cap.

9. Royals Coach Attacked

Being an MLB coach is supposed to involve strategy and a fair amount of arm-waving. Defending yourself from blows by idiotic fans is not in the job description. Tell that to the shirtless White Sox fan (and his son) who ran on to the field at U.S. Cellular in 2002 and began beating Kansas City Royals first-base coach Tom Gamboa.

Alternative Marriage

Regardless of your position on same-sex marriage, it's probably safe to say that few would consider the following marriages anything but alternative

Erika La Tour Eiffel In June 2008, a San Francisco woman legally changed her name to establish a bond with the famous tower after friends conducted a wedding between them. Eiffel complains, "The issue of intimacy—or rather lack of it—is forever present."

Eija-Riitta Berliner-Mauer This Swedish woman took the German name for the Berlin Wall after "marrying" it in June 1979. Says Mauer: "In Eastern cultures people routinely believe objects have souls."

Sharon Tendler In 2005, British-born Tendler married a male dolphin named Cindy. The monogamous type, Tendler calls herself a "one dolphin" woman.

Selva Kumar After stoning two dogs to death, Kumar, a Hindu, made amends by marrying a female dog in 2007. He hoped that the union would lift the "curse" that has followed him since his cruel act.

Mr. Tombe A council of local elders forced a Sudanese man known as Mr. Tombe to marry a goat after he was caught having sex with the animal in 2006.

Dauveed Mysterious Californian Dauveed popped the question to a mannequin named Clara in June 2009. While her response was presumably wooden, Clara apparently complied, and the two have made the Hollywood scene ever since.

Emily Mabou Ms. Mabou decided to marry a dog in 2009 after being mistreated by men.

Sagula Munda In 2009, the two-year-old Munda was married to a dog in eastern India. The reason? Villagers felt that the union would "ward off evil spirits and bad luck."

Phulram Chaudhary A Nepalese man married a female dog for good luck in 2004, only to die three days later. Sassy news agencies called it the "deadly consequences of marrying a bitch."

Presidentially Speaking

"Blessed are the young for they shall inherit the national debt."
—Herbert Hoover

"Things may come to those who wait,
but only the things left by those who hustle."
—Abraham Lincoln

"Never kick a fresh turd on a hot day."
—Harry Truman

"Always be sincere, even if you don't mean it."
—Harry Truman

"Any man who wants to be president is either
an egomaniac or crazy."
—Dwight D. Eisenhower

"My brother Bob doesn't want to be in government—
he promised Dad he'd go straight."
—John F. Kennedy

"We've uncovered some embarrassing ancestors in the not-too-distant past. Some horse thieves and some people killed on Saturday nights. One of my relatives, unfortunately, was even in the newspaper business."
—Jimmy Carter

"I do not like broccoli. And I haven't liked it since I was a little kid and my mother made me eat it. And I'm president of the United States and I'm not going to eat any more broccoli."
—George H. W. Bush

"You can put wings on a pig, but you don't make it an eagle."
—William Jefferson Clinton

"I have a different vision of leadership. A leadership is someone who brings people together."
—George W. Bush

"It's clearly a budget. It's got a lot of numbers in it."
—George W. Bush

"The fact that a man is a newspaper reporter is evidence of some flaw of character."
—Lyndon B. Johnson

How to Kill the Undead

It's getting so you can barely drive to a remote wooded location or let a teeny-weeny little mutant virus loose without attracting the undead. Zombies and vampires are seemingly everywhere, from big cities to rural hamlets, and from the frozen tundra to the blazing desert. A person needs to be prepared—knowing how to destroy the undead can prevent them from ruining your day.

I Have Seen the Enemy, and It Is Grandma

In order to kill the undead, it's first important to know which type of creature you're facing. For example, there are numerous types of zombies. Imagine how you'd feel if you thought you were facing the slow, shambling zombies from *Shaun of the Dead* or a George A. Romero flick and figured you could easily outmaneuver them, and instead they turned out to be the fast-paced zombies from the *Dawn of the Dead* remake. Wouldn't your face be red! (Granted, as they ate your brain.)

Vampires are similar: Some vampires turn into crispy critters in the sunlight. However, Dracula himself walked around London in the daytime. A vampire's aversion to sunlight is strictly a 20th-century invention.

By the same token, you should realize that any former affiliations you may have had with the undead have no meaning anymore. If you see grandma lurching toward the house or floating outside your window—and she's been dead since last May—it's likely she's not back to offer you a plate of fresh-baked chocolate chip cookies. Common sense is key.

Killing Them Softly... Sort Of

Weapons for taking down the undead abound. For zombies, the best weapon is a shotgun or any other type of firearm that can dispatch the creature with a headshot from a distance. (As Romero put it: Kill the brain, kill the ghoul.) Of course, loading up with fresh ammunition is annoying, which is why a machete is a popular choice. A chainsaw also works well, but with the price of gasoline nowadays, you may not want to waste it on zombies. A baseball bat, crowbar, or other bludgeoning implement also gets the job done, and you never run out of ammo.

Setting a zombie on fire may look pretty, but until the flames melt the brain, all you've really done is create a shambling fire hazard. The same for explosives—since a zombie's dead already, it will simply shrug off the loss of a limb or the inconvenience of shrapnel wounds.

When battling zombies, always wear tight-fitting clothing. Zombies are like babies; they'll grab whatever they can and stick it in their mouths. Your clothes should also be heavy, like leather, to provide bite protection.

Vampires: Old-School Slaughtering

Killing a vampire is more old-school, organic work. To kill a vampire, a stake made of aspen, ash, hawthorn, or maple through the heart usually does the trick. Decapitation also works; sometimes the head is placed under the arm or between the legs to make it harder for it to rejoin the body. Some Slavic traditions specify that only a sexton's or gravedigger's shovel can be used for this purpose, so plan accordingly. Burning a vampire can be effective, but it may take a while.

Unlike zombies, vampires can be deterred. A simple smearing of garlic often does the trick. According to legend, a vampire is compulsively neat, so throwing a handful of seeds, salt, or sand into its path will force it to pick up every grain before resuming its pursuit. Another legend says that a vampire will stop and read every word of a torn-up newspaper thrown in its way.

However, there is no word as to how well this works with an illiterate vampire.

Now That Would Have Been a Great Photo!

If only we had a camera—and a time machine—to capture these historic events. Unfortunately, each took place prior to the development of modern photography in the 1820s.

1. The Big Bang No need for flash photography at the Big Bang...though the images may have been overexposed.

2. Dinosaurs Doesn't matter if they're from the Triassic, Jurassic, or Cretaceous period, they would've looked awesome!

3. Neanderthals Their ability to make fire and advanced tools would have made a great "how-to" book filled with step-by-step instructions and illustrations.

4. Egyptian Pyramids Another great "how-to" book!

5. Birth of Christ Whatever your religious beliefs, you have to admit that this would have been the ultimate baby album.

6. Destruction of Pompeii Spectacular color photography would have emerged from that fateful day in A.D. 79—provided the photographer didn't get too close to Mount Vesuvius.

7. Charlemagne Is Crowned It's not every day that someone becomes Holy Roman Emperor.

8. Magna Carta Is Signed And history is made.

9. **Mona Lisa Is Painted** Maybe it's a good thing there was no photography in 1503; Leonardo da Vinci would have gotten off too easy.

10. **Christopher Columbus "Discovers" the New World** Send a couple of snapshots back to Queen Isabella and let her know you're okay.

11. **Henry VIII of England** Acting as official royal wedding photographer to King Henry VIII would surely have kept any shutterbug busy.

12. **The Pilgrims' First Thanksgiving** Pilgrims and Indians—what's not to love?

13. **Declaration of Independence** Benjamin Franklin could have called in some favors from his days as a newspaper editor to get a photographer into the 1776 signing.

14. **War of 1812** We could use a couple of photos of the rockets' red glare and the bombs bursting in air to accompany the lyrics to "The Star-Spangled Banner."

15. **George Washington's First Presidential Inauguration** Hail to the chief!

Steven Sasson, an engineer at Eastman Kodak, produced the first prototype digital camera in 1975. Weighing eight pounds, the camera took 23 seconds to capture its first image.

"A person is neither whole nor healthy without the memories of photo albums. They are the storybook of our lives. They provide a nostalgic escape from the tormented days of the present."
—Patrick Garry

Wacky Jelly Belly Flavors

There was a time when root beer was considered an exotic flavor for a jelly bean. Jelly Belly candy makers have since raised the bar for strange flavors—especially with some of their most recent selections.

- Pickle
- Black Pepper
- Booger
- Dirt
- Earthworm
- Earwax
- Sausage
- Rotten Egg
- Soap
- Vomit
- Sardine
- Grass
- Skunk Spray
- Bacon
- Baby Wipes
- Pencil Shavings
- Toothpaste
- Moldy Cheese
- Buttered Popcorn
- Dr. Pepper
- Jalapeño
- Margarita
- Spinach
- Cappuccino
- Peanut Butter
- Café Latte
- 7UP
- Pomegranate
- Baked Beans

The Impossible 'Possum

Let's face it: Opossums are weird. But here are some interesting facts that might change your mind about the unique opossum.

- Opossums are the only marsupial (a mammal that carries its young in a pouch) native to North America.

- The word *opossum* comes from the Algonquin word *apasum,* meaning "white animal." Captain John Smith used "opossum" around 1612, when he described it as a cross between a pig, a cat, and a rat.

- Although it is often colloquially called the " 'possum," the opossum is completely different from a possum, an Australian marsupial.

- The opossum's nickname is "the living fossil," as it dates back to the dinosaurs and the Cretaceous Period, 70 million years ago. It is the oldest surviving mammal family on Earth.

- When cornered, opossums vocalize ferociously and show all 50 of their teeth, which they have more of than any other mammal. But they are not fighters and prefer to run from danger.

- If trapped, they will "play 'possum," an involuntary response in which their bodies go rigid, and they fall to the ground in a state of shock. Their breathing slows, they drool a bit, and they release smelly green liquid from their anal sacs. This is enough to convince most predators the opossum is already dead, leaving it alone.

- Despite their predilection for eating anything—including rotting flesh—opossums are fastidious about hygiene. They bathe themselves frequently, including several times during each meal.

- Opossums are extremely resistant to most forms of disease and toxins, including rabies and snake venom, the latter probably due to their low metabolism.

- The idea that opossums mate through the female's nostrils is a myth. Although the male opossum has a forked (bifid) penis, he mates with the female in the normal manner.

Memorable Fast-Food Mascots

The Big Boy

The Big Boy, a 12-foot statue of a chubby boy that stands outside Big Boy restaurants, is considered one of the first fast-food mascots. The grinning boy, with the words "Big Boy" stamped across his chest, sports red-and-white overalls and holds a triple-decker hamburger in his hand. No wonder he's so big.

Speedee

No, this isn't the Alka-Seltzer mascot. McDonald's originally had its own Speedee mascot, a chef with a hamburger for a head. McDonald's dropped Speedee to avoid any legal battles with Alka-Seltzer. The chain's new mascot, Ronald McDonald, has done pretty well: A poll once found that 96 percent of children recognized the burger-slinging clown.

The Taco Bell Chihuahua

You may not know that the Chihuahua that famously promoted Taco Bell products was named Gidget. You also may not know that Gidget passed away in July 2009 after suffering a stroke. She was 15.

Pizza Hut Chef

Many fast-food mascots have been discontinued because they were deemed insulting to different ethnic groups. Pizza Hut, for instance, once featured an Italian chef tossing a dough ball. The chef was replaced by the chain's "red roof" logo because PepsiCo, which had purchased Pizza Hut, was concerned that the mascot was too cartoonishly Italian.

Colonel Harland Sanders

Not many mascots are real people, but Harland Sanders, the mascot and founder of Kentucky Fried Chicken, is. Sanders lacked an advertising budget when starting his restaurant chain. To save money, he became his chain's own mascot.

Wimpy

Wimpy Grills, which closed in 1978, featured the hamburger-loving Wimpy character from the Popeye comic strip as its mascot. The restaurant, which had 1,500 outlets across the United States at one time, closed after the death of its founder, Edward Vale Gold. Gold had specified in his will that he wanted all Wimpy's outlets closed once he died.

The Tastee-Freez Twins

Female Tee and male Eff represent soft-serve ice-cream chain Tastee-Freez. The twins have ice cream running down their heads, with Tee sporting strawberry and Eff dripping chocolate.

Iam Hungry

If you blinked, you might have missed this fast-food mascot. Iam Hungry was a floating ball of fuzz with orange arms that tried desperately to mooch McDonald's meals from Ronald McDonald. McDonald's introduced the mascot in 1998 and dumped him in the early 2000s.

The Noid

The Noid, an odd creature with rabbit ears who wore a tight red latex suit, appeared in commercials for Domino's Pizza in the 1980s and 1990s. The creature only communicated with odd grunts and groans and ranks as one of the creepiest of fast-food mascots.

The Sleepy Mexican

Here is another example of a mascot that was dumped because it was racially offensive. Taco Bell used a Siesta-enjoying Mexican figure as its mascot until PepsiCo bought the chain. PepsiCo replaced the mascot with the now-familiar mission bell logo.

Who Knew?

Taking a Shine to Aluminum Foil

You've got it in your kitchen, and you use it all the time there. But the kitchen isn't the only place for that handy roll of shininess. Aluminum foil is perfect for dozens of other projects and fixes around the house. Who knew?

- Most pets hate the feel and sound of aluminum foil. If you don't want your dog or cat on the furniture, place sheets of aluminum foil on the cushions. Birds don't like aluminum foil, either, so hang a few strips where you don't want feathered friends to roost.

- Doesn't it always happen that you have a three-inch piece left at the end of your aluminum foil roll? Don't throw it away! Fold it a few times and cut it with scissors for a nice, sharp blade.

- In the fall, wrap delicate saplings with a couple passes of heavy-duty aluminum foil to keep mice and other plant-killing varmints from nibbling on your baby trees. Remove foil in the spring.

- Out of wrapping paper? A sheet of aluminum foil makes fine in-a-pinch gift wrap. Bonus: You won't need tape.

- Take your foil camping! A few sheets of heavy-duty aluminum foil laid on the ground will keep your sleeping bag dry. Foil on a fish hook may help land the big one.

- Make gold and silver jewelry and silverware look new again. Wrap them in an aluminum foil pouch filled with weak saltwater. Leave overnight. The next morning, admire the shine.

- Wrinkle a handful of aluminum foil and rub carefully (it can scratch!) to clean bumpers, golf club shafts, and anything else made of chrome.

- Aluminum foil makes a great temporary palette for your budding artist. It can also be used for rainy-day sculpting contests. And aluminum foil can be spray-painted. Who knew?

Film Flops

Just because a movie features a big name doesn't necessarily mean that it will make a lot of money. In fact, some of the previous decade's most talked about motion pictures didn't even come close to earning back what it cost to make them. And the awards for biggest flops go to . . .

- *Battlefield Earth* (2000). Do the math: John Travolta + a mediocre story by L. Ron Hubbard = box office failure. Cost to make: $75 million. Domestic gross: $21 million.

- *Catwoman* (2004). Warner Bros. ponied up $100 million to make this Batman spin-off, which starred Halle Berry in the titular role. Domestic gross: $40 million.

- *Gigli* (2003). Few people could pronounce the title of this romantic comedy starring Ben Affleck and Jennifer Lopez; fewer went to see it. Cost to make: $54 million. Domestic gross: $6.1 million.

- *Grindhouse* (2007). Despite a huge advertising blitz around codirectors Quentin Tarantino and Robert Rodriguez, this stylized double-feature sank at the box office. Cost to make: $67 million. Domestic gross: $25 million.

- *Land of the Lost* (2009). This comedy, based on the '70s kids' program, proved that Will Ferrell doesn't always mean big box office. Cost to make: $100 million. Domestic gross: $65 million.

- *Rollerball* (2002). Audiences actively avoided this remake of the '70s sci-fi classic, resulting in a domestic gross of just $19 million. Cost to make: $70 million.

- *The Adventures of Pluto Nash* (2002). This sci-fi comedy starring Eddie Murphy takes the prize for biggest loser, bringing in a minuscule $4.4 million against a budget of $100 million.

- *The Invasion* (2007). Not even Nicole Kidman could save this remake of *Invasion of the Body Snatchers*. Cost to make: $80 million. Domestic gross: $15.1 million.

- *Town & Country* (2001). Warren Beatty's name used to mean box office gold. Sadly, this uninteresting comedy proved the sheen is gone. Cost to make: $90 million. Domestic gross: $6.7 million.

Strange but True Inventions

Pierced Glasses

Tired of your glasses slipping down your nose? Try pierced glasses—spectacles that connect to a piercing surgically implanted into the nose. Invented by James Sooy in 2004, these glasses appeal to body modification artists.

The Bulletproof Bed

Are you consumed with fearful thoughts when you go to bed? Perhaps you'll rest more peacefully in a bulletproof bed. The Quantum Sleeper's coffinlike design protects from attacks, fires, and natural disasters with its airtight and waterproof interior. The bed features an air filtration system and can be fitted with DVD screens, a refrigerator, and even a microwave!

The Portable Crosswalk

There never seems to be a crosswalk when you need one, and nobody wants to break the law by jaywalking. Instead, use a portable crosswalk, a vinyl sheet that can be spread across a busy street to ensure your safety as you make your way through traffic. Though its legality may be in question, it will certainly stop traffic...we hope.

Sauce-Dispensing Chopsticks

Need to shave time from your daily schedule? Try sauce-dispensing chopsticks for the sushi eater in a rush. No longer do you have to waste valuable seconds dipping your food into the soy sauce—just squeeze the end of the stick and the liquid flows right onto your food! The utensils cost about $20, but can you really put a price on time-saving of this magnitude?

The Drymobile

In this day and age, everyone is looking for ways to save time and energy. Now you can do both with the Japanese Drymobile. Hang your clothes from a rack that fits on top of your car, and your clothes will be dry in no time as you run your daily errands...unless, of course, it starts to rain.

One-Cut Nail Clippers

Staying well groomed can be quite time-consuming. But now one task can be shortened with one-cut nail clippers. A series of five clippers are positioned over the toes or fingernails, allowing the user to cut all five nails at once.

The Gas Grabber

Sometimes you just can't blame the dog. For those occasions, turn to the Gas Grabber, a charcoal filter that slips into your underwear to cover up those social faux pas. The filter was originally developed by the British to guard against nerve agents.

The Grin Grabber

Some people just don't smile enough, so it's the Grin Grabber to the rescue! Attach a hook to each side of your mouth, grasp the string, and yank. The pulley system will lift the corners, and soon you'll be beaming from ear to ear!

The Snot Sucker

No tissue? No problem! The WIVA-VAC Nasal Aspirator uses vacuum power to clean up a runny nose. Perfect for children on the go; just slip the tapered end into a nostril and suck the snot right out!

The Daddy Nurser

Men can experience the joy of motherhood with the Daddy Nurser, a pair of milk-filled orbs that connect to a man's chest to mimic the act of breast-feeding. If only they could invent a way for men to give birth!

Deadliest Creepy Crawlies

Insect stings kill between 40 and 100 Americans every year.
But in other parts of the world, bugs kill many times that number.
Here are some of the most fearsome.

- **Locusts** Individually, locusts are just weird-looking grasshoppers. But when they swarm, look out! Locusts can rapidly devastate huge regions of farmland, leading to mass starvation.

- **Mosquitoes** Believe it or not, mosquitoes are responsible for more deaths than any other creature. The reason? They spread a wide variety of potentially deadly diseases including malaria, which kills an estimated two million people annually.

- **Africanized Bees** Big honeybees with a really bad attitude, Africanized bees attack with little provocation. Worse, when one bee stings, it releases a chemical that provokes the entire nest.

- **Fleas** Little more than a nuisance today, fleas are one of history's greatest mass killers. Fleas are thought to have wiped out one-third of the population of Europe through the transmission of bubonic plague in the 14th century.

- **Brazilian Wandering Spider** The most venomous spider in the world, this deadly nocturnal hunter likes to hide in banana bunches during the day. One bite, and you're in big trouble.

- **Black Widow** Another deadly arachnid, the black widow's venom is more powerful than that of the cobra or the coral snake.

- **Sydney Funnel-Web Spider** Indigenous to Australia, this venomous spider's fangs are strong enough to puncture shoes.

- **Tsetse Fly** This harmless-looking bug is responsible for spreading sleeping sickness throughout Africa, resulting in hundreds of deaths each year.

Con Talk

As long as there has been greed, there have been con artists. In fact, the games cons play have a language all their own.

- The **shill** is important to many con schemes because he's the confederate who draws the sucker to the bait. The shill is also called the **roperor stooge.**

- **Cooling the mark**—This remains the most important part of any confidence game, as it allows the victim, or **mark,** to depart the scene feeling like he got lucky, when in fact, he's been taken.

- The **Big Store con** made famous in the movie *The Sting* was based on reality. Involving high overheads and multiple confederates, this con is directed at a single mark—often another con man—for a big payoff. One Chicago-based con man, Yellow Kid Weil, staffed a fake bank with prostitutes and fellow con artists in order to take a corrupt businessman. Of course, most cons aren't that elaborate.

Smaller Scale Cons

Short cons come in all sizes and flavors. They're the bread and butter for many con artists because they can be carried out quickly and inexpensively. Among these are:

- **Chugging**—Hustling donations to a fictitious charity. Currently used for fake disaster relief donations.

- **The Gypsy Switch**—Involves switching something valuable for something worthless. This con is probably the origin of the adage, "If it seems too good to be true, it probably is."

- **True Believer Syndrome**—Fake swamis, palm readers, and psychics love naïve marks afflicted with this "syndrome," because it means they keep coming back for more. Repeat business is always better than a one-time con.

20 Can't-Miss Items from the Johnson Smith Company

Launched in Chicago in 1914, the Johnson Smith Company has been providing the world with whimsical gift ideas for nearly a century. The next time you're struggling to find that perfect gift for the person who has everything, why not consider one of these essential items?

1. *A Christmas Story* Leg Lamp Bobble Head

As if life isn't complicated enough.

2. Acre of Pacific Ocean

Finally! Something useful! One acre of Pacific Ocean floor situated somewhere between California and Hawaii. Stake your claim for 20 bucks, and build the island that you deserve.

3. Animal Sounds Clock

Each hour sounds with a different animal call, including a bison, camel, and panda. Listed (in all seriousness) in the company's catalog under "Useful Things."

4. Butt Cheek Boxers

These clever underwear look like an exposed bum—the perfect gift for the shy exhibitionist in your life.

5. Dog Mustache Disguise

Presumably for those days when your underage dog wants to buy liquor or cigarettes, this rubber fetch ball comes complete with a handlebar mustache attached.

6. Disappearing Ink

A classic prank for the seven-year-old in everyone!

7. Fake Vomit

Another classic prank, this item features a vividly written catalog description with the selling point: "Almost turns your stomach... it's so realistic. The 'gloopiest' look."

8. Fanny Bank

Yes, gentle reader, it's exactly what it sounds like: a toy bank that allows its owner to insert coins into a strategically placed slot. The payoff? Inappropriate bodily function sounds!

9. Flatulence, Flatulence, and More Flatulence

Apparently, nothing is funnier than farting. This explains why the company produces such items as a remote-control fart machine, fart powder, fart spray, a farting gnome, a fart pen, a remote-controlled farting bear, and that old standby—a whoopee cushion.

10. Flavored Body Pens

Chocolate- or strawberry-flavored—perfect for those days when you can't find anything else in the fridge to eat.

11. Gag GPS System

Nothing screams "hilarious" like becoming hopelessly lost at night in a strange area while your GPS unit makes wisecracks.

12. Hunk Ironing Board Cover

So... people still iron, huh?

13. Jiggle Jugs

Anatomically correct female anatomy made out of soft vinyl and equipped with a motion detector. The company's online

catalog proclaims that the item is "fun for...(the) office..."
Wanna bet most HR and legal departments disagree?

14. Meowing Cat Pencil Sharpener

Now *this* is something that will be fun for the entire office!
Also available in barking dog.

15. Nose Shower Gel Dispenser

It looks like nasal discharge but it's not! (Ha ha ha ha! Get it?)
Seriously though, this nose dispenses shower gel. Why exactly,
no one knows.

16. Phony Brick

What every litigious society needs—a fake brick to throw at
passersby.

17. Ponytail Cap

Turns any well-groomed young man into an aging hippie.

18. Shocking Pen

Guaranteed to discourage pen thieves! The ballpoint
pen apparently "shocks" (but does not electrocute) any
ne'er-do-well.

19. World's Largest Flask

Able to transport 64 ounces, this flask sends a clear-cut message: "What drinking problem?"

20. X-Ray Glasses

We'll save you some heartache on this one: They don't actually
work.

Boy, Am I Stuffed!

Eating: It's not just for amateurs anymore.

In an age when everything from dancing to weight loss has become a competition, it should come as no surprise that eating is now a spectator sport. Indeed, an eclectic array of contests have been held in recent years, with trophies and large cash prizes going to those who can consume the most food in a given time. Here are just a few of the wackier world records, courtesy of the International Federation of Competitive Eating:

- **Baked beans:** 6 pounds in 1 minute, 48 seconds (Don Lerman)
- **Butter:** 7 quarter-pound sticks in 5 minutes (Don Lerman)
- **Chicken wings:** 7½ pounds in 12 minutes (Joey Chestnut)
- **Corned beef sandwiches:** 16¾ sandwiches (6 ounces each) in 10 minutes (Patrick Bertoletti)
- **Cow brains:** 57 (17.7 pounds) in 15 minutes (Takeru Kobayashi)
- **Doughnuts:** 49 glazed doughnuts in 8 minutes (Eric Booker)
- **Eggs:** 65 hard-boiled eggs in 6 minutes, 40 seconds (Sonya Thomas)
- **Grilled cheese sandwiches:** 47 in 10 minutes (Joey Chestnut)
- **Haggis:** 3 pounds in 8 minutes (Eric Livingston)
- **Hamburgers (Krystals):** 103 in 8 minutes (Joey Chestnut)
- **Hot dogs:** 68 Nathan's Famous Hot Dogs (with buns) in 10 minutes (Joey Chestnut)
- **Jalapeño peppers (pickled):** 247 in 8 minutes (Rich "The Locust" LeFevre)
- **Jambalaya:** 9 pounds in 10 minutes (Sonya Thomas)
- **Maine lobster:** 44 lobsters (11.3 pounds of meat) from the shell in 12 minutes (Sonya Thomas)

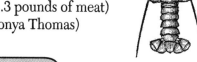

- **Matzo balls:** 21 baseball-sized matzos in 5 minutes, 25 seconds (Eric Booker)
- **Mayonnaise:** 4 bowls (32 ounces each) in 8 minutes (Oleg Zhornitskiy)
- **Nigiri sushi:** 141 pieces in 6 minutes (Timothy Janus)
- **Oysters:** 552 in 10 minutes (Sonya Thomas)
- **Pancakes:** 3 pounds of pancakes and bacon in 12 minutes (Crazy Legs Conti)
- **Peanut butter and jelly sandwiches:** 42 in 10 minutes (Patrick Bertoletti)
- **Pickles (sour):** 2.99 pounds in 5 minutes (Cookie Jarvis)
- **Pizza:** 47 slices in 10 minutes (Patrick Bertoletti)
- **Pumpkin pies:** 4⅜ Entenmann's pumpkin pies in 12 minutes (Eric Booker)
- **Ramen noodles:** 10.5 pounds in 8 minutes (Timothy Janus)

- **Shrimp:** 4 pounds, 15 ounces in 12 minutes (Erik "The Red" Denmark)
- **Sweet corn:** 314 ears in 12 minutes (Crazy Legs Conti)
- **Tamales:** 71 in 12 minutes (Timothy Janus)

❖ ❖ ❖

"I don't get crazy with it. The competitive eating thing is a weekend hobby."
—Ian Hickman

Real Names of the Rich and Famous

"A rose by any other name" is supposed to smell as sweet, but while that may be true in love, it isn't always so in show business. Below are the real names of some famous faces—see if you can match the real name to the alias.

1. Reginald Kenneth Dwight	a. John Wayne
2. Paul Hewson	b. Cary Grant
3. Mark Vincent	c. Woody Allen
4. David Robert Jones	d. Elton John
5. Caryn Elaine Johnson	e. Mark Twain
6. Nathan Birnbaum	f. Freddie Mercury
7. Archibald Leach	g. Bob Dylan
8. Eleanor Gow	h. George Michael
9. Samuel Langhorne Clemens	i. Whoopi Goldberg
10. Tara Patrick	j. Bono
11. McKinley Morganfield	k. Jason Alexander
12. Farrokh Bulsara	l. Demi Moore
13. Frances Gumm	m. Vin Diesel
14. Robert Allen Zimmerman	n. George Burns
15. Demetria Gene Guynes	o. David Bowie
16. Marion Morrison	p. Muddy Waters
17. Allen Konigsberg	q. Judy Garland
18. Georgios Panayiotou	r. Elle MacPherson
19. Jay Scott Greenspan	s. Carmen Electra

1–d; 2–j; 3–m; 4–o; 5–i; 6–n; 7–b; 8–r; 9–e; 10–s; 11–p; 12–f; 13–q; 14–g; 15–l; 16–a; 17–c; 18–h; 19–k.

Don't Let the Bedbugs Bite...

Good night, sleep tight. Don't let the bedbugs bite! For decades, bedbugs were all but extinct in many places. But recently, increased travel and less toxic modern pesticides have allowed a resurgence of these creepy crawlies.

- When full of blood, bedbugs can swell as large as three times their normal size.

- It takes a bedbug five minutes to drink its fill of blood.

- A female bedbug can lay as many as 5 eggs per day and 200 to 500 eggs in her lifetime.

- When bedbugs bite, proteins in their saliva prevent the wound from closing.

- Bedbugs can consume as much as six times their weight in blood at one feeding.

- Normally, a bedbug is brown. After eating, however, its body appears dark red.

- Bedbugs are nocturnal—they become active when humans are sleeping.

- Bedbugs only eat once every seven to ten days.

- In recent years, calls to pest-control companies about bedbugs have increased by more than 70 percent.

- Other names for bedbugs include "mahogany flats," "redcoats," and "chinches."

- Bedbugs molt five times before reaching adulthood.

- Bedbugs migrated from Europe to the United States during the 1600s.

- Contrary to popular belief, the presence of bedbugs does not indicate a dirty house.

It Happened in...August

- Stop and think about this: The first lighted traffic signals were installed in Cleveland, Ohio, in August 1914.

- In August 1861, Congress enacted the Revenue Act of 1861, which became the first income tax law. By law, incomes over $800 were taxed 3 percent.

- In August 1977, Elvis died. Or so they say...

- The world's last quagga—a uniquely striped subspecies of African Plains zebra—died in an Amsterdam zoo in 1883. Because of a quirk in language (the word *quagga* in Afrikaans referred to any strangely striped zebra), few then understood that the death of the mare meant extinction of the species.

- Snow fell in the Grand Canyon area in August 2009, and that's a good thing. Firefighters were battling a blaze in that area, and the white stuff helped quell the hot stuff.

- Copy that: Thomas Edison patented the mimeograph machine in August 1876, and generations of former schoolkids will never forget the smell of fresh ditto copies.

- The Factory Act of 1833 was passed in Great Britain. Among other things, it limited work hours for 14- to 18-year-olds to 12 hours a day, and it outlawed hiring children younger than age 9 in the textile industry.

- A very reluctant Clark Gable accepted the role of Rhett Butler in August 1938. He obviously gave a damn in the end.

- August is What Will Be Your Legacy Month, National Win with Civility Month (isn't that nice?), and—this will make you smile—Happiness Happens Month.

Odd Celebrity Deaths

Their lives may have been glamorous, but some celebrity deaths are downright bizarre.

John Bonham

Led Zeppelin's drummer famously died in 1980 after choking on vomit, reportedly following 40 shots of vodka. (The official cause of death was pulmonary edema—fluid in the lungs—caused by inhalation of vomit.)

Tommy Dorsey

A heavy meal and sleeping pills do not mix, as the Big Band bandleader learned in 1956 after he choked to death in his sleep.

Isadora Duncan

The dancer was strangled in 1927 when her flowing scarf was caught in a wheel of her moving automobile.

Peg Entwistle

Entwistle's sad demise in 1932 is noteworthy for its location. A wannabe starlet who never really shined, Entwistle climbed to the top of the "Hollywood" sign in California and flung her body to the ground.

Jimi Hendrix

What is it with rock icons and their vomit? Hendrix: 1970.

Steve Irwin

Wrestling crocodiles, reptiles, and other beasties was all in a day's work for "The Crocodile Hunter," yet death came at the end of a stingray's barbed tail while Irwin was snorkeling in 2006.

More Box Office Disasters

Cutthroat Island

Some movies are so dismal, they bankrupt an entire company. Such was the case with the Geena Davis pirate movie *Cutthroat Island*. With a budget of $115 million, this 1995 movie made only $10 million at the U.S. box office. In the process, it bankrupted production company Carolco Pictures. In fact, *Guinness World Records* ranks *Cutthroat Island* as the biggest money loser of all time.

Howard the Duck

There was a time when comic book superheroes didn't guarantee big grosses. *Howard the Duck,* the 1986 movie based on a wisecracking, cigar-smoking duck created by Marvel Comics, offers proof. The movie had a budget of $38 million but only made $16 million at the domestic box office.

Bad reviews sunk this film, and many critics still place it on their lists of all-time worst movies. Executive producer George Lucas made some questionable choices, including spending $2 million on a duck suit that looked like something from a bad Godzilla movie.

Speed Racer

Speed Racer was supposed to be one of the breakout hits of the 2008 summer movie season. Instead the film, directed by the Wachowski brothers of *Matrix* movie fame, ranked as the biggest loser of that summer.

Speed Racer cost $120 million to make but earned only $44 million at the box office. The film is considered a technological marvel, but its bright colors and endless onslaught of computer-generated effects gave audiences headaches. After bad word of mouth, the crowds stayed away. It took just 60 days to shoot *Speed Racer.* They may rank as the costliest 60 days in Warner Bros. history.

Cybernetic Stars: The Robot Hall of Fame

Robotlike machines date back nearly 2,000 years to the ancient Greeks, who designed impressive automatons—mechanical human and animal figures that moved as though they had a mind of their own. But these were really glorified wind-up toys. True robots—machines that can sense and respond to their environment independently—weren't a reality until the mid-20th century. In the short time since then, engineers have created countless robots with a wide range of abilities. Here are some of the more notable machines.

The First Robots

The first true robots were Elmer and Elsie, two machines created in the 1940s by neurophysiologist William Grey Walter. Each of Grey's bulky robots, which he called *tortoises,* had three wheels, a light-detecting photoelectric cell, electric sensors that detected contact with other objects, a rechargeable telephone battery, and an electronic circuit comprising two vacuum tubes enclosed in a clear plastic shell. The robots would move toward light sources and retreat when the light got very bright or when they encountered obstacles. When Walter attached lights to each of them, they would even dance with each other.

The Smallest Robot

In the future, we may think nothing of microscopic nanobots fixing up our bodies and cleaning our houses. But today, it's very difficult to shrink robotic technology. There are a few possible smallest bot champs, depending on how loosely you define "robot."

The smallest contender, developed at Dartmouth, measures 250 micrometers by 60 micrometers—about the width of a human hair. It's a tiny silicon strip that moves along like an inchworm by alternately extending and scrunching itself. However, it only works when placed on a grid of electrodes, which provide power and guide the robot's motion. So, it's not a truly autonomous robot.

In 2007, roboticists at the Technion-Israel Institute of Technology announced a robot with similar constraints: a millimeter-long machine designed to crawl through blood vessels. In this case, an external magnetic field powers and guides the robot.

The smallest fully autonomous robot with a built-in power supply is a tracked vehicle developed at Sandia National Laboratories. The microbot is one centimeter tall and a quarter of a cubic inch at the base—small enough to literally turn on a dime. It boasts 8 kilobytes of brain power, runs on 3 watch batteries, and can zip along at 20 inches per minute.

The Deadliest Robots

As of 2009, the U.S. military had 12,000 robots on the ground and 7,000 in the air. The deadliest of the bunch are the Predator and the Reaper uncrewed aircraft. The military initially used the $4.5 million Predator as an unarmed reconnaissance drone, loaded with cameras and sensors that acted as soldiers' eyes in the sky. But after 9/11, the military reconfigured it to carry two laser-guided Hellfire missiles. The Predator's newer, bigger cousin, the Reaper, can carry 14 Hellfire missiles or four missiles and two 500-pound bombs. Most of the 200 Predators and 30 Reapers in the U.S. fleet are controlled via satellite by crews sitting in front of computer screens in a base outside Las Vegas, thousands of miles from the action. The drones handle some tasks autonomously, but human controllers always decide whether to attack possible targets. The total Predator and Reaper body count isn't clear, but the Air Force says that in 2007 and 2008, the drones fired missiles in 244 missions in Afghanistan and Iraq. Drones have taken out at least 11 al-Qaeda leaders.

The Top Android

Honda bills its 4'3" ASIMO as "the world's most advanced humanoid robot," and most people would agree. The culmination of more than 20 years of research and development, ASIMO can walk, dance, climb stairs, and respond to commands. With a top speed of 3.7 miles per hour, the current version also holds the record as fastest robotic runner.

Scaring Up Some Halloween Trivia

The scariest day of the year isn't so frightening to either retailers or children. That's because, no matter what the economy is doing, Halloween continues to grow. Here are some fascinating facts about the only holiday in which werewolves, vampires, and ghosts are not only tolerated but are the guests of honor.

- Don't be surprised to see more than a few witches this Halloween. In 2008 (the most recent year for which data was available), 14.9 percent of adult Halloween revelers planned to don the black hats and broomsticks. Pirates, too, are popular with adults, with 4.4 percent grabbing eye patches, peg legs, and swords.

- The top-rated children's costume in 2008 was the princess, with 10.5 percent of young trick-or-treaters living the life of royalty for the day. Spider-Man was also popular, with 3.5 percent of children selecting the superhero's distinctive red-and-blue duds.

- Halloween isn't just for kids. An estimated 51.8 million adults planned to wear a costume for Halloween in 2008.

- The odds are good that Batman showed up at your door. The Dark Knight ranked as the sixth most popular costume for adults, the eighth most for children, and the sixteenth most common for trick-or-treaters of the four-legged variety.

- Did you spot Barack Obama, John McCain, or Sarah Palin walking the streets of your neighborhood on Halloween? An estimated 574,000 adults said they were planning to dress as political figures in 2008.

- Halloween is big business. Total Halloween spending in 2008 was estimated at $5.77 billion. The average U.S. resident planned to spend $66.54 on the holiday. That's a lot of candy corn! Consumers also spent an estimated average of $24.17 on Halloween costumes, $20.39 on candy, $18.25 on decorations, and $3.73 on greeting cards.

- Not everyone spends the same amount of money on Halloween. Men, for instance, spent an estimated $50 on the holiday in 2008. Women, though, spent just $43 on the big day. Those revelers younger than 45 spent an average of $55 each, while those older than that spent an estimated $38 on average.

- Maybe it's because they get more trick-or-treaters? City dwellers spent more on Halloween in 2008 than did their peers in the suburbs. Urbanites spent $51 on average, while those living in the suburbs spent just $43 on average.

- Small chocolate bars remain a favorite of trick-or-treaters. According to 75 percent of consumers, bite-size chocolate treats are their favorite Halloween candy.

- Watch those sticky-fingered parents! A whopping 90 percent of parents admitted to stealing sweets from their kids' trick-or-treat bags. Only 18 percent, though, wanted to steal licorice. The majority (70 percent) of adults said they most liked to snatch bite-sized chocolate bars. No word on whether their children were looking when they did this.

- A total of 36 million trick-or-treaters from ages 5 to 13 hit the streets on Halloween in 2007 in the United States.

- How dangerous is Halloween? The number of motor vehicle deaths increases an average of 30 percent when Halloween falls on a Friday, Saturday, or Sunday.

- Candy corn, that staple of Halloween candy, has been around for more than 100 years. Credit George Renninger, an employee of the Wunderlee Candy Company, with inventing candy corn in the 1880s. The Goelitz Candy Company, better known today as the Jelly Belly Candy Company, first started making candy corn in 1900 and still produces the treat today.

- Want to guarantee some shaving cream on your car? Give trick-or-treaters fruit or pretzels. Children rank fruit and salty snacks as their least favorite Halloween "treats."

Weird Web Buys

Today's consumers have few qualms about purchasing goods online.
As it turns out, there are some truly bizarre cyber-bargains
to be had at the touch of a keypad.

The Anti-Ticket Donut

Catering to the stereotype of the donut-loving cop, this product (a fake donut available in chocolate or "sprinkle") retails for $9.95, fits easily into a glove compartment, and is designed to dissuade hungry police officers from issuing traffic tickets.

Bacon Strips Adhesive Bandages

Who needs plain old pink bandages when you can dress your wounds in simulated bacon? This novelty item (you get 15 strips for about five bucks) could be seen as a key argument against unchecked capitalism, but apparently the market is there for this meat/medical supply hybrid.

Fish 'n' Flush

The family john can be an ugly piece of porcelain. So why not arrange to have a fully functioning tropical fish tank built into the back of it? As an added benefit, goldfish funerals will be remarkably convenient.

Flatulence Filters

The "TooT TrappeR" is a charcoal filter shaped like a seat cushion that's designed to silence and deodorize unwanted outbursts. It comes in gray or black and makes a rather awkward Christmas gift.

Garden Gnomes in Compromising Positions

Not the normal garden variety of gnome, these lewd lawn statues depict one gnome burying another, a gnome "dropping a moon," and other assorted indecencies—and you thought all they did was hold shovels and wheelbarrows!

Ghost in a Jar

One of eBay's zaniest offerings was an alleged spirit trapped inside a glass jar. Fourteen bids were registered by people hoping to have their very own pet poltergeist.

Gourmet Oxygen

Although it's likely intended to be a novelty item, "Big Ox" brand oxygen, which comes in flavors such as Tropical Breeze, Mountain Mint, Citrus Blast, and Polar Rush, may provide a sinister glimpse of future consumer goods in a world with depleted natural resources.

Mint-Flavored Golf Tees

It's important to have fresh breath when you're out on the links, and these tees will help—as long as you don't mind sucking on sharpened sticks of wood. A word of caution: Only use them once, or the dirt gets in the way of the mint flavor.

Shoot the Poop

Sick of carrying around a plastic bag when walking your pooch? Try shooting your dog's poop with Poop-Freeze, which forms a "white crusty film" over the droppings and solidifies them for easy pickup. It's up to you whether you want to dispose of it or put it in your prized pet's baby book.

Stainless-Steel Lollipops

The Zilopop is a German product that promotes fresh breath through the frequent licking of a cold steel circle. After a two- to four-minute suck on this lollipop look-alike, mouth odors are neutralized. And it's reusable! Unlike the Tootsie Pop, no amount of licking will ever get you to the center of a Zilopop.

Strange Catastrophes

Life is full of surprises, some less pleasant than others. From beer floods to raining frogs to exploding whales, headlines continually prove that truth is sometimes stranger than fiction.

The London Beer Flood

In 1814, a vat of beer erupted in a London brewery. Within minutes, the explosion had split open several other vats, and more than 320,000 gallons of beer flooded the streets of a nearby slum. People rushed to save as much of the beer as they could, collecting it in pots, cans, and cups. Others scooped the beer up in their hands and drank it as quickly as they could. Nine people died in the flood—eight from drowning and one from alcohol poisoning.

The Great Siberian Explosion

Around 7:00 A.M. on June 30, 1908, 60 million trees in remote Siberia were flattened by a mysterious 15-megaton explosion. The huge blast, which occurred about five miles above the surface of Earth, traveled around the world twice and triggered a strong, four-hour magnetic storm. Magnetic storms occur about once every 100 years and can create radiation similar to a nuclear explosion. These storms start in space and are typically accompanied by solar flares.

The 1908 explosion may have started with a comet of ice, which melted and exploded as it entered Earth's atmosphere. Or, it may have been an unusual airburst from an asteroid. Others believe that the source was a nuclear-powered spacecraft from another planet. However, no physical evidence of the cause has ever been found.

The Boston Molasses Disaster

On an unusually warm January day in 1919, a molasses tank burst near downtown Boston, sending more than two million gallons of the sticky stuff flowing through the city's North End at an estimated 35 miles per hour. The force of the molasses wave was so intense that it lifted a train off its tracks and crushed several buildings in its path. When the flood finally came to a halt, molasses was two to three feet deep in the streets, 21 people and several horses had died, and more than 150 people were injured. Nearly 90 years later, people in Boston can still smell molasses on sultry summer days.

It's Raining...Frogs

On September 7, 1953, clouds formed over Leicester, Massachusetts —a peaceful little town near the middle of the state. Within a few hours, a downpour began, but it wasn't rain falling from the sky. Thousands of frogs and toads dropped out of the air. Children collected them in buckets as if it was a game. Town officials insisted that the creatures had simply escaped from a nearby pond, but many of them landed on roofs and in gutters, which seemed to dispute this theory. It is still unclear why the frogs appeared in Leicester or why the same thing happened almost 20 years later in Brignoles, France.

Oregon's Exploding Whale

When an eight-ton sperm whale beaches itself in your town, what do you do? That's a question residents of Florence, Oregon, faced in November 1970. After consulting with the U.S. Navy, town officials decided to blow up the carcass with a half ton of dynamite. Spectators and news crews gathered to watch but were horrified when they were engulfed in a sandy, reddish mist and slapped by flying pieces of whale blubber. A quarter-mile away, a car was crushed when a gigantic chunk of whale flesh landed on it. No one was seriously hurt in the incident, but when the air cleared, most of the whale was still on the beach. The highway department hauled away the rest.

The Torino Impact Hazard Scale is used to categorize the chances of an asteroid or comet hitting Earth. The scale goes from zero to ten, with zero being no risk and ten being a certain collision, with global catastrophe imminent.

Bringing the World to Chicago

The 1893 World's Columbian Exposition, also known as the Chicago World's Fair, was the largest event of its kind ever held. The Fair was so expansive—more than 200 individual buildings spread over 633 acres, with exhibits from 36 foreign nations and 46 U.S. states and territories—that organizers estimated a visitor would have to walk for three weeks and cover more than 150 miles to see every exhibit.

The Fair opened on May 1, 1893, and proved to be a huge success, with more than 27.5 million admissions over its six-month run. People happily paid 50 cents each (25 cents for children) to see a world of things they'd never seen before. Among the more unusual attractions were:

- The first Ferris wheel, constructed by George Ferris at a cost of $250,000. Each of its 36 cars held 60 passengers. Cost: 50 cents per ride (this was in addition to the entrance fee).

- The Streets of Cairo, a detailed representation of the Egyptian capital manned by real Egyptians brought over specifically for the Fair. The most popular attraction: camel rides.

- Buffalo Bill Cody's Wild West Show. Cody gave 318 shows over six months and pocketed nearly $1 million.

- A "palace of corn" built in the Pompeian style of architecture, as part of the Iowa exhibition.

- A British cannon surrendered at Yorktown during the Revolutionary War.

- A mammoth skeleton (part of the Smithsonian exhibit).

- A life-size silver statue of Christopher Columbus. The Fair celebrated the 400th anniversary of Columbus's voyage to the New World.

- The largest telescope in the world (at the time) and a print of the first photograph of the moon.

Zippo's Most Popular Lighters

*Since the first Zippo lighter was sold in 1932,
over 475 million of the windproof lighters have been made.
Over the years, Zippo has embellished their basic lighter with
hundreds of different designs. So, of those half a billion
lighters, which designs have been the most popular?*

For many people, basic is best. Two of the most popular designs
have been available since the 1930s and were named for their prices.
No. 200 sold for $2.00 while No. 250 sold for $2.50. In 75 years,
prices of No. 200 and No. 250 have changed but their names
haven't—they now cost $15.95 and $18.95. Other popular designs
include:

- American eagle
- American flag
- Brass
- Elvis Presley
- Engine turned design
- Four-leaf clover
- Harley-Davidson motorcycle
- Matte colors
- Military, all branches
- Playboy
- State designs—West Coast states, Hawaii, and Guam (a U.S. territory) are most popular because of Japanese tourists who are eager to prove to friends that they have traveled to the United States (even Guam, which is only 1,607 miles—a four-hour flight—away from Japan).
- Statue of Liberty
- Venetian design

O Christmas Tree...

Getting ready to deck the halls? Before you trim that tree, spruce up your knowledge of this holiday centerpiece.

Origins

According to horticultural experts, the use of trees to spruce up a winter holiday dates back thousands of years. The ancient Egyptians celebrated the winter solstice by adorning their homes with date palm leaves, and the Romans enjoyed a seasonal festival called Saturnalia that included decorating one's home with tree branches and lights and exchanging gifts. Sound familiar?

Christmas Trees by the Numbers

50: the number of states that grow Christmas trees; Oregon is the recognized leader, followed by North Carolina

60–70 million: the number of Christmas tree seedlings planted annually

28.2 million: the number of live Christmas trees purchased each year

$1.03 billion: the retail value of those live Christmas trees

7 years: the average age of a Christmas tree when it's harvested for sale

500,000: the number of acres in the United States dedicated to growing various types of Christmas trees

200: the average number of Christmas-tree-related fires reported each year

How the Christmas tree came to America is open to debate. Some historians believe it arrived with Hessian troops during the Revolutionary War. Others believe it started when German immigrants settled into Pennsylvania and the surrounding states.

The commercial Christmas tree industry as we know it today began in 1851, when an enterprising farmer named Mark Carr had the brilliant idea to take two sleds full of evergreens to New York City. He quickly sold them all, and by 1900, the home Christmas tree had become an established tradition.

The National Christmas Tree

The first National Christmas Tree was a 48-foot balsam fir, erected by the District of Columbia Public Schools on the Ellipse south of the White House in November 1923. About 3,000 spectators gathered that Christmas Eve at 5:00 P.M. to watch President Calvin Coolidge and his wife, Grace, stroll from the White House to the tree. The president then pressed a button to activate the 2,500 electric red, green, and white bulbs on the tree, winning cheers and applause from the cold but excited crowd. Coolidge was especially pleased that the tree came from his home state of Vermont.

The first Christmas tree was decorated in Riga, Latvia, in 1510.

The first printed reference to Christmas trees occurred in Germany in 1531.

In 1856, Franklin Pierce became the first president to place a Christmas tree in the White House.

Every day, an acre of Christmas trees provides enough oxygen to support 18 people.

Institutions of Higher Chicanery!

When it comes to clever pranks, some colleges and universities get an A+!

Practical jokes aren't part of the curriculum at most colleges and universities, but that hasn't stopped generations of students from perpetrating some very clever pranks. Here are seven of the most impressive:

1. Football rivalries have sparked some genuinely notable pranks over the years. During the 1961 Rose Bowl game between the Washington Huskies and the Minnesota Golden Gophers, for example, students from Caltech cleverly switched the colored placards that were distributed to spectators sitting on the Washington Huskies' side of the field. As a result, instead of hailing the Huskies when held up on cue during halftime, the placards spelled out "CALTECH." The prank was viewed by millions on television and is still considered one of the most impressive (and elaborate) college stunts ever.

   Yale University students perpetrated a similar prank against archrival Harvard University during the annual Yale–Harvard football game in 2004. Instead of reading "GO HARVARD," the collective cards read "WE SUCK."

2. In 1933, the staff of the Harvard *Lampoon* took it upon themselves to steal the Massachusetts Sacred Cod, a five-foot-long carving that traditionally hangs over one entrance to the Massachusetts State House. When no one was looking, the students simply cut down the fish, hid it in a flower box, and casually strolled away. A few days later, after a lot of hubbub, two *Lampoon* staffers, wearing disguises, returned the cod to the Harvard chief of police.

3. The United States isn't alone in its love of a good college prank. In 1958, students at Cambridge University successfully placed an Austin Seven automobile atop the roof of the Senate House. The students needed just one night to place the car, but it took civil planners a week to figure out how to get it down. Amazingly,

the pranksters were never caught, though they did finally reveal themselves during a reunion dinner in 2008.

4. The more difficult a prank, the better, as evidenced by a 1988 endeavor in which students at Rice University successfully turned the one-ton statue of William Marsh Rice so that it faced the university library instead of having its back to it. The stunt was an amazing feat of engineering that went unappreciated by school officials, who forced Patrick Dyson—one of the students involved in the prank—to pay to have the statue returned to its original position. However, Dyson didn't have to pay a penny out of his own pocket; his fellow students raised the money for Rice's turnaround by selling commemorative T-shirts.

5. More recent college pranks often take advantage of new technologies. In 2006, students at UC Berkeley pulled a fast one on USC basketball star Gabe Pruitt by enticing him with an attractive girl named Victoria via Facebook. Victoria didn't really exist, but Pruitt didn't know that until a game in which UC students started chanting "Victoria! Victoria! Victoria!" and Pruitt's cell phone number, which he had divulged to his nonexistent paramour. The chanting continued throughout the game and truly rattled Pruitt, who shot just 3 for 13 that day.

6. In 1993, three Ohio State University students sent out a fake news release promoting a program to donate guns and ammunition to the homeless, backed by a nonexistent organization called Arm the Homeless Coalition (ATHC). Many news organizations, agencies, and prominent individuals fell for the prank and expressed their outrage by condemning the ATHC. The students finally confessed to the hoax, saying they were just trying to draw attention to the issues of guns and violence, the homeless, and media manipulation in society, but others soon took up the "cause" with similar pranks around the country.

7. Not all college pranks go as planned. In 1958, students at UCLA plotted a devious caper against archrival USC that involved dumping hundreds of pounds of manure from a rented helicopter on to USC's fabled Tommy Trojan statue. Unfortunately for the pranksters, the pull of the helicopter's rotors sucked the manure back into their faces and dropped very little on their intended target.

Correct Change Only!

From live bait to neckties, you can buy it all from the world's vending machines!

Vending machines are ubiquitous in today's society—almost every city street corner, it seems, has at least one machine selling something or other. Most vending machines offer the kind of stuff you'd normally expect, such as soft drinks and snacks. But depending on where you live, vending machines can sell much, much more.

Get Your Holy Water Here!

Most people consider vending machines a modern convenience, but the concept is actually eons old. The very first vending machine was developed in the first century A.D. by Hero of Alexandria, a talented engineer who invented a device that dispensed holy water when a coin was inserted into it. The coin landed on a pan attached to a lever, which opened a valve and dispensed a fixed amount of water. A counterweight then pulled the lever back into position, stopping the flow.

It was a pretty ingenious device, but it didn't really catch on; centuries passed before vending machines as we know them really caught on with the general public. The first modern vending machine was installed in London in the 1880s and dispensed postcards. The first American vending machine, introduced in 1888, sold chewing gum at train stations.

Today, you can buy almost anything from a vending machine. Here's a list of some of the more bizarre items sold via vending machines in the United States and abroad:

- **Medical Marijuana** That's right, you can buy dope from vending machines at certain dispensaries in California, but it's not as simple as you might think. You'll need a prescription from a physician noting your medical need, and you'll be fingerprinted by a security guard before being allowed to purchase a vacuum-sealed packet of medicinal weed.

- **Live Bait** Anglers around the United States who can't wait for the bait shop to open can now buy night crawlers from converted sandwich machines. Don't worry about a mess—the night crawlers are delivered in sealed plastic bags containing oxygen tablets.

- **Soccer Balls** How many times have you had to cancel your soccer game for lack of a ball? In New York City, such crises are easily averted by vending machines that sell Nike soccer balls for just $20. Game on!

- **Fresh-Baked Pizza** People love pizza but hate waiting around. The solution? Wonder Pizza, a vending machine that bakes a hot, nine-inch pizza in just minutes. The downside? You get a pizza made by a vending machine.

- **Men's Ties** Appearance is everything in Japan, especially if you're a businessman on the go. But what if you spill soy sauce on your tie during lunch and have a meeting with the big boss immediately afterward? No problem. Just drop a few coins in a nearby vending machine and—voilà!—you get a brand-new tie, ready to wear.

Only in Japan...

The Japanese are absolutely passionate about their vending machines, the sales from which total more than $50 billion a year. What can you buy from a vending machine in the Land of the Rising Sun? A better question would be: What *can't* you buy? A recent survey found vending machines selling the following items. Buyer beware!

- **Farm-Fresh Eggs** For those times when you just don't feel like walking that extra block to the nearest grocery.

- **Umbrellas** For rainy days and Mondays.

- **Hot Ramen Noodles** Since ramen noodles are a staple among college students, one has to wonder why these machines haven't popped up on college campuses in the United States.

- **Hot Popcorn** And from Hello Kitty, no less!

- **10-Kilo Bags of Rice** To go with your vending machine eggs, maybe?
- **Fishing Equipment** Includes a rod, line, and lures. Don't worry: You can get bait from that vending machine over there.
- **Toilet Paper** It's about time someone came up with this idea!
- **Beer** Nothing like cutting out the middle man.
- **Pornography and Sex Toys** As a plus, the machine allows the purchaser to sidestep the embarrassment of interacting with another human for this exchange.
- **Designer Condoms** A nice complement to your vending machine pornography and sex toys.
- **Fresh Flowers** We'd suggest picking up some flowers to go along with the items above. You can never go wrong with flowers!
- **Frequent Flyer Miles** Japan Air Lines (JAL) has a machine that reads a credit card and boarding pass and issues frequent flyer miles.
- **Dry Ice** Sold at supermarkets for keeping frozen food cold until the customer gets home.
- **Water Salad** Don't feel bad, we don't know what this is, either. But if you want it, there's a machine that will sell it to you.
- **Rhinoceros Beetles** In the United States, people squash weird bugs. In Japan, they keep them as pets. And apparently buy them from vending machines.

❖ ❖ ❖

"I like vending machines, because snacks are better when they fall. If I buy a candy bar at the store, oftentimes I will drop it so that it achieves its maximum flavor potential."
—Mitch Hedberg

❖ ❖ ❖

"Change is inevitable—except from a vending machine."
—Robert C. Gallagher

Alien's Eye View: What You Can See From Space

Contrary to popular belief, the Great Wall of China isn't the only human creation visible from space. Astronauts can spot many structures, including airports and bridges. The Wall doesn't even stand out: It's thousands of miles long, but it's only about 15 feet wide and it matches the color of the surrounding terrain. Some astronauts claim they've seen it, but China's first astronaut couldn't find it, and you can bet he was really searching. No humanmade structure is visible from the moon, but sightseers can pick out notable landmarks from low orbit.

- **The Great Malls of China** At least China can take solace that the world's biggest malls—the 7.1-million-square-foot South China Mall and the 6-million-square-foot Golden Resources Mall, not far from the Great Wall—are visible from orbit.

- **The Pyramids of Giza** Like the Great Wall, the pyramids match their surroundings, but they cast distinctive angular shadows that make them stand out.

- **The Millennium Dome** London's big white $1.22-billion dome (now called the O2) covers over 80,000 square meters and is fairly conspicuous in its location next to the Thames River.

- **Palm Jumeirah** It's hard to miss this 12-square-mile artificial island in the shape of a palm tree, which is located off the coast of Dubai.

- **Mega Fireworks** Speaking of the Palm Jumeirah, the opening party for the Atlantis Resort on the island included a fireworks display big enough to entertain people in orbit.

- **Colonel Sanders** Zeroing in on the alien demographic, in 2006 KFC created an 87,500-square-foot portrait of the Colonel in Rachel, Nevada, made from 65,000 square tiles.

Fabulous Last Lines

"I'll go home, and I'll think of some way to get him back!
After all, tomorrow is another day!"
Gone with the Wind (1939)

"Goodbye, Mr. Chips. Goodbye."
Goodbye, Mr. Chips (1939)

"And oh, Auntie Em—there's no place like home."
The Wizard of Oz (1939)

"Louis, I think this is the beginning of a beautiful friendship."
Casablanca (1942)

"Look, Daddy. Teacher says, every time a bell rings,
an angel gets his wings."

"That's right, that's right. Attaboy, Clarence."
It's a Wonderful Life (1946)

"Shane. Shane! Come back! 'Bye, Shane."
Shane (1953)

"I'm a man!"
"Well, nobody's perfect."
Some Like It Hot (1959)

"You finally really did it. You maniacs! You blew it up!
God damn you! God damn you all to hell!"
Planet of the Apes (1968)

"Forget it, Jake. It's Chinatown!"
Chinatown (1974)

"This was the story of Howard Beale, the first known instance of a
man who was killed because he had lousy ratings."
Network (1976)

"Rorrrrrwwl!" (as growled by Chewbacca the Wookiee)
Star Wars (1977)

"The horror. The horror."
Apocalypse Now (1979)

"Roads? Where we're going, we don't need roads."
Back to the Future (1985)

Behind the Best-Selling Posters of All Time

No teenager's room is complete without a poster or two. You remember your own favorites. You might even have them rolled up in your attic. But did you know... ?

- The photographer behind Farrah Fawcett's iconic, number-one-selling poster was hired to do a bikini shot with the actress. Fawcett didn't bring a bikini, but she had this red swimsuit, and the photographer had a Mexican blanket to use as a background. Sales: as high as 12 million copies.

- Actresses can be directed, snakes cannot. Thus, the famous poster image of Nastassja Kinski "wearing" a boa constrictor took over two hours to capture while the photographer waited for the snake to cooperate. Kinski lay naked on the cement the entire time until the snake finally slithered over the proper parts for the right shot. Sales: unknown.

- The famous poster of Marilyn Monroe with a billowing white dress wasn't originally intended to become a poster. Monroe was filmed walking over a subway grating in *The Seven Year Itch*; the shot was turned into a picture that still graces walls and halls. Sales: millions of copies.

- Bo Derek's romp on the beach in a Blake Edwards movie was another shot that wasn't originally meant as a poster. Bo Derek posters from her movies *Bolero* and *Tarzan the Ape Man* were also best-sellers. Sales: way more than 10.

- A fortuitous out-of-this-world photograph resulted in another of the best-selling posters of all time. NASA's *Apollo 17* astronauts snapped a picture of Earth from the vantage point of space to result in the famous so-called "Blue Marble" poster. Sales: unknown.

Travel Guide: By the Numbers

Of course there's more to a city than its crime rate, air pollution levels, and water quality. But when you're planning a trip or considering a move, these measures are sure to be high on your list. As this look at each end of the scale demonstrates, there's an astounding gap between the top and the bottom.

Cleanest

In 2007, *Forbes* published a list of the 25 cleanest cities (which actually included 26 cities because there was a tie for 25th place). The editors based the list on how well cities handled problems such as sanitation, energy production, recycling, and transportation—data they gathered from consulting firm Mercer's in-depth studies of 300 cities. Here's a summary of their conclusions:

- Canada dominated the list, claiming top honors with Calgary and nabbing four other spots (Ottawa, Montreal, Vancouver, Toronto).

- The United States ranked second overall. Honolulu nabbed the #2 spot, and Minneapolis, Boston, Lexington, and Pittsburgh also made the list.

- Overall, ten European cities made the list, and Switzerland took three spots (Zurich, Bern, and Geneva).

- Japan grabbed three spots (Katsuyama, Kobe, and Omuta), but no other Asian countries made the list.

- Only two cities below the equator made the list—Auckland and Wellington, both in New Zealand.

Dirtiest

- *Forbes* has also published a less flattering list, ranking the 25 dirtiest cities. The 2008 list was based on Mercer's profiles of how 215 cities handled waste management, air pollution, disease, water cleanliness, and hospital care. As you might expect, the list was dominated by cities in impoverished third-world countries: Baku, in the former Soviet Republic of Azerbaijan, claimed the top spot, thanks to extreme air pollution from many years of oil drilling. Almaty, in the former Soviet Republic of Kazakhstan, also made the list, as did Moscow, which has severe air pollution.

- African countries dominated the list, taking 16 spots. In most of these cities, the biggest problems are poor waste management in high population areas, which leads to severely polluted water supplies.

- Water pollution also put two Indian cities on the list (Mumbai and New Delhi), as well as Dhaka in neighboring Bangladesh.

- The only cities in the Americas that made the list were Port au Prince, Haiti, and Mexico City, Mexico.

- In a 2007 article, *Forbes* named smoggy Los Angeles the dirtiest U.S. city.

Safest and Deadliest

- As part of their 2008 "Quality of Living" report, Mercer identified the cities with the highest and lowest "personal safety rankings." Their criteria included crime rate, law enforcement effectiveness, stability, and quality of relationships with other countries. Here's a look at the two extremes on their list: The tiny European country Luxembourg's capital city, Luxembourg, scored the highest on personal safety.

- Helsinki, Finland, tied for second place with three Swiss cities (Bern, Zurich, and Geneva).

- The report ranked Baghdad, Iraq, as the most dangerous city, followed by Kinshasa in the Democratic Republic of Congo; Karachi, Pakistan; Nairobi, Kenya; and Bangui, in the Central African Republic.

- And what about the United States? Every year, CQ Press ranks the safety of U.S. cities with populations greater than 75,000, based on crime statistics gathered by the FBI (specifically, per-capita rates of murder, rape, aggravated assault, robbery, burglary, and car theft). Here's a summary of the 2008–2009 report's conclusions: Ramapo, New York, made the top of the safe list, with only 688 reported crimes and no murders reported in 2007.

- Second place went to Mission Viejo, California, which had taken first place in the previous year's report.

- The report ranked New Orleans as the most dangerous city, with 19,034 reported crimes and 209 murders.

- After New Orleans, the report listed Camden, New Jersey; Detroit, Michigan; St. Louis, Missouri; and Oakland, California, as the most dangerous U.S. cities.

Ten Countries with Most Readers

Country	Avg. Hours Spent Reading per Week
1. India	10.7
2. Thailand	9.4
3. China	8.0
4. Philippines	7.6
5. Egypt	7.5
6. Czech Republic	7.4
7. Russia	7.1
8. Sweden (tied)	6.9
France (tied)	6.9
10. Hungary	6.8

You Live Where?
Some Silly City Names

Angel Fire, New Mexico

Angels Camp, California

Bear, Delaware

Benevolence, Georgia

Black River, New York

Blue Earth, Minnesota

Boring, Maryland

Bread Loaf, Vermont

Bumble Bee, Arizona

Busti, New York

Buttermilk, Kansas

Buttzville, New Jersey

Cheddar, South Carolina

Chipmunk, New York

Church, Iowa

Climax, Georgia

Conception, Missouri

Convent, Louisiana

Deadman Crossing, Ohio

Devil's Slide, Utah

Devils Den, California

Devil Town, Ohio

Frogtown, Virginia

Green Pond, New Jersey

Half Hell, North Carolina

Hooker, Oklahoma

Horneytown, North Carolina

Intercourse, Pennsylvania

Jackass Flats, Nevada

Lizard Lick, North Carolina

Monkeys Eyebrow, Kentucky

Mosquitoville, Vermont

Nirvana, Michigan

Oatmeal, Texas

Ordinary, Virginia

Pie, West Virginia

Pray, Montana

Rainbow City, Alabama

Red Devil, Alaska

Sandwich, Massachusetts

Santa Claus, Indiana

Silver Creek, Washington

Spider, Kentucky

Success, Missouri

Suck-Egg Hollow, Tennessee

Tea, South Dakota

Ticktown, Virginia

Toast, North Carolina

Just the Facts:
Arlington National Cemetery

Arlington is much more than just a cemetery—it's a tribute to those who fought for freedom. Here are eight intriguing facts you probably didn't know.

1. The 200-acre tract was officially designated a military cemetery on June 15, 1864, by Secretary of War Edwin Stanton. Prior to becoming a cemetery, it was a plantation that belonged to Confederate General Robert E. Lee. The property was confiscated by the U.S. government during the Civil War.

2. More than 300,000 people are buried there. They represent all of the nation's wars, from the Revolutionary War to the wars in Iraq and Afghanistan.

3. Those who died before the Civil War were reinterred after 1900.

4. Arlington National Cemetery boasts the second largest number of burials (for a national cemetery in the United States), after Calverton National Cemetery near Riverhead, New York.

5. An average of 28 funerals per day are conducted at Arlington National Cemetery. The flags on the cemetery grounds are flown at half-mast from a half-hour before the first funeral of the day until a half-hour after the final funeral.

6. The remains of an unknown serviceman from the Vietnam War, interred in 1984, were disinterred in 1998 after being positively identified as Air Force 1st Lt. Michael J. Blassie.

7. The Tomb of the Unknowns is guarded 24 hours a day by members of the 3rd U.S. Infantry, also known as "The Old Guard." They began guarding the tomb on April 6, 1948.

8. Among the famous people buried in Arlington National Cemetery are presidents William Howard Taft and John F. Kennedy, explorers Robert Peary and Matthew Henson, mystery writer Dashiell Hammett, and band leader Glenn Miller.

When Celebs Go Bad!

Back in the day, celebrities were publicly pilloried for their bad behavior. Today, a well-publicized arrest and brief stint in jail might seem like a smart career move. Here are just a few of the rich and famous who have had brushes with the law.

Ozzy Osbourne

In 1982, the Black Sabbath front man and reality TV superstar angered Texans everywhere by drunkenly urinating on a wall at the Alamo. Osbourne was banned from the city of San Antonio for a decade but later made amends by donating $20,000 to the Daughters of the Republic of Texas to help restore the fabled landmark.

Matthew McConaughey

In October 1999, following a noise complaint, McConaughey was found by police sitting naked in his home playing the bongos. The cops also found the actor's stash, which led to McConaughey being arrested for marijuana possession and resisting arrest. The drug charges were later dropped, and McConaughey was fined $50 for violating a municipal noise ordinance.

Winona Ryder

In December 2001, Ryder was nabbed for shoplifting merchandise at the ritzy Saks Fifth Avenue store in Beverly Hills. She was convicted of grand theft and vandalism but received a relatively light sentence: three years probation and 480 hours of community service and restitution.

Nicole Richie

In February 2003, the daughter of singer Lionel Richie was charged with heroin possession and driving with a suspended license. Three years later, she was arrested again for driving under the influence. Her sentence: four days in jail. Actual time served: 82 minutes.

Natasha Lyonne

Known for such films as *Slums of Beverly Hills* (1998) and *American Pie* (1999), Lyonne was arrested in December 2004 after verbally attacking her neighbor, breaking the neighbor's mirror, and threatening to harm the neighbor's dog. A warrant was issued against the troubled actress in April 2005 for failure to appear before a judge, and a second warrant was issued in January 2006. In December 2006, Lyonne was finally sentenced to a conditional discharge.

Paris Hilton

Over the years, Hilton has been charged with a variety of crimes, including driving under the influence of alcohol and driving with a suspended license (twice). In June 2007, the hard-partying hotel heiress finally received her due when she was sentenced to 45 days in jail, though she was quickly released because of an undisclosed medical condition. Instead of doing her time in the slammer, Hilton was given 40 days house arrest with a monitoring device.

Lindsay Lohan

In July 2007, the former child star was found by police in a Santa Monica parking garage engaged in a heated argument with a former assistant. She failed a sobriety test, and police also found a small amount of cocaine on her person. Lohan pleaded guilty to cocaine possession and driving under the influence and was sentenced to one day in jail, community service, and three years probation. Actual time spent behind bars: 84 minutes.

Bill Murray

In 2007, during a trip to Sweden, the former *Ghostbuster* and *Saturday Night Live* funnyman was charged with driving under the influence—while driving a golf cart. He refused to take a breath test but signed a document saying he had been driving drunk. He was allowed to leave the country without punishment.

It Happened in...September

- So, like, it was gnarly when the *Third New International Dictionary (Unabridged)* hit the stacks in 1961, and a bunch of teacher dudes holla'd about slang being included. But the suits that made the book said it was all groovy and everybody should just chill.

- Alan Hale Jr. was about to skip his career in Hollywood until Sherwood Schwartz decided to test Hale for a role in a new series he was casting. In September 1962, Hale was hired as the Skipper on *Gilligan's Island.*

- New York Jets player Steve O'Neal kicked the longest punt in pro football history—98 yards—in a 1969 game against the Denver Broncos.

- Take it *all* off: KISS band members appeared for the first time sans makeup for an MTV interview in September 1983.

- Don Claps, a real estate agent from Colorado, did 1,293 cart-wheels in one hour on *Live with Regis and Kelly* in September 2006. Give him a hand!

- An arresting fact: The world's first known female police officer was hired in Los Angeles in September 1910.

- Georgia Governor Jimmy Carter filed a report in September 1973 on a UFO he claimed he'd seen two years previously. Naysayers scoffed, saying that it was a ruse to gain votes for a planned presidential bid. That argument never held water, however, as aliens were constitutionally barred from voting.

- September is Be Kind to Editors and Writers Month (we like this one!), National Chicken Month (so take a chicken to lunch), and Self-Awareness Month (you know who you are).

Less than Heroic Heroes!

Not every character in spandex can save the day.
Here are five less-than-super heroes and villains.

1. Brother Power, The Geek (DC Comics) Brother Power came to life as a "puppet elemental" when lightning struck a tailor's mannequin covered with hippie clothing. He wandered California helping his fellow flower children take on "the man" but he failed to take off with readers and was canceled after two issues.

2. Dracula (Dell Comics) This second-rate batman was a descendant of the original Dracula. Hoping to clear the family name, he developed a serum out of bat blood that could heal damaged brain cells but was transformed into a bat himself when he accidentally ingested some of the elixir. However, rather than biting necks like his blood-thirsty ancestor, this Drac used his newfound powers to fight crime. Even diehard superhero fans found the concept ridiculous; the series was quickly canceled.

3. Tin (DC Comics) The Metal Men were good-guy robots made from various elements, including gold, iron, and mercury. Among the group was Tin, perhaps the most irritating superhero ever created. Weak and insecure, all he did was complain about how useless he was, forcing the other Metal Men to save his tin butt on a regular basis.

4. Starro (DC Comics) Super villains come in all shapes and sizes. Starro was . . . a giant intergalactic starfish. True, he could exert mental control over others and fire death rays from his appendages, but he was still just a starfish.

5. Stilt-Man (Marvel Comics) Stilt-Man, who regularly battled Spider-Man and Daredevil, had hydraulic stilts that allowed him to tower 60 feet in the air. Why his foes simply didn't knock him over and kick his keister remains one of comicdom's great mysteries.

Death—Isn't It Ironic?

No matter who you are, it's inevitable: Your time on this earth will end. But some people have a way of shuffling off this mortal coil with a bit more ironic poignancy.

- In 1936, a picture of baby George Story was featured in the first issue of *Life* magazine. Story died in 2000 at age 63, just after the magazine announced it would be shutting down. *Life* carried an article about his death from heart failure in its final issue.

- In the early 1960s, Ken Hubbs was a Gold Glove second baseman for the Chicago Cubs. The young standout had a lifelong fear of flying, so to overcome it, he decided to take flying lessons. In 1964, shortly after earning his pilot's license, Hubbs was killed when his plane went down during a snowstorm.

- While defending an accused murderer in 1871, attorney Clement Vallandigham argued that the victim accidentally killed himself as he tried to draw his pistol. Demonstrating his theory for the court, the lawyer fatally shot himself in the process. The jury acquitted his client and Vallandigham won the case posthumously.

- Private detective Allan Pinkerton built his career on secrecy and his ability to keep his mouth shut. However, biting his tongue literally killed him when he tripped while out for a walk, severely cutting his tongue. The injury became infected and led to his death in 1884.

- When he appeared on *The Dick Cavett Show* in 1971, writer and healthy living advocate Jerome I. Rodale claimed, "I've decided to live to be a hundred," and "I never felt better in my life!" Moments later, still in his seat on stage, the 72-year-old Rodale died of a heart attack. The episode never aired.

- South Korean Lee Seung Seop loved playing video games more than anything. His obsession caused him to lose his job and his girlfriend and eventually took his life as well. In August 2005, after playing a video game at an Internet café for 50 consecutive hours, he died at age 28 from dehydration, exhaustion, and heart failure.

- Jim Fixx advocated running as a cure-all, helping develop the fitness craze of the late 20th century. However, in 1984, he died from a heart attack while jogging. Autopsy results showed he suffered from severely clogged and hardened arteries.

- Thomas Midgley Jr. was a brilliant engineer and inventor who held 170 patents. After contracting polio at age 51, he turned his attention to inventing a system of pulleys to help him move around in bed. In 1944, he was found dead, strangled by the pulley system that he had invented.

- At least two of the Marlboro Men—the chiseled icons of the cigarette culture—have died from lung cancer. David McLean developed emphysema in 1985 and died from lung cancer a decade later. Wayne McLaren portrayed the character in the 1970s, and although he was an antismoking advocate later in life, he still contracted cancer. Despite having a lung removed, the cancer spread to his brain, and he died in 1992.

- Author Olivia Goldsmith wrote *The First Wives Club*, a book that became an icon for older women whose husbands had tossed them aside for younger trophy wives. A generation of women embraced their wrinkles and weren't afraid to let the world know. Ironically, Goldsmith died while undergoing cosmetic surgery.

- Shortly before he died in a high-speed car crash, James Dean filmed a television spot promoting his new film *Giant*. The interviewer asked Dean if he had any advice for young people. "Take it easy driving," he replied. "The life you save might be mine."

"The supreme irony of life is that hardly anyone gets out of it alive."
—Robert A. Heinlein

18 Famous Sidekicks

As fearless, funny, or heroic as a protagonist may be, everyone needs a hand from time to time. Many of the leading men and women in literature, television, and cinema have had a trusty sidekick. See if you can match these faithful friends.

1. Don Quixote	a. Little John
2. Snoopy	b. Boo Boo
3. Ken Hutchinson	c. Babe
4. Fred Flintstone	d. Tinkerbell
5. D. J. Tanner	e. Ed McMahon
6. Archie Andrews	f. Ethel Mertz
7. Dorothy Gale	g. Goose
8. Robin Hood	h. Scooby-Doo
9. Yogi Bear	i. Tonto
10. Maverick	j. Jughead Jones
11. Peter Pan	k. Kimmy Gibbler
12. Batman	l. Dave Starsky
13. Shaggy	m. Barney Rubble
14. Paul Bunyan	n. Toto
15. Sherlock Holmes	o. Robin
16. Johnny Carson	p. Sancho Panza
17. Lucy Ricardo	q. Dr. Watson
18. The Lone Ranger	r. Woodstock

1–p; 2–r; 3–l; 4–m; 5–k; 6–j; 7–n; 8–a; 9–b; 10–g; 11–d; 12–o; 13–h; 14–c; 15–q; 16–e; 17–f; 18–i

Bragging Rights

The Most Expensive Baseball Card

A 100-year-old baseball card turns grown men into little kids.

Honus Wagner was either the most noble of all early 20th-century baseball players—a man who cringed at the thought of his likeness being used to hawk a tobacco product—or a guy who was ticked that he wasn't getting a big enough share of the profits.

Regardless of the reason, the "Flying Dutchman" pitched a fit when the American Tobacco Company, a cigarette manufacturer, released its T206 series of tobacco cards in 1909. Approximately 50 cards picturing Wagner in uniform with the Pittsburgh Pirates are estimated to have made it to cigarette packs back in the day before being yanked. Only a tiny percentage of those 50 made it to the late 20th-century marketplace.

Flash-forward a hundred years, and that T206 card, the "Holy Grail" among baseball card collectors, is considered the most valuable card of all time. One such exemplar has been owned by hockey Hall of Famer Wayne Gretzky, who—along with a business partner—purchased the T206 card for $451,000 in 1991. Gretzky later sold it in 1995 for $500,000 to Wal-Mart, which used it as part of a store promotion. The winner—a Florida postal worker—was thrilled…until she had to sell it to cover the taxes on her good fortune.

And so Wagner's travels continued as the card was auctioned for $640,000 and again on the online auction site eBay for almost twice that: $1.27 million. Oh, but the news just keeps getting better, as an anonymous collector with gobs of money shelled out $2.35 million for this cardboard classic in 2007. Looking to make a quick buck, that same collector turned around and sold it six months later…for a record $2.8 million.

Somewhere, a 110-year-old man is kicking himself for sticking *his* Honus Wagner card in the spokes of his bicycle.

It Happened in... October

- Ya gotta love politicians! In 1949, an amendment to a 1938 law allowed minimum wage to go from 40 cents to a whopping 75 cents an hour.

- Coleco (remember them?) released the Adam computer, touted as a complete device with everything a family could ever need for home computing in 1983. For $600, you also received a printer, cassette tape drive, and 64K RAM.

- Write this down: Though it had been developed many years earlier, the first ballpoint pen went on sale in the United States in October 1945 at a cost of almost $15 each.

- The American Wife Carrying Championships are held each October at the Sunday River Resort in Maine. The 278-yard course includes an uphill run, waist-deep water, and hurdles. Contestants don't have to be legally married; the winner gets beer plus cash.

- Good morning, Bunny Rabbit! TV's *Captain Kangaroo* debuted in October 1955. *The Mickey Mouse Club* also debuted that month.

- Johann Deisenhofer, Robert Huber, and Hartmut Michel won the 1988 Nobel Prize for chemistry "for the determination of the three-dimensional structure of a photosynthetic reaction centre," according to a press release. But you already knew that, right?

- *Geographically Speaking* became the first TV show with a commercial sponsor (Bristol-Myers) in October 1946.

- October is National Roller Skating Month, Talk About Prescriptions Month, National Go on a Field Trip Month (so get going), and Liver Awareness Month (and be aware).

Who Let the Dogs Out?

Dogs and humans have been palling around for eons. Though the exact timetable remains somewhat controversial, existing evidence suggests that dogs have been domesticated for at least 30,000 years. Today, approximately 45 million American households have dogs.

Dogs, Dogs Everywhere

There are literally scores of recognized breeds of dogs throughout the world, with new breeds being developed all the time. The American Kennel Club currently recognizes 163 breeds, with 12 additional breeds given partial status in the Miscellaneous class.

The most popular breed changes over time, but the Labrador retriever has enjoyed the number one spot for several consecutive years. In 2007, some of the most popular American dog names were Max, Molly, Jake, Lucy, Bailey, Buster, Cody, Bear, Princess, and Angel.

Dogs by the Numbers

24: the largest number of puppies ever recorded in a single litter. The big event occurred in January 2005 to a Neapolitan mastiff owned by Damian Ward and Anne Kellegher of Manea, United Kingdom. Twenty of the pups survived.

29 years, 5 months: the age of the oldest dog ever recorded, an Australian cattle dog named Bluey owned by Les Hall of Rochester, Victoria, Australia.

8 years, 190 days: the longest time a dog has spent on "death row." Word, a Lhasa apso owned by Wilton Rabon of Seattle, Washington, was incarcerated following two biting incidents, but he was eventually released to a sanctuary.

1,000+: the number of Americans who require medical care for a dog bite each day.

Lotto Trouble!

Everyone fantasizes about winning the lottery and living the good life. But for every lucky winner who achieves the dream, there's another whose life is turned upside down. Here are ten true-life lottery horror stories that will make you think twice about buying that scratch-off ticket.

1. In 1988, William Post won $16.2 million in the Pennsylvania Lottery. Unfortunately, Post's good luck brought out the worst in his friends and family, including his brother, who tried to have Post killed for the inheritance. Post survived his brother's murderous intent only to be successfully sued by a former girlfriend for a share of his winnings. Post spent his money like a drunken sailor until he was $1 million in debt and forced to declare bankruptcy. When he died in 2006, Post had been living on his Social Security for several years.

2. Everyone believes that winning the lottery will bring an end to their problems, but for Billie Bob Harrell Jr., that wasn't the case. After scoring $31 million in the Texas Lottery, Harrell spent big on cars, real estate, and gifts for family and friends. But wealth apparently couldn't buy the happiness Harrell was seeking, so he took his own life just two years after cashing that winning ticket.

3. Evelyn Adams was a two-time winner, hitting it big in the New Jersey Lottery in 1985 and 1986 for a total of more than $5 million. But Adams couldn't control her gambling habit and quickly frittered her winnings away on the slots. (She also gave away large sums to family and friends.) By 2001, the former multimillionaire had gone from riches to rags and was living in a trailer.

4. Willie Hurt won $3.1 million in the Michigan Lottery in 1989. Two years later, he was penniless and facing a murder charge after squandering his fortune on a divorce and crack cocaine.

5. Jeffrey Dampier won a whopping $20 million in the Illinois Lottery and spent lavishly on friends and family—including his

sister-in-law, Victoria Jackson. Hungry for a bigger chunk of Dampier's fortune, Jackson and her boyfriend lured Dampier to Jackson's apartment, then kidnapped and murdered him. Jackson was sentenced to life in prison without parole.

6. In December 2002, West Virginian Jack Whittaker won $314 million in the largest undivided Powerball jackpot in lottery history. He had nothing but good intentions for his money and gave generously to his church, his friends, and various civic organizations. But trouble seemed to follow Whittaker after he won the big one. Strangers hounded him for money, and some even threatened his family when he refused. He was hit with a variety of lawsuits and once was robbed of $500,000 in cash. But the greatest tragedy was when Whittaker's teenage granddaughter died of a drug overdose, her habit funded by the generous allowance she received from her grandfather.

7. Wanda Rickerson won more than half a million dollars in the Georgia Lottery in 2003. Three years later, the former sheriff's office administrative clerk was ordered to pay $84,000 to Columbia County after pleading no contest to theft and insurance charges. Rickerson's crime? Embezzling $56,000 from an inmate trust account she supervised at the Columbia County Detention Center.

8. An anonymous British man who won a sizable fortune in the national lottery was the victim of a home invasion following his windfall. Masked thugs wielding machetes burst into the man's home and held him, his wife, and his young son at knifepoint while they ransacked the place. The thieves escaped with jewelry and numerous personal items.

9. In 2001, Victoria Zell and her husband won an $11 million jackpot in the Minnesota Lottery. But Zell's good fortune didn't last long. In 2005, she was sent to prison for an alcohol-related car crash that killed one motorist and paralyzed another.

10. Michael Carroll's $17 million fortune couldn't keep him out of prison either. In 2006, the British lottery winner was sentenced to nine months in the hoosegow for going berserk in a disco.

Who Knew?

Pantyhose—Not Just for Legs

Every woman—and not just a few men—knows that pantyhose can make legs look oooh-la-la. But not every woman (and very few men) knows that there are many other things hose can do. Who knew?

- Did you lose something small and hard to find? Slide a length of pantyhose over your vacuum cleaner's hose, secure it tightly with rubber bands, and carefully vacuum where you think the lost item might be. The hose will keep the item from being sucked up into the bag.

- Cut an old piece of pantyhose slightly larger than your new hairbrush. Push the bristles through the hose. When it's time to clean the brush, just pull the old pantyhose off and refresh it with a new piece.

- Keep pantyhose in the craft room. When shredded, it works great for stuffing soft toys. Cut the pantyhose into small squares for use instead of cotton balls. Pantyhose wrapped and rubber-banded around a wooden stick makes an inexpensive, in-a-pinch paintbrush. Use a clean piece of pantyhose to test your sanding job for snags.

- Line your houseplant's pots with pantyhose to prevent soil loss from the bottom of the pot. Cut pantyhose into strips and use them to tie seedlings to posts or to tie bundles of brush. Wider strips attached to stakes can be used as a "hammock" for melons or large produce in the garden. Or leave the legs intact, hang the hose so mice can't reach it, and store seeds in them for the winter. (This works great for storing onions and potatoes at the end of the growing season, too.)

- Use recycled pantyhose as mesh bags in the laundry room. Just cut off a length of leg, drop in your delicates, and wash as usual. Use the other leg as a back-scrubber: Insert a bar of soap or two, tie a knot at both ends, and scrub-a-dub-dub. Who knew?

Five Reasons People Think Nixon Was a Crummy President

Nixon claims the dubious honor of being the only U.S. president to resign from office. Before his hasty exit, his approval rating plummeted to a dismal 23 percent. Here's why:

1. **Watergate** On June 17, 1972, five men were caught breaking into Democratic Party offices at The Watergate complex. They were there to bug phones and photograph private documents to help Nixon win reelection. Damning testimony and Nixon's own recordings of Oval Office conversations implicated the president in a cover-up conspiracy. Nixon resigned before he could be impeached.

2. **Vietnam** In his 1968 campaign, Nixon promised to end the war. Yet, during his first term, he expanded U.S. combat operations into neighboring Cambodia, which had long been neutral, and authorized secret bombings there.

3. **The Economy** When Nixon took office, unemployment was at 3.3 percent. It rose to 9 percent in 1975, in the aftermath of his presidency. Inflation jumped from 5 percent to 12.1 percent while he was in office. The economy saw an upturn just before the 1972 election, but by the time Nixon left office, the nation was in a recession.

4. **The Plumbers** Before Watergate, Nixon assembled a Special Investigation Unit (SIU)—better known as "The Plumbers"—to stop White House leaks. The SIU specialized in illegal capers, including breaking into Daniel Ellsberg's psychiatrist's office to dig up dirt after Ellsberg released classified Vietnam documents.

5. **His Big Mouth** Because of the Watergate investigation, Nixon was forced to hand over around 3,700 hours of Oval Office recordings. The recordings released to the public painted Nixon as devious, anti-Semitic, paranoid, and exceptionally foul-mouthed.

But Somebody's Got to Do It...

So Monday comes around too soon for you. You've got a lousy boss, a rotten job, and a terrible way to make a living. Before you give your two week's notice, you might want to consider how bad you really have it. After all, you could have one of these jobs...

- **Breath Odor Evaluator** Next time you move in for a kiss, you can thank the people who sniff morning breath, garlic breath, smoker's breath, and bad denture breath to assess the effectiveness of mouthwash, mints, and toothpaste. Come to think of it, both the kisser and the kissee have a lot to be thankful for.

- **Porta-Potty Supplier** They supply those smelly little shanties for county fairs, concerts, rallies, parades, and other events. Not so bad, huh? Don't forget that somebody's got to clean them when the fun is done.

- **Dog Food Tester and Dog Sniffer** Most dogs will eat anything, right? Unfortunately, Fido can't tell you whether or not something tastes yummy. Enter the dog food tester, who checks for taste, consistency, and crumbliness (because dog owners hate a mess). On the other side of the kennel, someone gets paid to take a whiff of Rover's breath to be sure his fangs are in good shape after he's eaten the dog food. Sit. Stay. Good.

- **Biohazard Clean-Up Crew** These folks have strong arms and stronger stomachs. Their job is, among other things, to clean up bodies that have lain for days or weeks in one spot, homicides (after the police are through with the crime scene), and the aftermath of suicide.

- **Diener** Dying for a new job? Check out a career as a diener. The diener prepares dead bodies (in any state of decomposition) for autopsies so the coroner can do his or her job more efficiently.

- **Jobs in Underwear** Someone has to design the tighty whities and thongs of tomorrow. There are also jobs available for people who make undies with special charcoal filters so that the excessively flatulent don't offend. And somebody's got to test those undies, too.

- **Beer Tester and Ice Cream Tester** Sounds like a great job until you understand that they don't get to swallow the samples. They only get to taste, then they have to spit it out. Drat.

- **Chewing Gum Remover** Remember sticking your ABC (already been chewed) gum under the park bench, on the sidewalk, to a tree, beneath a desk? Well, somebody's got to remove it so you can do it again.

- **Bovine Artificial Inseminator and Semen Collector** Moooove over if you think you might like these careers. Semen collectors collect bull ejaculate so that valuable cows can be impregnated with the right genes. To get that job done, AIs have to stick their hand, um, well, up inside…you know. Or maybe you don't want to know.

- **Magician's Assistant** Not a bad way to make bucks, unless the boss decides he might want to try his hand (and your head) at being a knife thrower, too.

- **Mosquito Researcher** It's not like you can call a mosquito and she'll come running, right? Nope, mosquito researchers generally offer themselves up as bait to get skeeters to bite. Not surprisingly, such researchers are slapped with mosquito-borne illnesses quite often.

- **Hazardous Materials Diver** Love the water? Can't wait to take a quick, refreshing dip? Then grab your swimsuit and more: Hazmat divers swim beneath sewage and toxic spills to find bodies, evidence, and other items that need to be recovered in the muck and murk. They also work to clean up toxic accidents in bodies of water.

- **Feces Collector** Within the Hindu caste system, there are untouchables within the untouchables. Called *safai karamchari,* their job is to pick up human feces and carry it away from homes and public buildings. They're paid very little, if at all. So stop complaining about your job, okay?

The Gold of Little Golden Books

Little Golden Books first hit the literary world in 1942. Back then, the books cost just 25 cents each and were an instant hit—more than 1.5 million copies were printed in their first five months. By the time Little Golden Books celebrated its 60th birthday in 2002, more than two billion of them had found their way to children and their parents. So which are the best and brightest titles? And which are just a little weird? You'll have to read on to find out.

The Poky Little Puppy This remains the best-selling Little Golden Book of all time. The odds are good that you read this book when you were a child; more than 15 million copies of *The Poky Little Puppy* have been sold since the book was first published in September 1942 as part of the original 12 Little Golden Books.

The story itself is a classic: A puppy who dawdles on his way home is consistently rewarded despite his meandering ways, getting extra treats such as custard even after he arrives home long after his fellow dogs. But in the end, the puppy's bad habit finally catches up to him: The dog has to go to bed without any strawberry shortcake. Even worse, his fellow puppies fill their stomachs with the treat before they head off to sleep.

The Little Red Hen This book was also part of the first set of Little Golden Books released in 1942. The story is a classic tale about the benefits of hard work. The hen of the title busies herself making a loaf of bread. But none of her animal friends are willing to help pick the wheat, travel to the mill, or bake the bread. Once the delicious bread is baked, though, the hen has the last laugh. She asks the lazy animals if any of them would like to help her eat the bread. They all volunteer this time, but the hen refuses their help and eats the bread alone with her chicks.

Doctor Dan, The Bandage Man Many Little Golden Books have been used to teach children not to be afraid of medical professionals. *Doctor Dan, The Bandage Man* was one of the more unusual.

Released in 1951, the book came with Johnson & Johnson Band-Aids glued to the right side of its title page. The book made history as one of the first examples of a joint effort between a corporation and a publishing company. It sold 1.75 million copies in its first printing.

Little Lulu and Her Magic Tricks This book, released in 1954, had a huge first printing of 2.25 million copies. Part of the appeal was the small package of tissues attached to its front cover. The book explained how children could make toys from the tissues. Lulu even made it on *The Arthur Godfrey Show,* a popular television show, during its first month of release.

Scooby-Doo: The Haunted Carnival Several top-selling Little Golden Books have featured popular television or cartoon characters. Scooby-Doo is no exception. In 2000, *Scooby-Doo: The Haunted Carnival* ranked as the third best-selling hardcover children's title of the year, according to *Publishers Weekly.*

Seven Little Postmen Little Golden Books highlighting different professions have always been popular. The books have featured firefighters, police officers, and doctors, of course. But one of the most popular profession-focused books is *Seven Little Postmen*, published in 1952. This popular book tells the tale of how seven hardworking postmen deliver a letter from a little boy to his grandmother.

The Original Dozen

The first 12 Little Golden Books, published in 1942, were:

1. *Three Little Kittens*
2. *Bedtime Stories*
3. *Mother Goose*
4. *Prayers for Little Children*
5. *The Little Red Hen*
6. *The Alphabet A–Z*
7. *Nursery Songs*
8. *The Poky Little Puppy*
9. *The Golden Book of Fairy Tales*
10. *Baby's Book*
11. *The Animals of Farmer Jones*
12. *This Little Piggy*

Really Stupid Hazing Incidents

Ahhh…college. Institutions of higher learning, preparing the leaders of tomorrow. Oh, and along the way showing that some students can be really, really stupid—especially when it comes to hazing. Sadly, some incidents of abuse lead to death. Other times, people just look really foolish. (Not surprisingly, many of these initiations involved booze.)

1. **Egg on His…Everything** A University of Michigan freshman nearly froze to death in 1980 after he consumed a large amount of alcohol and then was stripped; shaved; covered with jam, eggs, and cologne; and shoved outside in near-freezing temperatures for more than an hour.

2. **No More Cold Steel on Ice** Administrators at Kent State University in Ohio canceled the 1988 hockey season after a dozen players violated various university hazing laws. The students allegedly shaved the heads and bodies (again with the shaving!) of teammates. One student nearly died after being forced to drink alcohol.

3. **Compromising Positions** The men's soccer team at the University of Washington was placed on probation in 1997 after its members taped three rookie players to a luggage cart after posing them in…ahem…compromising positions.

4. **Tastes Like Chicken** A veteran baseball coach at the University of Wisconsin-Stout was suspended in 1997 after senior members of the team encouraged rookie teammates to eat goldfish during a road trip.

5. **Can't Touch This** In 1999, a state investigator confirmed a complaint of "improper sexual touching" and alcohol consumption made by members of the hockey team at the University of Vermont.

6. **Shocking** Several frat boys at Stetson University in Florida were expelled from their fraternity after shocking pledges with an electrical device in 1980.

7. **No More Male Bonding** The University of Vermont's 1999–2000 men's hockey season was canceled after freshmen said that they were forced to wear women's underwear and parade in a line where they were forced to hold each other's...manhood.

8. **Deadly Turn of Events** The death of a Chico State University freshman drew national headlines in 2005 when he died of brain swelling from water intoxication after being forced to drink from a five-gallon water bottle. He was also covered in urine and feces.

9. **Out of Tune** Even members of the marching band get in on the hazing freak show. Members of the Southern University marching band in Louisiana were hospitalized after partaking in an initiation. According to reports, at least one of the men was beaten more than 50 times with a two-by-four. Seven students were arrested.

10. **No Comment Necessary** One Web site (which may or may not be serious) offers fraternities some "helpful hints" on ways to initiate pledges. Among them: paddling bare bottoms, forcing pledges to drink bodily fluids, and placing objects where objects should NOT be placed.

11. **The Smoot** Not every hazing incident leads to death or pending lawsuits. Witness the case of Oliver Smoot, MIT class of 1962, whose participation in a freshman hazing stunt led to a unit of measurement being named in his honor. In October 1958, his frat buddies used the 5′7″ Smoot to measure the Massachusetts Bridge. His exact height equaled one smoot (the bridge measured 364.4 smoots and one ear). For some reason, almost all MIT students know this.

"You cannot do hazing. If you're stupid enough to do hazing now... you'll pay the price."
—Don Cherry

Behind the People of Our Time

TIME *magazine awards its prestigious Person of the Year award annually. Take a look back through time to see who has made the cut.*

First Person Chosen Charles Lindbergh was the first person to make a solo nonstop flight over the Atlantic Ocean. In the same year, he was chosen as *TIME*'s first Man of the Year (1927).

First Non-American Chosen Mohandas Gandhi was chosen as Man of the Year in 1930. The following year, French politician Pierre Laval, who was later executed for high treason, was the first European picked. In 1935, Haile Selassie I became the first African chosen.

First Woman of the Year Between the time that King Edward abdicated the throne for the woman he loved (1936) and the day that he married her (1937), divorcée Wallis Simpson was chosen as *TIME* magazine's first Woman of the Year.

First Nonhuman Chosen Despite cries of outrage from fans and purists, *TIME* magazine chose the computer as Machine of the Year in 1982.

Biggest Controversies Over the years, *TIME* magazine has taken the most flack for three choices: Adolf Hitler was chosen Man of the Year in 1938; Joseph Stalin in 1939 and 1942; and the Ayatollah Khomeini in 1979.

Chosen More than Once: Joseph Stalin, George Marshall, Harry S. Truman, Winston Churchill, Dwight Eisenhower, Franklin Delano Roosevelt, Lyndon Baines Johnson, Richard Nixon, Ronald Reagan, Deng Xiaoping, Mikhail Gorbachev, Bill Clinton, The American Soldier, and George W. Bush.

Oddest, Broadest Choice: Congratulations! You were chosen in 2006. The wide net was cast to represent individual use, creation, and content of the World Wide Web.

15 Phobias You Obviously Don't Have

You might be scared of spiders (arachnophobia). Maybe shedders make you shudder (doraphobia, or the fear of fur). Maybe you've always wondered why hippopotomonstrosesquippedaliophobia describes the fear of long words. But it's a sure bet these 15 fearsome phobias don't make your heart race.

So you've got this great new book in your hands. Well, wanting to read *Armchair Reader™: Vitally Useless Information* means you don't suffer from gnosiophobia (fear of knowledge) or sophophobia (fear of learning).

Because you comprehend these words now, somebody must've taught you how to read, which means you don't have scolionophobia (fear of school). With all that learning you had to do, it's a good thing you never suffered from phronemophobia (fear of thinking) or ideophobia (fear of ideas), right?

Since you're holding this book, you obviously aren't concerned about bibliophobia. That's the fear of books. It's pretty safe to say you don't have the fear of words (verbophobia and/or logophobia), either. And because a book is made of paper, it's not likely you have papyrophobia, which is the fear of—you guessed it—paper.

When you read, you need good light, of course; otherwise, you couldn't see the page. That means you don't suffer from photophobia, which is the fear of light, nor do you need to worry about optophobia (fear of opening your eyes). And speaking of this page in your hand, it's easy to see that neither the page itself nor the ink frightens you. That means you don't have to be concerned about leukophobia (fear of the color white) or melanophobia (fear of the color black).

Don't look now. Okay, it's safe, so take a peek at the bottom of the page. There, right in the middle. See that? Whew, you don't have numerophobia or arithmophobia (both describe the fear of numbers).

Now, isn't this fun? Sure it is, which means you don't suffer from geliophobia (fear of laughter), and you surely don't ever have to worry about panophobia (fear of everything).

Lefty Trivia:

Facts about Left-Handedness

- There is no standard for what constitutes left-handedness, making research into handedness difficult.

- Left-handed adults find many workplaces inefficient or dangerous because they're designed for right-handed people.

- Around 10 percent of the population is left-handed.

- Famous lefties include Mark Twain, Whoopie Goldberg, Ronald Reagan, George H. W. Bush, Bill Clinton, Jay Leno, Julia Roberts, Oprah Winfrey, John McCain, and Barack Obama.

- More men than women are left-handed.

- Left-handers are more likely to stutter, have dyslexia, and suffer from allergies.

- International Left-Handers Day is August 13, and was first celebrated in 1976.

- Homosexuals are 39 percent more likely to be left-handed or ambidextrous.

- Lefties are three times more likely to become addicted to alcohol or other substances.

- The term *southpaw* was first used to refer to left-handers in the 1890s.

- At one time, teachers would force students to write with their right hands, even when left-handed. Luckily, that bias is changing.

- Lefties might be better in hand-to-hand combat.

- Researchers at Oxford University have found a gene for left-handedness.

- Scientists have found that handedness develops *in utero.*

- The hair of right-handed people swirls clockwise on the top of their head, but the hair of left-handed people can swirl in any direction.

- Lefties tend to perform better on IQ tests.

It Happened in...November

- In order to entice audiences to theaters, Hollywood introduced a major studio film (*Bwana Devil*) in 3-D in November 1952. Despite the fact that polarized glasses tacked a dime onto the admission price, box office records were shattered.

- Readers of *Billboard* magazine voted Elvis Presley the most promising country/western singer in November 1955.

- A fact that sticks to the roof of your mouth: John Kellogg filed for a patent for making peanut butter in November 1895.

- Jules Leotard performed the first flying trapeze act in public in November 1859 at the Cirque Napoleon in Paris. He was wearing—guess what?—a leotard, a garment he designed.

- District of Columbia residents were allowed to vote in a presidential election for the first time in November 1964, thanks to the 23rd Amendment. Before the amendment's passage, D.C. residents were only allowed to cast ballots for delegates and party officials for the two major political conventions.

- Hola! Bonjour! Guten Tag! Buongiorno! World Hello Day began in November 1973 and is celebrated every November 21. The goal of the day is to greet ten people in any language, all in the name of peace.

- More than six inches of snow fell on Tucson, Arizona, on November 16, 1958, making it the earliest and heaviest snow in that city to date. The white stuff closed roads and knocked down power lines.

- November is National Inspirational Role Models Month, Lifewriting Month, National Pomegranate Month, Family Stories Month, and Prematurity Awareness Month.

Presidential Pets

More than two dozen children, both children and grandchildren of presidents, have called the White House home. And along with clothes, toys, and schoolbooks, the First Families have brought their pets to the White House.

During some administrations the White House has resembled the National Zoo. President Theodore Roosevelt and his six children assembled the largest menagerie: dogs, cats, birds, guinea pigs, rats, a badger, a pig, a flying squirrel, a rabbit, horses, and snakes. Algonquin, their Icelandic pony, was famous for his elevator ride (at the urging of young Quentin) to visit Archie, confined with the measles in an upper-floor bedroom.

Soviet Union Premier Nikita Khrushchev gave Caroline Kennedy a puppy called Pushinka. Her mother Strelka was one of the first dogs in space. Since it was the height of the Cold War, the poor pup was checked for bugs—and not the kind with six legs. Pushinka and another Kennedy dog, Charlie the Welsh terrier, had four puppies, or pupniks as JFK called them.

Although dogs are the most common White House animal, many exotic animals have wandered the halls as well. In 1929, Herbert Hoover's son, Allan Henry, brought a pair of alligators with him. They weren't even the first alligators to call the White House home. When the Marquis de Lafayette visited the White House in 1826, he brought along a gator who lived in the East Room for two months.

In 1863, a friend sent the Lincolns a live turkey for Christmas dinner. Before the ax could fall, son Tad named the newcomer Jack. And if you've got a name, you're a dinner guest, not a dinner entrée. Jack wasn't the only dinner-turned-pet. Upon receiving a raccoon for his Thanksgiving dinner, Calvin Coolidge promptly named her Rebecca. Rebecca had an annoying habit—unscrewing lightbulbs as she wandered through the White House.

One day, strollers on Pennsylvania Avenue witnessed President Benjamin Harrison barreling down the street brandishing a cane. He was in pursuit of the family goat. Whiskers had made a break for freedom—while harnessed to a cart containing several of the president's grandchildren!

Getting Carded

Back when you were a kid, Grandma used to send you a birthday card with a Washington inside. You were happy to get the dollar, but you probably didn't give much thought to the card itself. Let's change that, shall we?

- The very first greeting cards were believed to have been sent by the Chinese and early Egyptians thousands of years ago. The Germans made woodcut cards in the 1400s, and at least one English paper Valentine survives from that century.

- By the mid-1800s, greeting cards were enormously popular in Europe, inexpensive to create and send, and an important keepsake for the recipient.

- The notable exception to that paper happiness was the Penny Dreadful Valentine card, which cost one cent. As the name implies, these cards were nasty: The pictures and verse were insulting, and the cards were generally delivered to someone the sender disliked. Penny Dreadfuls (also known as Vinegar Valentines) were (un)popular starting in the 1850s.

- Though Louis Prang is usually said to have started the greeting card industry in the United States in 1856, Esther Howland was hand-making Valentines in Massachusetts four years earlier. Prang, however, developed a lithographic method of card-making that made his products more vivid and more in demand.

- Only a few years before Prang started his business, the first Christmas cards had appeared in London. By the late 1800s, both Brits and Americans were exchanging Yuletide greetings among friends. Back then, Christmas cards were elaborate, unusually shaped, and featured artwork by popular artists of the times.

- In the early part of the 20th century, many American greeting card companies formed to meet the demand of the public. Patriotic and war-themed greetings were trendy during World War II, and greeting cards with humor made their entry in the 1950s. By the 1980s, greeting card manufacturers were mass-producing cards for every imaginable holiday, as well as for no holiday at all!

Hooray for Hollywood!

What is now the Hollywood Walk of Fame was conceived in 1958 as a permanent tribute to Hollywood's most celebrated personalities. A groundbreaking ceremony was held on February 9, 1960, and stars for the first 1,558 individuals were unveiled 16 months later. Administered by the Hollywood Chamber of Commerce, the Hollywood Walk of Fame was designated a cultural/historic landmark by the City of Los Angeles in 1978.

A Star Is Born

The Walk of Fame is comprised of five acres of bronze stars, each embedded in pink terrazzo and surrounded by charcoal terrazzo squares. The recipient's name is engraved on his or her star, along with an emblem identifying the category for which he or she has been honored: motion pictures, television, radio, recording, or live theater.

The Hollywood Walk of Fame can be found on both sides of Hollywood Boulevard, from Gower to LaBrea, and on both sides of Vine Street, from Yucca Street to Sunset Boulevard.

Walk of Fame by the Numbers

2,500+: the number of stars created when the Walk of Fame was dedicated in 1960

3.5 miles: the distance you will have to walk if you want to see every star along the Walk of Fame's path

3: the number of Hollywood canines who have stars dedicated to them: Strongheart, Lassie, and Rin Tin Tin

$25,000: the sponsorship fee to receive a star on the Hollywood Walk of Fame (You didn't think they were free, did you?)

Four Really Famous Movie Stars Who Do Not Have a Star

Clint Eastwood

Jane Fonda

Mel Gibson

Robert Redford

When You Wish Upon a Star...

Receiving a star on the Hollywood Walk of Fame isn't as simple as just requesting one. There are strict criteria:

Professional achievement

Longevity of five years in the field of entertainment

Contributions to the community

An agreement to attend the dedication ceremony

Nominations, which are accepted by the Hollywood Chamber of Commerce during a specific 60-day nomination period, must be approved by the Walk of Fame Committee. Often, several annual nominations are required before a star is approved.

Walk of Fame Who's Who

- Singing cowboy Gene Autry is the only personality to have a star dedicated to him in all five categories.

- Singer John Denver was awarded a star in 1982. However, it had not been officially dedicated at the time of his death in 1997 because Denver had yet to schedule the required personal appearance.

- Fictional personalities who have received a star on the Walk of Fame include Big Bird, Mickey Mouse, Bugs Bunny, the Simpsons, and Donald Duck.

- The crew of *Apollo 11*, the first crewed mission to the moon, are honored with individual stars, all located at the intersection of Hollywood and Vine.

- Ronald Reagan is one of only two California governors to be honored with a star on the Walk of Fame. The other is Arnold Schwarzenegger. Reagan is also the only U.S. president to be so honored.

- Not all stars are located on a sidewalk. Boxing legend Muhammad Ali's star can be found mounted on a wall at the Kodak Theater because he insisted that he not be walked upon.

- In 2004, Mary-Kate and Ashley Olsen, then 18, became the youngest recipients in any category to receive a star on the Walk of Fame.

- Hollywood isn't the only city with a Walk of Fame; Palm Springs, California, boasts a "Walk of Stars" along Palm Canyon Drive. Approximately 300 movie stars and other notables are honored there, including Frank Sinatra, Elvis Presley, Marilyn Monroe, and Bob Hope.

Stop, Thief!

Over the years, four stars have been stolen from the Hollywood Walk of Fame. The stars of James Stewart and Kirk Douglas were swiped by an unscrupulous contractor after they had been removed during a construction project. One of Gene Autry's five stars was also absconded with during a construction project; it later turned up in Iowa. And in November 2005, thieves sawed Gregory Peck's star right out of the sidewalk. It was replaced in September 2006.

"Is Hollywood the cruelest city in the world? Well, it can be. New York can be that, too. You can be a Broadway star here one night, and something happens, and out—nobody knows you on the street. They forget you ever lived. It happens in Hollywood, too."
—Buster Keaton

Hurricane 101

Hurricanes are huge tropical storm systems that can measure up to 600 miles across. Powerful winds (ranging from 75 to more than 200 miles per hour), flooding rains, and huge storm surges can leave utter devastation in their wake.

A Storm by Any Other Name...

Hurricanes are only called by that name in the Atlantic Ocean, Gulf of Mexico, and the Eastern Pacific Ocean. In the Western Pacific Ocean, such storms are called *typhoons.* In the Indian Ocean, the Bay of Bengal, and Australia, they are known as *cyclones.*

Hurricanes by the Numbers

1953: the year the U.S. Weather Bureau started giving hurricanes women's names. Previously, they were named by the phonetic alphabet (Able, Baker, Charlie)

5: the number of categories in the Saffir-Simpson Hurricane Wind Scale

6 months: the length of the official "hurricane season" (June 1–November 30). The Eastern Pacific hurricane season extends from May 15 through November 30

8,000: the estimated number of deaths caused by the unnamed category 4 hurricane that ravaged Galveston, Texas, on September 8, 1900

$25 billion: the estimated amount of damage caused by Hurricane Andrew, which struck Dade County, Florida, in 1992

$75 billion: the estimated amount of damage caused by Hurricane Katrina, which devastated New Orleans and the Mississippi Gulf Coast in 2005

Sabaku! Sabaku! Sabaku!

(Translation: Sell! Sell! Sell!)

*Once they make it to the "big time" (or even close to the big time),
most actors declare that they are too good for lowly commercials.
But apparently Japanese commercials are a whole different story.
A slew of actors, including Oscar winners, have signed contracts
restricting their ads to Japan, filmed bizarre spots speaking really
bad Japanese, and pocketed obscene amounts of money for the
pleasure. So who's selling what?*

1. Which movie star, philanthropist, and super-dad wins the prize
   for most Japanese advertising campaigns—including those for
   Edwin jeans, Rolex, Honda, and coffee?

       a. Ben Affleck   c. Mel Gibson

       b. Brad Pitt   d. Paul Newman

   Answer: b.

2. First he was fighting hams in his movies, then he was selling them
   in Japan. Perhaps because even his English is often undecipher-
   able, the director of the commercial limited him to one Japanese
   word: *osebo*. Who is the osebo man?

       a. Ed Norton   c. Sylvester Stallone

       b. Ralph Macchio   d. Tom Cruise

   Answer : c.

3. Before he entered politics, which movie star sold noodles, Direct
   TV, Sky TV (Japan's HBO), beer, and—the perfect match for
   him—Vfuyy, an energy drink/potency drink?

       a. Arnold Schwarzenegger   c. Fred Thompson

       b. Clint Eastwood   d. Jesse Ventura

   Answer: a.

4. Known in the United States for promoting environmental causes, this Hollywood star was the Japanese face of the gas-guzzling Suzuki SUV.

      a. Cameron Diaz   c. Leonardo DiCaprio

      b. Ed Norton   d. Martin Sheen

Answer: c.

5. Although his most famous character preferred gin, which star promoted Japanese scotch—as well as Ito hams and Mazda?

      a. Alan Alda   c. Kevin Spacey

      b. Daniel Craig   d. Sean Connery

Answer: d.

6. Not only did this American sweetheart sell Nohohon—a canned chrysanthemum and dandelion tea—in Japan, but she also "went to the mats" to prevent Westerners from finding out—even taking legal action against Web sites that mentioned it.

      a. Brooke Shields   c. Celine Dion

      b. Catherine Zeta-Jones   d. Meg Ryan

Answer: d.

7. She may be one of the richest women in Hollywood but that didn't stop her from appearing in ads for the Aeon School of English Conversation.

      a. Cameron Diaz   c. Nicole Kidman

      b. Jennifer Aniston   d. Oprah Winfrey

Answer: a.

8. Japanese ad execs are famous for matching the right star with the right product. So what beverage did Harrison Ford sell?

      a. Go-Go Tea   c. Mt. Rainier coffee
         (carbonated iced tea)

      b. Kirin Lager   d. Suntory (diet beer)

Answer: b.

The Way the Future Wasn't...
Life on the Moon?

When Neil Armstrong landed on the moon on July 21, 1969, and uttered his famous phrase, "That's one small step for man; one giant leap for mankind," millions of people asked, "Can shopping malls be far behind?" Suddenly, living on the moon seemed a very real possibility. Yet as of 2009, only 12 people have ever set foot on the moon. What happened to lunar colonies?

Back in 1954, science-fiction author Arthur C. Clarke predicted future moon dwellers would inhabit inflatable igloos heated by nuclear power. During the early '60s, several aerospace engineers proposed building underground bases beneath the moon's inhospitable surface. Robert Wilson and Jack LaPatra combined these two approaches with their 1968 design for Moonlab, a multilevel structure that would feature an astronomical observatory and a lunar farming community. They believed their colony could be fully functional and capable of supporting 24 residents by 1984.

University of Utah plant science professor Frank Salisbury went even further. His 1991 article *Lunar Farming* took readers on an imaginary tour of "Lunar City" in the year 2019. This thriving colony had over 100 residents engaged in growing dozens of crops, among them peanuts, sugarcane, wheat, rice, potatoes, and spinach.

Unfortunately, it doesn't look like we're going to catch up to Salisbury's vision within the next decade. The sheer cost of establishing a moon colony has proven daunting, and new problems keep cropping up. In addition to extreme temperatures and the general lack of elements such as carbon and nitrogen that are essential to life, colonists would also have to contend with falling meteorites and gritty moon dust gumming up the workings of all their machines.

However, those still eager to become lunar pioneers may have reason for hope. In September 2009, scientists working on a joint venture between NASA's Moon Mineralogy Mapper and India's Chandrayaan-1 announced that they had discovered water on the moon. Details are still forthcoming, but it's possible that humankind may yet make that leap to living on the moon.

It Happened in . . . December

- Cabbage Patch Kids appeared on the cover of *Newsweek* magazine in December 1983. By the end of the year, some three million dolls had been sold, but holiday shoppers still clamored for the homely toys.

- In December 1969, guitarist Jimi Hendrix told a Toronto court that he had "outgrown" drugs. He was subsequently found not guilty of possession.

- *The Teletubbies* went to the top position in the UK charts in December 1997 with the single "Teletubbies Say Eh-Oh." They beat out Janet Jackson, the Spice Girls, and other popular artists.

- And you think you're lucky? Angelo and Maria Gallina each won a different lottery on the same day in December 2002, winning $126,000 in the first jackpot and $17 million in the second lottery. The odds of it happening are an estimated 1 in 24 trillion.

- A one-eyed "Cyclops" kitten was born in late December 2005 in Oregon. Despite round-the-clock TLC, the pussycat perished within 24 hours of birth.

- Let's toast to this: Prohibition ended in December 1933—just in time to ring in the New Year.

- Neither snow, nor rain, nor all that other stuff: The first International mail-by-dogsled left Maine for its Montreal destination in December 1928. Most of the journey was over snowless ground.

- December is Bingo's Birthday Month (B-seven. That's B . . . seven), National Tie Month (Won't Dad be surprised?), National Write a Business Plan Month, 3D (Drunk and Drugged Driving) Prevention Month, and Spiritual Literacy Month.

Ten Alleged Cases of Feral Children

According to legend, ancient Rome was founded by twin brothers Romulus and Remus, who had both been nursed by a female wolf. Since then, there have been hundreds of stories about children being raised by animals. Some of these reports are simply hoaxes. In other cases, the children are not literally feral but are the victims of abusive parents. There are, however, some surprising incidents in recent history that could give the phrase "a walk on the wild side" a whole new meaning.

1. In 2007, a boy approximately ten years old was reported to be living among wolves in the Kaluga Region of Central Russia. He was captured and sent to an orphanage in Moscow, but he managed to escape and is still thought to be living in the wild.

2. Traian Caldarar of Brasov, Romania, became lost and lived among stray dogs between the ages of four and seven. In 2002, he was discovered and returned to his mother. He eventually relearned human language and became a normal boy again.

3. In 2004, social workers found seven-year-old Andrei Tolstyk living in an abandoned house in Bespalovskoya, Siberia, with only a dog for company. They believe he had survived there for almost seven years after his alcoholic parents deserted him when he was an infant. He was placed in an orphanage but reportedly never learned to speak.

4. One of Russia's most famous "wild boys" not only lived with dogs, he actually became leader of his pack. In 1998, six-year-old Ivan Mishukov was finally separated from his beloved pack of stray dogs and placed in a Moscow orphanage. Because he had only been living among the dogs for two years, he was able to relearn language fairly rapidly.

5. Abandoned by her parents at the age of three, Oxana Malaya of the Ukrainian village of Novaya Blagoveschenka spent five years among wild dogs. Rescued at the age of eight in 1991, she eventually acquired language skills and was featured in a 2004 Discovery Channel documentary on feral children.

6. In 2000, ten-year-old Alex Rivas was found among a pack of 15 wild dogs on the outskirts of Talcahuano, Chile. Social workers believe he had been living with the pack for about two years and may have even suckled milk from one of the female dogs. At the childcare center, he could communicate in basic Spanish. He also liked to draw pictures of his favorite subject—dogs.

7. Not all feral children live among canines. Several have been discovered in the company of nonhuman primates. A seven-year-old girl known only by the name Baby Hospital was discovered living among wild chimpanzees in Sierra Leone in 1984. She reportedly never learned how to speak, though she did cry—a trait unusual in feral children.

8. Saturday Mifune of Kwazulu-Natal, South Africa, lived with a tribe of wild chimpanzees for at least a year. Found in 1987 at the age of five, he was placed in an orphanage. Even after living among humans for a decade, he still behaved in a chimplike fashion, leaping from furniture and clapping his hands to his head when disturbed. He died in 2005 of unreported causes.

9. Two-year-old Bello of Nigeria lived with a band of chimpanzees for a year after his parents abandoned him. In 1996, villagers discovered him and placed him in an orphanage. Reports indicate that he never learned how to speak.

10. John Ssabunnya lived with a colony of African Green Monkeys after his parents died in the Ugandan civil war. He was found in 1991, at the age of six, and placed in an orphanage. At 14, he joined the Pearl of Africa Children's Choir, a group dedicated to raising funds for Africa's orphans.

Mad about
MAD Magazine

For those who know it only by reputation, MAD *is a satire magazine that makes fun (of the PG-13 variety) of anyone or anything, from Saddam Hussein to pop culture to the British royal family. It's a thick-skinned reader's hoot and a touchy reader's cerebral hemorrhage.*

MAD has been *MAD* since the early 1950s, but its prehistory extends back to the darkest days of the Great Depression. Its emblem, Alfred E. Neuman, dates back even further.

Contrary to popular belief, iconic publisher William "Bill" Gaines didn't invent *MAD.* His father, Max Gaines, pioneered newsstand comic books in the mid-1930s as cheap, commercially viable amusement for children. Son Bill was an eccentric prankster, the type of kid peers might label "Most Likely to Publish an Iconoclastic Satire Mag." Upon his father's tragic death in 1947, Bill inherited the family comic book business, Educational Comics (EC). He steered EC to stand for Entertaining Comics: a publisher of garish horror comics veering into sardonic social commentary.

In 1952, Bill's early collaborator Harvey Kurtzman proposed a new comic called *MAD,* which would poke fun at just about anything. Kurtzman's brainchild was a success, and in 1955 Bill allowed Kurtzman to convert *MAD* from comic book to magazine. Kurtzman left EC shortly thereafter, but their creation still thrives more than a half century later.

Two Types of *MAD*

As a comic book: #1 (October–November 1952) through #23 (May 1955)

As a magazine: #24 (July 1955)–present

MAD Mascot Alfred E. Neuman

- Motto: "What, me worry?"
- First appearance in *MAD*: #21, March 1955
- First cover to prominently feature Alfred's face: #30, December 1956
- First artist to draw Alfred: Norman Mingo
- Ten other artists who have drawn Alfred for the cover: Kelly Freas, Jack Rickard, Jack Davis, Mort Drucker, Mort Kuntzler, Bob Jones, Al Jaffee, Sergio Aragones, Richard Williams

From Cover to Cover

- Only president since 1960 *not* to be featured on the cover: Gerald Ford
- Pop star with the most cover appearances: Michael Jackson (five appearances in four issues: #251, #277, #420, #438)
- Most controversial cover: #166 (April 1974). Featured a hand giving the middle finger. Angry retailers refused to stock it, and the issue was returned by the box load. It is now a rare collector's item.
- Only cover drawn by an ape: #38 (March 1958), painted by celebrity chimp J. Fred Muggs.

MAD Magazine and *Star Wars*

- Number of covers to feature the *Star Wars* franchise: 9.
- Between them, George Lucas and Steven Spielberg have purchased the original art to 11 *MAD* covers featuring their movies.
- An attorney for Lucas Films once sent Bill Gaines a threatening letter following a parody of one of the *Star Wars* films. At the same time, Gaines received a letter from George Lucas praising the same parody. An amused Gaines settled the issue by sending a photocopy of Lucas's letter to the attorney with a note reading: "Take it up with your boss."
- Number of *MAD* editors who have worked for Lucas Films: 1 (Jonathan Bresman)

Bet You Didn't Know...

- In its September 24, 1956, issue, *TIME* Magazine referred to *MAD* as "a short-lived satirical pulp." *MAD* celebrated its 500th issue in April 2009.

- *MAD* was once sued by renowned songwriter Irving Berlin over a series of song parodies "sung to the tune of..." Berlin lost. The case, which went all the way to the U.S. Court of Appeals, helped establish satire as protected speech.

- Issue #161 (September 1973) was *MAD*'s best-selling issue ever, with more than 2.5 million copies sold.

- Freelance contributor Dick DeBartolo has been published in every consecutive issue of *MAD* since #103.

- Notable humorists who have been published in *MAD*: Ernie Kovaks, Bob & Ray, Orson Bean, Wally Cox, Henry Morgan, Jean Shepherd.

- *MAD* publisher Bill Gaines loved practical jokes. In one memorable incident, he filled the office water cooler with white wine. In another, Gaines terrorized a young employee in the magazine's mail room by pretending to be his own evil twin.

- *MAD* has been associated with only one motion picture, *MAD Magazine's Up the Academy* (1980). It was a critical and commercial flop.

- Gaines rewarded his most prolific freelance contributors with all-expenses-paid trips to various locations around the world. During a trip to Haiti, he learned that the magazine had a single subscriber there, so he arranged for the group to drop by the individual's house so Gaines could personally present him with a subscription renewal card.

- *MAD Magazine* didn't contain outside advertising until issue #403 (March 2001).

Rodent Fun Facts!

Because who doesn't want to know more about rodents?

Rodents are some of the most common animals on the planet. In fact, nearly half of all mammal species on earth are rodents. Did you know…

- Mice can get by with almost no water; they get most of the moisture they need from the food they eat.

- Rats have been known to chew through wood, glass, cinderblock, and lead.

- Mice become sexually mature at six to ten weeks and can breed year-round. Female mice average six to ten litters annually.

- If a pair of mice started breeding on January 1, they could theoretically have as many as 31,000 descendants by the end of the year.

- The bubonic plague pandemic that killed millions throughout Europe in the mid-1300s was predominantly caused by fleas carried by rats.

- The largest rodent in the world is the capybara. Indigenous to South America, it can measure as large as 4 feet in length and 20 inches in height.

- The world's 4,000 known rodent species are divided into three suborders: squirrellike rodents (*Sciuromorpha*), mouselike rodents (*Myomorpha*), and porcupinelike rodents (*Hystricomorpha*).

- According to the Centers for Disease Control and Prevention, more than 45,000 Americans are bitten by rats each year.

- Rodents in the United States spread a horrifying array of diseases, including bubonic plague, murine typhus, salmonellosis, trichinosis, and hantavirus.

- Rats are the NBA stars of the rodent world. They can jump three feet straight up and four feet outward from a standing position.

- Approximately 20 percent of fires of unknown origin are believed to be caused by mice and rats chewing through electrical wires.

- Rats can enter a building through a hole just half an inch in diameter.

Bragging Rights
Loudest Noises

What is the loudest noise ever? The answer is subjective, but here are a few impressive noisemakers of note.

Krakatoa When this volcano erupted on August 27, 1883, scientists estimated the volume at 180 decibels. The cataclysmic blast was so loud that it was heard nearly 3,000 miles away.

Fireworks Though fun to look at, fireworks can reach a deafening 150 decibels at the bursting point. Luckily, that's usually far, far away.

One-Ton Bomb Anyone standing within 250 feet will experience 210 decibels. But that's probably the least of your worries.

Tunguska Blast On June 30, 1908, a comet or meteor exploded over the uninhabited Tunguska region of Russia with the force of a 1,000-megaton bomb. The blast flattened trees for miles, and scientists have estimated the noise at between 300 and 315 decibels—almost certainly the loudest single event in history.

Gunfire Markspeople wear ear protection for a reason—gunfire can produce blasts as loud as 155 decibels.

Space Shuttle Launch NASA protocol requires that anyone watching a shuttle launch on site be a minimum of a half-mile away. Why? Because these space-faring juggernauts unleash an overpowering 170 decibels as they race toward the heavens.

Blue Whales When blue whales get to chatting, everyone's in on the conversation. That's because the cry of these massive animals can reach more than 185 decibels and can travel for miles through the water. As a result, the blue whale is regarded as the loudest creature on earth.

Noises by the Numbers

125 dB: the volume at which people begin to experience pain

190 dB: the volume at which most people's eardrums burst

198 dB: the volume at which death can occur

Index

Contributing Writers

Referring to himself as a "preposterous pile of protoplasm," **Jeff Bahr** remains an enigma. Frequent contributor to the earth-shattering Armchair™ series and author of *Amazing and Unusual USA*, this offbeat writer finds depth in the shallows, meaning in the meaningless, and hope in the hopeless. Fittingly, he considers himself as vitally useless as this book.

Diane Lanzillotta Bobis is a food, fashion, and lifestyle writer living in Glenview, Illinois.

Tim Frystak is a professional writer and editor with more than 20 years experience. He's worked in Chicagoland media, encyclopedia publishing, and as a copywriter.

Tom Harris is a Web project consultant, editor, and writer living in Atlanta. He is the cofounder of Explainst.com and was leader of the editorial content team at HowStuffWorks.com.

Noah Liberman is a Chicago-based sports, entertainment, and business writer who has published two books and has contributed articles to newspapers and magazines.

Matt Modica is a writer living in Chicago.

David Morrow is an accomplished writer and editor who has worked in the publishing industry for over 20 years. His recent work includes coauthoring *Florida on Film* and contributing to the reference guide *Disasters, Accidents, and Crises in American History*.

Dan Rafter is a freelance writer from Chicago, where he lives with his wife, two sons, and dog. He's written for the *Washington Post*, *Chicago Tribune*, *Phoenix Magazine*, and several trade magazines. He also writes comic book scripts for several independent comics publishers.

Terri Schlichenmeyer (The Bookworm Sez) writes book reviews and trivia for a living. Terri has been reading since she was three years old, and she never goes anywhere without a book. She lives on a hill in Wisconsin with two dogs and 11,000 books.

Pat Sherman is the author of several books for children, including *The Sun's Daughter and Ben* and the *Proclamation of Emancipation*.

Donald Vaughan originated on January 11, 1958. Since then, he has worked as a staff writer and editor and also as a freelance writer for an eclectic array of publications, including *MAD Magazine*, *The Weekly World News*, *Military Officer Magazine*, and *Nursing Spectrum*. Donald is also the founder of Triangle Area Freelancers. He lives in Raleigh, North Carolina, with his wife, Nanette, and their very spoiled cat, Rhianna.

Vivian Wagner teaches journalism at Muskingum University in New Concord, Ohio. She is a freelance writer and photographer and the author of *Fiddle: One Woman, Four Strings, and 8,000 Miles of Music*. Visit her Web site at www.vivianwagner.net.

Jodi Webb has written for many magazines including *GRAND, Grit, and Birds and Blooms*. While writing Pennsylvania trivia, her antidote for writer's block was baking—to her three children's delight! You can find her at www.jodiwebb.com.